...WE'VE GOT KID

MW00966087

Dear Readers,

photo by eventworks.ca, 416-482-3984

Clockwise from top right:
Shari, Elisa, Dani, Sydney, Adam, Jamie, Daniel, Heidi

Here at Help!...We've Got Kids, we are celebrating our 13th year in print ... and instead of being a young, upstart publication, we are now considered to be an official "teenager". Initially, we spent quite a bit of time explaining to people who we were and what we did. Now, we are happy to say that our advertisers and readers are wonderful research assistants. They know that we will be helpful to new businesses so when they hear of one, they tell the owners to call us. This has allowed us to make the book as comprehensive and useful as possible. Thanks for your continued assistance in this area - please…keep it up!

In the past 13 years, we have had an extraordinary response to our print directory, and more recently, we have seen a remarkable growth in our online directory. The Help! site currently receives over a million hits per month as parents discover that it is an excellent adjunct to the print edition. Readers say they enjoy having the print edition near the phone (and they love the coupons) and they also welcome the chance to look up something quickly online. The online Event Calendar and Bulletin Boards are also excellent ways to keep current.

This year, we have another new baby…our newsletter. The Help! e-newsletter was launched in early Spring 2006. It's FREE. The newsletter offers readers the opportunity to hear about new companies, upcoming events and many other topics of interest to Toronto parents - it is emailed 6-8 times per year. If you have not already signed up for it, please do so by visiting our website and clicking on the starburst.

All in all, we have grown up a lot in the past 13 years and are immensely grateful for your assistance and support during this time. We look forward to the many more years of being a valued part of your family.

Our best wishes for 2007.

Elisa & Shari

Elisa Morton Palter and Shari Wert
info@helpwevegotkids.com
416-444-7678

Dedication & Appreciation

Thanks to all of our families who have been wonderfully supportive, as always.

Special thanks to the people who've worked tirelessly to make this book possible:
Jan and Steve at Digitally Creative, Karrie for everything she does - she's a lifesaver
and a pleasure and Terri Lee for our great cover.

Copyright

Canadian Cataloguing in Publication Data

Help!...We've Got Kids.
Annual.

1995 ed.-
ISSN 1203-1836
ISBN 1-896208-22-3 (13th edition, 2007)

1. Children–Services for–Ontario–Toronto Region–Directories.
2. Children's paraphernalia–Ontario–Toronto Region–Directories.
3. Amusements–Ontario–Toronto Region–Directories.
4. Toronto Region (Ont.)–Directories.

FC3097.2.H45 1994/95-   917.13'541'0025   C97-302249-3

Cover Design: Terri Lee
Production: Digitally Creative
Printed and bound in Canada by Maracle Press
Paper used in this book is recyclable.

13 14 15 16 17 10 09 08 07 06

v

Table of Contents

Table of Contents

Mean Moms

Someday when my children are old enough to understand the logic that motivates a parent, I will tell them, as my Mean Mom told me:

I loved you enough . . . to ask where you were going, with whom, and what time you would be home. I loved you enough to be silent and let you discover that your new best friend was a creep.

I loved you enough to make you go pay for the bubble gum you had taken and tell the clerk, "I stole this yesterday and want to pay for it." I loved you enough to stand over you for two hours while you cleaned your room, a job that should have taken 15 minutes. I loved you enough to let you assume the responsibility for your actions even when the penalties were so harsh they almost broke my heart.

But most of all, I loved you enough . . . to say NO when I knew you would hate me for it. Those were the most difficult battles of all. I'm glad I won them, because in the end you won, too.

Was your Mom mean? I know mine was. We had the meanest mother in the whole world! While other kids ate candy for breakfast, we had to have cereal, eggs, and toast. When others had a Pepsi and an Oreo for lunch, we had to eat sandwiches. And you can guess our mother fixed us a dinner that was different from what other kids had, too.

Mother insisted on knowing where we were at all times. You'd think we were convicts in a prison. She had to know who our friends were, and what we were doing with them. We were ashamed to admit it, but Mother had the nerve to break the Child Labor Laws by making us work. We had to wash the dishes, make the beds, learn to cook, vacuum the floor, do laundry, empty the trash and all sorts of cruel jobs. I think she would lie awake at night thinking of more things for us to do.

She always insisted on us telling the whole truth. By the time we were teenagers, she could read our minds and had eyes in the back of her head. Then, life was really tough! Because of our mother we missed out on lots of things other kids experienced. None of us have ever been caught shoplifting, vandalizing other's property or been arrested for any crime. It was all her fault.

Now that we have left home, we are all educated, honest adults. We are doing our best to be mean parents just like Mom was.

I think that is what's wrong with the world today. It just doesn't have enough mean moms!

-Author unknown, received via email

Special note to readers:

• FREE LISTINGS: Our goal is to make our directories as comprehensive as possible so they are useful to parents like us. We offer free listings to all eligible companies - if you would like to be listed, or you know of a company that should be included, please contact us. Some companies choose to have additional exposure with either a boxed listing or a display ad but they are under no obligation to do so.

• WEBSITE: www.HelpWeveGotKids.com is updated daily with listings, a calendar and a bulletin board for parent to parent comments. - check it out! The information is different from the book as some companies may choose to augment their exposure in one but not the other so check both for maximum information.

• COUPONS: Don't forget to check out the money-saving coupons at the back of the book.

• COMMENTS: As always, we do not endorse any of the companies listed - you should research and ask for references from any company you choose to use - and please, we appreciate hearing both good and bad experiences.

• UPDATED LISTINGS: New companies pop up every day, and others, for a variety of reasons, close their doors. This year, we have over 400 companies that were not in last year's book. That's why when people ask us if they should buy a new book every year, we tell them DEFINITELY!

• SUMMER FUN GUIDE: We would like to remind you that Help! also publishes The Ontario Summer Fun Guide. Fun Guides are available at no charge at Esso stations and participating attractions during the summer or check out www.summerfunguide.ca, for a comprehensive guide to family summertime fun. The Summer Fun Guide website also has a calendar of events that runs all year.

After School & Weekend Activities

While some may debate about the appropriate quantity of afterschool programs, no one can say that afterschool programs in and of themselves are a bad thing. Kids can all benefit from finding some activity which allows them to be creative, be intellectually challenged or just burn off their excess energy. There is no limit to the range of programs available from science, animation, and trumpet lessons to cooking, Parisian French and Yoga. Both parents and children will find something to their liking here.

You will find the following sub-categories in this section: Clubs, Dance, Drama & Performing Arts, Languages, Multi-disciplinary Centres & Specialty Programs, Music, Yoga.

$COUPON$ Look for this company's coupon at the back of the book

■ Clubs

Boys & Girls Club of East Scarborough
100 Galloway Rd, Scarborough, Ont, M1E 1W7. • 416-281-0262 •
Programs for children and youth birth to 18 yrs. • &.

$COUPON$ Fun & Fitness Club at Club Candy Castle
1 DeLisle Avenue (Yonge & St. Clair), Toronto, Ont • 416-962-2639 • www.clubcandycastle.com
Variety of club classes for children 2 to 12 years of age. **Look for our ad in the Birthday section. See coupon section for valuable savings.**

Girl Guides Of Canada - Ontario Council
14 Birch Ave, Toronto, Ont, M4V 1C8. • 416-920-6666 •
Experience the fun, friendship and new adventures of Girl Guides. Programs available for girls aged 5-18.

Scouts Canada
265 Yorkland Blvd, 2nd Fl, North York, Ont, M2J 5C7. • 416-490-6364 or 888-726-8876 •
Coed programs run in 235 communities throughout Metro Toronto: Beavers, Cubs, Scouts, Venturers, and Rovers. Also camps. • Ages: 5+ • &.

■ Dance

Academy Of Spanish Dance
401 Richmond St W, Ste B104, Toronto, Ont, M5V 3A8. • 416-595-5753 •
Flamenco, Spanish classical and regional dances of Spain. • Ages: 6-15.

$COUPON$ All That Dance
630 Magnetic Dr Unit D, North York, Ont, M3J 2C4. • 416-663-1212 • www.allthatdance.ca
Jazz, ballet, tap, hip hop and acrobatics. Qualified, personable instructors. Newly renovated facility. **Look for our ad in the Parent/Tot section. See coupon section for valuable savings.**
Ages: 2+ • Visa, Debit, Cheque.

Allegro Dance School
50 Esna Park Dr, Toronto, Ont, L3R 1E1. • 905-477-7146 • www.allegrodanceschool.ca
Classes for all ages in: Ballet, Modern, Jazz, Tap, Hip Hop & more!

Ardyth Johnson School Of Highland Dancing
432 Parliament St., Toronto, Ont, M5A 3A2. • 416-966-4511 •
Learn recreational or competitive Scottish dancing.

After School & Weekend Activities

Attitudes Dance & Performing Arts Studio
2800 John St, #6, Markham, Ont, L3R 0E2. • 905-513-1213 • www.attitudesdance.com
Whether dancing for fun, exercise, hobby, or career, our classes are based on fun and enjoyment.
We have a friendly staff that is motivated to help you increase confidence. Classes for Children,
Teens and Adults. Beginner to Advanced. • Ages: 5+.

Ballet Creole
375 Dovercourt Rd, 2nd floor, Toronto, Ont, M6J 3E5. • 416-960-0350 •
Contemporary African/Caribbean dance and drumming. Ages 5+. Saturdays.

Canada's National Ballet School
400 Jarvis St, Toronto, Ont, M4Y 2G6. • 416-964-3780 • www.nbs-enb.ca
The Associates Program: boys and girls aged six to 17-years. After-school and Saturday dance
classes: September-June.

Canadian Dance Teachers' Association
905-564-2139 •
Information on qualified Member Teachers in all disciplines of dance.

Coysh School Of Dance
St Paul's United Church, 200 McIntosh St, Scarborough, Ont, M4E 1N9. • 416-694-9083 •
We teach Royal Academy syllabus in ballet and Canadian Dance Association in jazz and tap. •
Ages: 3+ • Cheque • Mon-Fri: 4-9.

Dance Art Studio - Ballroom & Latin Dance Lessons
10 East Wilmot St Unit 21, Richmond Hill, Ont, L4B 1G9. • 416-878-4443 • www.danceart.ca
Hustle, Cha Cha, Samba, Rumba, Jive Pasodoble, Waltz, Viennese Waltz, Tango, Foxtrot, Quickstep,
Swing, Mambo, Salsa, Hustle, Meringue, Hip-hop, Ballet, Tap, Etc. Award Winning Studio.

Dance Ontario Association
55 Mill St, Case Goods Bldg, Ste 304, Toronto, Ont, M5A 3C4. • 416-204-1083 •
Referral service for teachers, dance schools and choreographers.

$ COUPONS$ Dance Place, The
2 locations: Etobicoke & North York, • 416-633-2726 • www.danceplace.ca
Recreational & Competitive Ballet, Tap, Jazz, Hip Hop, Acro, Creative & Modern and Music
Theatre. Annual Showcase. Competition Program. Body Conditioning. Great Summer Dance
Camps. Ages: 3 - adult. Beginners to advanced. Examinations. Parking. **Look for our ad in this section.**
See coupon section for valuable savings. • Cheque.

East York Performing Arts Centre
1351 Woodbine Avenue, Toronto, Ont, M4C 4G4. • 416 422-5920 •
www.eastyorkperformingarts.com
Under the direction of Amanda Ramrup and an experienced faculty of qualified instructors, our
goal is to provide East York and metro Toronto with the finest dance, vocal, and drama instruction
in the greatest variety of styles. • Ages: 2 1/2 - teens.

Fairyland Dance Academy
1183A Finch Ave W, Unit 1 and 2, Toronto, Ont, M3J 2G3. • 416-663-1700 •
Kinderdance, Ballet, Jazz, Hip Hop. • Ages: 2.5+.

After School & Weekend Activities

Children's Ballet and Dance Programs

Ballet classes with piano accompaniment.
Other classes: PowerBoys, Hip Hop Street Dance,
F.A.M.E. and an exciting Summer Program.

www.foresthilldance.com | 416-962-2639

1 DeLisle Avenue (Yonge & St.Clair) Toronto

Groove School of Dance

Let your child explore their
creativity and build self confidence
through dance, music and drama.

• Ballet • Jazz
• Irish • Tap • Hip Hop
• Break-dancing • Acro

A.M. and P.M. Programs Available
Ages 2 mos to Adults

Ask about our dance classes & birthday parties

416-919-2914

Forest Hill Dance

1 DeLisle Avenue (Yonge & St. Clair), Toronto, Ont • 416-962-2639 • www.foresthilldance.com
Children's Ballet and Dance Programs. With piano accompaniment. Classes include PowerBoys,
HipHop Street Dance, F.A.M.E., Cardio Power and an Exciting Summer Program. **Look for our ad in
this section.**

Front and Centre Dance Academy

875 Eglinton Ave W, Unit 7, Toronto, Ont, M6C 3Z9. • 416-916-3687 •
www.frontandcentredance.com
Dance classes in Ballet, Jazz, Hip Hop, Tap, Musical Theatre, Lyrical, Acro, and adults. Fun and
creative daytime classes for 3-5 yrs. Birthday Parties. Summer camp programs-dance, drama,
arts and crafts. Professional, dynamic instructors with a passion for dance.

$COUPON$ Groove School of Dance

53 Burnaby Blvd (St Margaret's Church - Avenue Rd/Eglinton); Bayview/Lawrence; East York,
416-919-2914 •
Come explore your creativity & build self confidence through dance. Ballet, Jazz, Tap, Hip Hop,
Break-dancing & Acro. Classes for mom/babies. Toddlers to Adults. Birthday parties. **Look for our
ad in this section. See coupon section for valuable savings.**

Joy of Dance Studio

95 Danforth Ave, Third Floor, Toronto, Ont, M4K 1N2. • 416-406-3262 • www.joyofdance.ca
Ballet, Latin, Salsa, Jazz, Modern, Ballroom & more! Group or private lessons - learn the fine
points of dancing, leading, following, technique and timing, etc.   You can skip the theory and
come just for the joy of dancing. Highly trained staff available 7 days a week.

The Dance Place

Classical • Tap • Jazz • Acro • Hip Hop
Musical Theatre • Competition Training Programs
Ages 3-1/2 yrs to Adult
Dance 'n' Arts Camp (ages 5 - 15)
Toronto West & Etobicoke - 48 Fieldway Road (Bloor & Islington)
Toronto North & North York - 885 Sheppard Ave. W (near Wilson Hgts)

416-633-2726   www.danceplace.ca

After School & Weekend Activities

Martha Hicks School of Ballet

2384 Yonge Street, 2nd Fl, Toronto, Ont, M4P 2E0. • 416-484-4731 x224 • www.mhsb.ca
Classes in creative movement, ballet, jazz, tap, hip hop, modern, musical theatre and body conditioning. Fabulous year end recital. Great summer camp. Daytime classes for pre-school and
kindergarten children. 7 locations in North Toronto. Ages 3+. • *VISA*, ⊜, *Interac*, Cheque.

Pegasus Studios

361 Glebeholme Blvd (Danforth & Coxwell), Toronto, Ont, M4C 1T9. • 416-469-2799 •
www.pegasusdance.com
RAD ballet, Jazz, Hip Hop, Tap, Modern dance, Musical Theatre & Yoga 4 Kids. Pilates and adult programs. Childhood Expressions program for children aged 2.5-4 yrs combining music, dance and art.
Summer Creative Arts Camps. In operation since 1986. • Ages: 2.5+ • *VISA*, ⊜, ▓, Cheque.

Performing Dance Arts Inc

250 Trowers Rd, Unit 4, Woodbridge, Ont, L4L 5Z6. • 905-856-1030 •
www.performingdancearts.ca
Most successful dance studio in North America. Professional Tap, Jazz, Ballet, Hip Hop instruction. Winners of Miss Dance of Canada and Mr Dance of Canada. • Ages: 4+.

Pia Bouman School for Ballet and Creative Movement

6 Noble St (Queen St W & Dufferin), Toronto, Ont, M6K 2C6. • 416-533-3706 •
www.piaboumanschool.org
Professional dance school since 1979. Courses include: Music & Movement and Early Dance
(2-6 yrs), Ballet (to RAD Grade 8) and Creative Movement (6-18 yrs), Improvisation and
Contemporary (Young Adults), Pre-Professional Program (to Advanced RAD), Virtuosity, STOTT
Pilates, Adult Classes, Summer Program, Performance Company-YMI Dancing.

Reach Dance Academy

70 Newkirk Road Unit 38 , Richmond Hill, Ont, L4C 3G3. • 905-918-4900 •
www.reachdanceacademy.com
Jazz, Tap, Ballet, Musical Theatre, Acro, Lyrical, Hip Hop, Mother/Daughter Belly Dancing, Adult
Salsa, Performance Company. • Ages: 2yrs. - Adult.

Royal Academy Of Dance

1200 Sheppard Ave E, ste 500, Toronto, Ont, M2K 2S5. • 416-489-2813 • www.radcanada.org
Contact us for a Royal Academy of Dance teacher in your area, or visit us at www.radcanada.org.

School of Canadian Children's Dance Theatre

509 Parliament St, Toronto, Ont, M4X 1P3. • 416-924-5657 •
Creative dance, RAD ballet, tap, jazz, & hip hop.

School Of Toronto Dance Theatre, The

80 Winchester St, Toronto, Ont, M4X 1B2. • 416-967-6887 •
Creative movement and modern classes.

$ COUPONS $ Seneca College Community Sport & Recreation; Dance Program

Newnham Campus, 1750 Finch Ave E, • 416-491-5050 x2301 •
www.senecac.on.ca/home/kidstuff/comrec
Excellent instruction by certified dance instructors in ballet, jazz, tap and hip-hop for children.
Latin/salsa, ballet, jazz, hip-hop, ballroom and dance orientale for adults too! Fun and fitness for
all. **Look for our ad in the Camp section. See coupon section for valuable savings**. • Ages: 3+ • *VISA*,
⊜, ▓, *Interac* • Mon-Tue: 5:45-9:30, Thu-Fri: 5:45-9:45, Sat: 9-3, Sun: 9:30am-9:15pm.

Star Academy

4637 Kingston Rd, Unit 6, Scarborough, Ont, M1E 2P8. • 416-283-2572 •
Offering: Ballet, Tap, Jazz, Hip Hop, Swimming lessons.

Thornhill School Of Ballet

Studio: 11 Glen Cameron Rd, Unit #14, Thornhill, Ont, L3T 4N3. • 905- 882-9796 •
www.thornhillschoolofballet.ca
Since 1968. We take special care with our youngest dancers, insuring they get the happiest,
healthiest introduction to the art. We believe that a child's first years in the dance class are the
most important in forming a healthy self image and strong appreciation for music and dance. •
Ages: 2 1/2 - teens. • VISA, Cheque.

Turning Pointe Academy of Dance Ltd

105 Vanderhoof Ave, unit 1, Toronto, Ont, M4G 2H7. • 416-696-7466 • www.turningpointe.ca
Ballet, Tap, Jazz, Acro, Hip Hop and Musical Theatre. Quality dance training in a fun and friendly envi-
ronment with an emphasis on individual achievement. Community involvement throughout the year.
Recreational and amateur programs with an annual year-end recital for all students. • Ages: 3+.

■ Drama & Performing Arts

Actors On Camera

416-694-9994 • actorsoncamera@rogers.com
Classes explore acting and auditioning for film and TV. Beginner and advanced levels available.
Summer day camps offered. Improve vocal expression and improvisation skills. Develops self-
confidence and focus. Emphasis on creativity and fun. • Ages: 6-17.

Annagram Productions; Anna Chatterton

416-792-9409 •
Experienced acting coach for auditions. Professional working actor uses fun and creative approach.

Aspire Studio

Yonge & Steeles Area, Toronto, • 416-569-7866 •
Imagine...Express...Create! Unique, dynamic, and individualized drama classes.

$COUPON$ Avenue Road Arts School

460 Avenue Rd, Toronto, Ont, M4V 2J1. • 416-961-1502 • www.avenueroadartsschool.com
High quality and innovative programming in the visual and performing arts - all in a warm and sup-
portive environment. Drama, musical theatre and acting for television offered Monday-Saturday.
Advanced programs by audition only. Small class sizes, highly qualified artist/instructors. **Look for
our ad in the Art section. See coupon section for valuable savings.** • Ages: 9mos-adult • VISA, ⊕,
Interac, Cheque • Mon-Thu: 8:30-8, Fri: 8:30-6:30, Sat: 8:30-5:30.

Bonnie's School of Speech and Drama

15 Burnaby Blvd, North York, Ont, M4R 1B5. • 416-489-4236 •
Poetry speaking, reading aloud, public speaking (impromptu and prepared talks), characterization
(performing parts from plays), storytelling, and improvisation. • Ages: 6+.

Canadian Children's Opera Chorus

227 Front St E, Toronto, Ont, M5A1E8. • 416-366-0467 •
For kids who love Music and Drama! Call for auditions or upcoming performances. • Ages: 5-16.

$COUPON$ Children's Arts Theatre School

6+ Locations across the GTA, including Mississauga/Oakville • 416-533-6755 •
www.catsdrama.com
Children are introduced to a form of improvisational training producing a more alive, spontaneous,
in-the-moment actor. Our programme aims to stimulate the imagination, encourage self-expres-
sion and discover the fun & creativity of theatre. Outstanding final performance! Classes after-
school & Sat. Voted "Best Drama School in Toronto". **Look for our ad in this section. See coupon
section for free introductory lesson.** • Ages: 3+.

After School & Weekend Activities

Children's Television Studios
1498 Yonge St, Toronto, Ont, M4T 1Z6. • 416-922-2564 •
Kids create, produce & perform in their own TV commercials, features & interviews.

Doogster Productions Inc
368-415 Jarvis Street, Toronto, Ont, M4Y 3C1. • 416-972-6997 • www.doogsterproductions.com
Dynamic Theatre Classes & Birthday Parties! Classes taught by "Professionally Trained Actors" with years of experience in the "Business". Programs: Early Stages ages 3-7, Musical Theatre ages 7-12 or 13-18, Theatre for Pre-Teens ages 8-12. **Look for our ad in this section.**

$COUPONS$ Drama Mamas, The
515 St. Germain Avenue, Toronto, Ont, M5M 1X3. • 416-256-1308 • www.thedramamamas.com
Creative drama, storytelling, role playing, movement, music and crafts. **Look for our ad in the Parent/Tot section. See coupon section for valuable savings.** • Ages: 18 mos+.

DramaWay
416-614-1078 x2 • www.dramaway.com
Offers structured sessions and workshops focused on creative expression. Drama classes for ages 3 and up. Also catering to individuals with special needs.

East York Performing Arts Centre
1351 Woodbine Avenue, Toronto, Ont, M4C 4G4. • 416 422-5920 •
Finest dance, vocal, and drama instruction in the greatest variety of styles. • Ages: 2 1/2 - teens.

Kids on Broadway
416-237-9738 •
Intensive musical theater performing program. • Ages: 9 - 13.

Kingsway Conservatory of Music
3086 Bloor St W, Toronto, Ont, M8X 1C8. • 416-234-0121 • www.kingswayconservatory.ca
Introductory classes to Performance Skills (from 6 yrs) - course objectives include building language, communication, social skills, confidence, self-awareness - audition, festival & exam preparation - techniques include mime, improvisation, story-telling, characterization, interpretation, diction, staging & blocking and presentation skills.

Lorraine Kimsa Theatre for Young People Drama School
165 Front St E, Toronto, Ont, M5A 3Z4. • 416-363-5131 x242 •
Year-round classes available in three GTA locations. For ages JK to OAC. • Ages: JK-OAC • VISA,
🚇, ▨, Interac • ♿.

Mississauga Youth Theatre Company

Mississauga Area, • 905-949-6499 •
Outstanding productions/training/workshops/camps. Ages 7-25 yrs.

ShakespeareWorks

416-427-6282 •
Rehearse Shakespeare scenes with professional actors. • Ages: 8-19.

Stage Coach Theatre for Children

Various Mississauga Locations, • 905-566-9314 •
Summer Camps/Fall-Winter Performing Arts Programs. Ages 7-16.

Stand Up and Speak Inc

5100 Erin Mills Parkway, POB 53040, Mississauga, Ont, L5M 5H0. • 905-828-8333 •
Public Speaking Workshops for Kids! • Ages: 4-18.

Summer Movie Camps - The Acting Studio

6535 Millcreek Dr, Ste 59, Mississauga, Ont, L5N 2M2. • 905-813-3220 •
www.theactingstudio.ca
The Acting Studio was built by actors, for actors. All instructors at the Studio are working professionals. Ages 8 to Adult. Improv, Scene Study, Monologues, End of year performances. Improves Reading, Writing and Social Skills. FUN FUN FUN... • Ages: 8+.

Theatre Ontario

215 Spadina Ave, Ste 210, Toronto, Ont, M5T 2C7. • 416-408-4556 •
Resource centre for getting started in the theatre world.

Yonge Street Players Theatre School (since 1987)

416-823-5343 or 905-944-9995 • www.yongestreetplayers.com
YTV award for comedy (presented by Jim Carrey!). Comedy, improvisation, original plays, "Improv Olympics". 18th season of Improv. Ages: 6-16 yrs. Yonge and 401. For Toronto's seriously funny kids.

$ COUPONS $ Zodiactors

Convenient central Toronto locations. • 416-789-1989 • www.zodiaccamp.on.ca
Exposure to drama, dance and music. Participation in a mini Broadway-style show in a supportive, fun and stimulating environment. • Ages: 7-12 year olds (Grades 2 through 6). **Look for our ad in the camp section. See coupon section for valuable savings.** • *VISA*, ⊜, Cheque
Hours: Variable.

DOOGSTER
Productions Inc.

KEVIN PATTERSON
Teacher/Actor/Director/Producer/Member of C.A.E.A. and ACTRA

368 - 415 JARVIS STREET TORONTO ONTARIO M4Y 3C1
TEL 416 • 972 • 6997   CELL 416 • 970 • 6997
e-mail: info@doogsterproductions.com • www.doogsterproductions.com
► AFTERSCHOOL THEATRE PROGRAMS FOR KIDS ► PRE-SCHOOL THEATRE PROGRAMS
► THEATRICAL BIRTHDAY PARTIES ► CHRISTMAS CAROLING

After School & Weekend Activities

■ Languages

Ahavat Yisrael Hebrew School
416-781-8088 •
Finally, a Hebrew School you don't have to drag your child to! Hebrew Language, reading & writing, Jewish customs & holidays. Exciting holiday events - Chanukah performance, Purim Carnival, Mock Passover Seder and Tzedakah projects. Innovative Bar/Bat Mitzvah programs. Sundays only. • Other Locations: Thornhill/Richmond Hill, Bayview/York Mills & Bathurst/Lawrence • Ages: 5-13 • Sun: 10am-12:30pm.

French Programmes Français
12 Bannockburn Ave (Avenue Rd & 401), Toronto, Ont, M5M 2M8. • 416-789-7855 x308 • www.frenchprogrammesfrancais.com
Various ways to learn and love French: baby/tot classes; Cooking en Francais; March and Summer Camps; tutoring for all ages.

Hebrew Fun Time
224 Faywood Blvd, Toronto, Ont, M3H 6A9. • 647-285-7045 or 416-638-2014 •
Learning Hebrew through art, drama, music and movement. Enrich the Jewish holidays and traditions. Enhance creative thinking and self expression with art. Groups and individuals 6-12 years of age.

Ledbury Park Community Hebrew School Inc: The Hebrew School Kids Love!
Beth Radom Congregation, 18 Reiner Rd, Toronto, Ont, M3H 2K9 • 647-889-9511 •
Do your children love going to Hebrew School? Ours do! Ledbury offers once/week classes (4-6pm), JK-Gr 6, plus bar/bat mitzvah program, small class size, emphasis on Jewish heritage, arts & crafts, music. We welcome new students!

MLK - Multi Lingual Kids
416-223-3382 • www.multilingualkids.ca
A unique and inspired experience – Italian, French, Spanish, Mandarin or English. Songs, poems, rhymes, games and stories for parents and children from birth to 7 yrs.

Spanish for Children at the Canada - Mexico Cultural Exchange Centre
416-428-9000 • www.canadamexico.com
Spanish lessons for children age 18mos+. Classes held at University of Toronto, in York Region or in your own home. Give your kids the gift of another language while they have fun! • Ages: 18mos+.

Spanish Schoolhouse
180 Steeles Ave West, Unit 202, Thornhill, Ont, L4J 2L1. • 905-771-1136 •
Learn Spanish the fun way! Ages 4+ •

Temmy Latner Hebrew School
446 Spadina Rd, Suite 206, Toronto, Ont, M5P 2V6. • 416 483-0883 •
Exciting Hebrew School, Tuesdays in Forest Hill

■ Multi-Disciplinary Centres & Specialty Programs

$COUPON$ 5 Elements Camps & Workshops
416-423-8456 • www.5elements4girls.com
5 Elements is all about helping girls of all ages feel confident, strong and healthy. Our workshops encourage self-respect, positive body image and supportive relationships. The emphasis is on fun. The results are far reaching. **Look for our ad in the Camp section. See coupon section for valuable savings.** • Ages: girls 6 - 15.

After School & Weekend Activities

$COUPON$ Avenue Road Arts School

460 Avenue Rd, Toronto, Ont, M4V 2J1. • 416-961-1502 • www.avenueroadartsschool.com
High quality and innovative programming in the visual and performing arts - all in a warm and supportive environment. Drawing, painting, pottery, architecture, drama and musical theatre, offered after school and Saturdays. Small class sizes, highly qualified artist/instructors. **Look for our ad in the Art section. See coupon section for valuable savings.** • Ages: 9mos-adult • *VISA*, ⊕, *Interac*, Cheque • Mon-Thu: 8:30-8, Fri: 8:30-6:30, Sat: 8:30-5:30.

Behaviour Matters

1 Caldow Rd, Toronto, Ont, M5N 2P4. • 416-270-6610 •
Social skills and anger management groups for children, ages 6-12.

$COUPON$ Mad Science

1170 Sheppard Ave W, Unit 14, Toronto, Ont, M3K 2A3. • 800-630-4403 •
www.madscience.com/toronto
After school and lunch time programs. Lasers, rocketry, slime, chemical magic and tons more! **Look for our ad in the Birthday Parties section. See coupon section for valuable savings.** • Ages: 5-12 • Cheque.

Making Money-Smart Kids Inc.

50 Cedarland Drive, Etobicoke, Ont, M9A 2L1. • 647-436-8099 •
Money Management Courses for kids aged 7-12.

Miles Nadal JCC

750 Spadina Ave, Toronto, Ont, M5S 2J2. • 416-924-6211 •
Programs for children ages 0-12.

Mississauga Recreation & Parks

300 City Centre Drive, Mississauga, Ont, L5B 3C1. • 905-615-4100 •
www.mississauga.ca/rec&parks
Supervised recreation programs for a variety of interests and levels. Program areas include: arts, fitness, skating, sports, swimming and more! **Look for our ad in the Camp section.** • Ages: newborn-seniors.

National Film Board of Canada - Mediatheque

150 John Street (at Richmond - Osgoode Subway), Toronto, Ont, M5V 3C3. • 416-973-3012 •
www.nfb.ca/mediatheque
Interactive filmmaking workshops for children and youth, guided by professional instructors. Thousands of NFB films on personal viewing stations. Kid-friendly guided viewing programs available. 7 days a week! Call for more information and to book. • Ages: 6-16.

Royal Ontario Museum Saturday Morning Club

100 Queen's Park (Bloor St at Avenue Rd), Toronto, Ont, M5S 2C6. • 416-586-5797 •
www.rom.on.ca (ROMKids pgms)
Fun and Exciting eight-week programs based on the world-class collections of the ROM - perfect for the curious and creative child! • Ages: 5-14 • *VISA*, ⊕, ▓, *Interac* • Sat: 9am-noon • ♿.

smARTS Creative Learning Workshops and Programs

647-899-7857 •
Workshops in Art, Music, Drama and more! • Ages: 18 mos+.

Star Reach; Self-Esteem Seminars for Kids

416-787-7877 • www.SelfEsteemForTeensCanada.com
Are You Happy With Your Child's Confidence Level? Strong self-esteem means better grades, better relationships and a better life! Our interactive seminars boost children's self-esteem. Complimentary evaluation assesses your child's potential for success. Call or visit us online.

Studio 7

1977 Avenue Rd, Toronto, Ont, M5M 4A2. • 416-480-2902 •
Sewing and fashion design classes for kids and teens.

Young Filmmakers Workshop
416-690-4056 • www.youngfilmmakersworkshop.com
Filmmaking and animating camp offered weekly during July, Aug, and March break. After school, weekend, in the classroom workshops from Sept-June. • Ages: 10-16yrs.

■ Music

Allegro Music
2045 Avenue Rd, Toronto, Ont, M5M 4A7. • 416-483-7203 •
Lessons and rental of instruments. Rental of karaoke machines. • Ages: 5+.

Arts Integra Centre for Music and the Arts
132 Main St, Unionville, Ont, L3R 2G4. • 905-471-3001 •
Outstanding music lessons and drama classes. Markham.

Beach Music Arts Ltd
1928 Queen St E 2nd Fl, Toronto, Ont, M4L 1H5. • 416-698-3449 •
Private music lessons for young and older children.

Blue Moon Music School
P.O. Box 10555 - 998 Bloor Street West, Toronto, Ont, M6H 1L8. • 416-531-6668 •
Seriously Fun Music Experience for All Ages.

Brampton's Inter-National Music School and Fine Arts
905-791-6997 •
Music, dance, drama and art programs.

CATS Creative Music
100 Ravel Rd - Leslie and Finch, Toronto, Ont, M2H 1S9. • 416-564-5634 •
CATS Creative Arts & Technology School where the piano keyboard and computer are taught together. Students learn to play by ear first and by notation later allowing them to be creative and record and edit their music. • Ages: 6+.

Creative Vocalization Studio
707 Eglinton Ave. W, Toronto, Ont, M5N IC8. • 416-782-7944 •
Singing lessons. All Ages. Unique approach. Affordable.

Crescendo Music Services
94 Billings Avenue, Toronto, Ont, M4L 2S4. • 416-463-6054 •
Instrumental & vocal lessons - private or group.

Drummer's Choice
71 West Dr, Unit 41, Brampton, Ont, L6T 5E2. • 905-455-9884 •
Lessons on-site, sales, service and repair.

Eli Kassner Guitar Academy
9 Gibson Ave, Toronto, Ont, M5R 1T4. • 416-922-8002 •
World-famous guitar academy. Classical, jazz, rock, blues, folk, etc. • Ages: 4+ • Cheque.

Etobicoke Suzuki School Of Music
416-239-4637 • www.etobicokesuzukimusic.ca
Violin and cello instruction for children aged 3 and up. Private and group classes. Concerts and workshops. Parent attends lessons with child. • Cheque • ♿.

Frog Barn Productions
48 Redwood Ave, Toronto, Ont, M4L 2S6. • 416-803-8603 • www.frogbarnproductions.ca
Document the vocal progression of your child. Instruction and recording by professional recording artists producing a CD with songs performed and co-written by YOUR CHILD. Share it with family and friends for years to come. • Ages: 7-12 years.

After School & Weekend Activities

Gardner Piano, Guitar & Vocal Lessons: In-Home /Studio Service
416-467-7959 • www.brendacarol.com
Professional piano, guitar and vocal instruction since 1977. Customized curriculum or RCMT exam preparation available. Classical, Rock, Pop, Jazz & Blues. The emphasis is always on enjoyment & proper skill development. All private lessons. • Ages: 5+ • Cheque.

Jennifer Hu, Piano Teacher
416-792-1265 •
Private piano lessons. Located near Yonge/Sheppard. • Ages: 5+.

Kathryn Ladano - flute, clarinet and saxaphone lessons
416-249-4543 •
Private lessons on woodwind instruments and theory. • Ages: 8-18 yrs..

Kindermusik International
1064 Salk Rd., Unit 6 , Pickering, Ont, L1W 4B5 . • 1-800-628-5687 for the location nearest you •
A premier music and movement program for children from newborn - 7 years.

Kingsway Conservatory of Music
3086 Bloor St W, Toronto, M8X 1C8. • 416-234-0121 • www.kingswayconservatory.ca
Private Instruction: Piano, Voice, Guitar, Strings, Winds, Brass by professionals - Music for You & Your Baby (0-3 yrs), Eurhythmics/Kodály/Orff (3-10 yrs), Suzuki Violin (from 4 yrs), Kingsway Children's Chorus, Chamber Ensembles, Electronic Music, Theory, Drama - Performance/Ensemble Opportunities.

$ COUPON $ Music for Young Children®
1-888-474-1556 • www.myc.com
A keyboard-based music program that includes piano, singing, rhythm, theory, and composing. Group lessons with adult participation. Teachers throughout Canada and the USA. Wonderful introduction to music! **Look for our ad in this section. See coupon section for valuable savings.** • Ages: 3+.

Music Studio, The
6 Burnhamthorpe Rd, Toronto, Ont, M9A 5C9. • 416-234-9268 •
Professional, instrumental and vocal instruction. • Ages: 4+.

Musica Music School
88 Laird Drive, Toronto, Ont, M4G 3V1. • 416-696-0905 •
The music school with a difference! Private AND Group Lessons in Piano, Voice, Musical Theatre and Guitar seven days a week. Also the Leaside home of Music for Young Children® for parent-and-child programs. Free Parking. • Ages: 6 mths+ .

North Toronto Institute of Music
550 Eglinton Ave E, Toronto, Ont, M4P 1N9. • 416-488-2588 • www.ntimusic.com
High quality music instruction in most instruments, voice, theory and in jazz programs. Music theatre and pre-school classes available. Exciting faculty and student concerts. • Ages: Birth+.

North York Suzuki School of Music
348 Sheppard Ave E, North York, Ont, M2N 3B4. • 416-222-5315 • www.northyork-suzuki.com
Thriving Suzuki school offers lessons in violin, piano, guitar and cello. Experience the joy of learning to play an instrument! Highly trained, certified teachers. Friendly atmosphere for learning and loving music. Ask about our parent-toddler program. • Ages: 4+ • Cheque.

Ontario College of Percussion and Music
214 Laird Dr, Toronto, Ont • 416-483-9117 •
Private lessons in most musical instruments. Specializing in percussion. Established 1965.

After School & Weekend Activities

Ontario Registered Music Teachers Association (ORMTA)
416-694-0296 •
Instruction in piano, voice, guitar, violin, cello, woodwind, brass, theory and more.

Pat Doherty, Guitar Instructor
122 Cambridge Ave, Toronto, Ont, M4K 2L6. • 416-463-9126 •
Guitar lessons, age 4 to adult.

Royal Conservatory of Music Community School
90 Croatia St, Toronto, Ont, M6H 1K9. • 416-408-2825 •
Music classes. All ages. All levels. • Other Locations 850 Enola St, Mississauga.

Scratchlab DJ Institute
1170 Sheppard Ave W, Unit 32, Toronto, Ont, M3K 2A3. • 416-SCRATCH (727-2824) •
www.scratchlab.ca
Learn how to DJ from some of North America's top in the industry. For All ages and skill levels.

Stay at Home Music
905-881-3629 • www.stayathomemusic.ca
A music school that offers private in-home lessons for guitar, piano, keyboards, vocal, bass guitar
and drums for beginner, intermediate, and advanced level students. Experienced teachers.
Excellent references. Very flexible make up lesson and cancellation policy.

String Orchestra Academy
120 Longboat Ave, Toronto, Ont, M5A 4G3. • 416-875-3427 •
String orchestra academy. Classical music home. • Ages: 7+.

Check out our website
www.helpwevegotkids.com

...WE'VE GOT KIDS

YogaBuds™for Kids 5-13 years

- Classical Iyengar yoga blended with creative movement & art.
- Improves posture, strength and balance.
- Enhances self-esteem.

Kids & Parent-Child Classes & Workshops

Director: Temmi Ungerman Sears
Certified Iyengar Yoga Instructor
with over 25 yrs. experience

Call 416-785-7888
www.yogabuds.com   **YogaBuds**

Yamaha Music Schools

5075 Yonge St, 10th Fl, Toronto, Ont, M2N 6C6. • 416-224-5590 • www.yamaha.ca
Yamaha Music Schools offer quality music programs throughout the week. World renowned music courses for children of all ages. A unique, creative approach to teaching music and inspiring creativity. • Ages: 2+ • VISA, ⊖, ■■, Cheque • Mon-Fri: noon-9pm • &.

Yellow Dog Music

416 Moore Ave, Ste 301, Toronto, Ont, M4G 1C9. • 416-696-1226 • www.yellowdogmusic.ca
Innovative, alternative to traditional private music. • Ages: 5+.

▪ Yoga

Breathe Yoga Studio

2253 Bloor St W, Toronto, Ont, M6S 1N8. • 416-926-YOGA (9642) •
Yoga for Kids, Pre-natal, Moms N' Babes Yoga. • Ages: 1 mon-13yrs.

Village Yoga Studio

329 Lonsdale Road., 2nd floor, Toronto, Ont, M4V 1X3. • 416-487-2812 •
Classes/workshops including Mom & Baby, Prenatal.

Yoga 4 Kids

416-532-5988 • www.yoga4kids.org
Yoga 4 Kids is specifically developed to teach yoga and meditation to children of all ages and abilities. Yoga 4 Kids offers private Yoga Therapy to children with special needs. Workshops for adults too.

Yoga Sanctuary, The

95 Danforth Avenue Suite 301 • Toronto, Ont, M4K 1N2. • 416-461-6161 •
Pre-natal, Post-natal, kids Yoga. Ashtanga and Hatha.

$COUPON$ YogaBuds: Yoga for Kids, since 1997

416-785-7888 • www.yogabuds.com
Yoga classes/workshops for kids (5+) or parents & kids together (3.5+). **Look for our ad in this section. See coupon section for valuable savings.**

Yogaplay™

416-505-4997 •
Improve fitness, body awareness & self-esteem.

Amusement Centres

Look no further when you are searching for something to do on weekends, holidays or just a rainy afternoon. Glow in the dark mini golf and bowling are fun for old and young. Or, if you have a few more hours, visit one of the amusement centres and ride a bumper car or merry go round!

For the younger set, indoor playgrounds are a wonderful place for kids to test their independence. Because they are in a self-contained, safe space, kids can play by themselves while parents watch from a distance. Indoor playgrounds are great for kids to burn off steam and wonderful for parents who are looking to talk in full sentences to other adults going through the same experience. There are additional listings for indoor playgrounds found in the Birthday Parties section. Evening hours and casual drop-in play are available throughout the weekend as well as during the week. You must call for the hours at each specific location.

<u>Listings are divided into the following sub-categories:</u>
Amusement Centres, Bowling, Indoor Playgrounds, Mini Golf

$ COUPON $ Look for this company's coupon at the back of the book

▪ Amusement Centres

Chuck E Cheese
2452 Sheppard Ave E, Willowdale , Ont, M2J 1X1. • 416-497-8855 •
Where a kid can be a kid! • Other Locations: 4141 Dixie Rd, Mississauga 905-602-4090 • ᕫ.

Cummer Skateboard Park - Toronto's First
6000 Leslie St, Toronto, Ont, M2H 1J9. • 416-395-7803 •
Jumps, ramps, half-pipe, etc. Built for skateboarding. Public, free, unsupervised.

Douglas Snow Aquatic Centre
5100 Yonge St, North York, Ont, M2N 5V7. • 416-395-7585 •
Excitement year round. Leisure swims with a Tarzan rope or a giant, 3-story, tubular slide. FREE.

$ COUPON $ Fantasy Fair
500 Rexdale Blvd, Etobicoke, Ont, M9W 6K5. • 416-674-5437 • www.fantasyfair.ca
"Ontario's largest indoor amusement park". Located inside the Woodbine Centre. Nine exciting full-sized rides, including Spinner, Bumper Cars, Children's play village, family arcade, midway games and our newest thrilling adventure, "Fantasy Flight" – all under one roof. Open daily 11-7. Thurs. & Fri until 8pm. **Look for our ad in the Birthday Party Places section. See coupon section for valuable savings.** • ᕫ.

$ COUPON $ Funstation Funpark
5 York Gate Blvd (2 bl. E of Hwy 400, N of Finch), , • 416-736-4804 •
www.funstationfunpark.com
A 5-acre amusement park featuring Go-Karts, mini Go-Karts, two 18-hole miniature golf courses, batting cages and an arcade. Fun for the whole family. A great birthday party venue! Open April to October, weather permitting. Call for hours. **Look for our ad in the Birthday Parties section. See coupon section for valuable savings.** • Ages: 3+.

In Play Inc
16655 Yonge St, Unit 23, Newmarket, Ont, L3X 1V6. • 905-953-8299 •
Games, climbing, mini golf, parties. Great food & fun! • Ages: all.

Laser Quest
Laser Quest is the hottest live action laser tag game in town. You don't just play the game - you're in it! Brampton 905-456-9999, Richmond Hill 905-883-6000 and Toronto East 416-285-1333. • Ages: 7+ • ᕫ.

$COUPON$ Scooter's Roller Palace

2105 Royal Windsor Dr, Mississauga, Ont, L5J 1K5. • 905-823-4001 • www.scooters.on.ca
Birthday parties, roller skating/roller blading facility featuring public skating, skate rentals, artistic skating, lessons. DJ music, refreshments, arcade, and private party bookings. Call for hours. **Look for our ad in the Birthday Parties section. See coupon section for valuable savings.** • Ages: 6-60 &.

$COUPON$ Wave Pool, The

5 Hopkins St, Richmond Hill, Ont, L4C 0C1. • 905-508-WAVE (9283) • www.richmondhill.ca
Open year round, The Wave Pool offers safe family fun! Enjoy a Wave Swim with 4 foot waves, a 160 foot twisting water slide, swirl pool and more. **Look for our ad in the Birthday Parties section. See coupon section for valuable savings.** • *VISA*, ⊖, *Interac*, Cheque • &.

▪ Bowling

Bathurst Bowlerama

2788 Bathurst St, Toronto, Ont, M6B 3A3. • 416-782-1841 •
Computerized 5 and 10 pin cosmic bowling. Fun for the whole family. • *VISA*, ⊖, *Interac* •
Mon-Thu: 11-11, Fri-Sat: 11 am - 1 am, Sun: 11-11 • &.

Brampton Bowling Lanes

12 Beech St, Brampton, Ont, L6V 1V1. • 905-459-2711 •
The family FUN place! Bumper bowling, snack bar and 5-pin bowling. • Mon-Sun: 9am-11am • &.

Centre Bowl

4300 Cawthra Rd, Mississauga, Ont, L4Z 1V8. • 905- 306-0043 •
Family fun. Special events. Birthdays. 5-pin bowling.

Classic Bowl

3055 Dundas St W, Mississauga, Ont, L5L 3R8. • 905-607-2695 • www.classicbowl.com
Classic Bowl offers 60 10-pin lanes with computerized scoring in a smoke-free environment.
Bowling makes a great family outing. • Ages: 3+.

National Youth Bowling Council

250 Shields Crt Unit 10A, Markham, Ont, L3R 9W7. • 905-479-1560 •
Step into the world of youth bowling. • Ages: 4+.

Playtime Bowl

33 Samor Rd, Toronto, Ont, M6A 1J2. • 416-STRIKED •
Bumper bowling. Cosmic bowling. Birthdays too.

World Bowl

9 East Wilmot, Thornhill, Ont • 905-881-5927 •
5 0r 10 pin, bumpers and computerized scoring.

▪ Indoor Playgrounds

$COUPON$ Amazon Indoor Playground

Bathurst/St Clair 416-656-5832, Royal York Rd/Eglinton 416-245-1459, •
www.amazonindoorplayground.com
Infant friendly & Lots of fun! Changetables, Microwave, Couches, Climber, Ball pit, Slides, Blocks, Riding toys, Dress Up and more. Two for one Tuesdays! Great Visibility, Bright & Clean. **Look for our ad in the Birthday Party Places section. See coupon section for valuable savings.** • Ages: 12 mos- 12 yrs.

Bounce 'N' Play Indoor Playground and Birthday Party Centre

3250 Ridgeway Dr, #2 , Mississauga, , L5L 5Y6. • 905-820-2171 • www.bouncenplay.ca
Drop-in play Mon-Fri only $7.00. Jumping castles, Air hockey, Motor cycle, PS2, Game Cube, Toddler area, etc. • Ages: 1-10 • Mon-Fri: 9:30-3:30.

Amusement Centres

$ COUPON $ Bounce 'N' Play Indoor Playground - Woodbridge
71 Marycroft Ave, #20, Woodbridge, Ont, L4L 5Y6. • 905-850-7529 •
Unique 3 level play structure, glow in the dark maze, separate toddler area and much more. **Look for our ad in the Birthday Party Places section. See coupon section for valuable savings.** • Ages: 1-10.

It's Playtime Inc
1425 Danforth Ave, Toronto, Ont, M4J 1N3. • 416-465-6688 •
Drop-In, Private Parties and Group Bookings, Babysitting - 48 hours notice. • Ages: 7 and under.

$ COUPON $ Jiggles & Giggles Indoor Playground and Party Centre
120 Carlauren Rd, Unit #1 (Weston Rd. & Hwy 7), Woodbridge, Ont, L4L 8E5. • 905-264-8222 •
www.jigglesandgiggles.ca
Private birthday parties & daily drop-in play. Climbing towers, slides, large air bouncer, toddler area and much more. New, bright & clean, safe and uniquely designed play centre. **Look for our ad in the Birthday Parties section. See coupon section for valuable savings.**

$ COUPON $ Jungle Cubs Indoor Playground
1681 Bayview Ave, Toronto, Ont, M4G 2C1. • 416-322-6005 •
Age appropriate equipment, fun, clean, safe & relaxed atmosphere. Complementary beverages. Ages 6 months - 7yrs. **Look for our ad in the Birthday Parties section. See coupon section for valuable savings.**

KidsWorks Indoor Playground & Party Centre
105 Vanderhoof, Toronto, Ont, M4G 2H7. • 416-876-1235 • www.kidsworkstoronto.com
Attractions: 50 Tons of Sand, Climbing Castle, 2 Climbing Walls, 3 Slides, 2 Zip Lines, 3 Rope Swings, Toddler Centre, Playhouse. Ages Toddler to 7. **Look for our ad in the Birthday Party Section.** Ages: toddler-7. •

KinderGarden in the Beach, The
1A Hannaford St, Toronto, Ont, M4E 3G6. • 416-690-6628 • www.thekindergarden.ca
Creative play tailor-made for little sprouts! Pint-sized ballpit and slides, castle, log cabin, house centre, dress-up, puppets, computer corner and reading nook. Stories, songs and crafts for kids; coffee, tea and conversation for adults. Parties too! Call us for current hours, themes and events. Ages: 0-6.

Let's Have Fun Indoor Playground
1825 Dundas St E, Unit 13, Mississauga, Ont, L4X 2X1. • 905-206-0082 •
Choose from 2 private playgrounds with large eating area. • Ages: 1-10.

Lil' Explorers Clubhouse & Indoor Gym
190 Bullock Dr. Unit 10, Toronto, Ont, L3P 7N3. • 905-910-PLAY (7529) •
Large, clean, open-concept playground conveniently located in Markham.

Little Feet Fitness & Fun for Tots
1077 Boundary Rd, Unit 108, Oshawa, Ont, L1J 8P8. • 905-433-4668 •
Safe, fun environment specially designed for the little ones. • Ages: 0-4yrs.

$ COUPON $ MegaFun 4 Kids Indoor Playground
91 Rylander Blvd Unit 1, Scarborough, Ont, M1B 5M5. • 416-282-6531 •
www.megafun4kids.com
Clean, bright, colourful facility. Toys, ball pit, pirate ship, train track, mini kitchen, costume area, book corner and more. Birthday parties with exclusive use of the playground. 3 party packages. Characters available. Infant area. Special events. **Look for our ad in the Birthday Parties section. See coupon section for valuable savings.** • Ages: infants -7 • _VISA_, ⊕, ■, _Interac._

Pippi's World Indoor Playground and Birthday Party Centre

1381 Lakeshore Rd E, Mississauga, Ont, L5E 1G6. • 905-271-0642 •
Play, parties, special events, daycare available. Open 7 days/wk. • Ages: 0-7.

$ COUPONS Playground Paradise

150 Grenoble Dr, North York, Ont, M3C 1E3. • 416-395-6014 •
Play with us at Playground Paradise and give your child the time of their life! Two story play
structure, ball pit, slides. Great prices! **Look for our ad in the Birthday section. See coupon section for
valuable savings.**

$ COUPONS Playhouse Indoor Playground

321 Rexdale Blvd, Unit 1, Etobicoke, Ont, M9W 1R8. • 416-745-4333 • www.playhouseip.ca
Come play in our large open concept playground. Multi-level play chalet, train rides, parents'
lounge and much more! Call or visit website for hours. **Look for our ad in the Birthday Party Places
section. See coupon section for valuable savings.** • Ages: 8 • _VISA_, ⊖, _Interac_.

Small Wonders Discovery Centre

140 Capitol Court, Mississauga, Ont, L5T 2R8. • 905 696-6817 • www.playatsmallwonders.ca
Small Wonders is the ultimate place for your little one to play! Small Wonders 10,000 square
foot facility is safe, clean and fun! Pretend and perform in the castle, play on the slides and
climbers in our park, ride cars & bikes on the raceway, or check out our live pet shop. We have it
all! • Ages: 0-8 years..

Spunky Monkey Indoor Playground & Party Centre

1550 16th Ave, Building "A" - Units#11 & #12, Richmond Hill, Ont, L4B 3K9. • 905-737-2335 or
1-877-737-2335 •
Daily playtime, kids' programs, camps and private parties. Infant play area. Kindermusik. • Ages: 0-8yrs.

Stomp 'N Romp Playhouse

158 Anderson Ave, Units 11 & 12, Markham, Ont, L6E 1A9. • 905-201-2626 •
Indoor playground and party centre for kids.

▪ Mini Golf

$ COUPONS Funstation Funpark

5 York Gate Blvd (2 bl. E of Hwy 400, N of Finch), , • 416-736-4804 •
www.funstationfunpark.com
A 5-acre amusement park featuring two 18-hole miniature golf courses. Open April to October,
weather permitting. **Look for our ad in the Birthday Parties section. See coupon section for valuable
savings.** • Ages: 3+.

Junkyard Jake's Mini-Golf (at the Practice Tee)

6380 Hurontario St (Just N. of the 401), Mississauga, Ont, L5W 1N3. • 905-564-3383 •
Outdoor mini-golf and driving range. Fun for the whole family!

Putt-N-Play Entertainment Centre

14 McEwan Drive Unit #4, Bolton, Ont, L7E 1H1. • 905-857-8989 •
18 Hole, indoor, glow in the dark, professional mini putt series.

Putting Edge: Glow-in-the-Dark Mini Golf

1 (888) 544-9262 for the location nearest you. • The ultimate Glow-in-the-Dark mini golf experience.

Timber Creek Miniature Golf & Fun Center

12772 9th Line, Stouffville, Ont, L4A 7X3 • 905-642-5174 • www.timbercreekgolf.ca
Fun-filled outdoor attraction for families. Two spectacular one-of-a-kind miniature golf courses
among waterfalls, rivers and even shipwrecks. A jumping castle, inflatable slide, games barn, batting cages, driving range and dairy bar make for a full day of fun. Birthday party packages available. • Ages: 3-65.

Art: Activities, Lessons & Supplies

Arts and crafts allow your children to express themselves creatively. Some of the children have real artistic inclinations and others just want to get messy. Both are great reasons to pursue art activities. Art is all about expression and creativity, not proficiency.

This category includes places where your child can take lessons in Scrapbooking, Cartooning, photography, drawing, ceramics, sculpture and so much more. In addition, paint your own ceramics studios are a great place for parties and rainy days.

<u>You will find the following sub-categories in this section:</u>
Art/Craft Classes, Craft Supplies, Paint Your Own Ceramics, Scrapbooking

$COUPON$ Look for this company's coupon at the back of the book

▪ Art/ Craft Classes

$COUPON$ Academy of Artisans
490 Eglinton Ave West, 2nd fl, Toronto, Ont, M5N 1A5. • 416-322-9997 •
www.academyofartisans.com
Fully equipped studios. Cooking, Baking, Stained Glass, Jewellery, Photography, Knitting, Sewing, Painting, Cartooning, Sculpture, Basketry, Mosaics, Wood Carving and more! Hands-On. Fun. Professional instructors. Low student:teacher ratios. **Look for our ad in the Birthday Party Places section. See coupon section for valuable savings.** • Ages: 4+.

All Fired Up Paintable Ceramics
8 & 10 Brentwood Rd N, Etobicoke, Ont, M8X 2B5. • 416-233-5512 •
Pottery classes for both kids and adults. Ages 4+.

Art Club for Kids
369 Walmer Road, Toronto, Ont, M5R 2Y3. • 647-283-4944 • www.artclubforkids.info
Imagine, create, experiment and learn in a small class environment, where children will explore different media, cultures and artists. • Ages: 4-9.

Art Gallery Of Ontario - Art Classes
317 Dundas St W, Toronto, Ont, M5T 1G4. • 416-979-6608 • www.ago.net
The Anne Tanenbaum Gallery School offers children's art classes, youth programs and adult courses. Drawing, painting, printing, sculpture and multimedia courses are available. All classes visit the Gallery's collections and exhibitions. • VISA, ⊖, ▦, *Interac* • ♿.

Art Garage Inc, The
2188 Queen St E, Toronto, Ont, M4E 1E6. • 416-686-0960 • www.theartgarageinc.com
Fun Art Workshops for Kids aged 1.5-16 years. Interactive atmosphere. Artwork is displayed in a gallery setting. Programs include Drawing Painting, Ceramics, Cartooning, Sculpture & more.

Art Smart
416-657-1696 • www.puppetadventure.com
Awesome in-home art classes with a professional artist. Painting, drawing, puppetry & much more! New! Kid Vid - video production & graphic design workshops for kids. Ages 5+.

Art Works Art School
2451 Bloor St W at Jane, Toronto, Ont, M6S 1P7. • 416-766-0662 •
After school & weekends. Cartooning, photography, drawing, painting, sculpture, etc. • Ages: 3+.

Art: Activities, Lessons & Supplies

$COUPONS Avenue Road Arts School

460 Avenue Rd, Toronto, Ont, M4V 2J1. • 416-961-1502 • www.avenueroadartsschool.com
High quality and innovative programming in the visual and performing arts - all in a warm and supportive environment. Drawing, painting, pottery, architecture, drama and musical theatre, offered after school and Saturdays. Small class sizes, highly qualified artist/instructors. **Look for our ad in this section. See coupon section for valuable savings.** • Ages: 9mos-adult • *VISA*, ⊖, *Interac*, Cheque • Mon-Thu: 8:30-8, Fri: 8:30-6:30, Sat: 8:30-5:30.

Barishev School of Fine Art

2965 Kingston Rd, Ste 2A , Scarborough, Ont, M1M 1P1. • 416-471-4731 •
Drawing, painting, composition, architectural design and more!

Beaux Arts School of Creative Learning

202 Parkhurst Blvd, Toronto, Ont, M4G 2G3. • 416-421-0773 •
Experimenting with art in a friendly, supportive environment.

Brainwaves Knitting School - Private, Group & Family Classes

416-489-1945 •
A warm, friendly atmosphere where kids can explore the fun of this timeless craft. Programs also available for AD/HD. Ages 5 & up.

**Avenue Road
Arts School, n.,**

Definition:
1. a nurturing place engaging children and teens of all ages in innovative arts programs
2. a provider of the latest approaches in art & drama
3. a place where every child feels like a star

Programs in the Visual & Performing Arts

460 Avenue Road, Toronto, ON, M4V 2J1
416-961-1502
www.avenueroadartsschool.com

Avenue Road Arts School

Art: Activities, Lessons & Supplies

$COUPON$ Gymboree Play and Music Programs
Central Toronto 416-410-6FUN, Thornhill (905) 707-1420,
Bloor West /Etob/Miss/Oakville (905) 542-PLAY • www.gymboree.com
Unleash your child's imagination in a world of hands-on discovery that includes exploration at our tactile table to life-size drawings on the wall. Come paint, draw, sculpt and create with us! **Look for our ad in Parent/Tot section. See coupon section for valuable savings.** • Other Locations: Call 1-800-520-PLAY. • Ages: 18 mos. - 5 yrs. • *VISA*, ⊕, *Interac*, Cheque.

$COUPON$ Klim School of Art
1238 Centre St, Thornhill, Ont, L4J 3M9. • 905-882-0884 • www.klimschoolofart.com
Klim offers small, intimate art classes to children and adults. We also offer animation, birthday parties, Creative Works summer programs, March Break, Passover and Winter Camp, extra-curricular programs and portfolio preparation. Stretch your imagination and creative abilities with Klim today. **Look for our ad in the Birthday Parties section. See coupon section for valuable savings.** • Ages: 4-18.

Lynrich Arts
93 Green Lane, Thornhill, Ont, L3T 6K6. • 905-771-0411 •
Art Parties, Art Camp, Art Classes, Art Supplies.

McMichael Canadian Art Collection
10365 Islington Ave, Kleinburg, Ont, L0J 1C0. • 905-893-1121 •
Weekend programs and year round family activities..

$COUPON$ MESSY HANDS Art Studio
2501 Rutherford Rd, Unit 27, Bldg B, Richmond Hill, • 905-303-MESS (6377) •
www.messyhands.com
Dive in & explore creativity! Small, intimate art classes in our inspiring studio atmosphere! Many drawing, painting, sculpting & multimedia classes for ages 2-102! **Look for our ad in the Birthday Parties section. See coupon section for valuable savings.**

Pegasus Studios
361 Glebeholme Blvd (Danforth & Coxwell), Toronto, Ont, M4C 1T9. • 416-469-2799 •
www.pegasusdance.com
Mixed Media Art, Painting & Drawing for 6 yrs and up. Childhood Expressions programs for 2.5-4yrs. combining music, dance and art. Summer Creative Arts Camps. Small Classes. In operation since 1986. • *VISA*, ⊕, ▓, Cheque.

Pottery, The
498 Runnymede Rd, Toronto, Ont, M6S 2Z5. • 416-690-9475 • www.thepottery.ca
Children's and adult pottery lessons, birthday parties. • Ages: 5+.

Progressive Art for Progressive Kids!
Beaux-Arts Brampton Gallery
70-74 Main St. N. , Brampton, Ont, L6V 1N7 . • 905-460-1606 • www.beaux-artsbrampton.com
Six fun-filled courses; cartooning to painting, six weeks each, taught by professional artist, Saturdays during school year, gallery visits, artist interviews and more! • Ages: 8-12.

Sew Be It Studio
2156 Yonge St, Toronto, Ont, M4S 2A8. • 416-481-7784 • www.sewbeitstudio.com
We are a fully equipped studio located in Central Toronto. We offer classes and workshops in sewing, beading, quilting, knitting, and all craft related activities. Our class size is small and intimate to inspire our student's imagination.

Art: Activities, Lessons & Supplies

$COUPON$ Wanda's Creative Clay
416-885-0885 • www.wandascreativeclay.com
Sculpey/FIMO Clay..it's fun, it's easy. Create a masterpiece at lunch! **Look for our ad in the Birthday section. See coupon section for valuable savings.**

▪ Craft Supplies

Canco Canada
31 Madawaska Ave, Toronto, Ont, M2M 2R1. • 416-229-6297 • www.cancoshop.ca
A leader in the supply of high quality arts & crafts products. Premier graphite and colored pencils at competitive prices. Three series of pencils - from beginner to artist quality.

Craft & Hobby Emporium
75 Dolomite Drive, Toronto, Ont, M3J 2N1. • 416-665-0504 •
We specialize in children's arts and crafts supplies.

J & J Crafts
93 Green Lane , Thornhill, Ont, L3T 6K6. • 905-707-7960 •
Arts & crafts supplies at wholesale prices.

Lewiscraft
416-291-8406 for a location near you •
Fun and Creative Kids' Craft Products.

Sassy Bead Co
2076 Yonge St, Toronto, Ont, M4S 2A3. • 416-488-7400 • www.thesassybeadco.com
Beads, accessories, jewellery school, workshops, birthday parties.

▪ Paint Your Own Ceramics

All Fired Up Paintable Ceramics
8 & 10 Brentwood Rd N, Etobicoke, Ont, M8X 2B5. • 416-233-5512 • www.afu-ceramics.com
Paint your own ceramics! No appointments are required! Great for any age! Birthday parties, camps and summer fun. • *VISA*, ⬤, *Interac* • Tue: 11-6, Wed: 11-9, Thu: 11-6, Fri: 11-9, Sat: 11-6, Sun: 12-5.

Bisque It Pottery Painting
8 - 9200 Weston Road, Woodbridge, Ont, L4H 2P8. • 905-303-6333 • www.bisqueit.com
Bisque It is a fun & funky pottery studio where you can paint functional, fabulous, personalized pottery for your home and gifts. Walk-ins Welcome! No experience necessary. All supplies & tips provided. • Ages: 5+.

$COUPON$ Clay Room, the
279 Danforth Ave, Toronto, Ont, M4K 1N2. • 416-466-8474 • www.theclayroom.ca
Creative clay parties. Paint your own ceramic parties, in store / take home. Birthday Parties. Bridal showers. Corporate parties. Baby prints. Walk In. Summer and School Break Clay & Craft Camps. Assortment 300+ items. School Rates. Sat & Sun 11am - 6pm, July - Aug (Mon - Fri) 11am-8pm, Sept - June (Tue - Fri) 12 - 8pm, open Monday in Dec. **Look for our ad in the Birthday section. See coupon section for valuable savings.** • *VISA*, ⬤, *Interac*, Cheque.

DIY Dishini Canada Ceramics Studio
132 Main St (Danforth and Main Street), Toronto, Ont, M4E 2V8. • 416-686-1278 •
www.diydishinicanada.com
Do It Yourself Ceramics. Colourful Clay Material. Classes & Parties. We guarantee you'll like it!

Art: Activities, Lessons & Supplies

Glazed Expressions Ceramics Studio
324 Guelph Street, Georgetown, Ont, L7G 4S8. • 905-877-2224 •
Enjoy a fun-filled, creative session. Create your own unique masterpiece.

Mess for Fun Ceramic Studio
73 Alness St, North York, Ont, M3J 2H2. • 416-736-7101 • www.messforfun.com
Ceramic painting is a great way to get your creative juices flowing! Wide variety of ceramic pieces and colours to choose from. No experience necessary. Assistance provided. • Ages: 3+.

Pottery Painting Place
2021 Williams Pkwy E, Unit 2, Brampton, Ont, L6S 5P4. • 905-792-2942 •
Birthday Parties, Home Parties, Guide Groups, Schools.

$COUPON$ Pottery-A-Go-Go
416-658-4545 • www.potteryagogo.com
We come to you. Paintable ceramics and clay. Anytime. Anywhere. Small or large groups. **Look for our ad in the Birthday Parties section. See coupon section for valuable savings.** • Ages: 1+.

Your Fired ...
10178 Yonge St, Richmond Hill, Ont, L4C 1T6. • 905-737-8944 •
Make a memory with one of our ready to paint pieces.

▪ Scrapbooking

Designs by Veronica
60 Lodgeway Drive, Maple, Ont, L6A 3S5. • 416-702-3669 • www.designsbyveronica.ca
I do private classes, group classes and albums for my customers.

Let's Scrap Inc
416-225-1255 •
Scrapbooking! It's the latest craze! • Ages: 7+.

Photoscrapbooking
38 Macauley Dr, Thornhill, Ont, L3T 5S5. • 905-764-1293 •
Meaningful, everlasting albums. Your precious family memories.

Scrapbooking Birthday Parties with Rochelle Simon
416-460-5707 •
Create keepsake albums at a Creative Memories party/workshop.

Scrapbooks by LauraLinda
905-294-4541 •
Professional scrapbook artist & consultant.

thank you for mentioning that you found it in

HELP! ...WE'VE GOT KIDS

Attractions & Family Outings

The city of Toronto has much to discover. The GTA has world recognized museums and galleries, several of which are currently being renovated or refurbished to make them even more incredible. Toronto also has many exciting sports teams: the Blue Jays, the Raptors, the Maple Leafs, as well as professional lacrosse teams, minor league hockey, soccer... something for every taste in every season. We also have excellent and well maintained historical sites which can show you how life used to be or take one of many scenic or historical train rides offered.

For those of you who prefer outdoor fun, there are many seasonal activities offered like the Maple Syrup Festival, Kite Flying Exhibits, Wagon rides, etc.

Check your local newspaper or call Ontario Travel at 1-800-668-2746 for detailed information on Special Events, Festivals and Activities taking place around Ontario. Or, pick up our other publication, The Ontario Summer Fun Guide at Esso Stations provincewide. It is also available online at www.SummerFunGuide.ca.

You will find the following sub-categories in this section:
Attractions & Family Outings, Conservation Areas, Farms are Fun

---

$ COUPONS $ Look for this company's coupon at the back of the book

---

▪ Attractions & Family Outings

African Lion Safari
1386 Cooper Rd, Cambridge, Ont, N1R 5S2. • 519-623-2620 or 800-461-WILD (9453) • Drive through wildlife park with 1,000 exotic animals.

Air Canada Centre Tours
416-815-5982 •
Visit the home of the Maple Leafs and Raptors.

Air Combat Zone Inc
5170 Dixie Rd, Unit 101, Mississauga, Ont, L4W 1E3. • 905-602-4775 •
Air Combat Zone puts YOUR family behind the controls of high performance CF-18 jet combat flight simulators. • Ages: 10+.

Art Gallery Of Ontario - Family Programs
317 Dundas St W, Toronto, Ont, M5T 1G4. • Family Fun Hotline 416-979-6615 • www.ago.net
Dragon Wagon, our interactive play station by artist Kim Adams, has a variety of activities - all included with general admission and free for children 5 and under! Also, enjoy Family Sundays from November to March. • *VISA*, ⊜, ▦, *Interac* • ᴕ.

$ COUPONS $ Bata Shoe Museum, The
327 Bloor St W, Toronto, Ont, M5S 1W7. • 416-979-7799 • www.batashoemuseum.ca
Come with your teacher, family or friends to find the smuggler's shoes, chestnut crushing spiked clogs and space boots in our shoebox! We're one of the best places to learn, explore and create. Free for kids under 5. **Look for our ad in this section. See coupon section for valuable savings.** • *VISA*, ⊜, ▦, *Interac* • Mon: 10-5 June/July/Aug, Tue-Wed: 10-5, Thu: 10-8, Fri-Sat: 10-5, Sun: 12-5 • ᴕ.

Bingemans
425 Bingemans Centre Dr, Kitchener, Ont, N2B 3X7. • 519-744-1231 •
Waterpark, FunworX, go-karts, golf, camping resort.

Black Creek Pioneer Village
1000 Murray Ross Pkwy, Toronto, Ont, M3J 2P3. • 416-736-1733 • www.blackcreek.ca
Experience life in the 1860s. Explore authentically restored heritage homes, shops and gardens.
History comes alive as interpreters in period dress demonstrate how settlers lived and worked in
rural Ontario. • 𝘝𝘐𝘚𝘈, ⊕, ▇, *Interac*, Cheque • ♿.

Bowmanville Zoo
340 King St E, Bowmanville, Ont, L1C 3K5. • 905-623-5655 • www.bowmanvillezoo.com
Awesome AnimaTheatre Shows - June, July and August. Exciting Elephant Rides, Animal
Encounters, Carnivore Feedings, Wildwood Cat Walk, Safari Patio Cafe, amazing Zoovenir Shop,
42 acre parkland, 300 celebrity critters & much more...Open Daily May-Sept, Oct 7,8,9. •
Ages: 1-12 • ♿.

Burd's Trout Fishing
13077 Hwy 48 , Stouffville, Ont, L4A 7X3. • 905-640-2928 •
Stocked pond. Bait. Rod rentals. Fun for all ages.

Campbell House Museum
160 Queen Street West, Toronto, Ont, M5H 3H3. • 416-597-0227 •
A unique glimpse of life in York in 1822.

Casa Loma
1 Austin Terrace , Toronto, Ont, M5R 1X8. • 416-923-1171 • www.casaloma.org
Toronto's famous castle. Secret passages, tunnels and more.

CBC Museum
in the Canadian Broadcasting Centre, 250 Front St. W. (across from CN Tower), • 416-205-5574 •
www.cbc.ca/museum
Fun displays bring CBC history to life. • Mon-Fri: 9-5, Sat: 12-4.

Centreville Family Amusement Park
Toronto Island, Toronto, Ont, M8Z 2T7. • 416-203-0405 • www.centreisland.ca
Enjoy a relaxing, fun-filled day in our turn-of-the-century village. 30+ Rides and attractions. Good
food and games. Catch the Centre Island ferry at Bay & Queens Quay. Open 10:30 am until dusk
every day from Victoria Day until Labour Day. • 𝘝𝘐𝘚𝘈, ⊕, *Interac*.

CN Tower
301 Front St West, Toronto, Ont, M5V 2T6. • 416-86-TOWER (86937) • www.cntower.ca
Celebrating 30 years! World's Tallest Building and Wonder of the World - Toronto's "must-see"
for kids of all ages.

Colborne Lodge in High Park (1837)
Colborne Lodge Drive, High Park, Ont • 416-392-6916 • www.toronto.ca/culture/museums.htm
Charming historic 19th century country home in picturesque High Park. • Ages: 6-12.

Crawford Lake
Steeles Ave @ Guelph Line, • 905-854-0234 •
Reconstructed Iroquoian Village, trails, lake, Niagara Escarpment.

Downey's Farm Market and Winery

13682 Heart Lake Rd (N of Brampton), Caledon, Ont, L7C 2J5. • 905-838-2990 • www.downeysfarm.on.ca
Birthday parties, school tours, u-pick strawberries and raspberries, Easterfest, Strawberryfest, corn maze, Pumpkinfest, farm animals, wagon rides May to December. • Ages: 2-12yrs.

Fish 4 Trout

Milton area, 20 min. from the Airport, • 416-587-9739 • www.fish4trout.ca
3 acre pond stocked with 1,000 rainbow trout. No fishing license required. Bait, rental equipment, food, clean washrooms. Breakfast served while you fish. &. Families, singles, friends & groups welcome. Open weekends 7:30 am - 1:30 pm.

Franklin Children's Garden on Toronto Island

Access Toronto, 416-338-0338 • Dig! Play Hide & Seek! Learn about wetlands! Climb! Discover!

$COUPON$ Funstation Funpark

5 York Gate Blvd (2 bl. E of Hwy 400, N of Finch), • 416-736-4804 • www.funstationfunpark.com
A 5-acre amusement park featuring Go-Karts, mini Go-Karts, two 18-hole miniature golf courses, batting cages and an arcade. Fun for the whole family. A great birthday party venue! Open April to October, weather permitting. Call for hours. **Look for our ad in the Birthday Parties section. See coupon section for valuable savings.** • Ages: 3+.

Gibson House (1851)

5172 Yonge St, North York, Ont, M2N 5P6. • 416-395-7432 •
www.toronto.ca/culture/museums.htm
Beautiful historic home depicts Toronto's rural past. Birthdays parties. Summer camp. Hands-on activities. • VISA, ⊕, *Interac*, Cheque.

Harbourfront Centre

235 Queens Quay W, Toronto, Ont, M5J 2G8. • 416-973-4000 • www.harbourfrontcentre.com
Fun and inspiring kids' programs year-round: free ZOOM! Family Sundays with Music with Bite, Gallery Kids, and more; jam-packed March Break and Summer Camps; free skating on the Natrel Rink all winter; and our incredible Milk International Children's Festival of the Arts every May! •
VISA, ⊕, ▦.

High Park Zoo

Deer Pen Rd (Bloor & High Park) , Toronto, Ont • 416-392-1111 •
See deer, yaks, llamas, peacocks and many more animals in our paddocks. Large, unique children's play area too. Nature walks available all year round. FREE. Entrances at Bloor St West (West of Keele St) and High Park Blvd and Parkside Drive. Follow signs to Grenadier Cafe (parking available) then walk across the street to Deer Pen Rd. Zoo is located at the end of the road. Open 7:30 - dusk every day.

Historic Fort York (1793)

100 Garrison Rd, Toronto, Ont, M5B 1N2. • 416-392-6907 •
www.toronto.ca/culture/museums.htm
Birthplace of Toronto, features original War of 1812 buildings. • Ages: 6-12.

Historic Sites & Museums of Toronto

Operated by the City of Toronto, Culture Division, , • Events Hotline: 416-338-3888 •
www.toronto.ca/culture/calendar.htm
The City of Toronto operates many historic museums, including Fort York, Colborne Lodge in
High Park, Gibson House, Mackenzie House, Montgomery's Inn, Spadina Museum: Historic
House & Gardens, Scarborough Historical Museum and Todmorden Heritage Museum & Arts
Centre, and more!

Hockey Hall of Fame

BCE Place, 30 Yonge St, Toronto, Ont, M5E 1X8. • 416-360-7765 • www.hhof.com
A thrilling experience awaits your family – games to play, The Stanley Cup and other trophies,
theatres and an awesome collection of hockey sticks, pucks and sweaters from around the
world! Experience the new 'NHL ZONE'. • **VISA**, ⊕, ■ • Mon-Fri: 10-5, Sat: 9:30-6,
Sun: 10:30-5 • &.

Holocaust Education & Memorial Centre of Toronto

4600 Bathurst St, North York, Ont, M2R 3V2. • 416-635-2883 x153 • www.jewishtoronto.net
Educational programs. Guided tours available for groups.

Jewish Discovery Museum

Bathurst Jewish Community Centre, 4588 Bathurst St, North York, Ont, M2R 1W6. •
416-636-1880 x 390 • www.bjcc.ca
Interactive exhibits about Jewish culture, history and values. Enjoy arts & crafts, special event
Sundays, school tours and birthday parties. • Ages: 0-6yrs • **VISA**, ⊕, Cheque • Mon-Wed: 11-4,
Thu: 10-1, Sun: 11-4.

Jungle Cat World Zoological Park

3667 Concession 6 RR 1, Orono, Ont, L0B 1M0. • 905-983-5016 •
Most unique and exciting Zoological Park.

KiddingAroundToronto.com

www.kiddingaroundtoronto.com
Visit www.KiddingAroundToronto.com for a fantastic local calendar of infant and child-friendly
events, activity suggestions, articles, reviews and much more!

Markham Museum

9350 Hwy 48 (2 km N of Hwy 7), Markham, Ont, L3P 3J3. • 905-294-4576 •
www.markhammuseum.ca
25 acres of parkland, hands-on children's gallery, pond, orchard & beautiful gardens. Tour the historic village or ride a heritage carousel. Applefest in September, Family Camp-in, Friday night marketplace & more! Corporate events & Birthday parties. Open year-round.

Martin House Museum of Doll Artistry

46 Centre St, Thornhill, Ont, L4J 1E9. • 905-881-0426 •
Canada's largest selection of dolls, teddy bears, miniatures & dollhouses. • &.

Medieval Times Dinner & Tournament

Exhibition Place, Dufferin Gate, Toronto, Ont, M6K 3C3. • 416- 260-1234 •
An exhilarating combination of fun, feasting and fighting . • **VISA**, ⊕, ■, *Interac* •
Wed-Thu: 7:00pm, Fri-Sat: 7:30pm, Sun: 3:30pm • &.

Mountsberg Wildlife Centre
S of 401 on Guelph Line, W of Campbellville, , • 905-854-2276 •
Maple syrup, daycamp, raptor centre, Christmastowne.

National Film Board of Canada - Mediatheque
150 John Street (at Richmond - Osgoode Subway), Toronto, Ont, M5V 3C3. • 416-973-3012 •
www.nfb.ca/mediatheque
Hands-on animation workshops for families every weekend. Two hours; guided by professional
instructors. $5 per child, adults free. Thousands of NFB films on personal viewing stations.
Family-friendly guided viewing programs. 7 days a week! Call for information and reservations.

Northwood Buffalo and Exotic Animal Ranch
2192 Cookson Lane, RR2, Seagrave, Ont, L0C 1G0. • 905-985-2738 •
Petting zoo, lions, tigers, jaguars, kodiak, bears, wolves.

Olympic Spirit Toronto
35 Dundas St E, Toronto, Ont • 1-888-466-9991 or 416-360-8477 •
World's only Olympic themed attraction. 12 interactive games. • Ages: 3-18 • Tue-Sat: 10-6.

Ontario Place
955 Lakeshore Blvd W, Toronto, Ont, M6K 3B9. • 416-314-9900 or 1(866) ONE-4-FUN •
Enjoy more than 100 days of summer fun. • Ages: 3+ • 𝗩𝗜𝗦𝗔, ⊝, ▮▮ • ᕋ.

Ontario Science Centre
770 Don Mills Rd, North York, Ont, M3C 1T3. • 416-696-3127 • www.OntarioScienceCentre.ca
Over 600 interactive exhibits, daily demonstrations and programs. Check out our new permanent
exhibit hall - KidSpark - perfect for toddlers and kids up to eight years old. Also, enjoy an IMAX®
Dome film experience at the Shoppers Drug Mart® OMNIMAX® Theatre. • Ages: 2+.

Paramount Canada's Wonderland
Hwy 400 & Major Mackenzie Dr, 9580 Jane St, Vaughan, Ont, L6A 1S6. • 905-832-7000 •
The Best of Hollywood Entertainment - Now Playing!

Playdium
99 Rathburn Rd W (across from Square One), Mississauga, Ont • 905-273-9000 •
www.playdium.com
Your family can count on the ultimate entertainment experience at Playdium. From virtual racing
and white water rafting to batting cages, air hockey and more - our 40,000 square foot playground is ready for your family adventure! Open year round, 7 days a week. Call for hours.

Richmond Hill Live Steamers
McCowan Road N of Aurora Rd., • 905- 277-0969 •
Miniature train rides. All ages. Limited hours.

Ripley's Believe It or Not! Museum
4960 Clifton Hill, Niagara Falls, Ont, L2G 3N4. • 905-356-2238 •
Strange and unusual exhibits from around the world! Winter 10am-5pm, Summer 9am-1am.

Rogers Centre Tour Experience
1 Blue Jays Way, between Gates 1 & 2, Toronto, Ont, M5V 1J3. • 416-341-2770 •
www.rogerscentre.com
An exciting 1 hour "behind the scenes" guided tour of the world famous Rogers Centre. Tours
run daily, event schedule permitting. • ᕋ.

Royal Botanical Garden

PO Box 399 , Hamilton, Ont, L8N 3H8. • 905-825-5040 •
Treat your family to a Family Sunday Funday at the Gardens. Plus, sign your children up for our popular day camps and birthday parties.

Royal Ontario Museum (ROM)

100 Queen's Park (Bloor St W at Avenue Rd), Toronto, Ont, M5S 2C6. • 416-586-8000 •
www.rom.on.ca
Explore the ROM, Canada's leading international museum of world cultures and natural history, and discover a world of wonder, inspiration, excitement and delight.

South Simcoe Railway Heritage Corporation

Mill Street West, Tottenham, Ont, L0G 1W0. • 905-936-5815 • www.steamtrain.com
Bring the family for a scenic, narrated excursion aboard a vintage steam train! Excursions depart from the station in downtown Tottenham, 20 km west of Highway 400 on Highway 9. Gift shop and refreshments at the station; conservation area across the road features swimming, picnicking.

Timber Creek Miniature Golf & Fun Center

12772 9th Line, Stouffville, Ont, L4A 7X3 . • 905-642-5174 • www.timbercreekgolf.ca
37 holes of adventure mini golf, jumping castle, 20-foot slide, games barn, batting cages, driving range and dairy bar. 15 min. E of 404 and Stouffville Rd. • Ages: 3-65.

Toronto Argonauts Football Club

Rogers Centre, 1 Blue Jays Way Ste 3300, Toronto, Ont, M5V 1J3. • 416-341-ARGO (2746) •
Call for ticket information, game dates and times .

Toronto Blue Jays Baseball Club

1 Blue Jays Way, Ste 3200 (Rogers Centre), Toronto, Ont, M5V 1J1. • 416-341-1000, for tickets call 416-341-1234 • www.bluejays.com
See the Blue Jays play at Roger Centre. Tickets start at just $9.00! Saturdays are Jr. Jays Saturdays, kids 14 and under get to run the bases after the game! Ask about our children's discount! • Ages: all, Jr Jays 14 & under.

Toronto Botanical Garden

777 Lawrence Ave E (at Leslie), North York, Ont, M3C 1P2. • 416-397-1340 •
Nature mid-town! Bike paths, picnics, gardens. Teaching Garden. • &.

Toronto Island Park

416-397-BOAT (2628) • www.toronto.ca/parks
Hike, bike, blade, fish, paddle or picnic. Ferry terminal located at foot of Bay Street at Queen's Quay West.

Toronto Maple Leafs

40 Bay St., Toronto, Ont, M5J 2X2. •
Call Ticketmaster for ticket availability (416) 872-5000.

Toronto Rock

643 Yonge St 2nd Fl, Toronto, Ont, M4Y 1Z9. • 416-596-3075 •
Game tickets are available through Ticketmaster by calling 416-872-5000.

Toronto Zoo

361 A Old Finch Ave (Meadowvale Rd and Hwy 401), Scarborough, Ont, M1B 5K7. •
416-392-5929 •
New-"Zellers Discovery Zone". Open year round (except Dec. 25). • ▨, ⊖, ▨, *Interac* • &.

Toronto's First Post Office Museum

260 Adelaide St E, Toronto, Ont, M5A 1N1. • 416-865-1833 •
Write a letter with a quill, seal it with wax and mail it from this British Colonial post office (1833).
For $1 plus postage. • &.

Tourism Toronto

416-203-2500 •
Visit tourismtoronto.com for info on festivals, events, attractions.

Wasaga Waterworld

544 River Rd West, P.O. Box 230, Wasaga Beach, Ont, L9Z 1A3. • 705-429-4400 •
www.wasagawaterworld.com
Family water amusement park. Wave pool, water slides, bumper boats, video arcade, picnic
areas, 18 hole mini golf, kiddies pool & playground and much more! Visit one of our two waterparks located in the world's largest fresh water beach community - Wasaga Beach. Just 1.25
hours North of Toronto.

$COUPONS Wave Pool, The

5 Hopkins St, Richmond Hill, Ont, L4C 0C1. • 905-508-WAVE (9283) • www.richmondhill.ca
Open year round, The Wave Pool offers safe family fun! Enjoy a Wave Swim with 4 foot waves,
a 160 foot twisting water slide, swirl pool and more. **Look for our ad in the Birthday Parties section.
See coupon section for valuable savings.** • VISA, ⊛, Interac, Cheque • &.

Wild Water Kingdom

7855 Finch Ave W, Brampton, Ont, L6T 3Y7. • 905-794-0565 or 416-369-0123 •
Canada's largest outdoor water theme park.

Wild Zone Adventures: Ontario's Largest Indoor Amusement Park

567 Richmond St, Chatham, Ont, N7M 5K6. • 519-436-5504 or (888) 467-WILD •
www.wildzone.com
WildZone Adventures features 12 exciting rides and attractions, 18 hole indoor miniature golf, 24
lane, 10 pin bowling centre, Games Reserve with over 150 interactive video games, and 2 seasonal outdoor go-kart tracks.

York Durham Heritage Railway

905-852-3696 •
Heritage train ride through the Oak Ridges Moraine.

▪ Conservation Areas

Albion Hills Conservation Area

Highway 50, 10 km N of Bolton, , Ont, M3N 1S4. • 416- 667-6299 • www.trcaparks.ca
Swimming, sandy beach, mountain biking, campground, nature trails. Canada Day celebrations &
fireworks. Cross country skiing and rentals. Children's playground.

Boyd Conservation Area

Islington Ave. 5 km N of Hwy 7, , Ont, M3N 1S4. • 416-667-6299 • www.trcaparks.ca
Vaughan's Premiere Picnic Destination! Trails. Soccer field. Beach Volleyball. Bocce. Playground.

Bruce's Mill Conservation Area

Stouffville Rd, 3 Km E of Hwy 404, M3N 1S4. • 416-667-6299 • www.trcaparks.ca
York Region's natural Community Park. Enjoy the Sugarbush and More!

Glen Haffy Conservation Area

Airport Road, 10 km N of Caledon E, , Ont, M3N 1S4. • 416-667-6299 • www.trcaparks.ca
On the Niagara Escarpment. Enjoy nature trails, fishing ponds stocked with rainbow trout from
our hatchery, hatchery tours available for groups - please call ahead. Summer fishing derby.

Heart Lake Conservation Area

Heart Lake Road, 3 km N of Hwy 7, Ont, M3N 1S4. • 416-667-6299 • www.trcaparks.ca
Enjoy Brampton's natural recreation park. Swimming, sandy beach, nature trails, picnicking &
fishing. Non-motorized boating.

Kortright Centre For Conservation

9550 Pine Valley Dr, Woodbridge, Ont, M3N 1S4 . • 905-832-2289 • www.kortright.org
Discover the wonders of nature along scenic trails through forest, meadow, wetlands. Guided
walks everyday. Call for brochure or details. Events include: Maple syrup, kite festival, fall colours
and honey festivals. • Mon-Sun: 10-4.

Petticoat Creek Conservation Area

Whites Road, 1 km S of Hwy 401, Ont, M3N 1S4. • 416-667-6299 • www.trcaparks.ca
Home of Ontario's largest outdoor pool. Enjoy swimming in a pool the size of a Football field!
Life guards. Snack Bar. Playground.

Toronto and Region Conservation Parks

5 Shoreham Dr, Downsview, Ont, M3N 1S4. • 416-667-6299 • www.trcaparks.on.ca
For a wonderful outdoor family outing visit one of Toronto's many spectacular Conservation Parks
including Albion Hills, Boyd, Bruce's Mill, Glen Haffy, Heart Lake, and Petticoat Creek.

▪ Farms are Fun

Albion Orchards Apple Farm

West of Hwy 400 & King Side Rd. in Caledon, • 905-584-0354 • www.albionorchards.com
U-Pick Apples and Pumpkins right from patch. Wagon rides, hayland, birthday parties, baked
goods, school tours, gifts, Xmas trees. Clean family fun!

Andrews Scenic Acres

9365 10 sideroad, Milton, Ont, L9T 2X9. • 905-878-5807 • www.AndrewsScenicAcres.com
PYO farm, farm market, winery, playground, animals, school tours, hayrides, strawberries,
pumpkins, raspberries, blueberries, sweet corn. No entrance fee. Family fun! N of 401 on 10th
sideroad betw Trafalgar Rd & Reg Rd 25.

Brooks Farms

122 Ashworth Rd, Mount Albert , Ont, L0G 1M0. • 1-905-473-3920 •
Train rides, farm, animals, pig races and more!

Chudleigh's Apple Farm

RR 25, 3km N of 401, Milton, Ont • 905-878-2725 • www.chudleighs.com
100 acre farm. Apple picking and pumpkins in season. Play area for kids with 20' long slide. Farm
animals in summer and fall. Tractor wagon rides. Family entertainment area open July through
October, 10am-5pm. 20 min. from Pearson airport. Birthday parties & corporate events.

Downey's Farm Market and Winery

13682 Heart Lake Rd (N of Brampton), Caledon, Ont, L7C 2J5. • 905-838-2990 •
Birthday parties, Pumpkinfest, farm animals, wagon rides May to December.

Forsythe Family Farms

10539 Kennedy Rd, Unionville, Ont, L6C 1N8. • 905-887-1087 • www.forsythefamilyfarms.com
FARMS ARE FUN! Enjoy farm animals, hayloft, rope maze, tricycle track & playground. Weekend
wagon rides and Enchanted Forest. Barn market has great pies and produce. PYO strawberries &
pumpkins. October Harvest Festival. School tours available. Open May-Dec 24. Hours variable.
Please call. • Ages: 0-12 • *VISA*, ⊕, *Interac* • Hours: Variable • &.

Horton Tree Farms

1-800-420-7385 •
Christmas trees - December. Maple festival - March/April.

Pingles Farm Market

1805 Taunton Rd E, Hampton, Ont, L0B 1J0. • 905-725-6089 •
Pick your own apples, strawberries, pumpkins, weekend activities, farm animals, play area.

Pony Farm & Petting Zoo at Lionel's

11714 McCowan Rd, Stouffville, Ont, L4A 7X5. • 905-640-7669 • www.lionelsfarm.com
Introduce children to the sights, sounds, smells, culture, products and lifestyles of the farming
community. Visit our great petting zoo. Pony rides on Sundays. Call for hours. **Look for our ad in the
Birthday Party (Party Places) section.**

Puck's Farm

PO Box 284, Schomberg, Ont, L0G 1T0. • 905-939-7036 • www.pucksfarm.com
Country fun, farm animals & musical entertainment.

Puddicombe Estate Farms & Winery

1468 Hwy #8 , Winona, Ont, L8E 5K9. • 905-643-1015 • www.puddicombefarms.com
Train rides, Thomas & Train gift store, Farm animals, play areas, walking trails, PYO fruit, group
events & parties, cafe, winery. May-Dec 24, 9-5.

Riverdale Farm

201 Winchester St, Toronto, Ont, M4X 1B8. • 416-392-6794 •
Kids look eye-to-eye with pigs, goats, cows, horses, rabbits, swans and chickens in a farm-like
setting. Admission free. Arts & crafts, events, demonstrations & activities daily. • Free • &.

Whittamore's Berry Farm

8100 Steeles Ave. E., Markham, Ont, L6B 1A8. • 905-294-3275 •
Pick-your-own fun farm yard, Pumpkinland.

Bar/Bat Mitzvahs & Corporate/Family Events

This section is focused on those large events in our lives: family gatherings, office parties, Confirmations and Bar/Bat Mitzvahs (a Jewish boy is deemed a "bar mitzvah" when he turns 13 and achieves the status of adulthood and a Jewish girl becomes a "bat mitzvah" when she turns 12). Unlike birthday parties, these events are usually months if not years in the making. In this section you will find everything you need to create a wonderful event. This category includes DJ's, rentals, décor, invitations, caterers, as well as cotton candy machines, giveaways, magicians, and circus performers.

You will find the following sub-categories in this section:
Catering & Specialty Foods; Décor, Rentals & Florists; Entertainment & Games, Hair & Makeup; Invitations & Thank You Notes, Music & DJ Services, One of a Kind Gifts, Party Favours, Party Planners & Consultants, Photographers & Videographers, Venues.

$COUPON$ Look for this company's coupon at the back of the book

▪ Catering & Specialty Foods

At Sweetcakes
905-568-8435 or (800) 331-6037 • www.sweetcakes.ca
Custom designs and photo cakes. Advance notice. Pickup: Mississauga, Woodbridge, North York or delivery. • VISA, ⊕, ▓ .

Cakes By Robert
134 Doncaster Avenue, Unit #5, Thornhill, Ont, L3T 1L3. • 905-889-1448 •
Expertly Decorated Custom Cakes for any occasion. • Ages: 5-10.

CandyMan
3413 Bathurst Street, Toronto, Ont, M6A 2C1. • 416-789-7173 •
Candy floss, sno-cone, popcorn, doughnut machine rentals. All Kosher.

Chocolate Charm
3541 Bathurst St, Toronto, Ont, M6A 2C7. • 416-787-4256 • www.chocolatecharm.com
Choose from five sizes of Smash Cakes and hundreds of chocolate shapes. Closed Saturday but open Sunday (except July/Aug).

Cookies Cookies Cookies
905-780-8762 •
Personalized cookie place cards. Fabulous theme oriented centerpieces.

Debi Duz Chocolates
416-839-1313 •
Custom chocolate creations for all occasions. 100's of designs. Be creative!

Lesley's Party Sandwiches
905-660-0551 • www.lesleyspartysandwiches.com
Delicious finger sandwiches. Also fresh fruit - vegetables & dip - wraps - salads & cheese trays -ready to serve. Desserts & more. Pick up or delivery available.

Bar/Bat Mitzvahs & Corporate/Family Events

▪ Decor, Rentals & Florists

Balloon Bash Gifts & Baskets
7241 Bathurst Street Unit 13, Thornhill, Ont, L4J 3W1. • 905-707-8177 •
Party planning including balloon decor, centrepieces and sculptures. Delivery citywide. • *VISA*,
🌐, ▓, *Interac* • Mon-Wed: 9:30-7, Thu: 9:30-8, Fri: 9:30-5, Sun: 10-5:30.

Balloon King Party Centre
374 Bathurst St, Toronto, Ont, M5T 2S6. • 416-603-4347 • www.balloonking.ca
Balloon and party centre serving the public since 1966. Parties big or small...we serve them all.
Great selection. • Other Locations: Mississauga 905- 272-4430 • *VISA*, 🌐, ▓, *Interac* Mon-
Fri: 9-6, Sat: 9:30-5.

Balloon Trix
39 St. Paul St, Toronto, Ont, M5A 3H2. • 416-214-0414 • www.balloontrix.com
Balloon Trix has been specializing in private and corporate functions for 15 years. We would be
pleased to mix our ideas, with your creative input, so people will talk, and remember your event.

Chair-Man Mills
184 Railside Rd, Toronto, Ont, M3A 3R4. • 416-391-0400 •
Quality rentals for parties & special events.

Garden's Path Floral Studio
327 Queen St E, Toronto, Ont, M5A 1S9. • 416-466-0116 •
Specializes in affordable high-end floral designs.

IceCulture
Box 232, 81 Brock St, Hensall, Ont, N0M 1X0. • 1-888- 251-9967 • www.iceculture.com
Custom designed ice sculptures - themed centrepieces, drink luges, seafood presentations,
dessert displays, ice bars, corporate logos and decorative sculptures for flowers and candles.

Just Design Floral Studio
416-461-8793 or 647-295-6703 •
Just Design special event decor. Creative and custom designs. • By appointment

Micki's
131 Citation Dr, Unit 21, Concord, Ont, L4K 2R3. • 905-738-1161 •
Chair covers, tablecloths, draping.

Parterre Flowers
182 Davenport Rd , Toronto, Ont, M5R 1J2. • 416-966-8669 •
Fresh/Dried arrangements. All special events.

Periwinkle Flowers
1957 Avenue Rd, Toronto, Ont, M5M 4A3. • 416-322-6985 •
It happens only once. Make it special.

▪ Entertainment & Games

$COUPON$ A Dress Up Tea Party by Simply Delightful
905-821-7073 • www.simplydelightful.ca
Exclusive Fairy, Princess and Diva Pop-Star entertainment. Costume dress-up, make-up/nail polish, storytelling, games/prizes, dancing, parade/fashion show. Character appearances and birthday parties also available. **Look for our ad in Birthday Parties-Party Places. See coupon section for
valuable savings.** • Ages: 412 • *VISA*, 🌐, *Interac.*

Bar/Bat Mitzvahs & Corporate/Family Events

A Magic Carpet Ride with Three Funny Hats

416-652-8069 •
Musical Storytelling Trio for family/corporate events. International themes. Educational. Entertaining.

$COUPON$ A Topnotch Magician: W I J the Magician

416-809-6243 • www.magicandcomedy.ca
Make your special events unforgettable! Wij combines clever magic with witty patter that leaves audiences both mesmerized and howling with laughter. Professional magic for bar/bat mitzvahs, corporate events and family picnics. **Look for our ad in the Birthday Parties section. See coupon section for valuable savings.** • Cheque.

Adagio Dancers

416-962-6685 •
Specialty dance performances, interactive. Customized for your event.

All Star Game Rentals

905-897-6108 • www.topshotgta.com
At All Star Game Rentals, we bring the fun to you with our interactive sports game rentals including hockey, soccer, basketball. Free delivery within G.T.A. Check us out at www.topshotgta.com.

ARToonz

905-762-8970 •
Creates 100+ popular cartoons, anime, caricatures.

Caricatures Unlimited

416-242-8745 • www.caricaturesunlimited.com
Hilarious sketches of guests. Outstanding party entertainment! HUGELY POPULAR presentation can be made by using an OVERHEAD PROJECTOR!

Chris Klein Caricatures

416-391-3774 •
Fun, Creative Entertainment for any event.

Cuthbertson Entertainment & Events

40 Havenbrook Blvd, Toronto, Ont, M2J 1A5. • 416-496-8200 • www.cuthbertsonevents.com
Full service entertainment specialist. Show producers. Event management. We can find anything from a Live White Tiger to Butterflies or a White Grand Piano. Nothing is impossible. Over 40 years experience.

$COUPON$ D Jay The Entertainer

44 Water Wheelway, Toronto, Ont, M2H 3E4. • 416-494-3034 • www.djaytheclown.yp.ca
One of Toronto's top family entertainers. Guitar. Magic. Balloons. **Look for our ad in the Birthday Party Entertainment section. See coupon section for valuable savings.** • Cheque.

Debi Sander Walker Entertainment

905-275-4744 •
Mystery reader, sing-a-longs, just plain silliness.

Elaine Charal Positive Strokes Handwriting Analysis

416-446-2903 • www.elainehandwriting.com
One-on-one handwriting analysis that entertains, amazes and focuses on the dynamic strengths of your guests-everyone feels special and positive. Ages: Older children; mixed adult/children group.

$ COUPON $ Entertainment Ontario

125 Weldrick Rd Unit 16, Richmond Hill, Ont, L4C 3V2. • 905-770-0231 •
www.entertainmentontario.com
Put some fun in your function. **Look for our ad in this section. See coupon section for valuable savings.**

$ COUPON $ Farco Entertainment

905-761-0010 • www.farcoentertainment.com
Popcorn, snow cones, candy floss and jumping castle rentals. "For the best in entertainment, call now." **Look for our ad in this section. See coupon section for valuable savings**. • Cheque • Mon-Sat: 9-5, Sun: 9-12.

Golden Canadian Productions

14 Winfield Ave, Toronto, Ont, M6S 2J8. • 416-766-8494 • www.goldencdnproductions.com
Over 2,000 superb performers! DJ's, Magicians, Look-a-likes, Bands & Musicians, Caricatures & more. Sensible prices. Over 36 years serving our valued clients. TRY US, WE CARE! **Look for our ad in the birthday party section.**

Happy Time Clowns & Magicians

416-996-2020 or 877-777-4544 •
Family entertainers, clowns, magicians & more.

Hart Entertainment

43 Gurney Cr, Toronto, Ont, M6B 1S9. • 416-762-2200 •
Casinos, arcade games, inflatables & amusements. Brochure.

Hollywood Heaven Look-A-Likes & Entertainment

416-456-5773 •
Home of Canada's top celebrity impersonators singing LIVE for any event.

Jason Wilkins - Event Caricature Artist

705-741-4652 • www.jasonwilkinsstudios.com
Jason Wilkins Studios offers the very best in Event and Gift Caricatures services for your next corporate or private function.

JGardner Entertainment and Event Management Inc

86 Gerrard St E, Ste 20E, Toronto, Ont, M5B 2J1. • 416-506-1643 • www.jgardnerevents.com
We create spectacular events! Live entertainment, interactive children's crafts & games, themed decor and much, much more! Call to book your next event. Visit our website for fabulous event photos.

Comments? Questions? HELP! ...WE'VE GOT KIDS
We'd love to hear from you!
Email us at info@helpwevegotkids.com

Bar/Bat Mitzvahs & Corporate/Family Events

Little Miss Henna

905-731-0067 • www.littlemisshenna.com

Not just tattoos anymore. Call to book your function and inquire about our many new party serv-ices. Tattoos, sparkles, leather bracelets, beaded keychains, hairwraps, facepainting, biker bands, personalized trucker hats & flip-flops and stick on tattoos. "CALL NOW...DON'T WAIT". • Ages: 5+.

Magic By Jordan

905-764-8835 • Close-up magic for Bar/Bat Mitzvahs and corporate events.

Redline Promotions Party Rentals

530 Coronation Dr, Unit 1, Scarborough, Ont, M1E 5C8. • 416-284-0388 •
www.redlinepromotions.com

We rent Jumping Castles, Giant Slides, Ball Pits, Video Games, Candy Floss and Popcorn machines and more. Clowns & Magicians. Birthdays or any special event. **Look for our ad in the Birthday Party Rentals section.**

Rent a Party Entertainment

416-748-9283 or 416-949-9283 •

Game Rentals, Catering, Limo Service, Banquet Halls, Live Bands and more.

Sphere Entertainment

1397 Danforth Ave, Ste 2A, Toronto, Ont, M4J 1N2. • 416-461-1844 •
www.sphereentertainment.com

Since 1980, top musicians, magicians, clowns, psychics, idol contests, TV stars. Specializing in corporate family events and festivals/fun fairs.

Tara, Tarot Consultant & More

1792 Dundas St E, Toronto, Ont, M4L 1M3. • 416-461-1999 •

Professional, entertaining,Tarot, Astrology. Your event success.

$ COUPONS Tom's Amazing Cats

416-347-1153 • www.tvpuppetree.com

It's got Puppets. It's got Magic. It's feline fun for ALL ages. It's Amazing! (and it's affordable, too). **Look for our ad in the Birthday Party section. See coupon section for valuable savings.**

Top Talent Entertainment

905-770-7808 or 1-888-877-0939 • www.toptalent.ca

WE HAVE IT ALL ... SINCE 1984! DJ's, Caricaturists, Bands, magicians and more. **Look for our ad in the Birthday Party Section. See coupon section for valuable savings.** • 𝘝𝘐𝘚𝘈, ▓, Cheque.

$ COUPONS Tribus Body Art

416-538-0770 • www.tribusbodyart.com

Temporary tattoos applied by airbrush, all paints FDA approved. Enjoyed by all ages, for all occa-sions! **Look for our ad in this section. See coupon section for valuable savings.**

Zero Gravity Circus Productions

416-469-1440 • www.zerogravitycircus.com

Our troupe of professional artists offers high-impact solo acts, full-length shows or site animation using traditional and contemporary circus-style disciplines. Acrobats, aerialists, fire artists, stilts & more! Custom shows of all shapes and sizes! • Mon-Fri: 10-6.

Bar/Bat Mitzvahs & Corporate/Family Events

ART&MIS
Illustration & Design Studio, Toronto

Greeting Cards, Posters, Brochures,
Promotional Material,
Announcements, Invitations…

(416)8170726 • maryam@rogers.com • www.artandmis.com

▪ Hair & Make-up

Jeanette Pandev Make-up Artist
89 Elvaston Drive, North York, Ont, M4A 1N7. • 416-752-8007 •
Make-up for all your special occasions.

Jenine Seetner, Makeup Artist
416-730-9349 •
Bar/Bat Mitzvah, bridal, prom, graduation, portrait makeup.

▪ Invitations & Thank-you Notes

$ COUPONS Art & Mis
25 Birch Ave, Richmond Hill, Ont, L4C 6C4. • 416-817-0726 •
Art & Mis Creative Design Studio specializes in one-of-a-kind hand-drawn illustrations for greeting
cards, announcements, invitations! Call Maryam. **Look for our ad in this section. See coupon section
for valuable savings.**

Designs by Sharon - Invitations
Yonge & Steeles, Thornhill, Ont, L3T 1P3. • 905-881-5884 •
Custom & catalogue invitations, baby cards - affordable. • By appointment

Elegant Invitations
128 Invermay Ave, Toronto, Ont, M3H 1Z8. • 416-631-0366 •
Exquisite invitations, thank you notes, and more. Discount prices.

▪ Entertainment & Games ▪ Hair & Make-up ▪ Invitations & Thank You Notes ▪   37

Invitations By Barbara
146 Rimmington Dr, Thornhill, Ont, L4J 6K1. • 905-738-1232 or 905-738-8733 •
Invitations, baby cards, business stationery, accessories, custom, etc. Great Discounts!

ladybugs creative stationery
6 Old Park Rd, Toronto, Ont, M6C 3H3. • 416-783-8140 •
Fully customized creative invitations. Excellent prices. Personalized service.

Main Event Invitations, The
343 Wilson Ave, #304, North York, Ont, M3H 1T1. • 416-802-2254 •
Adorable birth announcements. Classic/funky Wedding or Bar/Bat Mitzvah invitations. Beautiful
thank you notes. Many unique designs to choose from. To suit any style or budget. Creative
ideas and personalized service. Discount prices. Kippas available. Call Renee to view samples -
By appointment only. •

moms2moms
905-887-7598 •
Unforgettable memories through photocards, lootbags & event planning.

Paper Expressions
50 Doncaster Ave, unit 7, Thornhill, Ont, L3T 1L6. • 905-764-9812 • www.paperexpressions.com
Custom and catalogue invitations, seating cards, thank-yous, baby cards, personalized sign-in
books and boards. Papers for creating your own invitations.

Penny People Designs
416-932-8688 • www.pennypeople.com
Personalized stationery never looked so cute! Visit us online to see our beautiful collection of stationery items. We offer fine paper products such as Invitations, Personal Stationery, NoteCards &
Announcements. Orders available for pick up in Toronto.

The Wrappers, Toronto's Fabulous Kids' Label Catalogue
416-250-6020 • www.thewrappers.ca
Address labels, Thank -You notes, notepads, stationery, luggage tags, fun labels, custom pillowcase, towels and more. All personalized with professionally created, funky and fabulous, colourful
graphics that kids and adults love! Choose the graphic that best describes your favourite activities and unique personality. Perfect for school or camp. Great gifts!

Your Little Characters
2934 Council Ring Rd, Mississauga, Ont, L5L 1L2. • 905-607-1348 •
Customized-designed birth announcements and photo invitations.

▪ Music & DJ Services

Dooley Kidshow Family Fun
905-936-9054 •
Hilarious songs, interaction & "Spontaneous Kidsband" instruments.

Living Rhythm
45 Steepleview Cr, Richmond Hill, Ont, L4C 9R3. • 647-444-DRUM (3786) •
www.livingrhythm.ca
Drum and shake up some fun for your party, family/community event, teambuilding or leadership
seminar! Instruments provided. For all ages.

Magen Boys High Energy Entertainment

2600 John St, #105, Thornhill, Ont, L3R 3W3. • 905-513-6464 • www.magenboys.com
Looking for some high energy entertainment? Magen Boys Entertainment is your number one source for disc jockeys, dancers, live music and specialty entertainers. MBE will make your party one to remember. Call now!

PressPlay Productions

416-590-0070 •
For the party of your life!

Sole Power Productions

416-663-SOLE (7653) •
Interactive DJ and live entertainment company.

Speak-Easy Jazz Band

416-782-9202 •
For parties, bar/bat mitzvahs and family events. • Cheque.

▪ One of a Kind Gifts

2 Fun Momz

11 Flanders Rd, Toronto, Ont, M6C 3K5. • 416-789-9801 •
Custom sign-in scrapbooks, photo albums and more... • Cheque.

Digital Scrapbooks by Skeilk

10 Connaught Ave, Gormley, Ont, L0H 1G0. • 905-888-5922 • www.skeilk.ca
Let us help you preserve your memories. We take your photos and convert them into customized attractive digital scrapbook layouts.

Eclectics Unique ArtWare - Thornhill

905-886-8843 • www.eclecticsartware.com
We "Bling Your Thing" with Swarovski crystals - DIY kits available; Swarovski "HeartBead" Pendants. "Sign-in" Caricature paintings, DIVA bags, ANYTHING!

Ketubah by Karny

416-497-9555 •
Ketubah, Bar/Bat Mitzvah Haftorah, Baby Naming Calligraphy

PSS Gifts (a Slick Marcom Co)

PO Box 429, Maple, Ont, L6A 1S3. • 416-433-0639 •
Creative, customized gifts for all ages.

Sugar Sugar Creative Videos

647-200-7290 • www.sugarsugarvideos.com
Creative Videos of Children. Dust off your rarely watched home videos and gather your favourite photos....We'll transform them into something you'll watch over and over again.

▪ Party Favours

Chocolate Charm

3541 Bathurst St, Toronto, Ont, M6A 2C7. • 416-787-4256 • www.chocolatecharm.com
Great selection of chocolate shapes, chocolate lollipops, DJ gifts and truffle box favours. Custom printing and seating tags too.

Bar/Bat Mitzvahs & Corporate/Family Events

Digital Memoreze - BUZ GLOWSTICKS!

14-3650 Langstaff Rd, Suite 201, Woodbridge, Ont, L4L 9A8. • 416-763-8244 • www.buz.ca
GLOWSTICKS! Wholesale! Great for Parties, Children's Events, Bar/Bat Mitzvahs & More!
Hours of Fun. Free Shipping. Secure Online Ordering. **Look for our ad in the birthday party section.**

eventworks: digital photo novelties

416-482-3984 • www.eventworks.ca
Eventworks specializes in onsite digital photography and event novelties. Photos are shot, combined with a custom border and framed at your event; making them the perfect keepsake.
Framed photos, magnets, mousepads, snowglobes, T-shirts, Event TV and more.

Incredible Novelties

155 West Beaver Creek Rd, Unit 9, Richmond Hill, Ont, L4B 1E1. • 905- 881-9900 •
Incredible Novelties is a one-stop-party-favour shop!

$ COUPON $ Loots

896 Eglinton Ave W, Toronto, Ont, M6C 2B1. • 416-787-5668 • www.loots.com
Bar/bat mitzvah centre for all the latest giveaways. Specializing in one of a kind grand prizes. **Look for our ad on the inside front cover. See coupon section for valuable savings.** • *VISA*, 🏧, 🏧, *Interac* •
Mon-Fri: 9:30-7, Sat: 9:30-6, Sun: 10:30-5.

Photo Key-Chains At Your Party or Event

416-782-9202 • hseigel@sympatico.ca
Our photographer attends your party, takes glorious colour photos of your guests, & while you
wait, mounts them into jewel-quality lucite photo keychains. Great for Lootbags! Birthday Parties,
Family Get-togethers, Company Picnics, Weddings/Bar Mitzvahs. Call for quote.

Taal's Treats

2225 Middlesmoor Crescent, Burlington, Ont, L7P 3X2. • 905-336-7299 •
Homemade chocolates for any special occasion.

www.UpAndComingEvents.MakesParties.com

416-665-6100 •
Order your party goods & novelties online.

▪ Party Planners & Consultants

A N D Logistix Inc

1345 St Clair Ave W, 3rd Fl, Toronto, Ont, M6E 1C3. • 416-593-7744 • www.andlogistix.com
Complete event management produced by certified professional. Our team will produce an event
suiting your needs and budget. Let's talk!

A Piece of Cake - Party Planning Services

905-737-7237 • www.a-piece-of-cake.ca
We plan and deliver on every detail, or just a few, to make your child's birthday as unique as they
are!

An Event to Remember

905-771-0038 •
Party consultants help ensure everything runs smoothly.

Gayle Kertzman Wedding and Special Event Planning

416-892-1240 •
Coordination of bar/bat mitzvahs and children's parties.

Heidi Gruenspan Wedding & Party Planner
248 Judith Avenue, Thornhill, Ont, L4J 7C7. • 905-738-5030 • www.heidig.ca
"Let's Plan the Perfect Party". Professional planner for all occasions.

Melodye Friedman Event Planner
905-737-2770 •
Planning custom events that reflect personal taste.

Ricky Bessner & Fern Cohen Party Planning
905-731-2005 •
Let us take the stress out of party planning. Leave the Meetings, Coordination, Vendors, Overseeing, Liasoning, Organizing, Supervising and Unexpected Occurrences to us. Be a guest at your own party!

Tamara Temes Party Consultant
905-770-7977 •
Stress free weddings and bar/bat mitzvahs.

Up & Coming Events
416-665-6100 • www.upandcomingevents.ca
CREATIVE & ORGANIZED...that's what it takes to plan a perfect party. Our personal service and attention to detail will guide you in planning your special event.

▪ Photographers & Videographers

Alexandra Chelsky- A.J. Productions
416-801-1609 •
Convert old photos to DVD slideshow, add your favourite music.

Avonhill Video
1912A Avenue Rd, Toronto, Ont, M5M 4A1. • 416-622-8908 •
Professional videos for all occasions. Tribute Videos. Reasonable rates.

Creative Kids by Piper Studio
238 Supertest Rd, Toronto, Ont, M3J 2M2. • 416-650-1868 • www.piperstudios.com
Imagination, originality and expression; 3 ingredients for exciting and fun photography. Available in vibrant colours or dramatic Black & White portraits. Custom work available. • VISA, ⊕,
Interac • Mon: 10-6, Tue: 10-8:30, Wed: 10-6, Thu: 10-8:30, Fri-Sat: 10-6.

Lisa Productions
905-764-1033 •
Creative, innovative, personalized videos. Reasonable tribute videos.

Manuela Stefan
250 St George Unit #306, Toronto, Ont, M5R 3L8. • 416-924-7457 •
A child's face is a canvas on which emotions are displayed each and every second. I want to write little stories of their days.

Video Affairs
1 Clark Ave W, Ste 302, Thornhill, Ont, L4J 7Y6. • 905-889-0909 •
Creative & professional digital video productions on DVD for $995.

Video Excellence Productions
94 Breckonwood Cres, Thornhill, Ont, L3T 5E8. • 905-731-4355 •
Producing videos Bar/Bat Mitzvah & Tribute videos since 1983.

Video Productions by Josh
905-709-9277 •
Only the best for your event.

■ Venues

A Yankee Lady Yacht Charters
Box 7093, Stn A, Toronto, Ont, M5W 1X6. • 416-868-0000 •
Private charters. Three vessels - 50, 100 and 300 capacity.

Alleycatz Restaurant & Jazz Bar
2409 Yonge St , Toronto, Ont, M4P 2E7. • 416-481-6865 •
Available for corporate parties, bar mitzvahs, etc. Live entertainment nightly.

Atlantis Pavilions at Ontario Place
955 Lakeshore Blvd W, Toronto, Ont, M6K 3B9. • 416-260-8000 X272 • Toronto's most magical
place on the waterfront.

Beach Blast Indoor and Outdoor Beach Volleyball
15 Leswyn Rd (401 and Allen Expressway), Toronto, Ont, M6A 1K1. • 416 633-5929 •
www.beachblast.ca
Make your kid's party the BEST PARTY of the year! The "BEACH MITZVAH" package is active,
fun and safe. Beach Parties for up to 500 people in our 30,000 sq foot facility. Custom packages
available. • Other Locations Polson Pier 416-222-3577 • *VISA*, ⊕, *Interac.*

Camp Green Acres
11123 Kennedy Rd, Markham, Ont, L6C 1P2. • 905-887-1400 • www.campgreenacres.com
A unique way to celebrate. Indoor/Outdoor. Games. Music. Dancing. Food and more.

$COUPONS Canadian Hockey Academy, The
1107 Finch Ave West, Toronto, Ont, M3J 2P7. • Toll Free: 1-866-782-2822 or 416-782-2822
www.futurestarsarena.com
Make your function a hockey/skating theme party! Fun & enthusiastic staff design a custom
event specially designed for you including an "NHL style" skills competition, 3 on 3 hockey tournament & on-ice games. We provide invitations, catering & all activities. **Look for our ad in this section. See coupon section for valuable savings.** • Ages: 4 - 21 • *VISA*, ⊕, ■, Cheque.

Capitol & York Event Theatres
York: 101 Eglinton Ave E, Capitol: 2492 Yonge St, Toronto, Ont, M4P 1H4. • 416-322-3322 x221 •
www.eventtheatres.com
The Capitol and York Event Theatres are the perfect venues for your unforgettable functions.

Casa Loma
1 Austin Terrace , Toronto, Ont, M5R 1X8. • 416-923-1171 • www.casaloma.org
Enjoy the exclusive use of three charming main floor rooms. Experience the unique ambiance of The
Great Hall with its 60 foot oak beamed ceiling and towering bay window. Accommodates 125 - 1000.

Eglinton Grand, The
400 Eglinton Ave W, Toronto, Ont, M5N 1A2. • 416-485-5900 •
A historical landmark exclusively yours for the evening.

Hockey Hall of Fame
30 Yonge St, Toronto, Ont, M5E 1X8. • 416-360-7735 • Unique venue for parties from 100 -1000 people.

Make your child's next
Bar/Bat Mitzvah a hockey
or skating theme party! Our
staff will design a custom
Bar/Bat Mitzvah party
specially for your child.

**1107 Finch Avenue West • Toronto • Ontario • M3J 2P7
Phone: 416-782-2822 • www.futurestarsarena.com**

Loots Lounge

1669 Bayview Avenue , Toronto, Ont, M6C 2B1. • 647-435-1049 • www.loots.com
Toronto's latest & coolest Bar/bat mitzvah & Sweet 16 venue at 1669 Bayview Avenue. Looks
like a real South Beach nightclub with a large dance floor, games area, lounge and bar. Turnkey
party and very affordable. • VISA, ⊕, ▨, *Interac* • Mon-Fri: 9:30-7, Sat: 9:30-6, Sun: 10:30-5.

Match Restaurant and Event Venue

177 Whitmore Rd, Woodbridge, Ont, L4L 6A6. • 905-850-5699 • www.matchbar.ca
The established uptown funky venue committed to surpassing your expectations for private and
corporate parties.

$COUPONS North Beach Indoor Volleyball Academy

74 Railside Rd, North York, Ont, M3A 1A3. • 416-446-0777 • www.northbeachvolleyball.com
Bar/Bat Mitzvahs and corporate events offered year round at North Beach. Featuring authentic
beach atmosphere, catering and entertainment options. Included in the surroundings are 1500
tonnes of sand, beautiful painted murals, music and activity directors for any theme. **Look for our
ad in the Birthday Party section. See coupon section for valuable savings.** • Ages: 4+.

Rinx

65 Orfus Rd, North York, Ont, M6A1L7. • 416-410-RINX (7469) •
Interactive, Exciting, Sports-themed Venue! • VISA, ⊕, ▨, *Interac.*

Sam & Pete's

70 Interchange Way, Vaughan, Ont, L4K 5C3. • 905-738-6001 •
We specialize in tailoring your event for success.

Toronto Centre for the Arts

5040 Yonge St, Toronto, Ont, M2N 6R8. • 416-733-9388 •
An ideal location for your next event. • Ages: 3-10.

Toronto Zoo

361 A Old Finch Ave (Meadowvale Rd and Hwy 401), Scarborough, Ont, M1B 5K7. •
416-392-5940 • Looking for a unique venue for your next event? Think Toronto Zoo. • ♿.

Birthday Parties

Birthdays are a very special day for every child. Our children start planning their next birthday immediately after they celebrate their current one. There are so many innovative, creative ideas in this section that parents no longer have to worry about how to top last year's party. Your child's party can be as hassle-free as you would like - in this chapter you can find everything from entertainment, party places, rentals, cakes, loot bags, cotton candy machines and more.

If you are organizing a party at home, consult the entertainers sub-category and if you prefer to let someone else deal with the mess, check the Party Places sub-category. Don't forget that you can also rent amusements, games or jumping castles for a backyard or community centre party. The ideas in this section allow parents to fulfill virtually any birthday wish for their child. Sports, activities, music, rock climbing, art...you'll find it all here.

In addition to what appears in this section, there are other chapters which can assist you in finding a perfect party for your child - check listings in Farms Are Fun!, Amusements (esp. bowling, mini golf), After School Lessons and Sports as many listees don't appear in multiple categories.

You will find the following sub-categories in this section:
Cakes & Cookies; Entertainment (fun parties that come to you!); Inflatables & Party Rentals, Party Places; Supplies, Decorations & Loot Bags. Enjoy your party!

$COUPON$ Look for this company's coupon at the back of the book

▪ Cakes & Cookies

At Sweetcakes
905-568-8435 or (800) 331-6037 • www.sweetcakes.ca
Large selection: DoraExplorer, SpongeBob and hundreds more. Any occasion. Custom designs and photo cakes. Advance notice. Pickup: Mississauga, Woodbridge, North York or delivery. •
[VISA], ⊕, ▪▪▪.

Bake It Healthy Natural Sweets & Healthy Treats
905-303-7589 •
Organic treats without sugar, eggs, dairy or wheat.

Barb's Sinful Cakes and Catering
Dufferin and King St W, Toronto, Ont • 416-535-2455 •
Nut Free! Catering, Character Cakes, Cookies, Chocolates!

$COUPON$ Cakes By Robert
134 Doncaster Avenue, Unit #5, Thornhill, Ont, L3T 1L3. • 905-889-1448 •
www.cakesbyrobert.com
Nut Free - Simply the Best! Cakes for all occasions. 1000's of designs. Edible Photo Cakes. Gourmet Cookies and Cookie Grams. **Look for our loot bag ad in this section. See coupon section for valuable savings.**

Cakes by Rochelle
905-762-1696 •
Gourmet cookies & cakes for all occasions. Nut free.

Cakes & Parties By Lisa

905-881-4046 •
You name it, we'll make it. Custom-designed cakes for all occasions.

Chocolate Charm

3541 Bathurst St, Toronto, Ont, M6A 2C7. • 416-787-4256 • www.chocolatecharm.com
Choose from five sizes of Smash Cakes and hundreds of chocolate shapes. Closed Saturday but open Sunday (except July/Aug).

Chocolicks Fun Factory

573 Eglinton Ave West, Toronto, Ont, M5N 1B5. • 416-485-2047 • www.chocolicks.com
ChocoLicks creates new and different, fun and funky products to awe kids and adults of all ages. Fabulous Smash Cakes, Caramel and Chocolate Popcorn, Candy Apples, Crazy Candy Creations and much more! Birthdays, Bar Mitzvahs, Corporate events etc. Call us for something different!
Look for our ad in the Supplies, Decorations & Loot Bags section.

Cookies Cookies Cookies

905-780-8762 •
THE MOST TALKED ABOUT COOKIES IN TOWN. Custom designed, personalized, decorated cookies. All occasion cookie gift baskets. Cookie centrepieces. People place cards. Wiggles, The Princesses, Sesame Street characters, Barbie etc. Great as cake toppers or party favours. Peanut free. Anything is possible!

Eat My Words

416-489-7700 • www.eatmywords.org
Delightfully decorative and divinely delicious special occasion cakes and cupcakes, delivered in a hatbox tied with ribbon. With every treat box order, a three course hot meal will be provided to Out of the Cold, a program run out of churches and synagogues that provides meals to those in need. Nut free, no preservatives.

Essence Cakes

3 Morley Cres, Brampton, Ont, L6S 3K8. • 416-821-6924 •
Yummy cupcakes, character birthday cakes & sugar cookies.

$COUPON$ Katie's Cakes

1531 O'Connor Dr, Toronto, Ont, M4B 2V7. • 416-757-6896 • www.katiescakes.com
Specializing in nut free children's cakes, cookies and chocolates. Always fresh. Any Theme. Shaped, 3-D or flat. Special Photo cakes. Customized with your party. This is your ultimate cake, cookie and chocolate destination. **Look for our ad in this section. See coupon section for valuable savings.**

▪ Entertainment

Birthday Parties

A Barbie Dress-up Tea Party!

The original real hair Barbie parties for over 12 years!

· A real hair Barbie and 2 dressing assistants · High heels, Crowns & wands
· Gloves, Purses, Feather boas · Large selection of gowns
· Manicures, Pedicures, Make-up · Furs, Jewellery
· Party favors for up to 15 children · Invitations
· Real fine bone china

416-221-5881

www.dressupteaparty.ca

$COUPON$ A Barbie Dress-up Tea Party by Party Productions

416-221-5881 • www.dressupteaparty.ca
Where were these parties when we were little?! Two hour dress-up party in your home!
Includes heels, purses, gloves, furs, jewellery, gowns, make-up, manicures, pedicures, birthday
gift and party favours. **Look for our ad in this section. See coupon section for valuable savings.** •
Ages: 3-12 • Cheque •

A Clown called Joey & Zan Zar the Genie

416-766-8494 • www.goldencdnproductions.com
Magic, Balloonology, Fire Eating.

$COUPON$ A Different Kinda Party

905-882-0611 • www.dkp.zip411.net
Experienced, professional entertainers of all kinds, ranging from Super Heroes and Characters to
Clowns and Magicians. We also provide unique, custom-made Piñatas and delicious Party
Sandwiches for kids and adults. **Look for our ad in this section. See coupon section for valuable savings.**

$COUPON$ A Drama Queen Birthday!

905-731-3374 • www.dramaqueens.ca
The Drama Queens are committed to providing parties that are fun and unique. SET-UP/CLEAN-
UP, BIRTHDAY MURAL, LOOT BAGS and CD SLIDESHOW included. PARTIES take place in the
comfort of your own home. **Look for our ad in this section. See coupon section for valuable savings.** •
Ages: 4-14.

A Different Kinda Party

Look-a-Like Characters

Barney • Shrek • Superman • Barbie • Elmo
Bob the Builder • Red Ranger
Spiderman • Batman • Puss-in-Boots
Strawberry Shortcake • Gingerbread
Lunette • Mr. Incredible
Willy Wonka • Chicken Little

• ENTERTAINERS FROM SUPER HEROES &
CHARACTERS TO CLOWNS AND MAGICIANS

• UNIQUE CUSTOM-MADE PINATAS   *And Lots More! Always adding new characters*

CALL SARI (905) 882-0611
www.dkp.zip411.net

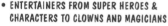

Check back of book for Coupon

THE MAGIC OF ROBERTO

Award Winning Performer

Professional • Reliable • Affordable

Rabbit, Doves, Illusions, Balloon Animals, Audience Participation, Magic Workshops, Educational Programmes, Comedy

"Have your child levitate at your party"

As seen on Discovery Channel, CBC, City TV and Roger's Cable

(905) 828-5577
TheMagicOfRoberto@hotmail.com

$ COUPON $ A Dress Up Tea Party by Simply Delightful

905-821-7073 • www.simplydelightful.ca
Exclusive Fairy, Princess and Diva Pop-Star parties/entertainment at our location or yours. Costume dress-up, make-up/nail polish, storytelling, games/prizes, dancing, parade/fashion show and tea parties. Character appearances, camps, cakes, balloons, loot bags also available. **Look for our ad in Birthday Parties-Party Places. See coupon section for valuable savings.** • Ages: 5-12 • *VISA*, *MC*, *Interac*.

A Family-Run Company: "Laugh Along Entertainment!"

416-694-6865 or 905-884-3725 • www.LaughAlong.com
Lunette & Mollee: Songs and Stories! Mama Make-Believe: Dress-Up Storytelling! Princess Penelope: Magic Show and Make-Up! Jelly Belly the Clown! Funky Fortune Tellers! Balloons! Face-painting! Interactive Magic! Musical Band! Crafts! "Custom parties created for your unique child!"

A Knit Magic Jewelry Party- Learn to Knit Beaded Treasures

416-489-1945 •
Knit Magic will bring fun to your party as kids create their very own knitted, beaded bracelets. Ages 8 & up.

A Nature Visit: Nature & Animal Presentations

30 Burnhamthorpe Road, Toronto, Ont, M9A 1G8. • 416-233-8548 • www.naturevisits.com
Nature & animal presentations for schools, birthday parties, corporations, etc.

A Piece of Cake - Birthday Planning Services

905-737-7237 • www.a-piece-of-cake.ca
Time to celebrate another special year of your child's life with the perfect party! We plan and deliver on every detail, or just a few, to make your child's birthday as unique as they are! A personalized party ensures lasting memories of their special day.

$ COUPON $ A Topnotch Magician: W I J the Magician

416-809-6243 • www.magicandcomedy.ca
Give your child memories of a birthday that will last a lifetime! Wij combines clever magic with witty patter that leaves audiences both mesmerized and howling with laughter. Professional magic for children's parties, birthdays, bar/bat mitzvahs. **Look for our ad in this section. See coupon section for valuable savings.** • Cheque.

A Ventriloquist Storytelling Party

416-781-5807 • Talking puppet/dummy adds joy to party.

$ COUPON $ Abracadabra, The Magic of Roberto

905-828-5577 •
Award winning performer. Interactive show. Live doves & rabbits. Prepare to be amazed! **Look for our ad in this section. See coupon section for valuable savings.**

The Drama Queens
Specialized Parties & Event Entertainment

Customize parties from a variety of fun options!
Day at the Spa ~ Crafty Couture ~ Create-A-Cookie ~ Dynamic Dance

Choosing from our many activities will surely make your child feel like royalty!
Call: 905.731.3374 or visit us online at www.dramaqueens.ca

$COUPON$ Alpha's Discovery Club Inc
416-410-2917 • www.alphasdiscoveryclub.com
Theme adventure parties! Dora Explores Jungle, Princess Dress-up, Be a Superhero, Under the Sea Spongebob/Nemo, Harry Potter's Magic, Pirate, Detective/Spy, 1st Birthday/Winnie the Pooh. **Look for our ad in this section. See coupon section for valuable savings.**

Amazing Jeff The Magician
905-839-7057 • www.magician.org/member/jeffsnape
Magician, clown, live bird and rabbit, Santa, balloons, comedy. Established 1989. In film, television, and live performances. All ages, all events, anywhere!

Amazing Magic of Danny Hamill
416-931-0099 • www.dannyhamill.com
30 years of magical entertainment! Danny will design a show specific to your needs - children's shows to adult shows. One of Toronto's foremost balloon artists!

An Astonishing Magic and Illusion Show! Ryan Wilson
264 Glenwood Cres, Bolton, Ont, L7E 1Z4. • 416-735-8343 • www.ryanwilsonmagic.com
Astonishing MAGIC SHOWS Kids birthday parties. Magic and illusion shows for all ages. Schools, corporate events, fundraisers, in your home. Incredibly affordable balloon animals and gummy bears for the kids. Starting @ $150.00.

thank you for mentioning you found it in

HELP!
...WE'VE GOT KIDS

Featured On Discovery Channel
Toronto's Favourite Magician "Wij"

Make your party this much FUN!
*Fun Interactive Children's Magic
*Balloon Animals *Magic Giveaways
(416) 809-6243
Www.magicandcomedy.ca

Birthday Parties

$COUPON$ Animals with Whimz at Whimz Studio
784 St. Clair Ave West, Toronto, Ont, M6C 1B6. • 416-656-7894 • www.whimzonline.com
Featuring Live Animals: Small Mammals, Reptiles, Amphibians, Bugs & Birds-from rabbit, hedgehogs and chinchillas to lizards, toads & snakes. All Hands-on and Very Busy. In your home or NEW!!! WHIMZ STUDIO (Bathurst & St. Clair location-lot parking by appt only). **Look for our ad in this section.**
See coupon section for valuable savings. • Ages: 1-16 • Cheque.

Anna Shmanna - the winsome clown
416-792-9409 •
Mesmerizing interactive clown show with props, music, balloons, face painting and much more! Professional actress and playwright. Great for Birthdays and Special Events.

Applefun Puppetry
416-895-3492 • www.applefun.ca
It's time to try something new! Hilarious, interactive shows, 45 minutes long. Entertainment even adults will enjoy. We come to you. • Ages: 1-8.

ARToonz
905-762-8970 • Learn to draw one of over 100 popular cartoons, anime, caricatures. Years of teaching experience in schools and parties. Each child makes a piece of art, toon-book, toon-shirt, toon-art. Toronto and York Region. Available for Schools, Daycares, Camps.

Auntie Jan's Parties
416 653 6248 • Reliable clowns and magicians, crafts, face painting and more! • Ages: 0-12.

Balloons & Magic by Gregory
416-657-6287 • Children have memories that last a lifetime when Greg brings his Amazing balloon art and award winning magic to their party.

Beading Bashes
416-488-6550 • Total fun with beads for everyone!

$COUPON$ Beadology for Kids
416-898-1347 • www.beadology.ca
Beads, Beads, Beads! Beadology brings a jewellery workshop to your party! Children design and create their own hand made gift to wear home! A rainbow of colours and all the skills make for one of the most creative birthdays ever! At Your Place or Ours!! Beadology Loot bags Included!
Look for our ad in this section. See coupon section for valuable savings.

Beads for your Needs
416-806-0427 • www.beadsforyourneeds.com
The children choose from a wide selection of beads and get to create their own beautiful piece of jewellery. It's always a great success and the children are delighted with their creation. $12 per child. • Ages: 6-15.

Birthday Party Doug
416-439-8133 • Interactive FUN parties with Super Heroes, Characters, Clowns, Magicians and much more! Balloons, Games - Completely interactive hour of fun.

Blossom the Clown
1-888-627-6690 • www.blossomtheclownbandb.com
Award winning professional, international clown. Parties, picnics, Xmas shows, gospel, all functions! Interactive shows include comedy, balloons, magic, storytelling, face-painting, audience participation, sight gags and more. For any size group. Group workshops also available. • VISA .

$ COUPONS Bugs Without Borders
416-788-4542 Sabeena or 416-573-5234 Nadine • www.bugswithoutborders.com
You're having a party, can we come? It's not just for two legged animals, is it? We would like to bring: Giant Millipedes, Hissing Cockroaches, Tree Frogs, Snakes, Salamanders, and more…
Look for our ad in this section. See coupon section for valuable savings.

Caricatures Unlimited
416-242-8745 • www.caricaturesunlimited.com
Hilarious professional entertainment for all occasions, all ages. Excellent original sketches of guests drawn quickly on paper or screen projection while everyone watches. Outstanding party entertainment and a souvenir too! • Cheque.

Catwalk Girls Modelling Parties & Workshops
905-876-4534 • For girls' birthdays and sleepovers ages 8+.

Celebrations Entertainment Co./Woodbridge Party Centre
4120 Steeles Avenue West, Units 1 & 2, Woodbridge, Ont, L4L 4V2. • 905-850-9193 •
Children's playground. Top quality kids' shows. Balloons, party supplies, costumes, lawn signs.

Ceramic Shop on Wheels
4 John St, Weston, Ont, M9N 1J3. • 416-433-0883 •
We come to You/You come to Us! Birthday parties for all ages.

Chandelle Productions
115 Madison Ave, Toronto, Ont, M5R 2S3. • 416-968-0563 •
Book Now! Magic, Juggling, Spiderman, Winnie & Cinderella.

We would like to introduce you to some of our friends, Giant Millipedes and Tree Frogs that will 'rock climb your arm', Snakes and Salamanders that will 'tickle you fearless', Tarantulas and Scorpions that will flabbergast you. A Chameleon that will change color right in front of your eyes!

If you have the backbone to host a spineless party for 40-50 minutes at your home for a bunch of kids then you're invited to bug us.

Book Your Party Today:

416-788-4542

www.bugswithoutborders.com
sabeena@bugswithoutborders.com

BUGS without Borders

Chester the Clown formerly Checkers the Clown
905-301-4877 •
For 10 years, Checkers provides phenomenal full time professional entertainment.

Children's Parties and Music Programs by Robyn (B.A., B.Ed.)
905-881-4699 • musicbyrobyn@sympatico.ca
Energetic singer/guitarist will keep your birthday guests thoroughly entertained and busy: singing, dancing, playing instruments and parachute games... • Ages: 6mos-8yrs • Mon-Tue: 4-9, Wed: 9-9, Thu: 4-9, Fri-Sun: 9-9.

Clay with Me - Thornhill
905-886-8843 • Create and play with Clay! Kids, Adults. • Ages: 4+.

Clowns at Party California
Serving Mississauga & surrounding areas, • 905 567 8912 •
"The best face painting." Incredible! Balloons. Magic.

Creative Clowns
125 Weldrick Rd, Unit 16, Richmond Hill, Ont, L4C 3V2. • 905-770-0231 •
www.entertainmentontario.com
Children's birthdays are our specialty. Quality professional entertainers for a wide range of social functions. Serving the surrounding Metro regions since 1985. Comedians, magicians, puppets, singers, costumed characters and more. Satisfaction guaranteed. References available. •
Ages: 0-10 • Cheque.

Creative Spark Ceramic Painting Parties

416-423-9605 • Bringing everything needed to paint keepsake masterpieces!

$ COUPON $ Creepy Crawlers Express Educational Presentations

1 Promenade Circle, PO Box 943, Thornhill, Ont, L4J 8G7. • 416-456-0262 •
www.creepycrawlers.ca
Let your children experience a birthday they will never forget! Four hands-on & interactive programs: Insects, Reptiles, Science, Furry Friends. Available for schools/daycares/camps. **Look for our ad in this section. See coupon section for valuable savings.** Ages 2-13.

Critter World: The Home of Travelling Critters

905-831-4470 • www.travellingcritters.com
A great hands on adventure for all, with over 30 different kinds of animals, cuddly to creepy.
Animal interaction. Questions & answers. Great for all ages!

$ COUPON $ Critters - Amazing Hands-on Animal Presentations

73 Baroness Cr, Toronto, Ont, M2J 3K4. • 416-494-0712 • www.critters.ca
For the most memorable birthday party ever. An entertaining, educational, hands-on experience
in your home. Touch and hold reptiles, bugs, birds, mammals, frogs and more. Plus schools (curriculum based) daycare, fun fairs and special events. Camps too. **Look for our ad in this section.
See coupon section for valuable savings.** • Ages: 2-12.

Voted Toronto's Best Entertainer 2004
Voted one of Toronto's Top Clowns 11 Years in a Row

Performed at over 6,000 fun-filled Birthday Parties!

D JAY THE CLOWN
(416) 494-3034
www.djaytheclown.yp.ca
A Real Clown Not a Clone

$COUPON$ D Jay The Clown
44 Water Wheelway, Toronto, Ont, M2H 3E4. • 416-494-3034 • www.djaytheclown.yp.ca
Award winning clown, author and teacher. D Jay performs a unique Clown show that your child
will love. Guitar music. Magic Tricks. Balloon Sculpture. Puppets. Imitations. Also available for
corporate events, promotions, picnics, Xmas. Classes in clowning and ballooning. Full time professional. **Look for our ad in this section. See coupon section for valuable savings**. • Ages: 1-90.

Donna's Driving Service
905-852-6746 •
Horse and carriage for all occasions.

Dragoon Puppet Theatre
416-657-1696 • www.puppetadventure.com
Terrific puppet shows! Music, humour, participation. Personalized, original stories. 1 hour show
that really keeps kids' attention! • Ages: 2-9.

DramaWay Birthday Celebrations - PartyWorks
416-614-1078 x2 • www.dramaway.com
Exciting and creative, child-centered, drama birthday parties in your home or an outside location.
Personalized themes. Dress-up. Creative movement. Storytelling. Puppetry and imaginative play.
Ages: 3+.

Dreams Revealed with Scott Dietrich
416-580-5522 or 866-686-2442 •
Award Winning Magician, audience participation, live bunny, balloon animals.

Entertainment Galore
29 Gladiola Court, Whitby, Ont, L1R 1N8. • 905-723-3175 •
Clown, magician and Santa.

$COUPON$ Entertainment Ontario
125 Weldrick Rd Unit 16, Richmond Hill, Ont, L4C 3V2. • 905-770-0231 •
www.entertainmentontario.com
Providing quality professional entertainment for over 18 years. Birthdays, Bar Mitzvahs, reunions.
Talented performers that suit your event. Clowns and magicians, carnival games, bouncing castles, candy floss, popcorn, balloon decorating and lots more. Since 1985. Phone for complete
brochure. **Look for our ad in the Bar/Bat Mitzvah section. See Coupon section for valuable savings.**

Birthday Parties

Excellent Enterprises (Dottie Dancer the Clown and Friends)
416-696-8822 •
Professionally clowning since 1983! Specializing in parties personally designed for your child.
Magic, Balloon Sculpting, Facepainting, Comedy, Children's Percussion Band, Sing-a-Long,
Games, Participation Songs, Storytelling, Temporary Tattoos, Puppets and More!

Exhale Mobile Spa - Spa Princess Birthday Parties
416-567-5032 • The Original Spa Princess Birthday Party • Ages: 6-12 yrs.

FaeryPixieGirl Creations
416-934-9624x1 •
Presenting, magical jewellery parties for kids. • Ages: 5+.

Fairy Tale Puppet Theatre
100 Bain Avenue Unit 37 Maples, Toronto, Ont, M4K 1E8. • 416-469-5342 •
www.fairytalepuppettheatre.com
Give your child a fairy tale birthday party with puppet shows and music. Hand made puppets in a
beautiful hand-painted theatre. Live music with banjo, guitar, singing popular and original songs.
Face-painting. Brochure available. • Ages: 3+ • Cheque.

Fairyland Theatre
1183A Finch Ave W, Unit 1 & 2, Toronto, Ont, M3J 2G3. • 416-663-1700 •
www.fairyland-theatre.com
Unique themed parties. Princess, Barbie, Fairy, Dora, Pirates, Spiderman, Harry Potter, Clowns,
Detective, Jungle Puppets, Santa Claus, Halloween and dance parties.

Magical Dan

Zan Zar the Genie

Joey the Clown

Speaking of Wildlife

Happy Jr.

Lenny G

Toyland Puppets

Notelpats the Magical Wizard

Golden Canadian Productions
"Over 2,000 superb performers!"
416-766-8494
www.goldencdnproductions.com

Princess Barbi

Disney Characters

Birthday Parties

Fantasy Fables Children's Entertainment Inc

905-847-4654 Oakville/Miss or 416-485-5048 Toronto • www.fantasyfables.com
Voted Best Entertainment Agency, City Parent. Disney Princess Parties: Cinderella, Sleeping Beauty, Little Mermaid, Snow White & more! We Bring The Magic To You! Since 1985.

$COUPON$ Farco Entertainment

905-761-0010 • www.farcoentertainment.com
Featuring Doo Doo the Clown and Dee Dee the Dancing Clown. Talented & professional clowns, magicians, children's singers and jugglers amaze and enchant audiences. Popcorn, snow cones, candy floss and jumping castle rentals also available. We "put a smile on the faces of children of all ages." **Look for our ad in this section. See coupon section for valuable savings**. • Cheque • Mon-Sat: 9-5, Sun: 9-12.

Feel The Beat

416-816-1533 •
Fun-tastic music & movement party with instruments, parachutes and more. • Ages: 1-6 • Cheque.

Fuzzy Buddies

905-508-0026 • www.fuzzybuddies.ca as
Stuff a friend parties at home. Everyone goes home with a new best friend, a stuffed animal they make.

Golden Canadian Productions

14 Winfield Ave, Toronto, Ont, M6S 2J8. • 416-766-8494 • www.goldencdnproductions.com
Over 2,000 superb performers! Clowns, Magicians, Puppet Shows, Look-a-likes (Snow White, Spiderman etc.), Animal Acts, Mirthful Musicians and more. Sensible prices. 36 years of professional service. TRY US, WE CARE! **Look for our ad in this section.**

Golden Opportunity Entertainment

1185 Kings College Dr, Oakville, Ont, L6M 2S5. • 905-845-9993 • www.goldenopportunity.biz
Ask about Magicians, Dora the Explorer, Elmo, Barney, Fairy Princesses, Super Heroes, Blue Dog, Barbie and more. Adult and teen impersonators also available.

Happy Time Clowns & Magicians

416-996-2020 or 877-777-4544 • www.happytimeclowns.com
Please visit our website where you will see pictures of our professional clowns and magicians. Fabulous family entertainers, some with live bunny rabbits. Professional mascots, Santa Claus, spider-guy, Dora and so much more!

Harvey the Magician

905-727-7782 • http://harveythemagician.tripod.com
This year, give the gift of MAGIC. The birthday child will be the star of a a fun-filled magic show featuring lots of comedy, laughter, audience participation and amazing magic. Magical memories at affordable prices!

Hello Nails

416-576-7673 • A mobile spa - Spa Princess Parties.

Hidee The Clown and "I'm Living Art"

416-282-1312 • www.imlivingart.com
Top Clown" Award! Magicians and princess parties too. See our incredible facepainters at many Toronto events.

Birthday Parties

World Play Theatre presents ... Songs & Stories with

James Funnyhat

For a Birthday Party that is fun, uplifting, and interactive, with
an international flavour.

- Ages 0-3: Music Circles
- Ages 3-6: Interactive Performances
- Ages 6-12: Performances & Workshops
- All Ages: Performances of Stories & Songs
from around the world

(416) 652-9403 • www.WorldPlayTheatre.com

Hollywood Heaven Look-A-Likes & Entertainment
416-456-5773 • Home of Canada's top celebrity impersonators.

It's a Girl Thing - Makeover Birthday Parties
905-336-3874 • In home spa birthday parties for girls of all ages!

$COUPONS James Funnyhat: Songs & Stories
416-652-9403 • www.WorldPlayTheatre.com
Fun, creative, and uplifting entertainment with an international flavour. Many fun programs for 0 -
12 year olds including music circles for the very young and workshops for 7 - 12 year olds. **Look
for our ad in this section. See coupon section for valuable savings. •**

$COUPONS Kayla
905-709-0234 • www.kaylamusic.ca
In-home birthday parties with Ontario's popular children's entertainer - Kayla. Lots of singing,
dancing, laughing and participation. Fun for parents and children. **Look for our ad in the Parent/Tot
section. See coupon section for valuable savings on a Kayla Birthday Party.** • Ages: 1-6 years •

$COUPONS Keri's Dancin' Kids (KDK)~Energized Entertainment
905-731-5146 • www.energizetheparty.com
Get the party started with high energy interactive dance. Add nail art, face paint and crafts. ENERGIZE
THE PARTY! **Look for our ad in this section. See coupon section for valuable savings.** • Ages: 5-11yrs.

Kid's Fun Factory--Science/Tech and Craft Adventures
416-239-6047 • www.thekidsfunfactory.com
TEDDY BEAR FACTORY: (ages 5-10) Design a T-shirt & make your own Teddy Bear! DINOSAUR
ADVENTURE (ages 5-10): Fossils, dig for bones, assemble a large dino. MOTORWORKS (Ages
7-11): Teams build & race wooden cars. • Ages: 5-9yrs.

Kid's Party Crew
416-456-7462 •
And now for something completely different! Exciting Mystery parties (ages 9+), Creative Craft
parties (ages 4-12), Fun Scavenger Hunt parties (ages 4-12). Any theme. In your home. Full set-
up and clean up. 60 - 90 minutes of fast-paced entertainment. • Ages: 4-12.

Kids Unlimited
905-471-5331, Markham • Children's entertainment. Readers Choice Award Winner.

Birthday Parties

Interactive Song & Dance Birthday Parties

Professional singer/songwriter Kayla plays guitar and entertains children with familiar songs & unique sound effects that grab kids' attention. A fun & lively show where everyone participates!

Music Circles

ph. (905) 709-0234

www.kaylamusic.ca

"As seen on Treehouse TV"

Laughing Trunk Inc , The - Creative Learning Centre
5602 10th line W, Unit 106, Mississauga, Ont, L5M 7L9. • 905-858-5884 •
www.thelaughingtrunk.ca
Add a trunk full of fun to your next party or occasion with creative arts and crafts. Join us at our centre or we can bring the fun to you. Workshops and camps also offered.

Lily-Belle
416-249-6978 • Clown, Magic, Dancing turtle, balloons, face painting.

Living Rhythm
45 Steepleview Cr, Richmond Hill, Ont, L4C 9R3. • 647-444-DRUM (3786) •
www.livingrhythm.ca
Drum and shake up some fun at your party! Instruments provided for an interactive journey of fun and games with rhythm. For all ages.

$COUPONS Lofty Entertainment
416-410-9248 • www.lofty.ca
Comedy magic shows, interactive disc jockey, unique balloon animals. **Look for our ad in this section. See coupon section for valuable savings.**

$COUPONS Loots Party Bus Co
896 Eglinton Ave W, Toronto, Ont, M6C 2B1. • 416-787-5668 • www.loots.com
It's so easy! Choose either the Disco Dance & Karaoke bus or the Glow-in-the-Dark Extreme Video Games bus. We'll show up at your chosen location and have a rockin' party entertained by our enthusiastic staff. Best of all, the mess is on us! **Look for our ad on the inside front cover. See coupon section for valuable savings.** • VISA , ⊖ , ■ , Interac.

• **Entertainment** •   59

INCLUDING:
* 4-Party Packages!
* Loot Bags

WE ALSO OFFER:
* School Workshops
* Special Events
* Preschool Programs
* Summer Camps

Give Mad Science® a call!

(800) 630-4403

www.madscience.org/toronto
birthdays@madscience.on.ca

Vortex Generators ● Chemical Reactions
Slippery Slime ● Light Shows
Rocket Launches ● Cotton Candy

$COUPONS Mad Science
1170 Sheppard Ave W, Unit 14, Toronto, Ont, M3K 2A3. • 800-630-4403 • www.madscience.com/toronto
High energy, interactive & hands on science birthday parties. Dry ice and bubbling potions, rockets and chemical magic. Four new party packages available. We'll bring the party to you! Loot bags available. We make your party experience fun and easy. **Look for our ad in this section. See coupon section for valuable savings**. • Ages: 5-12 • Cheque.

$COUPONS Madskills Soccer Programs
101 Chester Avenue, Toronto, Ont, M4K 2Z8. • 416-705-9090 • www.madskillsinc.com
Kick off your birthday with some entertaining soccer, skills tricks & ball control by professional soccer players. Fun parties and great prizes. **Look for our ad in this section. See coupon section for valuable savings.**

Magen Boys High Energy Entertainment
2600 John St, #105, Thornhill, Ont, L3R 3W3. • 905-513-6464 • www.magenboys.com
Are you looking for a birthday party that is like no other? We put on "High Energy" kids' parties for those of you that are looking for something cool and different. Our parties include music, dance, games, prizes, zany activities and more. Please inquire about our "Wrestlemania" kids' birthday shows.

Magic Dan
416-766-8494 • www.goldencdnproductions.com. Sensational comedy magic with lots of fun.

soccer B-DAY parties

amazing TRICKS & cool MOVES

THE FREESTYLERS
Madskills Inc.
Skills, Tricks & Ball Control

fun PARTIES & great PRIZES

ENTERTAINING for all AGES

CALL TO BOOK YOUR PARTY
416 705.9090
www.madskillsinc.com

Magical Clowns - Dilly Dally & Dumpling

905-826-3513 •
Birthday parties by Dumpling and Dilly Dally. Fun. Magic. Artistic face painting. Balloon sculptures. Nursery schools, seasonal parties, picnics, corporations. • Ages: 1-101.

$COUPON$ MESSY HANDS Art Bus

3 Buses to serve you across the GTA, • 905-303-MESS (6377) • www.messyhands.com
Get Inspired! Get messy! Get on the Art Bus! We park our funky, fabulous bus at your location. Parents relax inside while kids create on the art bus. Painting, clay sculpture, mosaics, tie dying, plush toy creation and more. Birthday parties also available at our Vaughan Art Studio. **Look for our ad in this section. See coupon section for valuable savings.** • Ages: 4+ • *VISA*, Cheque.

MESSY HANDS

Hop on the bus & create with us!

Art Bus
Studio Art Classes
Birthday Parties
Art Camps
Special Events
School Programs

2501 Rutherford Rd. Unit 27, Bldg.B
Vaughan, Ontario L4K 2N6

905-303-MESS
www.messyhands.com

Birthday Parties

Music With Simone
416-450-6391 •
Fun, interactive, age appropriate, music parties for kids aged 6 mos. - 5 yrs. Music, movement and participation. 40 minutes of a Musical Bonanza. Instruments for the kids and I play guitar. Fun for all.

My Party Animals
905-762-9799 • www.mypartyanimals.ca
Get ready for some interactive and educational fun with many different species of animals (snakes, birds, hedgehogs, rabbits, lizards and much more) We'll come to your birthday/event for a great experience no one will forget!

Mystic Drumz
416-494-5485 • www.mysticdrumz.com
Bring the rhythms of over 60 percussion instruments to your child's celebration. Unique, hands-on musical fun with the birthday child leading the group in an interactive, hour-long power-packed jam session. Lessons & workshops also available. Ages 4+.

Origami Magic by the Creative Learning Castle
416-693-4517 •
Kids create their own paper toys: Hopping Frogs, Flapping Birds, Airplanes, Jewellery & more. • Ages: 7+.

Papa's Kidz Trains
905-979-8525 • www.papaskidztrains.ca
An extraordinary interactive miniature electric model train layout with six different trains, 100 lights, 60 sounds & 12 animated motors. It's truly an exciting and magical adventure that children from 2-12 will love. Papa's Kidz Trains - where kids get to really play!

Par-T-Perfect Party Planners
Mississauga 905-593-8771, Oakville/Burlington 905-510-5102, • www.par-t-perfect.com
Year round party and event services. Our party leaders and characters will entertain your children while you relax. Inflatable rentals too. • Ages: 1-12 yrs.

$COUPON$ Party in the Kitchen!
106A Banff Road, Toronto, Ont, M4P 2P5. • 416-480-2772 •
Party in the Kitchen's cooking birthday parties provide everything you need for a fun and creative birthday party. From fun activities to goodie bags and from set-up to clean-up, we've got it all.
Look for our ad in this section. See coupon section for valuable savings.

Party on Productions
905-276-9230 • www.partyonproductions.ca
Great birthdays and parties in the comfort of your home. Complete set up and clean up. Fun themes that will engage and delight your children. Call today to reserve an unforgettable birthday!

Party Ponies, The
905-209-8847 • www.thepartyponies.ca
Pony rides at your home! Safe. Affordable. Fun! **Look for our ad in this section.**

Party With Me
905-763-6099 or 647-224-8386 • Specializing in children's parties.

Party With The Bead Girls
416-712-8934 - Sabrina • Fun beading parties for girls. Supplies included. • Ages: 8-18.

Birthday Parties

Looking For a Creative Birthday Party?
Party in the Kitchen all-inclusive cooking birthday parties for ages 4+.
Includes:

- Complete Set-up & Clean-up
- Reliable & Enthusiastic Staff
- Food (kids eat what they make)
- Craft activity & Goodie bags
- AND anything else you need for a creative & fun birthday party experience!

416 - 480 - 2772

party in the kitchen

children's all-inclusive cooking birthday parties

Patty Cakes Puppetry
905-637-7730 • www.pattycakespuppetry.com
Children share laughter; find joy in simplicity; and discover a whole new world through creativity and imagination. A unique, interactive experience includes a 40-minute show with dancing & audience participation. Imaginative & fun! Visit us online. Birthday Parties, Corporate Events, Special Occasions. • Ages: 6mos-13yrs.

Pet Shows on Wheels and NEW Reptile Shows on Wheels
705-737-5449 • Furry, feather, bug, reptile, amphibian creatures at your party. • Ages: 2+.

Petunia the Musical Magical Clown
905-455-3540 • www.petuniatheclown.yp.ca
Birthday party packages at reasonable rates. Magic. Balloon sculpting. Face painting. Sing A Longs and more. Specializes in Brampton and Mississauga area.

Philip & Henry Productions: Magicians and Ventriloquists
1-866-376-2033 • www.philipandhenry.com
Amazing Magic Show by Philip & Henry Productions Inc. at your location. We make the birthday child the star of the show with lots of laughter and participation. Reserve now before your date vanishes. "We bring the smile to your children anywhere in the GTA" Call Now! • Ages: 3+.

$COUPON$ Planet Dance Inc
905-709-2411 • www.planetdance.ca
Dance Birthday Parties at your location. Custom Designed Parties and Loot bags. Themes include; Interactive and Hip-Hop Dancing, Karaoke, Spa, Diva Nail Art, Glitter Make-up, Hula Hoop and Limbo Contests! School, camp and corporate shows available. **Look for our ad in this section. See coupon section for valuable savings.** • Ages: 5-14.

Look For the **Loots Entertainment** ad on the inside front cover!

The Party Ponies
"the most fun kids can have without leaving home"

Our Ponies Specialize in:
- In-Home Birthday Parties
- Daycare Centre Events
- Corporate Picnics
- Family Functions
- and more...

www.thepartyponies.ca
905 - 209 - 8847

Birthday Parties

Pony Farm & Petting Zoo at Lionel's

11714 McCowan Rd, Stouffville, Ont, L4A 7X5. • 905-640-7669 • www.lionelsfarm.com
Bring our ponies to your party (or do it at our place). **Look for our ad in the Party Places section.**

PonyPal Corral

(888) PONIES-8 •
Ponies, petting zoo, jumping castle and tents for your events. Great family fun! We come to you.
Call toll free. • Ages: 1+.

Pottery Painting Place

2021 Williams Pkwy E, Unit 2, Brampton, Ont, L6S 5P4. • 905-792-2942 •
Pottery painting parties at your location or ours!

$ COUPONS Pottery-A-Go-Go

416-658-4545 • www.potteryagogo.com
We bring the fun and creativity of a ceramics studio to you. Everything you need from brushes to
tablecloths is included. You choose the ceramics you wish to paint and we do the rest! **Look for
our ad in this section. See coupon section for valuable savings.** • Ages: 1+.

Princess Parties Plus

416-277-3346 • www.princesspartiesplus.com
We come to your PARTY/EVENT! Variety of parties: Princess, Fairy, Tea Parties, Diva Karaoke,
Spa Parties, Magic shows, Mad Monster Parties, Puppet shows ... Costumes, Crafts, Interactive
games & Music. Free birthday gift. Great for Girls & Boys. • Ages: 1-14.

Put On A Happy Face

17 Ridgefield Cres, Maple, Ont, L6A 1A8. • 905-832-8240 •
Face painting for birthday parties, fairs, corporate events, fundraisers.

Quality Clowns for a Low Price

416-577-KIDS (5437) • www.qualityclowns.com
Clowns and Magicians for birthday parties and special events. Balloon animals, Face Painting,
Amazing Magic Shows and more.

Raina's Rainbow Party-Sing Along Fun for Kids

416-527-2502 •
Specializing in traditional and popular songs. Kids interact with musical instruments to songs they
already know and love! Private parties. Special needs. Fundraisers. Corporate. Summer Music
groups. • Ages: 0-7yrs.

Rent a Party Entertainment

416-748-9283 or 416-949-9283 •
We offer the following services: Characters, Jumping Castles, Game Rentals, Hallowe'en
Costumes, Food Catering, Limo Service, Banquet Halls, Live Bands, Balloons, Loot Bags and
even a Fabulous, Fun Party Bus! Call Bill for more information.

Ron Guttman - The Party Magician

68 Edmund Seager Dr, Thornhill, Ont, L4J 4S5. • 905-889-5113 •
Magical entertainment for children of all ages. • Ages: 5+.

Rosanna's Creations

1967 Bur Oak Ave, Markham, Ont, L6E 1W4. • 416-414-0917 •
Facepainting for birthday parties and other events.

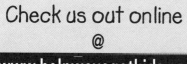

Scrapbooking Parties by Veronica
60 Lodgeway Drive, Maple, Ont, L6A 3S5. • 416-702-3669 • www.designsbyveronica.ca
All occasion scrapbooking parties, kids, adults, wedding, bridal showers. Enjoy a 2 hour class with Veronica Reis. We can do a 2 page layout or super-popular "Altered Paint Cans" for each child to take home. • Ages: 6+.

Sheltoons: Cartoon Fun For Kids
800-476-6910 •
90 minutes of total CARTOONTAINMENT! • Ages: 5-12 • Cheque • Mon-Sun: 9-6.

Sliders Clown & Jazz Band
416-782-9202 • Clown or jazz band for fabulous children's parties. (Adult parties too!)

Snazzy & Crampy Face-Painting Clown Duo
1792 Dundas St E, Toronto, Ont, M4L 1M3. • 416-461-1999 •
Detailed painting for Parties and Events.

Spa Birthday Parties for Kids
76 Roxborough Lane, Thornhill, Ont, L4J 4T4. • 905-482-9172 •
Craft, manicure, facial, massage, dress-up, fortune telling. • Ages: 3+.

Sparkles the Female Magician or Giggles the Magical Clown
416-759-5661 •
Less $. Less stress. More fun for you. Magic show, balloon animals, live rabbit, more!

Birthday Parties

Sphere Entertainment
1397 Danforth Ave, Ste 2A, Toronto, Ont, M4J 1N2. • 416-461-1844 •
www.sphereentertainment.com. Since 1980, top musicians, magicians, clowns and more!

$COUPON$ Steve's Magic
50 Jonathan Gate, Thornhill, Ont, L4J 5K2. • 905-889-6517 • www.stevesmagic.com
"Let me make your party MAGIC". Specializing in birthday parties, balloon animals, family picnics and
corporate functions. **Look for our ad in this section. See coupon section for valuable savings.** • Ages: 4+.

$COUPON$ Storylady
905-967-1139 • www.thestorylady.ca
Invite THE STORYLADY to your party for an unforgettable performance of stories, songs, surprises & super fun accompanied by puppets, music and drama. Ages 4 and up. **Look for our ad in this
section. See coupon section for valuable savings.**

Stuff a Friend with Jen - Stuffable Bear & Toy Parties!
47 Aspen Park Way, Whitby, Ont, L1N 9M6. • 905-665-7288 • www.stuffwithjen.com
We bring 'stuffing' adventures TO YOU! Awesome birthday parties where the 'lootbag' is an
actual hand-stuffed animal or doll.

Sunshine Enterprises: A Craft Birthday
905-889-6047 • Ceramic crafts in your home. Fun, inexpensive. • Ages: 5+.

$COUPON$ Super Science
2600 John St, Ste 106, Markham, Ont, L3R 3W3. • 905-479-4459 •
www.supersciencetoronto.com
Thrill your children with a Super Science Birthday at your location. Dry ice demonstrations, magic
potions, hair raising demonstrations, laser effects, outdoor rocket launches, make your own ooz-
ing putty and much more! Spectacular science entertainment! **Look for our ad in the Birthday Party
Places section. See coupon section for valuable savings.**

Tattoos & Sparkles by Sharon
416-783-9736 •
Amazing handpainted tattoos! Enhance your child's party!

$COUPON$ Tom's Amazing Cats
416-347-1153 • www.tvpuppetree.com
It's got Puppets. It's got Magic. It's feline fun for ALL ages. It's Amazing! (and it's affordable,
too). **Look for our ad in this section. See coupon section for valuable savings.**

$COUPON$ Top Talent Entertainment
905-770-7808 or 1-888-877-0939 • www.toptalent.ca
WE HAVE IT ALL…SINCE 1984! The finest in entertainment for ALL PARTIES AND
EVENTS…call or visit our website for details! **Look for our ad in this section. See coupon section for
valuable savings.** • VISA, [ ], Cheque.

Toyland Puppets
416-766-8494 • www.goldencdnproductions.com
Sensational, interactive, party fun with Puppets, Music and Magic.

Travelling Reptile Show, The
1-877-762-5355 •
Birthday parties, schools, corporate events, community events and children's clubs. See and
touch snakes, lizards, turtles, frogs, tarantulas, scorpions and alligators.

$COUPON$ Tribus Body Art

416-538-0770 • www.tribusbodyart.com
Temporary tattoos applied by airbrush, all paints FDA approved. Enjoyed by all ages, for all occasions! **Look for our ad in the Bar/Bat Mitzvahs & Corporate/Family Events section. See coupon section for valuable savings.**

Tricky Ricky

905-508-6750 •
Create happy memories for a lifetime. Laughter filled.

Try On Armour

524 Ridelle Ave, Toronto, Ont, M6B 1K8. • 416-787-3842, Doug •
Be a knight! Fun & educational. As worn at Casa Loma! • Ages: 5-14.

$COUPON$ Wanda's Creative Clay

416-885-0885 • www.wandascreativeclay.com
Are you looking for a unique birthday party idea, one where everyone will have a blast?
Sculpey/FIMO Clay... it's fun, it's easy and it's done in your own home. Try it, kids love it! It's the clay you make and bake. Great loot bag take home item. Call or visit us online. **Look for our ad in this section. See coupon section for valuable savings.** • Ages: 5+ • Cheque.

Birthday Parties

A CHECKER'S FUN FACTORY INC.
IF IT'S FUN...WE RENT IT!

BOUNCERS • GAMES • SLIDES • SUMO • DUNK TANKS • FUN FOODS • CLOWNS

COMPLETE CATALOGUE ON-LINE
www.rentfun.com
Call (416) 893 3866

■ Inflatables & Party Rentals

A Fun to Rent Inflatable Game Event: Checkers Fun Factory
416-893-3866 or 1 (877) We Rent Fun • www.rentfun.com
Our selection of amusements, inflatable rides, inflatable games, carnival games, and fun foods is one of the largest in Ontario. **Look for our ad in this section.**

$COUPON$ A to Z Fun Rentals
905-841-6484 • www.atozfunrentals.ca
Inflatable bouncers, slides, obstacle courses, mechanical rides, dunk tanks, carnival games, popcorn, sno cones, candy floss, lasertag, kids Go-Karts, BBQ's. Let us put the FUN in your event! Professional, friendly service guaranteed! **Look for our ad in this section. See coupon section for valuable savings.**

Al Gervais Chair & Table Rentals
74 Howden Rd, Scarborough, Ont, M1R 3E4. • 416-288-1846 •
Equipment rentals for children's tables, chairs and highchairs. •

Alltime Party Goods & Table & Chair Rental
3547 Bathurst St, Toronto, Ont, M6A 2C7. • 416-789-2710 •
Kid-sized tables and chairs. Party supplies.

Bounce 123
416-871-1602 • Selection of jumping castles. Set up & delivery.

Bounce House and Jumping Castles Rentals
1 Laura Sabrina Dr, Woodbridge, Ont, L4H1X2. • 905-893-4186 •
Children's party bounce house rentals. • Ages: 1-13yrs.

Fun Bounce House Rentals
416-779-3407 •
On a tight budget? Then search no further. We rent inflatable BOUNCE Houses at a low price. RESERVE Now!

$COUPON$ Great Canadian Amusement Company, The
79 Kincort St. Toronto, Ont. M6M 3E4 • 416-241-3309 or 1-800-567-3889 •
www.greatcanadianamusement.com
For the GREATEST birthday parties in town! We deliver - right to your door - Jumping castles, Games, Popcorn, Snocone, Candy floss machines as well as balloons and lootbags. Themed party supplies and game prizes also available. Call for FREE catalogue or visit our Interactive Showroom on our website. **Look for our ad in this section. See coupon section for valuable savings.** •
VISA, ⊕, ▦, *Interac*.

King of the Castle Jumping Castles
10 Munday Court, Bowmanville, Ont, L1C 4R7. • 416-289 4167 •
Jumping castle rentals, slides, cotton candy, carnival.

Kloda Productions & Entertainment
416-745-2882 • www.klodapro.com
Canada's largest fun party rental company with over 350 items including: Jumping castles, giant inflatable slides, obstacle courses, carnival games, popcorn, cotton candy & snow kone machines. Free colour catalogue. **Look for our ad in this section.**

KLODA PRODUCTIONS INC.   Tel: 416-745-2882
info@klodapro.com   www.klodapro.com

Merlins Party Bouncers
905-420-4008 or 888-285-7765 •
Google "Merlins Party Bouncers" for full details. • Ages: 2+.

Par-T-Perfect Party Planners
Mississauga 905-593-8771, Oakville/Burlington 905-510-5102, • www.par-t-perfect.com
Year round party and event services. Our party leaders and characters will entertain your children
while you relax. Inflatable rentals too. • Ages: 1-12 yrs.

Redline Promotions Party Rentals
530 Coronation Dr, Unit 1, Scarborough, Ont, M1E 5C8. • 416-284-0388 •
www.redlinepromotions.com
We rent Inflatable Bouncers, Jumping Castles, Giant Slides, Ball Pits, Video Games and more.
Clowns, Magicians & other entertainers. Birthdays or any special event. **Look for our ad in this section.**

■ Party Places

$COUPON$ 5 Elements Camps & Workshops
416-423-8456 • www.5elements4girls.com
Create a unique celebration at 5 Elements. Choose from an exciting list of themes from a spa
day or seasonal make-overs to a visual arts experience, your daughter and her friends will have
fun and learn new skills at the same time. **Look for our ad in the Camp section. See coupon section for
valuable savings.** • Ages: girls 6-15.

Birthday Parties

$COUPON$ A Dress Up Tea Party by Simply Delightful

905-821-7073 • www.simplydelightful.ca
Exclusive Fairy, Princess and Diva Pop-Star parties/entertainment at our location or yours. **Look for our ad in Birthday Parties-Party Places. See coupon section for valuable savings.** • Ages: 5-12 • VISA, Interac.

$COUPON$ Academy of Artisans

490 Eglinton Ave West, 2nd fl, Toronto, Ont, M5N 1A5. • 416-322-9997 • www.academyofartisans.com
Cooking, Cartooning, Silk Screen, Tie Dye, Pottery, Floor Cloths, Painting, Kites, Jewellery, Mosaics, Papier Mache, Stained Glass, Metal Sculpture and more!! Free invitations and party room. **Look for our ad in this section. See coupon section for valuable savings.** • Ages: 4+.

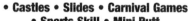

Birthday Parties

www.activekidszone.com
905-307-0707
2600 John St Unit 116. Markham, ON.

| Fun Zone | Cooking | Sports | Crafts |

Birthday Parties   **Special Events**
Childrens Programs   **Holiday and Summer Camps**

$COUPON$ Active Kids Zone

2600 John St, Unit 116, Markham, Ont, L3R 3W3. • 905-307-0707 • www.activekidszone.com
Sports, Crafts, Ceramics, Cooking and FunZone for the preschoolers. **Look for our ad in this section and the Camp section. See coupon section for valuable savings.** • Ages: 1-12 yrs.

Adventureland Playground & Party Centre

8051 Keele St, Units 1&2, Aurora, Ont, L4K 1Y9. • 905-760-PLAY (7529) or 866-515-7529 •
Now featuring Teddy Bear Parties. Private party rooms. Public play. • Ages: toddler-12 yrs.

Air Zone Party and Play Centre

1095 Kingston Rd, Pickering, Ont, L1V 2B1. • 905-839-1047 •
Party packages. Cake, food, pop and popcorn, lootbags, invitations and more! • Ages: 2-12.

airborne trampoline

3 locations: Woodbridge 905-850-8477, Mississauga 905-828-2412, Newmarket 905-836-9091 •
www.airbornetrampoline.ca
Host a trampoline party. Fully Coached, Catering Available. **Look for our ad in this section.** •
Ages: 4+ • *Interac*, Cheque.

All Fired Up Paintable Ceramics

8 & 10 Brentwood Rd N, Etobicoke, Ont, M8X 2B5. • 416-233-5512 • www.afu-ceramics.com
Looking for something unique to do for your birthday party this year? Come paint with us! Our reasonably priced party packages have something for everyone, from mugs to boxes to animals. Give us a call! All ages welcome! • *VISA*, ⊕, *Interac* • Tue: 11-6, Wed: 11-9, Thu: 11-6, Fri: 11-9, Sat: 11-6, Sun: 12-5.

$COUPON$ ALLtimate Party 'n Play

25C Mallard Rd, Don Mills, Ont, M3B 1S4. • 416-425-0098 • www.alltimatepartynplay.ca
Daily Play, Parties, Balloons, Lootbags, themed events. **Look for our ad in this section. See coupon section for valuable savings.**

$COUPON$ Amazon Indoor Playground

Bathurst/St Clair 416-656-5832, Royal York Rd/Eglinton 416-245-1459, •
www.amazonindoorplayground.com
Private, Fun, Family Parties are our Specialty! Climber, Ball Pit, Costumes, Soft Blocks, Infant Toys & More.*New* Karaoke, Fooseball & Air Hockey. Lots of Comfy seating. Bright & Clean. **Look for our ad in this section. See coupon section for valuable savings**. • Ages: 1-8yrs.

Birthday Parties

JUMP!
for the
"HEALTH"
of it.

Experience
the MOST EXHILARATING
Birthday or Holiday party!

airborne trampoline

6 Built-in trampolines
Party Rooms - Ages 4 and up
Certified Coaches

Woodbridge • 905-850-8477
Mississauga • 905-828-2412
Newmarket • 905-836-9091

www.airbornetrampoline.ca

$ COUPONS $ **Animals with Whimz at Whimz Studio**

784 St. Clair Ave West, Toronto, Ont, M6C 1B6. • 416-656-7894 • www.whimzonline.com
Featuring Live Animals: Small Mammals, Reptiles, Amphibians, Bugs & Birds-from rabbit, hedge-hogs and chinchillas to lizards, toads & snakes. All Hands-on and Very Busy. In your home or NEW!!! WHIMZ STUDIO (Bathurst & St. Clair location-lot parking by appt only). **Look for our ad in this section. See coupon section for valuable savings.** • Ages: 1-16 • Cheque.

Art Works Art School

2451 Bloor St W at Jane, Toronto, Ont, M6S 1P7. • 416-766-0662 • www.artworksartschool.com
Art parties. Choose from book-making, instruments, drawing, painting, print-making, sculpture, puppetry and more! Private decorated party room. Art classes, March break and Summer Camps too. • Cheque.

Bathurst Bowlerama

2788 Bathurst St, Toronto, Ont, M6B 3A3. • 416-782-1841 • www.bathurstbowlerama.com
Computerized 5 and 10 pin cosmic bowling. • 𝖵𝖨𝖲𝖠, ⊕, *Interac* • Mon-Thu: 11 - 11, Fri-Sat: 11 am - 1 am, Sun: 11 - 11 • ♿.

Bathurst Jewish Community Centre

4588 Bathurst St, North York, Ont, M2R 1W6. • 416-636-1880 x378 •
Stress & mess free. Includes cake, activities & instructors. • Ages: 2-11.

ALLTIMATE PARTY 'N' PLAY

CHILDREN'S INDOOR PLAYGROUND

Public Play available daily!
Party bookings available week nights and weekends too!
Come and join us for our monthly theme parties
VOTED #1 BY OUR PARENTS 2 YEARS IN A ROW

We are voted #1 Cleanest Playground by all our parents/visitors

25 Mallard Road, Unit C, Toronto ON M3B 1S4 (Don Mills and York Mills)
www.alltimatepartynplay.ca • alltimatepp@hotmail.com • 416-425-0098

Beach Blast Indoor and Outdoor Beach Volleyball
15 Leswyn Rd (401 and Allen Expressway), Toronto, Ont, M6A 1K1. • 416-633-5929 • www.beachblast.ca
High Energy Action Packed Parties led by our experienced and creative staff. Sand Games, Races, Volleyball, Treasure Hunts & more. Free invitations on website. Ideal for kids 3+. Let us tire your kids out! • Other Locations Polson Pier 416-222-3577 • Ages: 3-12 • *VISA*, ⊕, *Interac*.

Bead Cafe - Toronto's Bead Store
970 Eglinton Ave. W, Toronto, Ont, M6C 2C5. • 416-780-9889 • www.thebeadstore.ca
Awesome, fun, creative parties! They'll learn a new skill and take home a fine piece of jewellery they made themselves.

$COUPONS Beadology for Kids
416-898-1347 • www.beadology.ca
The Best Ever jewellery workshop birthday parties! **Look for our ad in the Birthday Entertainment section. See coupon section for valuable savings.**

Big Top School of Circus Arts
1105 Kerrisdale Blvd, Newmarket, Ont, L3Y 8W1. • 905-898-0699 • www.bigtopcircusschool.com
Memories! That's what birthdays are for. Memories of a juggling show, breathtaking trapeze, thrilling tight wire, and lots more! • Ages: 3+ • Fri: 4pm+, Sat-Sun: 12-9.

BIRTHDAY CLUB at Candy Castle
1 DeLisle Avenue (Yonge & St. Clair), Toronto, Ont • 416-96-CANDY (22639) • www.clubcandycastle.com
Design your own unique birthday party - pick your favorite theme. Play in the Candy Castle Giant Maze and enjoy lots of other activities. **Look for our ad in this section.**

Bisque It Pottery Painting

8 - 9200 Weston Road, Woodbridge, Ont, L4H 2P8. • 905-303-6333 • www.bisqueit.com
A fun, unique birthday just a paintbrush away! Paint pottery in our cozy studio … with music & time for pizza & cake!

Bobbins Sewing School

Woodbine & Danforth area, • 416 423 1305 •
Quilting workshops & sewing birthday parties! Machines & equipment provided.

BoNa Party Place Inc.

4945 Dundas St. W, Etobicoke, Ont, M9A 1B6. • 647-258-0459 • www.bonapartyplace.com
Check BoNa Island's village, bouncing castle, drive without a licence, check out the game stations and explore the BoNa Boat.

Bounce 'N' Play Indoor Playground and Birthday Party Centre

3250 Ridgeway Dr, #2, , Mississauga, Ont, L5L 5Y6. • 905-820-2171 • www.bouncenplay.ca
We have expanded!! Now 2 Private birthday party places. Huge 4 level structure w/ gang slides. Rock climbing. Pump it up (DDR), Jumping castles, Air hockey, PS2, Toddler area, etc. Exclusive private party. Bring your own foods. Drop-in play. Only $7.00. • Ages: 1-12 •
Mon-Fri: 9:30 - 3:30.

$COUPON$ Bounce 'N' Play Indoor Playground - Woodbridge

71 Marycroft Ave, #20, Woodbridge, Ont, L4L 5Y6. • 905-850-7529 • www.bounceandplay.ca
Unique 3 level play structure, slides, jumping castle, glow in the dark maze, video games, separate toddler area with a toddler jumping castle and much more...Lootbags and balloons. **Look for our ad in this section. See coupon section for valuable savings.** • Ages: 1-10.

Birthday Parties

Make your child's next Birthday a hockey or skating theme party! Our accommodating staff will design a custom Birthday party specially for your child.

1107 Finch Avenue West • Toronto • Ontario • M3J 2P7
Phone: 416-782-2822 • www.futurestarsarena.com

See our ad opposite the 1st Coupon page at the back of the book

www.sandylion.com

$COUPON$ Cakes By Robert
134 Doncaster Avenue, Unit #5, Thornhill, Ont, L3T 1L3. • 905-889-1448 •
www.cakesbyrobert.com • Kids have a blast making their own pizza, decorating cupcakes, creating ice cream sundaes, 2 hours of fun! Nut free facility. **Look for our loot bag ad in this section. See coupon section for valuable savings**. • Ages: 5-10.

Camp Green Acres
11123 Kennedy Rd, Markham, Ont, L6C 1P2. • 905-887-1400 • www.campgreenacres.com
A farm theme party suited for children 3-10 years old. Our staff will lead the 2 hour party: Visit with our barn animals, tractor pulled hayride, and our decorated party room are all a part of our country birthday bash!

$COUPON$ Canadian Hockey Academy, The
1107 Finch Ave West, Toronto, Ont, M3J 2P7. • Toll Free: 1-866-782-2822 or 416-782-2822
www.futurestarsarena.com
Make your child's next birthday a hockey/skating theme party! Fun & enthusiastic staff design a custom Birthday party specially for your child including an "NHL style" skills competition, 3 on 3 hockey tournament & on-ice games. We provide invitations, catering & all activities. **Look for our ad in this section. See coupon section for valuable savings**. • Ages: 4 - 21 • *VISA*, ⊕, ▓, Cheque.

Casa Loma
1 Austin Terrace , Toronto, Ont, M5R 1X8. • 416-923-1171 • www.casaloma.org
Explore a real castle for your child's birthday party. Specially Decorated Room. Photo opportunities with Kings, Queens and Wizard Cut outs. Available 7 days a week, January - October, for Parties.

Ceramic Shop on Wheels
4 John St, Weston, Ont, M9N 1J3. • 416-433-0883 • saudercam@netscape.net
We come to You/You come to Us! Birthday parties, Daycare, Schools, Churches, Scouting, Guiding, Seniors, Drop-ins, Lessons and Camps.

Children's Technology Workshop
109 Vanderhoof Ave, Toronto, Ont, M4G 2H7. • 1-866-704-2267 • www.ctworkshop.com
Animation, digital video production, and computer game making. Ages 6-14. **Look for our ad opposite the 1st page of the Table of Contents.**

Chuck E Cheese
2452 Sheppard Ave E, Willowdale , Ont, M2J 1X1. • 416-497-8855 •
Where a kid can be a kid! • Other Locations 4141 Dixie Rd, Mississauga 905-602-4090 • &.

Birthday Parties

Circus Gymnastics Programs for Moms & Tots and children of all ages.

Exciting Circus Shows
(in Oct, Dec & March)

Shows • Classes • Birthday Parties • Camps

2600 John St. (905)**479-2411**
Unit 204/205
www.wonderfulworldofcircus.com

CREATIVE CLAY PARTIES
MAKE & PAINT A MASTERPIECE
PAINT IT YOURSELF CERAMIC PARTIES
PRIVATE PARTY ROOMS

Birthday Parties • Corporate Parties
Baby Prints • Bridal Showers
In Store or Take Home Parties
Summer and School Break
Clay & Craft Camps
Assortment 300+ Items
Walk-in Welcome • Ages 5 – 105
School/Group Rates

279 Danforth Avenue Toronto
(between Broadview & Chester, we are closer than you think)
416-466-8474 • WWW.THECLAYROOM.CA

$COUPONS Circus Parties at Wonderful World of Circus

2600 John St, Unit 204, Markham, Ont, L3R 3W3. • 905-479-2411 • www.wonderfulworldofcircus.com • Show, parties & events in our gym or to go. With clowns, jugglers, trained dogs & birds, aerial gymnasts and much more! **Look for our ad in the Sports (Gymnastics) section. See coupon section for valuable section.**

Classic Bowl

3055 Dundas St W, Mississauga, Ont, • 905-607-2695 • Birthday bumper bowling at its best! • Ages: 3+.

$COUPONS Clay Room, the

279 Danforth Ave, Toronto, Ont, M4K 1N2. • 416-466-8474 • www.theclayroom.ca Creative clay parties. Paint your own ceramic parties, in store / take home. Birthday Parties. Bridal showers. Corporate parties. Baby prints. Walk In. Summer and School Break Clay & Craft Camps. assortment 300+ items. School Rates. Sat & Sun 11am - 6pm, July - Aug (Mon - Fri) 11am-8pm, Sept - June (Tue - Fri) 12 - 8pm, open Monday in Dec. **Look for our ad in this section. See coupon section for valuable savings.** • Ages: 6-12.

Cookerydoo

325 Roncesvalles Ave., • Toronto, 416-532-2232 • www.cookerydoo.com We offer uniquely creative cooking and craft parties for children of all ages. Our personalized parties are tailored to various interests and themes and can take place at our location or yours. We also offer classes, cookshops/craftshops, camps and child inspired catering. **Look for our ad in this section.**

CN Tower

301 Front St West, Toronto, Ont, M5V 2T6. • 416-86-TOWER • www.cntower.ca Spend your special day at the CN Tower and enjoy a private room, food, beverage, the Glass Floor and arcade.

Oodily doodily doo • Come try something new!

- uniquely creative cooking and craft parties for ages 3+, at our place or yours
- we also offer cookshops, craftshops, classes, camps and a kids cooking club
- child inspired catering
- gift baskets, loot bags

**325 Roncesvalles Ave. – 416.532.2232
or visit www.cookerydoo.com**

the
COOKERYDOO
Cooking & Crafts for Kids

Birthday Parties

JOIN US FOR A BIRTHDAY PARTY AT

AND FANTASY FAIR
SHOPPING'S NOT THE ONLY ATTRACTION

Ride the antique carousel or any of our 9 full-size rides. Enjoy the giant Play Village, exciting Family Arcade, Midway Games or shop in over 150 stores & services - All under one roof. Open year round 11-7 daily inside the Woodbine Shopping Centre on Rexdale Blvd, one km east of Hwy. 427

Birthday Child FREE with a minimum of 9 paying guests

WOODBINE CENTRE
and Fantasy Fair

(416) 674-KIDS (5437)
www.fantasyfair.ca

Discovery Gymnastics
205 Champagne Dr, Unit #5 (Finch & Dufferin), North York, Ont, M3J 2C6. • 416-638-3033 • Fun-filled gymnastics and trampoline birthday parties. • Ages: 3+.

DIY Dishini Canada Ceramics Studio
132 Main St (Danforth and Main Street), Toronto, Ont, M4E 2V8. • 416-686-1278 • www.diydishinicanada.com
Do It Yourself Ceramics. Colourful Clay Material. Wheel throwing, Figure & Toy Building and Jewelry Classes offered for kids/adults/seniors. Unique, Creative, Fun, Easy. Perfect for Birthday Parties or Special Events. We guarantee you'll like it!

Doogster Productions Inc
368-415 Jarvis Street, Toronto, Ont, M4Y 3C1. • 416-972-6997 • www.doogsterproductions.com
Our 2-hour themed Theatrical Parties will engage, amuse and delight kids aged 3-16! Professionally Trained Actors with years of experience in the Business. **Look for our ad in the After School Drama section.**

Douglas Snow Aquatic Centre North York Parks and Recreation
5100 Yonge St , North York, Ont, M2N 5V7. • 416-395-7585 • Exciting swim party! Tarzan rope, giant, tubular slide. Party room rental.

Dreams Indoor Playland
2701 Rutherford Rd, Maple , Ont, L4L 3N6. • 905-417-3962 • www.dreamsplayland.ca
A banquet hall for kids. 3 Large Private Party Rooms. Experience our new Princess Dress-up Room. Walk the Runway - Be a Star. Full catering available. Summer drop off arts and crafts program. • Ages: 1-9yrs.

$ COUPON $ Eunice's Swim School & Recreation Centre
2 locations: Don Mills/Sheppard & Allen/Eglinton, • 416-410-SWIM (7946) • www.euniceswimschool.com
Fun, flexible birthday pool parties - lifeguards available. Swim toys included. Warm pool temperature. One hour fun in the pool and one hour in party room. Gymnasium available at Don Mills location. **Look for our ad in the Sports (swim) section. See coupon section for valuable savings.** • VISA, ⊕, ▦, Cheque • ♿.

Fairyland Theatre
1183A Finch Ave W, Unit 1 & 2, Toronto, Ont, M3J 2G3. • 416-663-1700 • www.fairyland-theatre.com • Unique themed private parties with dressup, makeup, dance, games, where the birthday child is the star! Cinderella, Snow White, Arielle, Sleeping Beauty, Belle, Barbie, Ballerina, Pirate, Spiderman, Batman, Harry Potter, Peter Pan, and Teen Dance Parties.

Fantasy Castle - Children's Costume Party Centre

105 Vanderhoof Ave, Unit 8, Toronto, Ont, M4G 2H7. • 416-876-1235 •
www.fantasycastletoronto.com
Enter Fantasy Castle and enter the world of princes and princesses, kings and queens, dragons, fairies and knights. The magic begins the moment you enter our castle. Our costumed staff will greet your child and friends and help transform them into the characters of their choice. • Ages: 4 - 10yrs.

$COUPONS$ Fantasy Fair

500 Rexdale Blvd, Etobicoke, Ont, M9W 6K5. • 416-674-5437 • www.fantasyfair.ca
Birthday parties at "Ontario's largest indoor amusement park" inside Woodbine Centre. Nine full-sized exciting rides! Giant Children's Play Village, family arcade and midway games– all under one roof. Open daily 11-7. Thurs. & Fri until 8pm. **Look for our ad in this section. See coupon section for valuable savings.** • ♿.

Four Points by Sheraton Mississauga Meadowvale

2501 Argentia Road, Mississauga, Ont, L5N 4G8. • 905-858-2424 •
Pool parties, pizza parties and much more. • Ages: 5+.

Frozen Ropes Canada

2009 Wyecroft Road,Unit B, Oakville, Ont, L6L 6J4. • 905 847-7697 •
www.frozenropescanada.ca
Birthdays are a hit at Frozen Ropes. Throw the ultimate birthday party for your MVP and friends. Enjoy pro instruction, hitting, throwing, Speed Gun contests and more in our tunnels - and DQ cake in our party room. **Look for our ad in this section.**

Birthday Parties

$COUPONS$ Funstation Funpark

5 York Gate Blvd (2 bl. E of Hwy 400, N of Finch), • 416-736-4804 • www.funstationfunpark.com
A 5-acre amusement park featuring Go-Karts, mini Go-Karts, two 18-hole miniature golf courses, batting cages and an arcade. Fun for the whole family. A great birthday party venue! **Look for our ad in this section. See coupon section for valuable savings.** • Ages: 3+.

Funtastic Kids Indoor Playground

380 Dundas St E, Oakville, Ont, L6H 5K2. • 905-257-6500 •
Funtastic Kids Indoor Playground and Birthday Party Centre. • Ages: 0-6 years.

FunZone Party Centre Inc

3165 Unity Dr, Unit 2, Mississauga, Ont, L5L 4L4. • 905-608-ZONE (9663) •
www.funzonepartycentre.ca • Canada's new #1 Indoor Playground & Party Centre serving Mississauga & region. Obstacle courses, Little Mermaid & Sponge-Bob Bouncers, Inflatable Slide, Separate Toddler Area, Video Games, Table Games & more...Characters available. A World of Fun! • Ages: 1-10.

Gibson House (1851)

5172 Yonge St, North York, Ont, M2N 5P6. • 416-395-7432 •
www.toronto.ca/culture/birthdays.htm
Exciting, hands-on, activity-filled birthday party! Bake derby cakes over an open hearth, dye sheep's fleece, churn butter, dip candles. Party room. Loot bags. • *VISA*, *Interac*, Cheque.

Glaze Craze

7670 Yonge St, Thornhill, Ont, L3T 2C2. • 905-886-9009 •
Birthdays, corporate events, paint it yourself ceramics. • Ages: 4+ • *VISA*, *Interac* • Mon: 11-9, Tue: 11-10, Wed: 11-9, Thu: 11-10, Fri: 11-6, Sat-Sun: 10-6.

Grasshopper Playhouse

28 Crown Steel Dr, Unit 12, Markham, Ont, L3R 9Y1. • 905-944-9358 •
Private parties, ball pool, slides, riding cars, dress-up & loot bags. • Ages: 0-7 • &.

$COUPONS$ Groove School of Dance

53 Burnaby Blvd (St Margaret's Church - Avenue Rd/Eglinton); Bayview/Lawrence; East York, • 416-919-2914 •
Interactive dance parties. Crafts, dance, music, costumes & performance by the party children. **Look for our ad in the After School Activities category. See coupon section for valuable savings.** • Ages: 2+.

$COUPONS$ Gymboree Play and Music Programs

Central Toronto 416-410-6FUN, Thornhill 905-707-1420, Bloor West/ Etob/Miss/Oakville 905-542-PLAY • www.gymboree.com • We'll give your child the world's best birthday with a room full of specially designed play equipment and a teacher to lead great music and movement party activities. **Look for our ad in the Parent-Tot section. See coupon section for valuable savings.** • Other Locations: Call 1-800-520-PLAY. • Ages: 0-4 • *VISA*, ⊕, *Interac*, Cheque.

Historic Sites & Museums of Toronto

Operated by the City of Toronto, Culture Division, • Events Hotline: (416) 338-3888 •
www.toronto.ca/culture/birthdays.htm • Book FUN birthday parties at some of Toronto's historic houses and sites. Reasonable prices. Call or visit us online for details.

$COUPONS$ I Wanna B

1170 Burnhamthorpe Road West, Unit #29, Mississauga, Ont, L5C 4E6. • 905-270-9292 •
www.iwannab.ca • I Wanna B, is a unique private party center - where kids become Scientists, Chefs, Paleontologists, Hairstylists and so much more. **Look for our ad in this section. See coupon section for valuable savings.**

Birthday Parties

Private Parties at I Wanna B
Where playing grown-up is a party.

Firefighter - Your child is the hero as they turn on the sirens and race to participate in a pretend rescue.
The Cave - Kids crawl through tunnels to dig for dinosaur bones and treasure!
Scientist - Does your child want to learn the science behind volcanoes or slime?
The Salon - Style the hair of make-believe visitors and have light nail polish applied by an I Wanna B Host.

For more information
call 905 270-9292 or go to www.iwannab.ca

It's Playtime Inc

1425 Danforth Ave, Toronto, Ont, M4J 1N3. • 416-465-6688 • www.itsplaytime.ca
Let us host your next PRIVATE PARTY! Rock Climbing, Air Hockey, Soccer table, Karaoke, and more... Services available; Drop in, Baby-sitting, and Parties/Group Bookings. Mandarin lessons for parent and tot. Hours 9am-5pm. • Ages: 7 and under • Mon-Fri: 9-5, Sat-Sun: 10-8.

Jellybeenz Indoor Play and Party Centre

10 Bramhurst Ave, Units 13 & 14, Brampton, Ont, L6T 5H1 . • 647-273-0464 •
Indoor Activity Centre, Playground and Party Centre.

$ COUPON $ Jiggles & Giggles Indoor Playground and Party Centre

120 Carlauren Rd, Unit #1 (Weston Rd. & Hwy 7), Woodbridge, Ont, L4L 8E5. • 905-264-8222 •
www.jigglesandgiggles.ca
Private birthday parties & daily drop-in play. Climbing towers, slides, large air bouncer, toddler area, large private kitchen & more. Bright & clean, safe & uniquely designed. **Look for our ad in this section. See coupon section for valuable savings.**

$ COUPON $ Jungle Cubs Indoor Playground

1681 Bayview Ave, Toronto, Ont, M4G 2C1. • 416-322-6005 •
www.junglecubsindoorplayground.com
Children will have a ball celebrating in a fun, safe & relaxed atmosphere. To us every party is special. Our goal is to have you back. **Look for our ad in this section. See coupon section for valuable savings.** • Cheque.

VAUGHAN'S NEWEST INDOOR PLAYGROUND & PARTY CENTER
Large Climbing Towers | Slides | Air Bouncer | Toddler Area & More
Jiggles & Giggles
905.264.8222
120 Carlauren Rd. Unit 1, Woodbridge
www.jigglesandgiggles.ca

Jungle Cubs
Indoor Playground
www.junglecubsindoorplayground.com
• Daily Play! • Private Parties! • Kid Nights!
• Cakes! • Loot Bags! • Summer Camp!
1681 Bayview Ave. 416-322-6005

Birthday Parties

Just Bounce Trampoline Club
3731 Chesswood Dr, North York, Ont, M3J 2P6. • 416-635-0206 • www.justbounce.ca
8 TRAMPOLINES for your private super party!

Kiddyland Indoor Playground
50 Kennedy Rd S, Brampton, Ont, L6T 4B6. • 905-457-6170 •
Huge play area, arcade and birthday parties. • Ages: 1-12.

Kidnasium
745 Mount Pleasant Rd, 2nd Floor, Toronto, Ont, M4S 2N4. • 416-480-2608 • www.kidnasium.ca
Exciting interactive games and basic gymnastics hosted by qualified coaches. Mini trampoline, balance beams, climbing and jumping opportunities and more. Come visit our clean and inviting facility and see why birthdays are always a hit at Kidnasium! Private parties. • Ages: 18 mos. - 8 yrs. • *VISA*, ⊖, *Interac*, Cheque.

$COUPON$ Kids Kuts
728 St Clair Ave W, Toronto, Ont, M6C 1B3. • 416-658-3271 •
Birthday parties for girls. Hairdressing, makeup and manicures. Lots of Fun! **Look for our ad in the Hair Salons section. See coupon section for valuable savings.** • Other Locations 1010 Dreamcrest, Unit 10 Mississauga 905- 567-3476 • 占.

Kids Retreat Indoor Playground & Party Place
727 The Queensway, Etobicoke, Ont, M8Y 1L4. • 416-253-5437 •
Children's imaginations will be unleashed while they enjoy rock climbing, puppeteering, dress-up, zooming down the slide & much more! Call Us For Theme Parties, Balloons, Cakes, Loot Bags! Ask About Our Special Events Nights and Sitter Service!

KidsWorks Indoor Playground & Party Centre

105 Vanderhoof, Toronto, Ont, M4G 2H7. • 416-876-1235 • www.kidsworkstoronto.com
Attractions: 50 Tons of Sand, Climbing Castle, 2 Climbing Walls, 3 Slides, 2 Zip Lines, 3 Rope Swings, Toddler Centre, Playhouse. Ages Toddler to 7. **Look for our ad in this section.**

Kidz Castle Indoor Playground

2338 Major Mackenzie Dr, Unit 7, Maple, Ont, L6A 3Y7. • 905-417-2626 • www.kidzcastleplayground.com
Espresso Bar, Playpark, Climbing Wall, Toddler area, Air Bouncers, Movie/TV lounge, games & more. Private Parties for Birthdays & other occasions. Themed parties for older kids: Princess, Spa, Beading, Craft & Dance. Preschool Nursery class & Summer Camp. • Ages: 1-12.

Kinder Zone Indoor Playground

420 Hwy 7 E, Unit B101, Richmond Hill, Ont, L4B 3K2. • 905-882-8396 • www.kinderzone.com
Private birthday parties and play centre. Committed to offering; safe & clean environment, play & learn activities, best service, 100% customer satisfaction. • Ages: 1+.

KinderGarden in the Beach, The

1A Hannaford St, Toronto, Ont, M4E 3G6. • 416-690-6628 • www.thekindergarden.ca
Creative play tailor-made for little sprouts! Pint-sized fun: ballpit, slides, castle, log cabin, house centre, dress-up, puppets, crafts, computer corner and reading nook. Friendly, mature staff ensures your party is worry-free! • Ages: 0-6.

$COUPONS Klim School of Art

1238 Centre St, Thornhill, Ont, L4J 3M9. • 905-882-0884 • www.klimschoolofart.com
Klim offers birthday parties that allow kids to explore their creative and artistic talent. Various age-appropriate activities include clay (create your own pencil holder, mug, etc), painting, drawing and more. Invitations provided. 2 hours of fun! **Look for our ad in this section. See coupon section for valuable savings.** • Ages: 4-18.

Laser Quest

Brampton 905-456-9999, Richmond Hill 905-883-6000, Toronto East 416-285-1333, Mississauga 905-272-8000 • www.laserquest.com
Make Laser Quest your party headquarters for live action laser tag at its best! Enjoy two games, use the party room, get 241 passes for all and a free game pass for the birthday person. Open evenings and weekends, extended hours for school holidays. • Ages: 7+ • VISA, ⊕, ▨, *Interac* • ঌ.

Let's Have Fun Indoor Playground

1825 Dundas St E, Unit 13, Mississauga, Ont, L4X 2X1. • 905-206-0082 • www.letshavefun.ca
2 private playgrounds, large playstructure, glow in the dark basket ball, slides, bouncers, toddler area. FREE VIDEO AND AMUSEMENTS GAMES! • Ages: 1-10.

Birthday Parties

Lil' Explorers Clubhouse & Indoor Gym

190 Bullock Dr. Unit 10, Toronto, Ont, L3P 7N3. • 905-910-PLAY (7529) • www.lilexplorers.ca
Excellent location in Markham! Huge open-concept playground & party room. Private parties.
High-quality ASTM approved play equipment. *NEW* Now offering: Dance Birthday Parties suitable for children 6-14 years old. We also do amazing customized lootbags - we work with your budget! Daily play: Tues-Fri 10-3, Parties: Tues-Fri 3:30 - 8:00, Sat/Sun 10- 8.

Little Play House, Children's Indoor Playground & Party Centre

41 Gaudaur Rd, Vaughan, Ont, L4L 3R8. • 905-856-7600 •
10,000 square foot party and play centre in Vaughan. • Ages: 0-9 yrs.

$COUPON$ Loots Entertainment

896 Eglinton Ave W, Toronto, Ont, M6C 2B1. • 416-787-5668 • www.loots.com
The new Loots Lounge offers "tweens" a place to party. Fun crafts, dance games, karaoke, video, tournament play, and whoopee cushion competitions. Check out our games area, dance floor, light up soda bar and cool lounge. We provide invitations, drinks, snacks, prizes, entertainers, lootbags & more! **Look for our ad on the inside front cover. See coupon section for valuable savings.** • Other Locations 1669 Bayview Avenue 647-435-1049 • Ages: girls & boys 6-16 • *VISA*, ⊖, ▓, *Interac*.

Loots Lounge

1669 Bayview Avenue 647-435-1049 , Toronto, Ont, M6C 2B1. • 647-435-1049 •
www.loots.com
A brand new party entertainment venue specializing in the tween market 6 - 16. This party venue is built for kids but has the feel of a cool South Beach adult nightclub. Dance floor, games area and lounge holds 15 - 130 guests. Birthdays, Bar/bat mitzvahs and Sweet 16's. • *VISA*, ⊖, ▓, *Interac* • Mon-Fri: 9:30-7, Sat: 9:30-6, Sun: 10:30-5.

Lorraine Kimsa Theatre for Young People

165 Front St E, Toronto, Ont, M5A 3Z4. • 416-862-2222 •
Unique birthday party packages. For ages 3 and up. • *VISA*, ⊖, ▓, *Interac* • &.

Mackenzie House (1859)

82 Bond Street, Toronto, Ont, M5B 1X2. • 416-392-6915 • www.toronto.ca/culture/birthdays.htm
Play on a 19th century printing press, print a birthday souvenir, explore an 1859 house! • Ages: 8-12.

MadHatter's Tea Party, The

7676 Woodbine Ave, Unit 12, Markham, Ont, L3R 2N2. • 905-475-2854 •
www.toronto.com/madhatters
Birthday party service offering 6600 square feet of organized chaos since 1971! Invitations, pillow fights, a maze, games, facepainting, food, loot bags and supervision. Also providing themes and supplies for your home party. • Ages: 4-12 • *VISA*, ⊖, *Interac* • &.

Markham Museum

9350 Hwy 48 (2 km N of Hwy 7), Markham, Ont, L3P 3J3. • 905-294-4576 •
www.markhammuseum.ca
Markham Museum Birthday Parties! Packages can include, decorations, train/carousel rides, cake, themed activities, grab bags, village tours and even a sleep-over.

Martha Hicks School of Ballet

2384 Yonge Street, 2nd Fl, Toronto, Ont, M4P 2E0. • 416-484-4731 x224 • www.mhsb.ca
Birthday dance parties for children ages 5 and up. Choose from Jazz, Hip Hop or Ballet. 2 hour party with a performance at the end for parents. Centrally located at Yonge and Eglinton. Maximum 16 children. • *VISA*, ⊖, *Interac*, Cheque.

Visit Mississauga's

Look for our ad opposite the 2nd page of The Table of Contents

Affordable, convenient and fun for all ages.

MEGA FUN 4 KIDS
INDOOR PLAYGROUND
Daily Play and Birthday Parties
The Villages of Abbey Lane Plaza
91 Rylander Blvd. Scarborough,
ON M1B 5M5 Tel: (416) 282-6531
www.megafun4kids.com

$COUPON$ MegaFun 4 Kids Indoor Playground
91 Rylander Blvd Unit 1, Scarborough, Ont, M1B 5M5. • 416-282-6531 •
www.megafun4kids.com
Clean, bright, colourful facility. Toys, ball pit, pirate ship, train track, mini kitchen, costume area, book corner and more. Birthday parties with exclusive use of the playground. 3 party packages. Characters available. Infant area. Special events. **Look for our ad in this section. See coupon section for valuable savings.** • Ages: infant-7yrs • VISA, ⊖, ■, *Interac*.

Mess for Fun Indoor Playground & Ceramic Studio
73 Alness St, #3, North York, Ont, M3J 2H2. • 416-736-7101 • www.messforfun.com
A fun, new, indoor playground and paint-your-own ceramic studio that can host your child's next birthday! Open for walk-ins as well, but please call ahead. The fun never ends at Mess for Fun!

$COUPON$ MESSY HANDS Art Studio Birthday Parties
2501 Rutherford Rd, Unit 27, Bldg B, Richmond Hill, • 905-303-MESS (6377) •
www.messyhands.com
Embrace art and its many surprises. Leave the mess to us. Painting, clay sculpture, mosaics, tie dying, plush toy creation and more. All on the Art Bus parked inside our studio. Many party packages. **Look for our ad in the Birthday Entertainment section. See coupon section for valuable savings.** • Ages: 4+ • VISA, *Interac*, Cheque.

Mini Mania Indoor Playground & Party Palace Inc
61 Creditview Rd, Woodbridge, Ont, L4L 9N4. • 905-850-8980 • www.minimaniacenter.com
New, exciting, bright & clean, state of the art. A must see. CSA certified equipment and safety floors for your protection and peace of mind. Two completely private themed rooms. •
Ages: walking - 8yrs.

Mississauga Recreation & Parks - Birthday parties
300 City Centre Drive, Mississauga, Ont, L5B 3C1. • 905-615-4100 •
www.mississauga.ca/rec&parks
Celebrate your birthday at one of our community centres! Rent a pool, gym, arena or a room. Fun and exciting theme parties (Dinosaurs, Space, Fairy Princess) are available at some locations. **Look for our ad in the Camp section.**

Mississauga Valley CC - Terry Fox Wave Pool
1275 Mississauga Valley Blvd, Mississauga, Ont, L5A 3R8. • 905-615-4670 •
www.mississauga.ca/rec&parks
A multi-use facility which houses an ice rink, fitness centre, Mississauga's ONLY Wave pool and lots of outdoor amenities. Birthdays, summer programs, activities and fun! **Look for our ad opposite page 3 of the Table of Contents.**

Birthday Parties

Mookee's Indoor Playground
2700 Dufferin St, Unit #6, Toronto, Ont, M6B 4J3. • 416-789-0570 •
Toronto's newest party place! Fun-filled adventures. • Ages: 6mos-12yrs.

Nascar Speedpark
Vaughan Mills, 1 Bass Pro Mills Dr, Vaughan, Ont, L4K 5W4. • 905-669-7370 •
Birthday fun...NASCAR Style! • Ages: 4+.

National Film Board of Canada - Mediatheque
150 John Street (at Richmond - Osgoode Subway), Toronto, Ont, M5V 3C3. • 416-973-3012 •
www.nfb.ca/mediatheque
Entertaining two-hour animation workshops make a perfect birthday party for budding filmmak-
ers. Watch NFB animations, then make your own mini-movies! Available after school and weekends. Professional instructors. Affordable rates. Call for more information and to book.

Never Never Land Indoor Playground
8520 Jane St, Unit 6&7, Concord, Ont, L4K 5A9. • 905-761-1166 •
Separate age appropriate playgrounds. 2 Private party rooms. • Ages: 2-10.

$COUPON$ North Beach Dinosaur Dig
74 Railside Rd, North York, Ont, M3A 1A3. • 416-446-0777 • www.northbeachvolleyball.com
Book a Dinosaur Dig for your kids. Discover the thrill of digging up prehistoric skeletons. Kids
help put together different dinosaurs. Dinosaur exploration takes place in the 1500 tonnes of
sand around North Beach. For parties, clubs and school groups. Call us for dig details. **Look for
our ad in this section. See coupon section for valuable savings.** • Ages: 3-9.

$COUPON$ North Beach Indoor Rock Climbing Parties
74 Railside Rd, North York, Ont, M3A 1A3. • 416-446-0777 • www.northbeachvolleyball.com
Play in the sand or climb the mountains. North Beach now has indoor rock climbing for birthday
parties and group outings. **Look for our ad in this section. See coupon section for valuable savings.** •
Ages: 4+.

$COUPON$ North Beach Indoor Volleyball Academy
74 Railside Rd, North York, Ont, M3A 1A3. • 416-446-0777 • www.northbeachvolleyball.com
Kids love playing in our sand! Bring your group for an exciting, unique party supervised by our
fun, high-energy activities director. New rock climbing wall. **Look for our ad in this section. See
coupon section for valuable savings.** • Ages: 4+.

Olympic Spirit Toronto
35 Dundas Street East, Toronto, Ont • 1-888-466-9991 or 416-360-8477 • www.olympicspirit.ca
The world's only Olympic Themed Attraction featuring 12 interactive Summer & Winter Games
sports! Our Olympic Theatre shows our international award winning film The Calling and Our
downtown central location is perfect for hosting your next Birthday Party or special Team
Challenge.

Peanut Club Indoor Playground
2788 Bathurst St, Toronto, Ont, M6B 3A3. • 416-782-8735 • www.peanutclub.com
We cater to ages 6 months to 7 years. Motorized vehicles and train, play apparatus and kitchen,
baby area, slides, air hockey and so much more. Private parties, evenings and weekends. HAS-
SLE FREE and Free Parking.

Pippi's World Indoor Playground and Birthday Party Centre
1381 Lakeshore Rd E, Mississauga, Ont, L5E 1G6. • 905-271-0642 •
www.freewebs.com/pippisworld • Pippi's World offers PRIVATE, very affordable birthday party packages for 0-7 yrs. Great destination for Daycare Field Trips! Daily play, evenings and weekends too.
Frequent special events. Catering menu. Bouncy castle rentals. Free parking. • Ages: 0-7.

Birthday Parties

Play & Party-A-Saurus Indoor Playground
3355 The Collegeway, Mississauga, Ont, L5L 5G3. • 905-828-7088 •
The hottest playground in town. Jungle Jim, Toys, Carousel, Air hockey & soccer. Summer camp
program. • Ages: 1-7 • Cheque • &.

Play-A-Saurus
1107 Lorne Park Rd, Unit 9, Mississauga, Ont, L5H 3A1. • 905-274-1133 •
Indoor safe playground plus any occasion parties. • Ages: 1-9 yrs • &.

Playdium
99 Rathburn Rd W (across from Square One), Mississauga, Ont • 905-273-9000 •
www.playdium.com
Put your next party into high gear with the ultimate one-of-a-kind experience at Playdium! Value
packages for all ages and extreme fun with over 200 full interactive games in our 40,000 square
foot playground. Open year round, 7 days a week. Call for hours. • *VISA*, ⊖, ■■, *Interac*.

$ COUPONS $ Playground Paradise
150 Grenoble Dr, North York, Ont, M3C 1E3. • 416-395-6014 •
Party with us at Playground Paradise and give your child the time of their life! Two story play
structure, ball pit, slides - fully supervised by staff. Great prices! **Look for our ad in this section.**

$ COUPONS $ Playhouse Indoor Playground
321 Rexdale Blvd, Unit 1, Etobicoke, Ont, M9W 1R8. • 416-745-4333 • www.playhouseip.ca
Come play in our large open concept playground. We offer a variety of amusements for all ages
at affordable prices - multi-level play chalet, train rides, parents' lounge and much more! Open
for public play/private parties. Call for hours. **Look for our ad in this section. See coupon section for
valuable savings.** • Ages: 8 • *VISA*, ⊖, *Interac*.

Playtime Bowl
33 Samor Rd, Toronto, Ont, M6A 1J2. • 416-STRIKED •
The Ultimate in birthday party packages. Cosmic Bowling too • Ages: 3-13.

Pony Farm & Petting Zoo at Lionel's
11714 McCowan Rd, Stouffville, Ont, L4A 7X5. • 905-640-PONY (7669) • www.lionelsfarm.com
Ponies for birthday parties at your place or ours. Horse or Pony Haywagon/Sleigh Rides. School
tours. Visit our Petting Zoo! **Look for our ad in this section.**

Pony Parties at Silver Spur Ranch
11720 Hwy 27, Kleinberg, Ont • 416-283-5191 after 6pm • www.silverspurranch.ca
Birthday party packages from 1 to 13 years old including picnic area, chip wagon on site,
100 acres of scenic guided trails for all ages. Guided trails also available.

Pottery Painting Place
2021 Williams Pkwy E, Unit 2, Brampton, Ont, L6S 5P4. • 905-792-2942 • www.thepotterypaintingplace.com
The hottest place around for Birthday Parties, Family Time, Ladies night, Team Building, Bridal/Baby Showers. Fun, relaxing & creative. No experience required! Drop in and unleash the artist within. New Summer 2006 - we come to your home!

$COUPON$ Princess Palace Dress-Up Party Centre
241 Edgeley Blvd, Unit 5, Concord, Ont, L4K 3Y4. • 905-660-2215 • www.princesspalace.ca
From Dress-up, to Make-up to a Royal Tea Party, we will host your Enchanted Event. Leave the extras to us: cake, loot creations and balloon bouquets. Ages 3-9. Nut Free facility. Inquire about our Teen Glamour and Spa Parties ages 10-16. Save $35 when booking Mon-Fri. **Look for our ad in this section. See coupon for valuable savings.** ᵹ. • *VISA*, *Interac* • ᵹ.

Raceworld- Slot Car Racing Party Centre
7611 Pine Valley Dr. Unit 28, Woodbridge, Ont • 905-771-8982 • www.raceworldcanada.com
Exciting Model Car Racing fun for kids ages 5+. Safe and suitable for girls and boys. Party room. Groups up to 18 racers. Celebrating our 18th year! • Ages: 5+ • ᵹ.

Rainbow Cinemas
4 Locations: Promenade Mall 905-886-7464 , Woodbine Shoping Centre 416-213-9048, Fairview Mall 416-494-6848 and Market Square 416-214-7006, • www.rainbowcinemas.ca
Celebrate your child's birthday party Hollywood style at Rainbow Cinemas! Movie fun with the birthday child as the lead star! Family friendly prices. Call the Rainbow Cinema of your choice for movie details and to arrange the party! **Look for our ad in this section.** • *VISA*, ⊖, ▦, *Interac*.

Rainbow Play Systems of Ontario
28 Fulton Way, Unit 7, Richmond Hill, Ont, L4B 1E6. • 905-795-3999 •
www.rainbowofontario.com
An indoor playground, party room, video theater, enclosed toddler area bathrooms and infant change facility. While the children play, adults can relax with food & drinks in our lounge. Weekday and Weekend parties and School visits welcome. **Look for our ad in the Birthday section.** Ages: 4-8 • Tue-Fri: 10-3.

Rinx
65 Orfus Rd, North York, Ont, M6A1L7. • 416-410-RINX (7469) • www.ThinkRINX.com
In-line Skating, Lazer Tag, Cosmic Mini Golf, Bowling, Private Party Rooms,Whirly Ball & Ice Skating. • Ages: 5+ • *VISA*, ⊖, ■, *Interac*.

Rock Oasis Inc
27 Bathurst St, Toronto, Ont, M5V 2P1. • 416-703-3434 •
Rock climbing parties - Toronto and Ajax locations. • Ages: 6+. •

Sassy Bead Birthday Parties
2076 Yonge St, Toronto, Ont, M4S 2A3. • 416-488-7400 • www.thesassybeadco.com
Children choose from a huge selection of semi-precious, glass, plastic or wood beads in a variety of brilliant colors to create beautifully unique bracelets, necklaces, earrings, key chains and more. Maximum 10 children at our work table. Jewellery school & workshops also available. • Ages: 8+.

$COUPON$ Scooter's Roller Palace

2105 Royal Windsor Dr, Mississauga, Ont, L5J 1K5. • 905-823-4001 • www.scooters.on.ca
Birthday parties, roller skating/roller blading facility featuring public skating, skate rentals, artistic skating, lessons. DJ music, refreshments, arcade, and private party bookings. Call for hours. **Look for our ad in this section. See coupon section for valuable savings.**

$COUPON$ SCORE Birthday Bashes - Specializing in Sport Parties

905-709-6383 • www.scoredaycamp.com
Pick the sports of your choice for a hassle-free, FUN-ominal time! Choose from Floor/Roller Hockey, Soccer, Basketball & many more. Experienced, professional sports instructor. Great for boys & girls! Central location. Party room. Loot bags available. **Look for our ad in this section. See coupon section for valuable savings.** • Ages: 4-12.

Small Wonders Discovery Centre

140 Capitol Court, Mississauga, Ont, L5T 2R8. • 905 696-6817 • www.playatsmallwonders.ca
Sit back and relax! We will give you and your child a memorable party at an affordable price. Pretend and perform in the castle, play on the slides and climbers in our park, ride cars & bikes on the raceway, or check out our live pet shop. Theme parties available. • Ages: 0-8 years..

$COUPON$ Snugabug Portrait & Art Studios

1160 Clarence St Units 3 & 4, Vaughan, Ont, L4H 2V3. • 905-264-2640 •
www.snugabugportraits.com
Fun and creative birthday parties from dress-up to art parties. There's fun for all ages. Also offering art classes. **Look for our ad in the Photography section. See coupon section for valuable savings.**

$COUPON$ Solar Stage Children's Theatre Birthday Parties

100 Upper Madison, Concourse Level (Yonge/Sheppard), • 416-368-8031 •
www.solarstage.on.ca
We provide an exciting & fun-filled birthday/theatre experience! Group rates available. **Look for our ad in the Theatre & Concerts for Kids section. See coupon section for valuable savings.** • Ages: 2-10 • ♿.

South Simcoe Railway Heritage Corporation

Mill Street West, Tottenham, Ont, L0G 1W0. • 905-936-5815 • www.steamtrain.com
Celebrate a birthday or any other special occasion in a unique way with a Baggage Car Party aboard the steam train!

Birthday Parties

$COUPONS$ Sportball Canada

39 Glen Cameron Rd, Unit 8, Thornhill, Ont, L3T 1P1. • 905-882-4473 or 1-8-Sportkids • www.sportball.ca

High Energy multi-sports parties. Fun games encourage all guests' participation. Traditional birthday celebrations follow play. Enthusiastic coaches run your party from start to finish. **Look for our ad in the Parent/Tot section. See coupon section for valuable savings**. • Ages: 2 yrs+.

$COUPONS$ Sportplay Birthday Parties

Locations around the GTA or at a location of your choice, • 905-940-9481 or 1-866-940-9481 • www.sportplay.ca

Sportplay offers fun sport oriented parties for children 3-12 years. Choose your favourite sports and games. All equipment provided. Mature, experienced coaches provide leadership and supervision. **Look for our ad in this section. See coupon section for valuable savings**.

Spunky Monkey Indoor Playground & Party Centre

1550 16th Ave, Building "A" - Units#11 & #12, Richmond Hill, Ont, L4B 3K9. • 905-737-2335 or 1-877-737-2335 • www.spunkymonkeyplayground.com

A place for children to have fun and for parents to enjoy a stress-free environment. Daily/supervised playtime, kids' programs, camps and private birthday parties. Great party packages available. Infant play area. Kindermusik and other programs too! • Ages: 0-8yrs.

St Michael's Majors Hockey Club (OHL)

St. Michael's College School Arena, 1515 Bathurst St, Arena 2nd Fl, Toronto, Ont, M5P 3H4. • 416-651-8228 x207 • www.stmichaelsmajors.com
Bring your kids to an exciting Majors game! Special party room with player and mascot visits; optimum arena seating; exciting OHL action featuring future NHL stars. Great party rates. Pizza and cake available. Make sure to book in advance!

Stomp 'N Romp Playhouse

158 Anderson Ave, Units 11 & 12, Markham, Ont, L6E 1A9. • 905-201-2626 • www.stompnromp.com
Indoor playground and party centre. Lots of fun activities for kids. Give your children a PARTY they won't forget in our 5000 sq ft facility. Indoor play: Tu-Th 10-3, F-Sun 10-6.

Studio 7 - Sewing Birthday Parties

1977 Avenue Rd, Toronto, Ont, M5M 4A2. • 416-480-2902 •
Kids & teens will design, sew and make clothes or accessories in the studio to keep and take home. Parties, workshops and sewing classes. • Ages: 7+.

$ COUPONS $ Super Science

2600 John St, Ste 106, Markham, Ont, L3R 3W3. • 905-479-4459 • www.supersciencetoronto.com
At your location or our Super Science themed birthday party center, we provide the ultimate in science entertainment and education. **Look for our ad in this section. See coupon section for valuable savings.** • Ages: 6-12 yrs.

Thumbprint Adventures Birthday Parties

Central Toronto: 416-787-2882; Oakville: 905-845-6789 Bloor West Village: 416-787-2882, , • 416-787-2882 (V/TTY) • www.thumbprintadventures.com
Finally, exactly what you want for your child's special day. Embark on a spy mission, voyage with pirates, sleepover at a castle! Unique props, music, costumes and imagination make each adventure come to life! **Look for our ad in this section**. • Ages: 2-9yrs.

Timber Creek Miniature Golf & Fun Center

12772 9th Line, Stouffville, Ont, L4A 7X3 . • 905-642-5174 •
Fun-filled birthdays for kids of all ages. Two spectacular one-of-a-kind miniature golf courses among waterfalls, rivers and even shipwrecks. A jumping castle, inflatable slide, games barn, batting cages, driving range and dairy bar make for a full day of fun. • Ages: 3-65.

Tiny Tots Playground Inc
201 Eagle St, Newmarket, Ont, L3Y 1J8. • 905-954-0101 •
Private parties, daily play, indoor/outdoor facility. • Ages: 0-7.

Toronto Climbing Academy
100a Broadview Ave, Toronto, Ont, M4M 3H3. • 416-406-5900 •
2 hours of climbing. Gear provided. Certified instructors. • Ages: 6-12.

Town of Markham Recreation Department
101 Town Centre Blvd, Recreation & Culture Dept, Markham, Ont, L3R 9W3. • 905-477-7000 •
www.markham.ca
If you are looking for fun, safe and exciting activities, the Town of Markham offers a wonderful selection of great birthday choices including swimming, rock climbing, gymnasium rentals plus lots more.

Upstairs at Loblaws and RCSS
Specific locations across Ontario. • 1-800-296-2332 or 1-866-596-7277 •
Innovative, high quality, reasonably priced birthday parties. •

Vaughan Sportsplex
10 Westcreek Drive, Unit 12-15, Woodbridge, Ont, L4L 9R5. • 905-265-9115 •
www.vaughansportsplex.com
Coupon: $25 OFF - Sports birthday parties. Basketball, ball hockey rink, indoor soccer field, X-box lounge, referee, scoreboard - amazing birthday parties.

$COUPON$ Wave Pool, The
5 Hopkins St, Richmond Hill, Ont, L4C 0C1. • 905-508-WAVE (9283) • www.richmondhill.ca
Open year round, The Wave Pool offers safe family fun! Enjoy a Wave Swim with four foot waves, a 160 foot twisting water slide, swirl pool and more. Call for more information and swim schedules. **Look for our ad in this section. See coupon section for valuable savings.** • *VISA*, ⊖⊖,
Interac, Cheque • &.

Whirlyball
65 Orfus Rd, North York, Ont, M6A 1L7. • 416-787-5858 •
A new, exciting game played in Bumper Cars! Great birthday parties! • Ages: 9+.

Wiz Kids Activity Centre
484 Cosburn Ave, Toronto, Ont, M4J 2N5. • 416-425-8280 • www.go.to/wizkids
Private birthday parties. Great Craft Parties! Toddler area, arts & crafts, game tables, computer station. Preschool program - Ages 2+. Lootbags available. Drop in play.

Wonderkids Sports Center Inc
34 Doncaster Unit 9, Thornhill, Ont, L3T 4S1. • 905-881-8499 • www.wonderkids.ca
Fun filled birthday parties in the gym. Private and supervised. Trampoline, tarzan rope, rolling doughnut, parachute, rings and space trolley. • Ages: 3-10.

Your Fired ...
10178 Yonge St, Richmond Hill, Ont, L4C 1T6. • 905-737-8944 • www.yourfiredceramics.ca
Paint it yourself ceramics studio with more than 1000 different pieces. Birthday Party Packages. 2 separate party rooms or we'll close the whole store for big parties.

▪ Supplies, Decorations & Loot Bags

A New Take on Cake
905-881-9700 •
Personalized, customized paper cakes - a lootbag & cake in one!

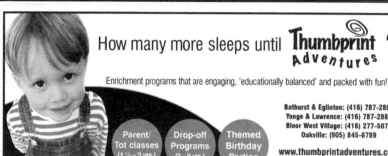

How many more sleeps until **Thumbprint Adventures**?

Enrichment programs that are engaging, 'educationally balanced' and packed with fun!

Parent/Tot classes (1 ½ – 3 yrs.)

Drop-off Programs (3 – 9 yrs.)

Themed Birthday Parties

Bathurst & Eglinton: (416) 787-2882
Yonge & Lawrence: (416) 787-2882
Bloor West Village: (416) 277-5075
Oakville: (905) 845-6789

www.thumbprintadventures.com

Giving children a chance to create, laugh and learn... one adventure at a time!

Balloon Bash Gifts & Baskets

7241 Bathurst Street Unit 13, Thornhill, Ont, L4J 3W1. • 905-707-8177 • www.balloonbash.com
Balloonagrams, custom lootbags from $3.99, novelties, plush, all occasion gift baskets. Party planning including balloon decor, centrepieces and sculptures. Delivery citywide. • ▨, ⊕, ▨, *Interac* • Mon-Wed: 9:30-7, Thu: 9:30-8, Fri: 9:30-5, Sun: 10-5:30.

Balloon Experts Ltd

190 Bullock Dr, Markham, Ont, L3P 1W2. • 905- 294-2300 •
Balloons, delivery, decorating services, party supplies.

Balloon King Party Centre

2 locations: Toronto 416-603-4347, Mississuaga 905-272-4430, , • www.balloonking.ca
Balloon and party centre serving the public since 1966. Parties big or small...we serve them all. Great selection. Bouquet and helium deliveries available. We also stock tableware, paper products as well as 100's of costumes! • ▨, ⊕, ▨, *Interac* • Mon-Fri: 9-6, Sat: 9:30-5.

Balloon Trix

39 St. Paul St, Toronto, Ont, M5A 3H2. • 416-214-0414 •
Balloon Trix has been specializing in private and corporate functions for 15 years.

Beads for your Needs - Loot Bag Bead Kits

416-806-0427 •
A kit full of everything you need to make beautiful Jewellery. • Ages: 6-15.

IT'S MAIN ATTRACTIONS INCLUDE:

- **4 Foot Waves**
- **160 Foot Twisting Waterslide**
- **Warm Water Swirlpool**
- **Sauna**
- **Free Parking**

York Region's FIRST & ONLY Indoor Wave Pool!

THE **Wave** POOL

905-508-Wave (9283)

Call for additional information or swim times.

5 HOPKINS ST., RICHMOND HILL
Southwest corner of Major Mackenzie and Yonge Street

Blue Sky Balloons
274 Jane St, Toronto, Ont, M6S 3Z2. • 416-761-9676 •
Party supplies. Loot bags. Balloon delivery/decorating.

$COUPON$ Cakes By Robert
134 Doncaster Avenue, Unit #5, Thornhill, Ont, L3T 1L3. • 905-889-1448 •
www.cakesbyrobert.com
Choose from our fabulous selection of Loot Bags or mix and match to create your own. Shop on
line for your convenience. Delivery Available. Pick-up together with your cake order - Perfect
enhancement to your party. **Look for our ad in this section. See coupon section for valuable savings.**

Chocolate Charm
3541 Bathurst St, Toronto, Ont, M6A 2C7. • 416-787-4256 •
Great selection of chocolate lollipop favours.

Chocolicks Fun Factory
573 Eglinton Ave West, Toronto, Ont, M5N 1B5. • 416-485-2047 • www.chocolicks.com
Kids love our yummy Chocolate and Crazy Candy lootbags! We create new and different, fun and
funky products to awe kids& adults of all ages. Smash Cakes, Caramel and Chocolate Popcorn,
Candy Apples, Crazy Candy Creations and much more! Birthdays, Bar Mitzvahs, Corporate
events etc. **Look for our ad in this section.**

Cocktails, Lootbags & Murder - Theme Party & Event Planning
519-371-8726 •
The most incredible unique party experience! Many cool themes, customized especially for you!

GlowSticks!

Parties - Fundraisers - Weddings - Bar/Bat Mitzvahs

Canada Wide Delivery

www.buz.ca • 416-763-8244

Cookies Cookies Cookies
905-780-8762 •
Custom cookies. Spiderman, Blue, Groovy Girls, Barbie, etc. Great party favours. Peanut free.

Digital Memoreze - BUZ GLOWSTICKS!
14-3650 Langstaff Rd, Suite 201, Woodbridge, Ont, L4L 9A8. • 416-763-8244 • www.buz.ca
GLOWSTICKS! Wholesale to You! 100 8" GlowSticks Per Tube (5 different colours) with connectors to make bracelets. Great for Parties, Children's Events, Bar/Bat Mitzvahs & More! Hours of Fun. Free Shipping. Secure Online Ordering. **Look for our ad in this section.**

Georgie Porgie *Loot bags* & Gift Baskets
416-892-0822 •
We create pre-filled, quality *loot bags* for all ages. • Ages: newborn to adult.

$COUPON$ It's My Party
423 Danforth Ave, Toronto, Ont, M4K 1P1. • 416-469-2223 • www.itsmyparty.com
Celebrating 10 years of serving the GTA! Specializing in Custom Loot Bags, Balloons & everything else to make your event a success!Check out our new pricing - Buy 12 items "Mix & Match" - Save 10% OR Buy 12 items "Same" - Save 20%. Metrowide Delivery & Decorating. Toronto's Best Halloween Store! Open 7 days. **Look for our ad in this section. See coupon section for valuable savings.** • VISA, ⊖, ▄, Interac • ♿.

Look For the
Loots Entertainment ad
on the inside front cover!

5,000sqft and 20,000 ITEMS!

It's My Party

**SAVE 10-20%
on Most items**
GTA Delivery

TORONTO'S
Celebration Store

423 Danforth Ave
416.469.2223
staff@itsmyparty.com
www.itsmyparty.com

Loot Bags • Party Supplies • Balloons • Candy • Costumes • Toys & Gifts
Jokes • Decorations • Greeting Cards • Helium • Weddings

Birthday Parties

Little Party Shoppe

2566 Yonge St, Toronto, Ont, M4P 2J3. • 416-487-7855 •
Party supplies, loot bags, helium balloons, gifts. • &.

$COUPON$ LootLady.com

1500 Royal York Rd, Etobicoke, Ont, M9P 3B9. • 416-828-4489 • www.lootlady.com
The best loot bags and gifts for the best kids! Curious George*Superman*Disney*Strawberry
Shortcake* Starwars & More. Kosher, Custom, & Corporate orders welcomed. Canada wide
delivery. Over 130 styles. **Look for our ad in this section. See coupon section for valuable savings.** •
Ages: 12 mos- 12 yrs..

$COUPON$ Loots

896 Eglinton Ave W, Toronto, Ont, M6C 2B1. • 416-787-5668 • www.loots.com
It's easy at the WORLD'S GREATEST LOOT BAG STORE. 125 age appropriate, beautifully packaged, themed loot bags. Newborn - adult. Themed cakes, party supplies, piñatas, helium balloons, craft activities, novelty candies, prizes, games and we even DELIVER! Corporate parties
are our specialty. **Look for our ad on the inside front cover. See coupon section for valuable savings.** •
VISA, ⊕, ▦, *Interac* • Mon-Fri: 9:30-7, Sat: 9:30-6, Sun: 10:30-5.

Loots by Lisa

905-884-7283 • Customized loot bags for all occasions.

Loots of Fun Lootbags

416-587-1430 • www.lootsoffun.com
Age-appropriate lootbags. Beautiful clear bags with colorful designs. Personalized with children's
names. Each lootbag is done with lots of thought and special care. Free delivery in the GTA

Party Agency Maria Monitos

1867 Bloor Street E Suite 701 , Mississauga, Ont, L4X 1T4. • 905-290-6027 •
Specializing in children's birthday parties. At your home or at a party location. Offering Adventure
theme parties, Entertainment, Decorations, Catering, Cakes, Table and chair rentals, Balloons,
Piñatas, Candy bags. Cake decorating classes. Spanish and English spoken.

Party In a Bag

7676 Woodbine Ave Unit 12, Markham, Ont, L3R 2N2. • 905-475-2854 •
www.toronto.com/madhatters
Prepackaged lootbags or custom lootbags starting at $2.50. Toys, girl's accessories, make-up,
stationery kits, slime, building toys, summer fun toys, cotton candy, chocolate and much much
more! We also carry a wide range of party supplies, helium balloons, theme packages and decorations. Since 1971. • Ages: 4-12 • VISA, ⊕, *Interac* • &.

Party In A Box

416-305-2345 • www.partyinaboxbypatricia.com
Your one stop party planning shop. Services include loot bags, partyware, decorations, balloons,
gift baskets, music classes, and face painting fun. Pick up or delivery available to your door. Free
balloon bouquet on orders over $75. To visit the showroom call 416-305-2345.

Party Packagers - 12 Super Store Locations!

www.partypackagers.com
A one-stop party supply superstore with an extensive line of Readymade Lootbags, Toys, Loot, Party
Supplies, Gifts, Balloons and Costumes at everyday BLOW-OUT prices! For kids and adults of all
ages. Tor: 416-785-4035, NY: 416-631-7688, Miss. South: 905-607-2789, Scarb: 416-293-2339, Bramp:
905-460-9720, Mark: 905-477-2808, Miss. North: 905-890-9229, Woodbridge: 905-265-2415,
Newmarket: 905-830-9446. Visit us online for all the locations. • VISA, ⊕, ▦, *Interac*

Party Place, The

25 Dennis Dr, Ajax, Ont, L1T 4A7. • 905-426-6724 •
We carry a variety of Licensed and Themed Party Supplies to complete your party.

$COUPONS Playhouse Indoor Playground

321 Rexdale Blvd, Unit 1, Etobicoke, Ont, M9W 1R8. • 416-745-4333 • www.playhouseip.ca
Awesome Loot Bags starting at $2! Customized for you. Huge selection! **Look for our ad in the Party Places section. See coupon section for valuable savings**. • Ages: 8 • *VISA*, ⊖, *Interac*.

Special Greetings

905-584-6990 •
8 foot lawn sign/ornament rental. Storks, penguins, flamingos, etc.

Themebag

2238 Dundas St W P.O. Box 59038, Toronto, Ont, M6R 3B5. • 416-828-7736 •
Themed loot bags for your children's parties.

$COUPONS Toytown

1754 Avenue Rd, Toronto, Ont, M5M 3Y9. • 416-783-8073 • www.toytown.ca
Exceptional selection of custom made lootbags at all prices. Your choice of hundreds of items, or let us decide! We fill our bags with quality! **Look for our ad in the Toy section. See coupon section for valuable savings**. • ♿.

Books

From picture books to interactive books, from classics to chapter books, children can all learn to love reading - it is often just a question of discovering the right type of book for your child. Don't worry if that perfect book is not one that is your cup of tea...it is more important THAT they read; WHAT they read shouldn't matter too much. The knowledgeable staff at your local bookstore is very experienced about how to find something to pique the interest of even the most stubborn non-readers.

Don't forget to check the Specialty and Personalized books section for great ideas for yourself or gifts.

LIBRARIES:

The Toronto Public Library is the largest public library system in Canada, with 98 branches and more than 3 million kids items to borrow or use in the library. Did you know that 24 hours a day, children can listen to stories over the phone in English, French, Cantonese, Italian, Mandarin, Polish, Portuguese and Spanish. The Dial-a-Story program is for kids up to age 12.

Each library has its own programs - check the website: www.tpl.toronto.on.ca for those at a library near you.. There is also a central information and Quick Reference phone line to tell you where various branches are, lending practices, reference info, etc. (416) 393-7131.

You will find the following sub-categories in this section:
Children's Bookstores, Specialty & Personalized Books

$ COUPON $ Look for this company's coupon at the back of the book

---

■ Children's Bookstores

Another Story
315 Roncesvalles Ave, Toronto, Ont, M6R 2M6. • 416-462-1104 •
Excellent multicultural, anti-bias children's books. Child friendly.

Bookman Textbook and Educational Outlet, The
4910 Yonge St, side door, North York, Ont, M2N 5N5. • 416-BOO-KMAN or (800) 461-8398 •
Textbooks used in all schools, grades pre-K to 12. Supplementary workbooks in all subjects. •
Other Locations 124 Portland St, Etobicoke • Ages: 2+ • *VISA*, ⊕, *Interac* • Mon-Sat: 10-6,
Sun: 12-5.

Children's French Bookstore
416-486-1131 •
French teacher owned and operated. Free consulting. By appointment only.

Flying Dragon Bookshop, The
1721 Bayview Ave, Toronto, Ont, M4G 3C1. • 416-481-7721 •
Books, storytime, gift baskets, registry, book clubs.

MABEL'S FABLES BOOKSTORE   662 Mt. Pleasant Rd., 416-322-0438   mabelsfables.com

$COUPONS Mabel's Fables Children's Bookstore

662 Mount Pleasant Rd , Toronto, Ont, M4S 2N3. • 416-322-0438 • www.mabelsfables.com
The most enchanting bookstore in Toronto. Toddler storytimes. Author visits. Loot bag certificates, baby baskets, etc. All our books are grouped into age departments from age "baby" to 14+. Everyone loves to visit the little bookstore for big readers. Call for store hours. **Look for our ad in this section. See coupon section for valuable savings.** • Ages: 0-12+ • *VISA*, ⊕, *Interac*, Cheque • &.

Parentbooks

201 Harbord St, Toronto, Ont, M5S 1H6. • 416-537-8334 • www.parentbooks.ca
Books for parents, professionals and kids on all topics of interest including childbirth, education, special needs, grief & loss, adoption and various parenting issues. Mail, e-mail and phone orders welcome. • *VISA*, ⊕, *Interac* • Mon-Sat: 10:30-6.

▪ Specialty & Personalized Books

Baby ... I Can Hardly Wait!, Samet Publishing
416-568-7163 •
A comprehensive diary and reference guide for expectant moms & newborns.

Inside Story Publishers - School Memory Album
905-881-9736 • ddanilewitz@rogers.com
Interactive school memory album. Beautifully designed. Functional. Has pockets for each grade to store reports and pictures. Place for parents and grandparents to write personal messages. Treasure this keepsake forever - a rich tapestry focussing on the whole child. From JK to Gr. 12.

Memory Collectors
422 St Clements Ave, Toronto, Ont, M5N 1M1. • 416-483-8743 •
Children's keepsake album for school memorabilia.

StoryTime
83 Dina Rd, Maple, Ont, L6A 1L7. • 905-832-3397 •
Personalized children's books including Disney. Lowest Prices! • Ages: 0-12 • Cheque.

Breastfeeding Support & Accessories

With today's short post partum hospital stays, there may be questions regarding breast-feeding that require professional assistance. While it seems that breastfeeding should be natural, if really isn't and both mother and baby often need help. Follow your instincts, if something doesn't feel right, it may be time to consult an expert.

$COUPON$ Look for this company's coupon at the back of the book

A Perfect Fit Innerfashions Boutique
17 Frontenac Ave, Toronto, Ont, M5N 1Z4. • 416-782-8378 •
Trained fit specialist will help you find "the perfect fit" in a bra! Extra specialty for nursing mothers: In addition to nursing bras, any bra can be converted into a nursing bra! For all your undergarments, bodyslimmers, lingerie accessories, sleepwear and swimwear needs. Sizes from 32AA - 46I.

Able Home Health Care
3537 Bathurst St, Toronto, Ont, M6A 2C7. • 416-789-5551 •
Complete line for all breastfeeding needs. Medela.

Ameda Breastfeeding Products (Manufactured by Hollister Ltd)
905-727-4344
800-263-7400 • www.hollister.ca
Hollister manufactures the ONLY milk collection kits that protect milk from bacteria, viruses and contaminants. These include the unrivaled Purely Yours™ personal breast pump and the Elite™ hospital-grade electric breast pump (available at rental depots). A complete line of breastfeeding accessories is also available.

Becoming Maternity and Parenting Centre
505 Eglinton Ave W Suite 401, Toronto, Ont, M5N 1B1. • 416-440-4020 •
www.becomingmaternity.com
Breastfeeding help and support in your home, hospital or our Centre provided by Certified Lactation Consultants. We also rent the latest hospital-grade pumps and baby weigh scales, and sell breastfeeding supplies, nursing bras and tank-tops.

Bestfeeding Services; Greater Toronto Area -Anne-Marie Desjardins
pager 416-295-8441 •
Breastfeeding & newborn care consultation. Medela breastfeeding products available.

Birth Solutions
416-802-0572 or 1-888-619-9945 • www.birthsolutions.info
We provide solutions to all your postpartum needs including Postpartum Doulas, Night Support, Breastfeeding Support, Happiest Baby Classes and more.

Breast is Best - Clothing for Nursing Mothers
905-837-5439 or (877- 837-5439 • www.breast-is-best.com
Offering Quality Breastfeeding Clothing at Affordable Prices Since 1995. We offer breastfeeding clothes, nursing bras, breast pumps, and other post-natal conveniences for today's busy nursing mothers.

Breastfeeding Centre for Families, Toronto East General
825 Coxwell - Main Floor G123, Toronto, Ont, M4C 3E7. • 416-469-6667 •
7 days/wk. 10 am - 3pm. Drop in. Bring OHIP card.

Childbirth and Parenting Centre St Joseph's Health Centre Breastfeeding Clinic

416-530-6367 • Prenatal and postnatal support and breastfeeding support.

City Pharmacy Breastfeeding Support & Supplies

238 Danforth Ave, Toronto, Ont, M4K 1N4. • 416-469-1898 •
Breastpump supplies, Sale/rental, AVENT and Ameda Egnell.

$COUPON$ Custom Comfort Care Inc

20 Bay St, Ste 1205, Toronto, Ont, M5J 2N8. • 416-703-2539 •
Skilled help with babycare & breastfeeding for new moms in your home, available 24/7. **Look for our ad in the Childcare section. See coupon section for valuable savings**.

$COUPON$ Diaper-Eez Breastfeeding Sales & Rentals

2309 Bloor St W, Toronto, Ont, M6S 1P1. • 416-604-0916 • www.diaper-eez.com
Make your breastfeeding experience easier with Pur-lan from Medela, Bravado Nursing Bras, Avent & Medela breastpumps & accessories, Nursing Pillows, Washable Breast Pads ... Medela breastpump rental station. **Look for our ad in the Diaper Stores & Services section. See coupon section for valuable savings**. • *VISA*, ⊕, ▓, *Interac*.

For Baby & You: Postpartum & Lactation Consultant Services

416-787-9849 • www.4babyandyou.com
Wendy Goodman, Registered Nurse & Certified Lactation Consultant, visits you in your home to help with breastfeeding problems, and any mother, babycare needs. Medela breastpumps (free demonstration) and "my breast friend pillow available".   Wendy also provides prenatal classes and doula services. • Ages: 0+ • Cheque • Mon-Sun: 9-9.

Gentle Mothering Breastfeeding Services

416-627-7485 • www.gentlemothering.ca
Providing Breastfeeding Support and Prenatal Breastfeeding Classes. Helping you have a positive Breastfeeding experience. Flexible packages to suit your needs. • Ages: 0-12mos.

La Leche League Of Metropolitan Toronto

416-483-3368 •
Specially trained experienced, breastfeeding mothers (volunteers) will answer breastfeeding questions or give information on local groups. Call for the volunteer nearest you.

Lydia Ling Breastfeeding Support

416-391-2123 •
Prenatal classes. Breastfeeding consultation & support.

Mark Levine & Associates
905-780-2468 •
Pediatric and Family Craniosacral therapy. Richmond Hill.

Markhambaby
10 Davidoff St, Markham, Ont, L6E 1J3. • 905-294-6234 •
Medela Breastpump sales and rentals and baby resources.

Maxi Mom & Me
4 Nomad Cres, North York, Ont, M3B 1S6. • 416-444-6884 •
Expert fittings for nursing bras, baby blankets etc. No GST. By app't. • Cheque.

Mothers Nest
2276 Queen St E @ Silverbirch. • 416-410-6914 •
mothersnestinc@sympatico.ca
Lamaze Birth Workshops. Breastfeeding Clinic & Home Visits. RN's, Certified Lactation
Consultants. 2276 Queen St E @ Silverbirch.

My Lil' Miracle & Indisposables™
1-877-218-0112 • www.mylilmiracle.com
Bravado nursing bras and full line of casual nursing wear. • Ages: 0-6 • 𝘝𝘐𝘚𝘈, ⊕, Cheque.

Newman Breastfeeding Clinic & Institute
Canadian College of Naturopathic Medicine, 1255 Sheppard Ave E, Toronto, Ont, M2K 1E2. •
416-498-0002 •
With Dr. Jack Newman and Edith Kernerman, IBCLC. For appointment, email
breastfeeding@ccnm.edu (see auto reply), or phone. OHIP Clinics most Tuesdays, Wednesdays
and Thursdays.

Pre & Postnatal Consulting Services
905-669-4358 • Breastfeeding consultation. Fee for home visit.

Public Health Nurses: Toronto Health Connection / York Region Health Connection
416-338-7600 - Toronto or 1-800- 361-5653 or 905-895-8004 - York Region •
www.city.toronto.on.ca/health•www.region.york.on.ca
Speak to a Public Health Nurse anytime between 8:30am-4:30 pm, Mon-Fri. For newborn care
and breastfeeding questions. Call with questions or for a home visit.

Region of Peel - Public Health
905-799-7700 • www.peelregion.ca
Breastfeeding information and telephone support from Public Health Nurses. Breastfeeding
Clinics - breastfeeding assessment, support and health education for parents with babies up to 6
weeks. For clinic hours and location, or to make an appointment, call Health Line Peel 905-799-7700.

Two-at-a-Time Nursing Pillow
416-248-1109 • Specially designed for mothers who are nursing multiples.

$COUPONS With Child
705 Pape Ave, Toronto, Ont, M4K 3S6. • 416-466-9693 • www.withchildonline.com
Personalized service. One stop shop for breastfeeding needs. Bravado nursing bras & breast-
pads, stylish nursing tops, Avent products, Medela breastpump rental/sales, books, general
breastfeeding support. For an unforgettable experience, visit our store. Delivery available. **Look for
our ad in this section. See coupon section for valuable savings**. • 𝘝𝘐𝘚𝘈, ⊕, *Interac*.

Camps

Ontario is known world-wide for its excellence and variety in summer camps. Children can choose from a day or specialty camp around the corner or a residential (sleepover) camp further afield. Some children welcome the opportunity to spend time away from home while others may be more comfortable playing away during the day but coming home each night. Talk to your children about what is right for them and don't assume that if one of your children wants to stay home, the others will too (or vice versa).

The annual Camping Guide, available on-line from the Ontario Camping Association at www.ontcamp.on.ca lists information on hundreds of accredited camps. It takes awhile to go through the accreditation process, so don't ignore camps that are not yet accredited. Instead, look for ones which meet your needs, then talk to camp directors, staff and other parents to check references. The OCA may be able to provide insight about camps that are in the process of accreditation as well.

March break and winter camps are increasingly popular. Kids have the opportunity to try a new sport, art or other activity for a week or two and parents without childcare can be assured that their kids are happy and active while off school. Many centres that teach gymnastics, trampoline, karate, arts & crafts, computers, reading & math and general sports offer camp programs too. Check the After School and Sports sections for camp ideas that may not be listed here.

<u>You will find the following sub-categories in this section:</u>
Camp Stuff & Labels, Day & Specialty Camps, Overnight Camps

$ COUPONS$ Look for this company's coupon at the back of the book

A Guide to the Best Summer Camps: www.ourkids.net
905-272-1843 x24
Profiles more than 180 of the leading Ontario and Quebec summer camps - Our Kids helps you find the right one for your child.

Ontario Camping Association
250 Merton St, Ste 403, Toronto, Ont, M4S 1B1. • 416-485-0425 •
Call for our free 74 page guide.

■ Camp Stuff & Labels
Camp Connection
Lawrence Plaza, 526 Lawrence Ave W, Toronto, Ont, M6A 1A1. • 416-789-1944 •
Not just for camp! • Other Locations: 7171 Yonge St, 905-707-0770 • Ages: 2+ • ♿.

Camp Essentials
2309 - 400 Walmer Rd., Toronto, Ont, M5P 2X7. • 416-923-2746 •
"Delivering the essentials for camp to your door"

Europe Bound /Hikers Haven
383 King St W, Toronto, Ont, M5V 1K1. • 416-205-9992 • www.europebound.com
Great camping gear at low prices! • Other Locations: 47 Front St E 416-601-1990, 166 South Service Rd E, Oakville 905-849-8928 • Ages: 0+ • Mon-Wed: 10-7, Thu-Fri: 10-9, Sat: 9-6, Sun: 11-5.

Camps

ladybugs creative stationery
6 Old Park Rd, Toronto, Ont, M6C 3H3. • 416-783-8140 • www.ladybugscreative.com
Unique, personalized stationery. Add your personal touch to create fabulous notecards, labels, stationary and more!

$COUPONS$ Loots - CAMP CARE PACKAGES
896 Eglinton Ave W, Toronto, Ont, M6C 2B1. • 416-787-5668 • www.loots.com
Send a gift of love. Cool camp care packages. We deliver! **Look for our ad on the inside front cover. See coupon section for valuable savings.** • 𝚅𝙸𝚂𝙰, ⊕ • Mon-Sat: 9:30-6 • ♿.

$COUPONS$ Lovable Labels Inc
1 City Centre Drive Suite 1010, Mississauga, Ont, L5B 1M2. • 1.866.327.LOVE (5683) • www.lovablelabels.ca
Personalized labels that stay put because kids' stuff doesn't! Sticker labels, shoe labels, iron-ons and unique bag tags. Bright, colorful and durable. **Look for our ad in this section. See coupon section for valuable savings.**

$COUPONS$ Mabel's Labels
866-306-2235 • www.mabel.ca
Dispatched within 24 hours! Mabel's Labels are the original Canadian-made Label! Iron-ons, Stickies, Bag Tags & more. Lots of cute icons. Dishwasher, microwave, laundry & kid tested! **Look for our ad in this section. See coupon section for valuable savings.**

Name Tapes: Quality Iron On Labels
101 Bideford Ave, Toronto, Ont, M3H 1K5. • 416-733-8188 • www.nametapes.ca
Large, easy to apply, iron on labels. Guaranteed to withstand camp washing. Designed to make mom's life easy. Ideal for camp and school uniforms. The larger size name tapes allow lost clothing to be easily identified. Tried and true! • Cheque.

NameLabels - Iron On Labels For Camp
2020 Bathurst Street, Ste 4, Toronto, Ont, M5P 3L1. • Toll free 1-86-MY-LABELS (1-866-952-2357) • www.namelabels.com
NameLabels.com manufactures iron on name tag labels for clothing identification. Our labels are great for Camps, Schools & long Term Care. Our name labels are one type that can either be ironed on or sewn into your clothes.

Stuck on You - Canada
1-866-904-9790 • www.stuckonyou.biz
Kids will never lose their belongings! Stuck-On-You produces a range of vinyl stick-on, fabric iron-on labels that are guaranteed to stick.

The Wrappers, Toronto's Fabulous Kids' Label Catalogue
416-250-6020 • www.thewrappers.ca
Address labels, notepads, notecards, stationery, luggage tags, fun labels, custom pillowcase, towels and more. All personalized with professionally created, funky and fabulous, colourful graphics that kids and adults love! Choose the graphic that best describes the child's favourite activities and unique personality. Perfect for school or camp. Great gifts too.

▪ Day, Specialty & Holiday Camps

Camps

$COUPON$ 5 Elements Camps & Workshops
416-423-8456 • www.5elements4girls.com
5 Elements promotes self-esteem through interactive experiences and discussions. From fashion to relationships, we'll equip girls with the skills to help them deal with the lives they're living now. And, excel in the lives they will grow into. The emphasis is on fun. The results are far reaching. **Look for our ad in this section. See coupon section for valuable savings.** • Ages: girls 6-17.

A.C.H.S. Sports Adventure, Wilderness, Paintball Camps
11191 Keele St N, Maple, Ont, L6A 1S1. • 905-832-8121 • www.achscanada.com
Since 1990 the ACHS has offered great and exciting camp programs for 8 -13 year olds which includes kayaking, canoeing, swimming, bike riding, golf, paintball, overnights, etc. • Ages: 6-13 • Cheque.

$COUPON$ Academy of Artisans
490 Eglinton Ave West, 2nd fl, Toronto, Ont, M5N 1A5. • 416-322-9997 •
www.academyofartisans.com
Arts & Crafts and Cooking camp programs. Fully equipped studios. Winter Break, March Break, Passover, P.D. Days & Summer. Weekly, Half day, full day. Snacks provided. **Look for our ad in the Birthday Party Places section. See coupon section for valuable savings**. • Ages: 4+.

$COUPON$ Active Kids Zone Summer Camp & Holiday Camp
2600 John St, Unit 116, Markham, Ont, L3R 3W3. • 905-307-0707 • www.activekidszone.com
Christmas, March & Passover Break Camps. Action packed days filled with Organized Indoor & Outdoor Sports & Games, Science, Magic, Crafts, Ceramics, Cooking & more! **Look for our ad in the Birthday section. See coupon section for valuable savings**. • Ages: 5-10 yrs.

airborne trampoline
3 locations: Woodbridge 905-850-8477, Mississauga 905-828-2412, Newmarket 905-836-9091 •
Summer, Christmas and March Break camps. Ages 6-15. Co-ed. **Look for our ad in the Birthday
Parties section.** • *Interac*, Cheque.

All Canadian Hockey School (Camp)
11191 Keele St N, Maple, Ont, L6A 1S1. • 905-832-8121 • www.achscanada.com
Since 1981, the ACHS has offered top quality hockey instruction to players from all over the
world 4 - 13 years old. • Ages: 6-13 • Cheque.

All Fired Up Paintable Ceramics
8 & 10 Brentwood Rd N, Etobicoke, Ont, M8X 2B5. • 416-233-5512 •
Summer and March break art camps for Ages 7+.

All-Star Sports Camp
11123 Kennedy Rd, Markham, Ont, L6C 1P2. • 905-887-1400 •
Toronto's Sports Day Camp - 11+ sports offered. • Ages: 6-15.

Art Club for Kids - Camp D'ete
369 Walmer Road, Toronto, Ont, M5R 2Y3. • 647-283-4944 • www.artclubforkids.info
Bilingual arts and crafts camp where children will explore different media, cultures and artists, in
a full and inspiring environment. New themes each week. • Ages: 6-9.

Art Gallery Of Ontario Camps

317 Dundas St W, Toronto, Ont, M5T 1G4. • 416-979-6608 • www.ago.net
Painting, drawing, printing, multimedia, sculpting, video and digital art in our spacious, light-filled studio. We balance art education and recreational games to provide a full experience for even the most energetic camper. July 4th to August 25th. • VISA, ⊜, ▦, *Interac* • ♿.

Arts Explorer Day Camp

2365 Bayview Ave - Crescent School, Toronto, Ont • 416-486-1716 •
Arts-based program. Sculpture, Dance, Painting, Drama & more! • Ages: 5+.

Arts Express

30 Twenty Eighth Street, Toronto, Ont, M8W 2Y6. • 416-239-3093 • www.ArtsExpress.ca
March Break and Summer camps in Drama, Dance and Art! Locations across the GTA. Creating a safe and comfortable environment where children explore their imaginations and build self-confidence. • Ages: 3-14 years.

$COUPON$ Avenue Road Arts School

460 Avenue Rd, Toronto, Ont, M4V 2J1. • 416-961-1502 • www.avenueroadartsschool.com
High quality and innovative programming in the visual and performing arts - all in a warm and supportive environment. Theme-based March Break & Summer Arts Camps for kids of all ages. Small class sizes, highly qualified artist/instructors. **Look for our ad in the Art section. See coupon section for valuable savings.** • Ages: 9mos-adult • VISA, ⊜, *Interac*, Cheque • Mon-Thu: 8:30-8, Fri: 8:30-6:30, Sat: 8:30-5:30.

Bathurst Jewish Community Centre - Centre Camp

BJCC, 4588 Bathurst St, North York, Ont, M2R 1W6. • 416-636-1880 x378 •
Swim, general and specialty programs! Break camps too! • Ages: 2.5-15yrs.

Bayview Glen Day Camp

275 Duncan Mill Rd, North York, Ont, M3B 3H9. • 416-449-7746 •
www.bayviewglendaycamp.com
Top quality camp since 1962, centrally located, excellent variety of activities, amazing ratios, lunch, towels, door-to-door transportation, air-conditioned buildings and outdoor pools. Great for ages 2-15 years. also offering: Munchkinland camp for babies - Ages 6 months-2yrs. **Look for our ad in this section.** • VISA, Cheque.

Big Top School of Circus Arts

1105 Kerrisdale Blvd, Newmarket, Ont, L3Y 8W1. • 905-898-0699 •
Have Summer and March Break at our little circus. • Ages: 6+.

THE BOULEVARD CLUB

Camp Boulevard

summer sports camps

tennis

sailing

rowing

swimming

badminton

peewee tennis

land multi-sports

water multi-sports

Information
416-532-3341 ext 134
camps@boulevardclub.com
www.boulevardclub.com
(online registration)

Also available
early drop-off
late pick-up
meal plan

Bisque It Pottery Painting
8 - 9200 Weston Road, Woodbridge, Ont, L4H 2P8. • 905-303-6333 • www.bisqueit.com
Create lasting memories at Bisque It Summer Camp! Pottery painting projects to inspire creativity & wonderful friendships while painting fabulous functional pottery to cherish at home or give as gifts. Weekly & Drop-in. Details: www.bisqueit.com

Bob Rumball Centre for the Deaf - SIGN OUT! Day Camp
2395 Bayview Ave, North York, Ont, M2L 1A2. • 416-449-9651 x137 or 416-449-2728 TTY •
www.bobrumball.org
A camp for hearing children who want to learn sign language. • Ages: 6-12.

$ COUPON $ Boulevard Club, The
1491 Lakeshore Blvd W, Toronto, Ont, M6K 3C2. • 416-532-3341 x114 •
www.boulevardclub.com
Eleven outstanding weeks of summer sports camp programs, utilizing all the sports facilities at The Beautiful Boulevard Club. **Look for our ad in this section. See coupon section for valuable savings.** Ages: 3-17 • Mon-Fri: 8:45-4.

$ COUPON $ Bugs Without Borders
416-788-4542 Sabeena or 416-573-5234 Nadine • www.bugswithoutborders.com
Imagine: Cozying up with a Corn Snake, snuggling with a Giant Millipede, leaping with a Tomato Frog, spinning with a Silk Worm, hissing with a Giant Cockroach, radiating with a Scorpion, can you handle more…? Summer and March Break Day Camps. **Look for our ad in the Birthday section. See coupon section for valuable savings.** • Ages: 4 - 13.

$COUPON$ Camp Edance

1238 Centre St, Thornhill, Ont, L4J 3M9. • 905-882-1679 • www.1camp.com
Dance plus traditional camping activities. Featuring jazz, hip hop, specialty dance and more.
Located in Thornhill. Great staff! **Look for our ad in the Day Camp section. See coupon section for valuable savings.** • Ages: 5-13.

$COUPON$ Camp Eden

1238 Centre St, Thornhill, Ont, L4J 3M9. • 905-882-1679 • www.1camp.com
Located in Thornhill, we provide a safe, structured, environment with stimulating and fun activities. Specialty Art or Dance camp. LIT Leadership programs. "The Art of Camp". **Look for our ad in this section. See coupon section for valuable savings.** • Ages: 3-13.

Camp eXL

570 Westney Rd South, Suite 25, Ajax, Ont, L1S 6V6. • 905-686-4800 •
Full day camp for children with special learning needs. Focus on Academics. • Other Locations
Richmond Hill • Ages: 4-10 years.

Camp Green Acres

11123 Kennedy Rd, Markham, Ont, L6C 1P2. • 905-887-1400 • www.campgreenacres.com
Traditional day camp in a country setting. Door to door transportation, daily swim instruction, amazing variety of activities - Sports and Horseback Riding Camp too! Half day programs for pre-nursery and nursery age. • Ages: 3-15.

Camps

Camp Northwood Preschoolers Only!

5 Locations covering North York, Thornhill & Markham: 416-492-7812 •
www.northwoodmontessori.ca
Our summer camp in July and August offers a safe, fun-filled program for children 18 mos-5
years. Exciting age appropriate activities keep our campers entertained for half or full days.
Extended hours and flexible scheduling are available. **Look for our ad in the Private Schools section.**
See coupon section for valuable savings. • Ages: 1.5-5yrs.

Camp Programs - Toronto Parks, Forestry & Recreation

416-338-4FUN (4386) • www.toronto.ca/parks
Summer, March Break and holiday camp programs. Fine arts, computers, gymnastics, sports, skiing, horseback riding, nature & environment and more.

Camp Robin Hood / Robin Hood Sports Academy

158 Limestone Cres, North York, Ont, M3J 2S4. • 416-736-4443 • www.camprobinhood.ca
Boys & girls 4-15 yrs. Variety of traditional camp activities. Twice daily swim instruction, specialized sport instruction in golf, baseball, soccer, tennis and personal challenge sports (mountain biking, inline hockey & climbing wall). Door to door transportation. Ask about our 'Parent & Child'
program. Camp site: Markham. • VISA, ⊕, Cheque • Mon-Fri: 8:30-5.

Canadian Hockey Academy, The

1107 Finch Ave West, Toronto, Ont, M3J 2P7. • Toll Free: 1-866-782-2822 or 416-782-2822
www.futurestarsarena.com
Year round hockey, goalie & skating school for the beginner to elite player. Small class size &
professional teachers with extensive experience. Ice rental, Private lessons, 3 on 3 Hockey
League, Summer, March Break, Xmas & Passover camps plus weekly classes. **Look for our ad in**
this section. See coupon section for valuable savings. • Ages: 4 - 21 • VISA, ⊕, ▉, Cheque.

Children's Arts Theatre School Summer Camp

6+ Locations across the GTA, including Mississauga/Oakville, • 416-533-6755 •
www.catsdrama.com
"Theatre under the stars". C.A.T.S. energetic theatre camps offer voice, physical theatre, storytelling, improvisation, stage combat, script-writing, comedy, Shakespearean training, creative
dance, visual arts, and an outstanding final performance. 2 week sessions. Free extended hours.
FREE C.I.T. Programme. **Look for our ad in the After School Activities (Drama) section. See coupon sec-**
tion for free introductory lesson. • Ages: 3+.

Children's Technology Workshop

109 Vanderhoof Ave, Toronto, Ont, M4G 2H7. • 1-866-704-2267 • www.ctworkshop.com
Holiday day camps run year round, Workshop Club, Academics, parties and group workshops.
Activities occur on and off the computer and include robotics, animation & digital video produc-
tion, digital art and computer game design. Campers choose "adventures" to suit age/ skill level.
Ages: 7-14. **Look for our ad opposite the 1st page of the Table of Contents.**

Circus Camp at Wonderful World of Circus

2600 John St, Unit 204-205, Markham, Ont, L3R 3W3. • 905-479-2411 •
www.wonderfulworldofcircus.com
Our programs include many activities such as trampolining, trapeze, training dogs and creating
shows for friends and family. Circus fun for everyone! **Look for our ad in the Sports (Gymnastics) sec-**
tion. See coupon section for valuable section. • Ages: 3-14yrs.

Clay Room, the

279 Danforth Ave, Toronto, Ont, M4K 1N2. • 416-466-8474 • www.theclayroom.ca
Summer and School Break Creative Clay & Craft Camps. Weekly -Day Sessions. Papier Mache,
Clay/ Pottery, Ceramics, Beading, Etc... **Look for our ad in the Birthday section. See coupon section for**
valuable savings.

Crestwood Valley Day Camp
In the fabulous valley at Lawrence and Bayview
Ages 2 1/2-10 yrs

- Superior camp experience
- Warm, caring, qualified staff
- 1/2, 3/4, or full days
- Door to door transportation

- Wholesome lunches and snacks provided
- 4 heated pools • Red Cross Swim Instruction
- Land Sports • Soccer Leagues • Climbing Wall
- Nature Farm • Computers • Fine Arts • Golf Instruction
- Musical Theatre • 4 day overnight camp experience
- Jewellery Shoppe • Leadership Training

www.crestwoodcamp.com

Baseball Training Camp
Basketball Clinics

416 **444-9595**

Crestwood Valley

411 Lawrence Ave E, Toronto, Ont, M3C 1N9. • 416-444-9595 • www.crestwoodcamp.com
Centrally located in a beautiful valley at Bayview and Lawrence. Talented specialists. Fine arts. Sports. Computers. Rock climbing wall. Introductory golf instruction. Superior swim program. 4 heated pools cater to every level. Nature farm. Specialized sports camps & leadership training. **Look for our ad in this section.** • Ages: 2.5-10.

$ COUPON $ Critters Camp

73 Baroness Cr, Toronto, Ont, M2J 3K4. • 416-494-0712 • www.critters.ca
A day camp like no other. 6-11 year olds learn about the Rainforest with live animals! **Look for our ad in the Birthday Parties section. See coupon section for valuable savings.**

$ COUPON $ Dance Place Summer Camp

2 locations: Etobicoke & North York, , • 416-633-2726 • www.danceplace.ca
The Broadway experience. Summer Dance & Performing Arts Day Camps. Ballet, Tap, Jazz, Drama, Music, Visual Arts. Recreational activities, swimming included. Certified Teaching Specialists. Fun for everyone. **Look for our ad in the After School section. See coupon section for valuable savings.** • Ages: 5-15.

Design Exchange Summer Camps

234 Bay St, P.O. Box 18, Toronto Dominion Centre, Toronto, Ont, M5K 1B2. • 416-216-2138 •
Fashion, toy design, graphic design, and more.

children's technology WORKSHOP™
Look for our ad opposite the 1st Table of Contents page

Camps

Discovery Gymnastics
205 Champagne Dr, Unit #5 (Finch & Dufferin), North York, Ont, M3J 2C6. • 416-638-3033 •
Winter, March Break, Passover Break and Summer Camps. Full or half day. Sign up for a day or
the whole week. • Ages: 3+ • Cheque.

Dreams Indoor Playland
2701 Rutherford Rd, Maple , Ont, L4L 3N6. • 905-417-3962 •
Summer drop off arts and crafts program. • Ages: 1-9yrs.

Dunlace Park Tennis Clinics & Camps
647-273-8206 •
Tennis Camps, All levels, Professionally Certified. FUN!

Elite Basketball Camps
Toronto, Richmond Hill, Etobicoke, Newmarket, Aurora Locations, • 905-326-9214 •
www.elitecamps.com
Elite Camps offers young athletes the opportunity to improve their basketball skills. Experienced
instructors will lead campers through skill-building sessions and competitive games. Elite Camps
is an accredited member of the Ontario Basketball Association and the Ontario Camping
Association and offers year round camps and weekly lessons. • Ages: 7-16.

Fairyland Theatre
1183A Finch Ave W, Unit 1 and 2, Toronto, Ont, M3J 2G3. • 416-663-1700 •
Theme camp with costume carnival, pirate & princess day. • Ages: 4-12.

Frozen Ropes Canada
2009 Wyecroft Road, Unit B, Oakville, Ont, L6L 6J4. • 905-847-7697 •
www.frozenropescanada.ca
Frozen Ropes makes camp a ball. Frozen Ropes offers proven instruction and top facilities for
players 8 to 16. Learn the fundamentals of catching, hitting, throwing and conditioning in age and
skill-appropriate groups. **Look for our ad in the Birthday section.**

$COUPON$ Fun & Fitness Club at Candy Castle
1 DeLisle Avenue (Yonge & St. Clair), Toronto, Ont • 416-962-2639 •
Full/half day camp -weekly themes. Sports/arts/computer/dance. **Look for our ad in the Birthday section. See coupon section for valuable savings**. • Ages: 4-9.

Gibson House (1851)
5172 Yonge St, North York, Ont, M2N 5P6. • 416-395-7432 • www.toronto.ca/culture/camps.htm
Have fun in the past this summer!

Glenbrook Day Camp
11737 McCowan Rd, Stouffville , Ont, L4A 7X5. • 905-640-2127 •
Nature, farm and adventure based programming. C.I.T. course!

Greg Salazar's Golf Academy
905-626-2658 • www.salazargolfacademy.com
Full and half day golf camp. Everything from the Fundamentals of the swing to rules and
etiquette. • From ages 8+. • Adult lessons available. • Ages: 8-17.

Gyros Gymnastics
2301 Keele St Unit 105, North York, Ont, M6M 3Z9. • 416-614-0521 •
Gymnastics Summer, Winter, March Break and Passover Camp! Full day and half-day programs.
Daytime, after school and weekend programs September to June. • Ages: 4yrs+ • _VISA_, Interac,
Cheque.

Hangar at Downsview Park, The
75 Carl Hall Rd, Downsview, Ont, M3K 2B9. • 416-638-8478 • www.hangarsports.com
Summer camp for kids who love SPORTS. • Ages: 5-14.

Harbourfront Centre March Break and Summer Camps
235 Queens Quay W, York Quay Centre, Toronto, Ont, M5J 2G8. • 416-973-4093 •
www.harbourfrontcentre.com/camps
One-of-a-kind experience at our unique waterfront location. OCA member.

Hillcrest Camp
59 Plymbridge Rd, Toronto, Ont, M2P 1A2. • 416-489-8355 • www.hillcrestcamp.ca
Our goal is to provide your child with an exceptional, well-rounded early camping experience within a safe, fun and supportive environment. Where every day is a special day. • Ages: 2 1/2 - 5.

Historic Sites & Museums of Toronto
Operated by the City of Toronto, Culture Division, • 416-338-3888 •
www.toronto.ca/culture/camps.htm
Experience wonderful hands-on March break programs and summer day camps at some of Toronto's most interesting and exciting historic houses and sites. Enjoy special events, archeological digs, crafts & tours. • 💳, 💳.

Hockey Toronto - www.hockeytoronto.com
416-631-4221 • www.hockeytoronto.com
Hockeytoronto.com is a comprehensive listing of all aspects of hockey in Toronto, the GTA and Ontario. Boys hockey, girls hockey, men's hockey, women's hockey and coed hockey. Hockey leagues, hockey tournaments, pickup hockey and hockey instruction. March Break hockey camps, Passover hockey camps and summer hockey camps.

$COUPON$ I Wanna B
1170 Burnhamthorpe Road West, Unit #29, Mississauga, Ont, L5C 4E6. • 905-270-9292 •
www.iwannab.ca
I Wanna B Camp. Children become Firefighters, Paleontologists, Hairstylists, Scientists and more. Activities, crafts, games and fun! Half and full day. Early and late pick up. Limited spaces.
Look for our ad in this section. See coupon section for valuable savings.

Joy of Dance Studio
95 Danforth Ave Suite 302, Toronto, Ont, M4K 1N2. • 416-406-3262 • www.joyofdance.ca
Learn stage acting, movement, ballroom, dance, musical theatre and more!

Camps

$ COUPONS $ Jungle Cubs Indoor Playground
1681 Bayview Ave, Toronto, Ont, M4G 2C1. • 416-322-6005 •
www.junglecubsindoorplayground.com
Summer Preschool Camp. Children will have fun playing while learning in a safe, clean &
relaxed atmosphere. A great way to get ready for school. **Look for our ad in the Birthday parties section. See coupon section for valuable savings.**

Just Bounce Trampoline Club
3731 Chesswood Dr, North York, Ont, M3J 2P6. • 416-635-0206 • www.justbounce.ca
8 TRAMPOLINES - We offer super Passover, March Break and Summer Day Camps!
Swimming, Arts & Crafts, Circus Arts, Outdoor Games AND Trampoline Instruction make for a
fun-filled day! 1:8 Instructor ratio. Come join us!

Kids Inc Day Camp
986 Flute Way, Mississauga, Ont, L5W 1S6. • 905-301-1414 •
Recreational summer day camp for children 4-14.

Kidsworld Day Camp & Funworld Day Camp (Bayview & York Mills)
416-785-4600 • www.kidsworlddaycamp.com
OUR 27th YEAR! Primary/preschool specialists. Door-to-door bussing. Instructional Swimming.
Arts. Sports. Skills Clinics. Daily Special Events. Hot lunches. As low as $185/wk. Ages:
Kidsworld- 3-5yrs. Funworld- 6-8yrs

KinderGarden in the Beach, The
1A Hannaford St, Toronto, Ont, M4E 3G6. • 416-690-6628 •
Creative play and themed activities tailor-made for little sprouts, aged 3-5.

Laughing Trunk Inc, The - Creative Learning Centre
5602 10th line W, Unit 106, Mississauga, Ont, L5M 7L9. • 905-858-5884 •
Hands-on creative learning during school breaks. • Ages: 3-12.

$ COUPONS $ Mad Science
1170 Sheppard Ave W, Unit 14, Toronto, Ont, M3K 2A3. • 800-630-4403 •
www.madscience.com/toronto
Spectacular hands-on science at several locations around the GTA. Choose from six theme
weeks, each with daily take-home activities such as rockets, space shuttles & birdhouses. It's a
fun, fascinating & educational world of science during week long sessions with real life Mad
Scientists. **Look for our ad in the Birthday Parties section. See coupon section for valuable savings.** •
Ages: 5-12 • Cheque.

Magic Forest Day Camp
416-425-5496 • www.magicforestdaycamp.com
Exciting outdoor adventures for young children including crafts, games, wading, sing-songs,
nature activities. Half and full day programmes available. • Ages: 3-8yrs.

Markham Museum
9350 Hwy 48 (2 km N of Hwy 7), Markham, Ont, L3P 3J3. • 905-294-4576 •
www.markhammuseum.ca • Summer, winter and holiday camps. Children, ages 4-12.

Martha Hicks School of Ballet
2384 Yonge Street, 2nd Fl, Toronto, Ont, M4P 2E0. • 416-484-4731 • www.mhsb.ca
Creative, energetic, fun and entertaining summer dance camp. Experience and enjoy the art of
dance, drama, arts and crafts and musical theatre. Highly trained teachers provide topnotch
instruction in an encouraging atmosphere. Ages 5-11.

Summer Camps!

- Full and half day camps such as adventure camps, sports camps, dance camps, and much more!
- Extended hours available
- Locations across Mississauga

Call **905-896-5883** for more details or consult our web site or **www.mississauga.ca/rec&parks**

MISSISSAUGA
Recreation and Parks
Leading today for tomorrow

$COUPON$ MESSY HANDS Summer Camp

2501 Rutherford Rd, Unit 27, Bldg B, Vaughan, • 905-303-MESS (6377) •
www.messyhands.com
Hands-on art programme promotes creativity, self-esteem & good friendships! Daily themes.
Draw. Paint. Sculpt. Drama. Visit the Art Bus! Richmond Hill, Woodbridge & Maple locations.
Look for our ad in the Birthday Parties section. See coupon section for valuable savings. • Ages: 3+.

Mississauga Recreation & Parks - Camp Programs

300 City Centre Drive, Mississauga, Ont, L5B 3C1. • 905-615-4100 •
www.mississauga.ca/rec&parks
Supervised Summer/March Break camps for a variety of interests. Camp areas include: adventure camps, sports camps, arts camps and much more! Full and half day options. **Look for our camp ad in this section.** • Ages: preschool to 14 yrs.

National Film Board of Canada - Mediatheque

150 John Street (at Richmond - Osgoode Subway), Toronto, Ont, M5V 3C3. • 416-973-3012 •
www.nfb.ca/mediatheque
Campers flex their creative muscles and learn professional filmmaking techniques in week-long day camps, learning all aspects of filmmaking and broadening their artistic horizons. Affordable rates. Call for more information and to book. • Ages: 3-16.

$COUPON$ North Beach Indoor Volleyball Academy (Since 1993)

74 Railside Rd, North York, Ont, M3A 1A3. • 416-446-0777 • www.northbeachvolleyball.com
Weekend volleyball camps & leagues are now available for ages 11yrs and up. Play bare feet on indoor beach courts. Christmas & Spring break camps give kids, five fun filled days ...of games and team building. **Look for our ad in this section. See coupon section for valuable savings.** • Ages: 4+.

We offer fun & exhilarating skills camps for kids on & off the sand. All sport & personal development programs are designed for children of similar age groups.

- **Sand Volleyball**
- **Boxing For Teens**
- **Peewee Volleyball**
- **4 on 4 Beach Soccer**
- **Beginner Rock Climbing**
- **Organized Dinosaur Digs**

Mention
" Help We've Got Kids"
and receive 10% off your
Christmas and March Break
camp registration

**North Beach Volleyball Academy
74 Railside Road, North York
(DVP & Lawrence)**

416 446 0777 or visit our website www.northbeachvolleyball.com

Ontario Science Centre

770 Don Mills Rd, North York, Ont, M3C 1T3. • 416-696-3256 • www.OntarioScienceCentre.ca
"OSCamp" is the Ontario Science Centre's popular summer day camp program. Campers participate in 'hands-on' science activities and workshops that will introduce them to various science
and technology concepts.

Par Golf Camps

821 Eglinton Ave W, Toronto, Ont, M5N 1E6. • 416-960-GOLF (4653) • www.learngolf.com
The only golf camp accredited by the OCA. Now in our 14th year, we offer 1, 2 and 4 week programs throughout the summer for boys and girls. Located on an 18 hole golf course. We offer
door to door busing throughout Metro. Adult programs available 7 days/week throughout the
summer. • Ages: 7-18 • *VISA*, ⊕, Cheque.

Party Ponies, The

2300 Rosebank Road North, Pickering, Ont • 905-209-8847 •
Pony rides at your home! Safe. Affordable. Fun! **Look for our ad in the Birthday Parties section.**

Pia Bouman School for Ballet and Creative Movement - Junior Programs

6 Noble St, Toronto, Ont, M6K 2C6. • 416-533-3706 • www.piaboumanschool.org
Summer Leaps and Summer Turns - Junior Programs (Ages for 4 to 11 years). 3 programs that
include different forms of dance, art and music. Younger students learn yoga, while older ones
explore African Dance. July 17 to 28. • Ages: 4-16.

Pia Bouman School for Ballet and Creative Movement - Pre-Professional Program

6 Noble St, Toronto, Ont, M6K 2C6. • 416-533-3706 • www.piaboumanschool.org
Summer Leaps and Summer Turns - Pre-Professional Program. (Ages 11 to 18 +) 2 levels
Stance, stamina and style are the focus of this program of Classical Ballet, Free Style Modern,
Improvisation, African Dance, Art and Percussive Instrumental Music. August 2 to 18. • Ages: 4-16.

$COUPON$ Planet Kids

1(877) 322-KIDS (5437) • www.planetkids.ca
Serving 2 000 families annually from Mississauga, Oakville, Burlington, Milton, Georgetown,
Brampton and beyond, with more than 30 exciting programs including Traditional, Theatre,
Film, Radio, Art, Horseback Riding, Construct It, Animal, Computers, Golf, Tennis, Lacrosse and
more! Transportation available. **Look for our ad in this section. See coupon section for valuable
savings.** • Ages: Kindergarten - Grade 11.

Power Soccer School of Excellence - Camps

905-829-0562 or 1-888-883-6712 • www.powersoccer.ca
March Break and Summer Soccer Camps. Learn soccer in a fun, safe atmosphere! Fun &
Fitness! Year round skill development Soccer School. Professional soccer coaching clinics for kids
aged 4-18. School of Excellence runs Fall, Winter & Spring programs. **Look for our ad in this section**

Renaissance Kids Camp

Avenue Rd & Eglinton Area, Toronto, Ont • 416-657-0220 • www.renaissancekidscamp.com
Activities include film, animation, martial arts, computer and sports. For ages 7-12. Professional
teachers, certified instructors and senior students will develop your child's talents.

Richmond Hill Country Club Day Camp

8905 Bathurst St (at Hwy 7), Richmond Hill, Ont, L4C 0H4. • 905-731-2800 x242 •
www.richmondhillcountryclub.com
Besides the beautiful natural environment, the Richmond Hill Country Club Day Camp offers an
indoor and outdoor swimming pool, outdoor tennis courts, gymnasium and an outdoor basketball
court plus a variety of art and science activities. • Ages: 2-14 • *VISA*, ⊕, ■, *Interac*, Cheque.

Rock Oasis Inc

27 Bathurst St, Toronto, Ont, M5V 2P1. • 416-703-3434 • www.rockoasis.com
Canada's largest rock climbing gym. Summer, March Break and PA days, we offer 1/2 day camps. Toronto and Ajax locations. • Ages: 6+. •

Royal Ontario Museum Summer Club

100 Queen's Park (Bloor St at Avenue Rd), Toronto, Ont, M5S 2C6. • 416-586-5797 • www.rom.on.ca (ROMKids Programs)
One of the city's most creative and diverse summer camps, offering an exciting array of fun, activity based programs inspired by the collections and research of a world-class museum. The ROM's fascinating galleries and authentic artifacts guarantee a camp experience that's hard to beat! • Ages: 5-16 • VISA, MasterCard, ■, *Interac* • Mon-Fri: 9-4 • ♿.

Ryerson University Sports Day Camp

350 Victoria St, Toronto, Ont, M5B 2K3. • 416-979-5000 x7360 • www.ryerson.ca/sportsandrec
Conveniently located in downtown Toronto. Sports & Recreation offers a variety of 1-week sports and activity programs designed for age groups 7-13; 10-13; 14-19 and 15-18. Camp activities include: swimming daily, basketball, volleyball, baseball, floor hockey, badminton, games and crafts. Visit us online! **Look for our ad in this section.**

S.A.C. Summer Camps

158 Limestone Cres, North York, Ont, M3J 2S4. • 905-727-6544 • www.sacsummercamps.com
Multi-sport adventure day camp includes a wide variety of sports. Specialty camps in science, film, arts, music, magic, computers and technology. Recreational swim. Hot and cold lunches provided daily. Optional bus transportation and after camp supervision available. • VISA, MasterCard, Cheque • Mon-Fri: 8:30-5.

Scarborough Historical Museum

1007 Brimley Rd, Scarborough, Ont, M1P 3E8. • 416-338-8807 • www.toronto.ca/culture/camps.htm
Children's summer and March break day camps in a historic setting. • Ages: 6-11 • VISA, MasterCard, Cheque.

$COUPON$ SCORE Day Camp

2760 Bathurst St., Toronto, Ont, M6B 3A1. • 905-709-6383 • www.scoredaycamp.com
Challenging and exciting programs. General day camp or specialty in sports, computers, science, art and drama. Pre-school camp. FUN-ominal Experience! **Look for our ad in the Birthday Parties (Party Places) section. See coupon section for valuable savings.** • Ages: 2 1/2 - 15.

Ryerson University Day Camps

RYERSON UNIVERSITY
STUDENT SERVICES

SPORTS DAY CAMP
- 7 - 13 year olds.
- One-week sessions, July - August.
- Variety of sports, arts & crafts, co-operative games.
- Swimming daily.

LEADERSHIP PROGRAM
- 14 - 18 year olds.
- Two-week session
- Program to develop team work and leadership skills.

BASKETBALL CAMP
- 7 - 18 year olds.
- One-week sessions, July - August.
- Have fun while developing basketball skills.

Ryerson University Day Camps 350 Victoria Street, Toronto, Ontario M5B 2K3
For more info: Tel: 416.979.5000 ext. 7360 Fax: 416.979.5364 E-mail rac@ryerson.ca **www.ryerson.ca/sportsandrec**

Camps

$COUPONS$ Seneca Summer Camps - Sports, Arts & Science

Newnham Campus, 1750 Finch Ave E, , • 416-491-5050 x2329 •
www.senecac.on.ca/home/kidstuff/camp
Caring for your children for 35 years. Excellent 1-week programs include Baseball, Basketball, Dance, Golf, Trampoline, Gymnastics, Cheerleading, Hockey, Soccer, Tennis, Multi-Sports, Science, Earth Watchers, Photography, Computer Animation or Game Design, Cartooning, Magic, Crime Scene, Rocketry, Robotics, Forensics & more. Certified, experienced staff. OCA accredited. **Look for our ad in this section. See coupon section for valuable savings.** •
Ages: 4 1/2 - 14 • VISA, ⊕, ■, Interac.

Shakespeare in Action

109 Gore Vale Ave, Toronto, Ont, M6J 2R5. • 416-703-4881 • www.shakespeareinaction.org
Two week fun-filled experience designed to bring Shakespeare Alive. Kids stage their own performance of a Shakespeare abridged play. • Ages: 7-12.

Small Wonders Discovery Centre

140 Capitol Court, Mississauga, Ont, L5T 2R8. • 905 696-6817 • www.playatsmallwonders.ca
Small Wonders Camp offers educational programs, arts & crafts, sports, and exciting field trips! Let your child learn and explore in a safe, clean and entertaining environment. Check out our super discounts. Extended hours are available. • Ages: 0-8 years.

Camps

$COUPONS Sportball Canada; Summer Camps
39 Glen Cameron Rd, Unit 8, Thornhill, Ont, L3T 1P1. • 905-882-4473 or 1-8-Sportkids •
Multi-sport camps offered during Summer/ December holidays/ March Break. **Look for our ad in
the Parent/Tot section. See coupon section for valuable savings.** • Ages: 2-8 yrs..

$COUPONS Sportplay Day Camp
Locations around the GTA, • 905-940-9481 or 1-866-940-9481 • www.sportplay.ca
Sportplay offers Summer, December and March Break DAY camps. Multi-sport instruction and
play including ball hockey, baseball, basketball, cooperative games, soccer, tennis, touch football,
track & field, volleyball and much more! Also craft, arts and nature activities. Ages 3-7 years old.
Half Day & Full Day options. **Look for our ad in this section. See coupon section for valuable savings.**

Summer Camp d'Ete
12 Bannockburn Ave (Avenue Rd & 401), Toronto, Ont, M5M 2M8. • 416-789-7855 x308 •
www.frenchprogrammesfrancais.com
Bilingual multi-faceted summer and March break camp. Activities include: cooking, computers,
art & crafts, drama, swimming, dance, sports, field trips and much more. Since 1996.

Sunnybrook Stables Ltd: Sunnybrook Park
1132 Leslie St (at Eglinton), Don Mills, Ont, M3C 2S7. • 416-444-4044 •
Summer riding day camp. 10 day sessions. Show on last day of camp. • Ages: 9-15.

Super Summer Soccer+ Camp: Royal City Soccer Club
1-800-427-0536 • Canada's largest grassroots summer soccer camp. • Ages: 5-13.

Toronto Lynx/Lady Lynx Soccer Camps
100 East Mall, Suite 11, Toronto, Ont, M8Z 5X2. • 416-251-4625 x31 •
Camps/events by top players in Canada. Ages 6+.

Toronto Tennis Camp
2 Elm Ave, Toronto, Ont, M4W 1N4. • 416-398-4826 •
Three tennis programs available. Co-ed. Ages: 5-15 years.

Toronto Zoo's Overnight Serengeti Bush Camp
Meadowvale Rd and Hwy 401, • 416-392-5947 •
www.torontozoo.com
Have an unforgettable experience and spend the night in the Toronto Zoo's African Savanna
within roaring distance of lions, hyenas and elephants. Tent accommodation, meals and full
educational program are all provided. Parents attend with children. • Ages: 6+ • *VISA*, ⊕,
■, *Interac* • ㅊ.

Toronto Zoo's Zoo Camp
Meadowvale Rd and Hwy 401, , • 416-392-5947 • www.torontozoo.com
Week long, summer day camp - perfect for children interested in animals. You'll amaze at how
much they learn! Designed to instill a love and enthusiasm for wildlife and nature. Informative
animal tours and encounters. Safe, friendly environment. ZooKids (4-5 yrs), ZooCamp (6-12 yrs),
BioCamp (13-16 yrs). • *VISA*, ⊕, ■, *Interac* • ㅊ.

Town of Markham Recreation Department
101 Town Centre Blvd, Recreation & Culture Dept, Markham, Ont, L3R 9W3. • 905-477-7000 •
www.markham.ca
If you are looking for fun, safe and exciting activities the Town of Markham offers a wonderful selection
of camps for ages 3 to 15 year olds. Sports Camps: basketball, hockey, golf, tennis and extreme sports.
General Camps: magic, dance , drama, computer, outdoor adventure camp and leaders in training.

University of Toronto - Camp U of T
55 Harbord St, Toronto, Ont, M5S 2W6. • 416-978-3436 • www.campuoft.ca
A wide variety of Sport Specific, Multisport, Leadership and Mini University camps in downtown
Toronto. Experienced and certified staff make a great camp! Over 20 years of experience. OCA
accredited. March Break camps also available. • Ages: 4-16 • *VISA*, ⊕, *Interac*, Cheque.

University of Toronto Power Music Camp

80 Queens Park, Toronto, Ont, M5S 2C5. • 416-978-3733 • www.music.utoronto.ca
An exciting music camp for students completing Grades 5 to 9. University of Toronto music faculty teach students to become Power Musicians. Students play in ensembles. Recreational activities round out the day. 2 one-week sessions in July. 9am-4pm daily. • Ages: 11-15.

University Settlement

23 Grange Road, Toronto, Ont, M5T 1C3. • 416-598-3444 x229 •
Aquatic, afterschool, camp programs for ages 4-13.

Upper Canada Day Camps

2900 John St, Unit 2, Markham, Ont, L3R 5G3. • 905-946-1113 •
www.uppercanadachildcare.com
Upper Canada is a growing family of day camps operating in North York, Thornhill, Vaughan, Markham, Maple, Stouffville, Aurora, Newmarket and Keswick. Exciting activities include two field trips per week, swimming, sports, arts and more. Call 905-946-9113 for the location nearest you. **Look for our ad in the Childcare section**. • Ages: 6-12 yrs..

Vaughan Sportsplex

10 Westcreek Drive, Unit 12-15, Woodbridge, Ont, L4L 9R5. • 905-265-9115 •
Kids sports facility with child/youth sized sports fields.

$COUPON$ Whimz Studio Creatures & Crafts Camp
784 St. Clair Ave West (west of Bathurst), Toronto, Ont, M6C 1B6. • 416-656-7894 •
www.whimzonline.com
Featuring Live Animals: Small Mammals, Reptiles, Amphibians, Bugs & Birds, plus a fabulous
craft program. Learn all about the animals in their natural habitat and in captivity plus lots of
hands on time while using your creative powers to make WHIMZ ANIMAL inspired crafts to take
home. Weekly Sessions- Half Days (a.m. or p.m.) Also: Parties & Classes. **Look for our ad in the
Birthday section. See coupon section for valuable savings.** • Ages: 4-12 • Cheque.

Wiz Kids Activity Centre
484 Cosburn Ave, Toronto, Ont, M4J 2N5. • 416-425-8280 • Half day camps. July & August. Ages 2+.

Wiz Kidz Day Camp
located in Leaside , • 416-425-5496 •
A unique summer learning experience for all campers! • Ages: 7-12yrs.

Yes I Can! Summer Camp
100 Ranleigh Avenue, Toronto, Ont, M4N 1W9. • 416-486-4911 •
www.yesicannurseryschool.com
Safe, shady no holds barred creative adventures coupled with indoor drama and music. Offered
by award winning preschool.

YMCA Day Camps
416-928-9622 • Super day camps, outdoor discovery camps, skills camps.

York Paediatric Therapy Services Inc
2 locations: Richmond Hill & Toronto, • Head Office: 905-737-9680 •
Fun printing/cursive handwriting camp. Two weeks/half days. • By appointment

Young Filmmakers Workshop
416-690-4056 • www.youngfilmmakersworkshop.com
Filmmaking and animating camp offered weekly during July, Aug, and March break. After school,
weekend, in the classroom workshops from Sept-June. • Ages: 10-16yrs.

$COUPON$ Zodiac Holiday Camps
Bayview/Lawrence location, • 416-789-1989 • www.zodiaccamp.on.ca
Campers, aged 2.5-12.5, participate in an awesome variety of Zodiac swim, sports, arts and other programs (extended day avail.) in our great Nov. and Mar. Break Camps. Half or full day. Flexible choice of
days. **Look for our ad in this section. See coupon section for valuable savings.** • VISA, ⊖, Cheque.

$COUPON$ Zodiac Swim & Specialty Camp
Bayview/Lawrence - Toronto French School Location, • 416-789-1989 • www.zodiaccamp.on.ca
Specialty program for campers 6.5-12.5 years old. Specialties include: Creatures & Creativity,
Land Sports, Science & Rocketry, Make & Bake, Performing Arts, Circus Arts, Extreme
Sports…plus more! Daily Zodiac swim. Half/full-day Kid-Vantage program for 2.5-6.5 year-olds.
Leadership programs available. **Look for our ad in this section. See coupon section for valuable
savings.** • Ages: 2.5-15.5 • VISA, ⊖, Cheque.

▪ Overnight Camps

Camp Gesher
City: 416-633-2511 Camp: 613-336-2583 • www.campgesher.com
Exploring Jewish life & culture through the camping experience. Exciting, fun activities. Great spirit.

Camp Wabikon
416-483-3172 • www.wabikon.com
Traditional summer camp. Established 1944. Co-ed, residential. International clientele. Full range
of land and water-based activities. Magnificent island location in beautiful Temagami, Ont.
Transportation provided. • Ages: 6-17.

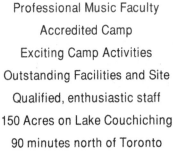

Camps

Camp Wahanowin

City Address: 227 Eglinton Ave W, Toronto, Ont, M4R 1A9. • 416-482-2600 or 800-701-3132 •
www.wahanowin.com
Celebrating our 53rd season! An exciting residential Sports & Arts Camp on Lake Couchiching.
Boys and girls ages 6-16. All Land & Water Sports, Water Slide, Climbing Centre & Zip Line, On-
Site 9 Hole Golf Course, Tennis, Ropes Course, Radio Station, Music Theatre and much more!
Look for our ad in this section.

Camp Walden

158 Limestone Cres, North York, Ont, M3J 2S4. • 416-736-4443 • www.campwalden.ca
An adventure in outdoor summer activity and self-discovery for boys and girls aged 7-16.
Campers and staff come together for summertime fun and excitement, developing skills, building
relationships and forming lasting friendships.

Camp White Pine

40 Lawrence Ave W, Toronto, Ont, M5M 1A4. • 416-322-6250 •
Co-ed residential children's summer camp in the Haliburton Highlands.   Ages 7 - 16.

Circle R Ranch

RR # 1, Delaware, Ont, N0L 1E0. • 1-877-844-8738 or 519-471-3799 • www.circlerranch.ca
Located 8 kms west of London. Western horseback riding- Learn to Ride & Care for Your Own Horse.
Also swimming, mountain biking, kayaking, bouldering wall, crafts and more! • Ages: 8-16 yrs.

Fraser Lake Camp

11737 McCowan Rd, Stouffville, Ont, L4A 7X5. • 905-642-2964 •
"Camping with a purpose since 1955." • Ages: 8-16.

Hollows Camp

3303 13th line, RR #3, Cookstown, Ont, L0L 1L0. • 905-775-2694 •
Riding Camp with full activities. 2 week programs. One week in Aug. • Ages: 7-14.

Medeba Summer Camp

PO Box 1435, West Guilford, Ont, K0M 1S0. • 1-800-461-6523 •
Traditional camp that specializes in adventure experiences. • Ages: 6-17.

National Music Camp of Canada

City Address: 227 Eglinton Ave W, Toronto, Ont, M4R 1A9. • 416-482-2475 or (800) 701-3132 •
www.nationalmusiccamp.com
A one-week summer camp dedicated to excellence in music instruction and amazing camp activities. For over 40 years we have provided an outstanding music experience balanced with exciting recreational activities led by qualified, caring professional musicians and enthusiastic recreational leaders. **Look for our ad in this section.** • Ages: 9-18.

Safari Zoo Camp, Jungle Cat World

3667 Concession 6 RR 1, Orono, Ont, L0B 1M0. • 905-983-5016 • www.junglecatworld.com
North America's most unique camp for children and teens. Fun & interactive programs that
encourage respect, understanding and care for wildlife and the environment. Hands-on activities
include: Jr. Zookeeping, falconry, hiking, mountain biking, canoeing, rock climbing, caving, swimming, waterslides, wilderness survival skills, eco-games, campfires, arts & crafts.

Sorcerer's Safari

389 Manor Rd E, Toronto, Ont, M4S 1S9. • 416-322-1442 •
Last week of Summer and March Break Magic Camps. Various locations. • Ages: 8-18.

YWCA Camp Tapawingo

177 Caledonia Rd, Toronto, Ont, M6E 4S8. • 416-652-9374 • www.ywcatoronto.org
A summer of adventure for girls. Swimming, canoeing, sailing, crafts, dance, kayaking and canoe
trips at our Georgian Bay location. • Ages: 6-15 • 𝗩𝗜𝗦𝗔, ⊖, ▓], Cheque.

Safety is something that should be taught to your kids but it is also something that should be modeled. Don't tell them to cross at the crosswalk instead of in the middle of the block, do it yourself. Teach them about wearing a helmet while biking and a seatbelt while driving by having the adults do it too. Start talking about safety as soon as possible. Tell them about "911" and when to use it. Talk about fire safety and what to do in an emergency. Practice evacuation procedures in your home. Discuss the internet and safe surfing habits.

Practice. Role play the situations and work on their responses.

Make sure your carseats and boosters are installed properly. For more information about carseats and boosters, call 1 (888) SAFE TIPS (723-3847) or visit www.safekidscanada.ca.

There are lots of listees in this category who can not only help you identify the dangerous stuff, but also have a variety of solutions to help keep your child safe.

Finally, keep emergency numbers in your home at your child's eye level. Ensure that the Poison Control Centre number and your home address are both posted near the phone. If at all possible, invest the time in a half or full day emergency first aid course. They are listed in the Health and Wellness section and may save a life one day!

Allied First Aid/CPR Training
905-391-6118 Pickering • Be prepared for emergencies. First aid/CPR courses.

Baby Barrier: Removeable Pool Safety Fence, A Division of Kiddie Proofers
3011 Dufferin St, S. of Lawrence 416-785-5437 & 3883 Rutherford Rd, (SW cornerWeston Rd) 905-851-5437, Toronto, • 416-785-KIDS (5437) or 1 (800) 601-KIDS • www.kiddieproofers.com Surround your pool with the lifeguard that is always on duty! Help prevent drowning accidents with our see-through and removable pool fence. Visit our Kiddie Proofers stores for Canada's most comprehensive line of pool, water & sun safety products. Fully insured & bonded. **See Kiddie Proofers ad for more information.** • *VISA*, ⊕, *Interac*.

$COUPONS$ Babyproofers/ www.babyproofers.ca
416-561-2524 • www.babyproofers.ca
Make your home safe for children. Home safety inspection and child safety education for you. Installation of magnetic locks, latches, hardware mounted stair gates, fireplace & electrical covers, removable pool safety fence and more. **Look for our ad in this section. See coupon section for valuable savings.** • Ages: 0-3 • Cheque.

Canadian Car seat Installation Centre (CCIC)
89 Research Rd, Toronto, Ont, M4G 2G8. • 416-422-CCIC (2242) • www.momstobeandmore.com/ccic
NEW SERVICE! The Canadian Car seat Installation Centre (CCIC) is new to the GTA. In Ontario 80% of car seats are incorrectly installed. Have your car seat professionally inspected or installed by our certified technicians. Call for appointment, or drop by. **Look for our ad in this section.**

Child Safety

Child Find Ontario
440A Britannia Rd E, Mississauga, Ont, L4Z1X9. • 1-866-Kid-Tips (866-543-8477) • www.ontario.childfind.ca
Offers hope and help to families by teaching how to keep children safe, and helping find them should they go missing. Free. Recognized by police, Kidcheck safety clinics. Admin: 9am - 5pm. Hotline open 24/7. • Ages: 0-18 yrs.

Consumer Product Safety, Health Canada
2301 Midland Avenue, , • 416-973-4705 • www.healthcanada.gc.ca/cps
Call regarding safety of cribs, toys, playpens, lighters, household chemicals, etc. It is illegal to sell unsafe products, new or used. Babywalkers are banned! • Mon-Fri: 8:30-4:30.

ENJO Cleaning - Lisa Borden
744 Briar Hill Ave, Toronto, Ont, M6B 1L3. • 416-785-3048 •
Clean without chemicals - protect your family home.

Internet Child Proofers
647-292-0759 • Internet proofing your family.

$COUPONS Kiddie Proofers
3011 Dufferin St, S. of Lawrence 416-785-5437 & 3883 Rutherford Rd, (SW corner Weston Rd) 905-851-5437, • www.kiddieproofers.com
Making homes and pools safer for children. Visit our stores to see Canada's most comprehensive line of child safety products & car seats. Home safety consultations and custom installation for your home and car. Canada's only fully insured and bonded child safety company. **Look for our ad in this section. See coupon section for valuable savings.** • *VISA*, ⊕, *Interac*.

Kids on the Go
416-605-1997 • Professional installation of children's car seats.

Maco Security Systems
416-540-4838 •
Sales and installation of cameras and equipment for covert surveillance of nannies. Standard alarm systems too. Visit our Toronto showroom - call for an appointment. • *VISA*, ⊕, Cheque.

MedicAlert
2005 Sheppard Ave E, Ste 800, Toronto, Ont, M2J 5B4. • 416-696-0267 or 800-668-1507 • www.medicalert.ca
MedicAlert®, a Canadian registered charity, is the leading provider of medical ID devices. Exciting sport and kids bracelets are now offered and are linked to our secure database that is accessible 24-7 through the MedicAlert Emergency Hotline.

Ontario Block Parent® Program Inc
902 Maitland St, London, Ont, N5Y 2X1. • 800-563-2771 •
A child safety program. Block Parents provide safe havens for children who find themselves in difficult, threatening or frightening situations.

Protect-a-Child
905-814-5747 • www.protectachild.com
The strongest and safest transparent removable pool fence with two exclusive patented safety features and shock resistant fiberglass super posts.

$COUPONS Safety Superstore
3 locations: Concord 905-761-SAFE (7233), Brampton 905-456-SAFE, Mississauga 905-828-SAFE, www.safetysuperstore.com
The best selection of new and innovative baby proofing products in Canada! Be sure your children are protected from all potential hazards. Very competitive prices. Friendly, personalized service. **Look for our ad in this section. See coupon section for valuable savings.** • *VISA*, ⊕, *Interac*.

V.I.P. Child Car Seat Rentals Inc
29 Steckley St, Aurora, Ont, L4G 7K6. • 905-713-0326 • www.vipchildcarseat.com
Renting children's car seats, play pens, strollers and high chairs. Equipment is safety checked. • Ages: 0-8.

This section is one of the most popular with parents but is also one of the few that we can't even attempt to make comprehensive. In fact, there could be a whole book which does nothing but lists licenced and unlicenced day care centres and providers in Toronto. We decided to focus this section mostly on larger companies which have multiple centres around the city, as well as organized (larger) homecare providers. There are a few registries as well as websites set up to connect parents with various types of childcare, from nannies to daycare. You might wish to check our bulletin board online as well, since childcare seems to be one of the hot topics among our online community members.

It is also worth calling Metro Children's Services at 392-5437 for their list of subsidized day care.

If you prefer to have your childcare come to you, we list nanny agencies that can provide live in and live out nannies. There are also several services which offer emergency or temporary in-home child care- a great idea for unexpected childcare needs like sick kids, respite, school strikes or even just a weekend getaway. We also have listings for baby nurses who can be an amazing help to parents during the first weeks when they come home from the hospital. Parents should ALWAYS ask for references with all of these services.

You will find the following sub-categories in this section:
Daycare and Home Childcare Centres, Emergency/Temporary Childcare & Baby Nurses, Nanny Services

---

$ COUPONS Look for this company's coupon at the back of the book

---

▪ Daycare & Home Childcare Centres

211 Toronto (Findhelp Information Services)
211 • www.211toronto.ca
Dial 211. Free childcare information 24 hours/day.

All About Kids; Quality Licensed Childcare
Multiple locations including: Markham, Central Toronto, North Toronto & Goodwood/Uxbridge , 416-977-0555 • www.allaboutkids.ca
Safe, cheerful environment. Kind, responsive teachers. Academic programming based in play. Web cameras (parent access only). Back-up care, before and after school care and extended hours also available. • Ages: 3mos-10yrs • Mon-Fri: 7:00 - 6:00.

Beaches Co-Operative Playschool
975 Kingston Road, Toronto, Ont, M4E 1T1. • 416-690 9935 •
Learning through play for children ages 2-4 1/2.

A licensed Non-profit agency since 1979. Warm, caring, homes in North York, Toronto, Scarborough, Thornhill, Richmond Hill, Maple and Markham

J&F Home Child Care Services

Caring Homes That Help Raise Caring Children

• Providers are educated in childcare and have First Aid/CPR Training
• Childcare consultants work with providers on programming, nutrition & safety issues
• Backup is available when your provider is ill or on vacation
• Income tax receipt given on a yearly basis.
• Monthly unannounced visits.
• Temporary care available

416-494-5898 jfhomechildcare@rogers.com www.j-f.ca

Building Blocks Montessori and Preschool

327 Bronte Street South, Unit 6, Milton, Ont, L9T 4A4. • 905-693-9620 • Open 7am-6pm. Fee assistance available. • Ages: 18 months-6 yrs.

Canada - Mexico Cultural Exchange Centre

416-428-9000 • www.canadamexico.com
FREE CHILDCARE in exchange for room and board. Reliable, intelligent, trustworthy and caring graduate students from Mexico. Candidates available year round. • Ages: NB+.

Child Care Info Peel

905-890-9432 or TTY 905-890-8089 • www.cdrcp.com
Free telephone information service on quality child care and subsidy. • Ages: 0-12.

Children's Magic Moments

98 Braemar Ave (Avenue Rd/Eglinton), Toronto, Ont, M5P 2L4. • 416-488-0114 • www.childrensmagicmoments.com
Licensed childcare ages 3 mos-6yrs. Bilingual JK/SK Enrichment program ages 2 1/2-5yrs.

Cliffwood Community Childcare Centre

140 Cliffwood Road, North York, Ontario, M2H 2E4. • 416-490-8848 •
Quality, licensed childcare ages 2.5 -12yrs. Subsidy Available. Qualified Staff. Nutritious Meals. Nurturing environment. Located in Cliffwood Public School. • Mon-Fri: 7:15 - 6.

Childcare

CozyKidz
416 532 7036 •
Experienced ECE; nurturing, cozy, educational, playful environment. • Ages: 1-12yrs.

Creditview Child Care Centre
1601 Eglinton Ave W, Mississauga, Ont, L5M 2B4. • 905-858-7860 •
Beside conservation area; Literacy program; ECE professionals.

Distillery District Early Learning Centre
55 Mill Street Building 9 Suite 200, Toronto, Ont, M5A 4R2. • 416-360-4042 •
www.distillerydistrictearlylearning.com
Our enriched curriculum is focused on child development through entertaining and educational
activities. Child care for ages 18 months - 5 years.

Eastbourne Daycare
416-488-6740 • Home Daycare. Educational program for 6m-3yrs.

Family Day Care Services
710 Progress Ave, Ste. 1, Toronto, Ont, M1H 2X3. • 416-922-3434 or 416-430-7406 •
www.familydaycare.com
Licensed childcare for children from infants to 12 years. 30 centres, 420 caregivers. Toronto East,
York and Peel regions. Safe, reliable, fun! Since 1851. **Look for our ad in this section.**

Fraser School Child Care
79 Manning St, Toronto, Ont, M6J 2K6. • 416-603-7372 • www.fraserchildcare.com
Cheerful, nurturing care in Queen West. Large, bright rooms, age-appropriate playground.
Experienced staff have been here for over 15 years! Flexible options: half-day, full-day, part-time
and nursery programs. Hours 7:30 - 6. • Ages: 2-6yrs.

It's Playtime Childcare Centre Inc
1423 Danforth Ave, Toronto, Ont, M4J 1N3. • 416-465-6688 • www.itsplaytime.ca
Specializing in part-time care. Includes catered snacks and lunches, p/up and d/off at Earl Haig,
Earl Beatty and RH McGregor. Mandarin lessons. Hours 8am-5:30pm. Fun and loving environment. • Ages: 2 1/2 to 5 yrs.

$COUPON$ J & F Home Childcare Services Incorporated
Head office: 211 Consumers Road, #205, Toronto, Ont, M2J 4G8. • 416-494-5898 • www.j-f.ca
Non-profit licensed agency celebrating 26 years of excellence. Where education and care go
hand in hand. Provides warm, caring, safe, supervised homes in North Toronto, North York,
Scarborough, Thornhill, Richmond Hill, Maple and Markham areas. **Look for our ad in this section.**
See coupon section for valuable savings. • Ages: 6 weeks - 12 years.

Childcare

Network Child Care Services

Child Care Services with a Difference!

We are proud to offer:

- Quality licensed child care services
- Six conveniently located Group Centre Programs for children aged 18 months - 5 years:

Ossington North,	next to Ossington Subway:	416-530-0722
Ossington South,	next to Ossington Subway:	416-536-2331
Wade Avenue,	next to Lansdowne Subway	416-537-0793
Metamorphosis,	next to Donlands Subway:	416-463-4429
St. Nicholas,	Finch Ave. E. and Kennedy Rd.:	416-850-5652
Just Kids,	Keele St. and Eglinton Ave. W.:	416-653-9944

- Home Based Child Care Programs in neighbourhood settings for children aged 6 months - 12 years: Covering the area bounded by Sherbourne St. to the West, Jane St. to the East, Lakeshore Blvd. to the South and North to Lawrence Ave.
- Enhanced programs (to meet every childs individual needs)

BEST START Programs (4 & 5 years old kindergarten children):
St. Nicholas Elementary Catholic School, 33 Amarillo Dr, Scarb
St. Aidan Elementary Catholic School 3521 Finch Ave. E.
St. Gabriel Lalemant Catholic School 160 Crow Trail, Scarb

Network Child Care Services
Call us today for a brochure at: 416-530-0722 or
e-mail us at: contact@networkchildcare.com • www.networkchildcare.com

Kateri Kids Childcare Centre
70 Margaret Ave, North York, Ont, M2J 4C5. • 416-496-2965 •
Licensed childcare for 2 1/2 - 12 years. Open 7am-6pm.

Kewpies Korner Private Home Daycare
(905) 896-1663 • Private home daycare. Ages 2-6. M-F 8am-5:30pm.

$ COUPON $ Little Tots Inc
2472 Cashmere Avenue, Mississauga, Ont, L5B 2S9. • 905-897-9888 •
Loving mother with 15 years experience provides summer, daily or before/after school care. First aid & CPR trained. Educational activities. Arts, Crafts, Reading, Outdoor play structure, Swings, Slide, Sandbox. Delicious Italian meals. Call Carmey. **Look for our ad in this section. See coupon section for valuable savings.**

Maple Preschool " Where learn & play go hand in hand."
9954 Keele St, Maple, Ont, L6A 5O3. • 905-832-2273 •
Since 1998. P/T available. Jolly Phonics. New playground. • Ages: 2.5-5yrs.

Mini Mania Day Nursery
61 Creditview Rd, Woodbridge, Ont, L4L 9N4. • 905-850-7002 • www.minimaniacenter.com
Family owned and operated for over 13 years. Quality childcare in a nurturing , academic and hygienic environment. Includes web cam & high security. F/T & P/T care available. Uniquely offering 4 season, indoor playground. Summer Day Camp. • Ages: 6 mos. - 6 yrs..

Mother of Carmel Childcare Centre
2599 Major Mackenzie Dr, Maple, Ont, L6A 1C6. • 905-303-1000 •
www.motherofcarmelchildcare.ca • A licensed centre providing a spiritual, loving, and positive learning environment for ages 2 1/2-5 yrs and 6-9 yrs.

Childcare

$COUPONS MyBabysitter.com

2000 Appleby Line, Ste 243, Burlington, Ont, L7L 7H7. • 905-331-5001 • www.mybabysitter.com
MyBabysitter.com is an online meeting place for families and childcare providers. If your family is
in need of a full or part time childcare, sign up today with www.mybabysitter.com. **Look for our ad
in this section. See coupon section for valuable savings**.

$COUPONS Network Child Care Services: Group Child Care Centres/Licenced Home Child Care Facilities

756 Ossington Ave (at Bloor), Toronto, Ont, M6G 3T9. • 416-530-0722 •
www.networkchildcare.com
Your Child is Our First Priority! Quality, licensed child care facilities/Enhanced programs/Music,
Movement, Drama & Creative art sessions incorporated into daily program, Kindergarten at off-
site public and separate schools/Professional On-site child care for trade shows and special
events. Nonprofit/subsidies available. **Look for our ad in this section. See coupon section for valuable
savings**. • Ages: 6mos-12yrs.

Pippi's World Indoor Playground and Birthday Party Centre

1381 Lakeshore Rd E, Mississauga, Ont, L5E 1G6. • 905-271-0642 •
www.freewebs.com/pippisworld
Pippi's World Indoor Playground also offers full time daycare for preschoolers 2.5-5yrs by ECE
teacher. Summer Day and Holiday Camps available. • Ages: 0-7.

PLASP Child Care Services

HO 121 Brunel Rd, Mississauga, Ont, L4Z 3E9. • 905-890-1711 • www.plasp.com
Early childhood development for children up to 5 years. 7am-6pm. 1/2 day care for kindergarten
children. Meals and snacks included.

St. Gabriel Child Care of Woodbridge

91 Fiori Dr, Woodbridge, Ont, L4I 5S4. • 416-850-3358 • Childcare centre for children ages 2.5-12 yrs.

Tracie's Home Daycare

2159 Pineview Dr , Oakville, Ont, L6H5M3. • 905-338-0620 •
Home daycare in Oakville.

Upper Canada Child Care Centres

Head office: 2900 John St, Unit 2, Markham, Ont, L3R 5G3. • 905-946-1113 •
www.uppercanadachildcare.com
A family of over 43 centres throughout York Region and the GTA, U.C.C.C. offers dynamic,
responsible, licensed quality care for ages 3 mos-12 yrs. Call 905-946-9113 for the location nearest you. **Look for our ad in this section.**

Order a copy for a friend
OR
order an extra copy for yourself

Help!... We've Got Kids is available at bookstores and kid-related stores
everywhere OR use the coupon at the back of this book and we'll mail
one right to you!

Tel: (416) 444-7678 ▪ Fax: (416) 444-1289
Email: info@helpwevegotkids.com

Little Tots Inc.
A Place to Grow
• Summer, Daily, Before & After School Childcare
• Large Playground
• Educational Program
• Music & Movement
• Indoor & Outdoor Activities
• Homemade Italian Meals
• First Aid & CPR trained
Give Your Child an Edge that Will Last a Lifetime!
Mississauga at Dundas & Mavis
Call Carmey:
905-897-9888 or 416-407-9007

Upper Canada Child Care

Non profit, government licensed quality care for ages 3 months to 12 yrs. 43 Centres located throughout North York, Thornhill, Markham, Vaughan, Stouffville, Newmarket and Keswick. Programs offered vary per centre.

Programs:
- Infant
- Toddler
- Preschool
- Before and After School
- Nursery School
- Summer Day Camp

Hours:
7:00 am to 6:00pm

Register today!

Call (905) 946-1113 for the Upper Canada Child Care Centre nearest you!

Uptown Yonge Preschool & Child Development Centre
1 Lord Seaton Road (North of Yonge&York Mills), Toronto, Ont • 416-602-9541 •
Half-day enriched preschool in North Toronto.

Waterfront Montessori Children's Centre
18 Wyandot Ave, Toronto, Ont, M5J 2B3. • 416-203-1017 •
Montessori/ECE on Toronto Island serving downtown families. • Ages: 2.5-5.

$COUPONS Wee Watch Private Home Day Care
1-800-663-6072 • www.weewatch.com
Licensed under the Day Nurseries Act, private home daycare is the preferred choice of parents due to: small numbers of children, family oriented settings and personalized attention. Safe and quality childcare services for over 18 years. Ask about our Wee Learn program. **Look for our ad in this section. See coupon section for valuable savings**. • Ages: 6wks + • Cheque.

YMCA Child Care
416-928-9622 •
Enriching environments for children aged six months to 12 years. Various locations across GTA.

▪ Emergency/Temporary Childcare & Baby Nurses

Network Child Care Services: Group Child Care Centres/Licenced $COUPONS Home Child Care Facilities
756 Ossington Ave (at Bloor), Toronto, Ont, M6G 3T9. • 416-530-0722 •
www.networkchildcare.com
Your Child is Our First Priority! Professional On-site care for trade shows and special events. **Look for our ad in the Childcare Section. See coupon section for valuable savings**. • Ages: 6mos-12 yrs.

A1 Baby Nurse
416-264-4458 •
Gentle hands baby nurse. Please feel free to call.

All About Babies
416-667-7695 or 416-220-2794 •
Specializing in infant & multiple birth support.

Alma Plummer, Baby Nurse & Newborn Care
416-789-1670 or 416-992-6319 •
Caregivers for newborn/mother's helper. 15 years experience.

Childcare

Babies R Beautiful
6000 Yonge St, Ste 409, Toronto, Ont, M2M 3W1. • 416-221-3989 •
Nursing & Postpartum Doula Services. Specialized Infant & Multiple Birth care. From hospital to home, private nursing and doula services offered with compassion and commitment.

Baby & Birth Support
905-882-9805 •
Day/Night post-partum care (Specializing in the care of multiples!). Breastfeeding & post-partum depression assistance. "Happiest Baby On The Block™" instructor." "WE'RE IN THE BUSINESS OF MOTHERING MOTHERS" in the GTA.

Birth Solutions
416-802-0572 • www.birthsolutions.info
We provide solutions to all your birth & postpartum needs including Birth & Postpartum Doulas, Night Support, Breastfeeding support and Happiest Baby Classes. We have extensive experience with multiples, special needs, postpartum depression, adoption and breastfeeding difficulties. Call 24/7.

$COUPON$ CanadianSitter.ca
1-866-221-7918 • www.canadiansitter.ca
Canadiansitter provides parents with an online connection to find mature babysitters. Our sitters are responsible and experienced. For occasional, part time and full time summer babysitters. Please log on to www.canadiansitter.ca. **Look for our ad in this section. See coupon section for valuable savings.**

Care-On-Call
14 Irwin Ave, Toronto, Ont, M4Y 1K9. • 416-975-1313 •
Experienced childcare - emergency, temporary, occasional and on-going.

Christopher Robin Babysitting Service
416-483-4744 • www.christopherrobin.ca
Caring for Toronto Children since 1953. Licensed, day, evenings, homes and hotels, temporary
live-in while you're away, First Aid, CPR, and Police Checks.

Comfort & Joy Newborn Care
416-901-6949 •
Warm, caring, nurturing baby nurse to help new moms and families with the first few days or
weeks. Multiple birth care experience and breastfeeding support. Day and night. References.
Reasonable rates for longer care you can afford. Advance booking required.

$COUPON$ Custom Comfort Care Inc
20 Bay St, Ste 1205, Toronto, Ont, M5J 2N8. • 416-703-2539 • www.customcomfortcare.ca
Nursing professionals providing "Care in a Crunch" for dependents, sick or well, all ages.
Work/Family conflicts. Overnight care during out-of-town travel. Short notice, short term nanny
replacement. Care and support of new mothers and babies. Ajax to Oakville. 24 hours, 7 days.
Look for our ad in this section. See coupon section for valuable savings.

Childcare

$COUPONS Gini Caring Helpers - Summer Nannies From Quebec
3-1750 The Queensway, Suite 314, Etobicoke, Ont, M9C 5H5. • 416-255-3838 •
Help! The summer is here! Do you need a nanny only for the summer and would like your children to learn or practice French 2 hours per day? We have the solution! Summer Quebec nannies available. May-August inclusive. **Look for our ad in this section. See coupon section for valuable savings.** • Cheque • By appointment.

$COUPONS Improv Care Services for Children
1009 Scarlett Rd, Toronto, Ont, M9P 2V3. • 416-243-3285 • www.improvcare.ca
Ideal for busy parents and families. In your home infant, child and adolescent care. ECE's, CYC's, teachers and RN's. Of special interest to those in the arts and entertainment, sports and hospitality industries, busy parents in general. **Look for our ad in this section. See coupon section for valuable savings.** Ages: 0-18.

In A Pinch
416-785-3939 • www.inapinch.ca
Your Temporary Care solution! Emergency short term care at a moment's notice or Babysitter for a night out. Baby nurses too. All Caregivers are fully screened. Day & night help available, short and long term care provided. **Look for our ad in this section.**

Lisa's Overnight Getaways
905-881-4046 •
Need a weekend getaway? Call Lisa for reliable babysitting services.

Marcy Cares
416-281-0880 • www.marcycares.com
Postnatal care - Newborns - Emergency care in home. Birth to 12 years. Seven days per week. Live in. Days/Nights. Over 23 years experience. Specializing in multiple births and colicky babies. Breastfeeding support and consultation. Visit our website for more information. • Ages: 0-12.

Maternal Infant & Child Ltd
416-733-7718 •
Childbirth, postpartum, multiples, breastfeeding and night support.

Maxine's Multiple Birth Newborn Care
188 Parkview Cres, Newmarket, Ont, L3Y 2C8. • 416-668-9957 •
ECE Specializing in Newborn-Infant care for Twins and Triplets. 10 Years experience with Multiples. Assist with breastfeeding, circumcision care, bathing, outings, sleep issues, day and night support. Extensive preemie care expertise. References and receipts available. Call Maxine.

Medals International Services
416-630-3546 •
Newborn care provider (baby nurses). Single and multiple births. Assist with breastfeeding, bath and all other care for baby. Available for 24 hour care or nights/days only. Short term or long term. 10 years experience and references. Call Joan.

My Nanny Called in Sick
www.MyNannyCalledinSick.com
MyNannyCalledinSick.com: Find occasional babysitters or full-time childcare in your own neighbourhood by exact distance from home and payrate. Sitter On-Call List.

Sleep Doula, The
1-877-ZZ-DOULA (416-929-7809) • www.sleepdoula.com
Need Sleep ? We provide sleep solutions for baby & you. The Sleep Doula provides physical, emotional & educational support to exhausted parents while solving their baby's sleep problems. In-Home Consultations & Support. • Ages: 0 -18months.

▪ Nanny Services

ABC Nannies Canada Inc.
416-850-5595 •
Nanny & caregiver agency. Over 10 years experience. Member of BBB.

Akemi's Household Professionals Agency Inc
92 Stuart Avenue, Toronto, Ont, M2N 1B4. • 416-322-3003 •
Completely screened. Nannies/Governess, Laundress/Ironer, Drivers/Chauffeurs, Special Needs, Housekeepers/Cleaners, Chefs/Cooks, Companion for Elderly/Healthcare Aides, Midwives/Nurses. Over 10 Years Agency Experience. Live ins, Live outs. Full time, part-time and temporary. Locally and internationally. Serving the GTA.

Amethyst Domestic Help
416-659-1233 or 519-943-0600 •
Nannies, Local/Overseas Sponsorships. No registration fee.

$COUPON$ Au Pair Canada® division of Be International Recruiting Inc.
45 Sheppard Ave East, Ste 900, Toronto, Ont, M2N 5W9. • 416-590-7429 or 877-242-7706 •
www.aupair.ca
Need a nanny? Call us! We find the best nannies in the World! Nannies from 42 countries, including Canada and US. Thorough screening process. Guarantee from 6 to 12 months. Testimonials available from previous clients. **Look for our ad in this section. See coupon section for valuable savings.**

Childcare

Canadiannanny.ca
1-866-221-7918 • www.canadiannanny.ca
Canadiannanny provides parents with an online connection to find part time and full time nannies. Both Live-in and live-out nannies available. Thousands of nannies to choose from. The most economical and effective method to find a nanny. For more information please log on to www.canadiannanny.ca.

$COUPON$ Custom Comfort Care Inc
20 Bay St, Ste 1205, Toronto, Ont, M5J 2N8. • 416-703-2539 •
60-minute seminar. Critical steps to screening and hiring nannies or temporary childcare workers. **Look for our ad in this section. See coupon section for valuable savings.**

Diamond Personnel Inc
4841 Yonge Street, Unit B2, Toronto, Ont, M2N 5X2. • 416-730-8866 •
www.diamondpersonnel.com
Nannies, homecare and household help. Live in/live out. Local and overseas. Specializing in permanent placements. **Look for our ad in this section.**

Distinction Home Care Services
2995 Bathurst Street, Toronto, Ont, M6B 3B3. • 416-789-9433 • www.distinctionhomecare.com
Providing honest and dependable caregivers. Nannies. Companions. Geriatric Care. Housekeepers. Drivers. Live-in/live-out, full/part time. "Applicants are welcome". BBB member.

Educare: Nanny Training Services, Dr. Tracy Friedman M.S.W, Ed.D
3219 Yonge St, Ste 139, Toronto, Ont, M4N 2L3. • 416-638-5575 • tracyfriedman@rogers.com
Work With a Specialized Family Therapist. Nanny Screening, Problem Solving and Parenting Training Services. Done In The Privacy of Your Own Home.

$COUPON$ Elite Care ™ division of Be International Recruiting Inc.
45 Sheppard Ave East, Ste 900, Toronto, Ont, M2N 5W9. • 416-850-1011 • www.needananny.ca
We have the ELITE Nannies. Our unique program can recruit an exceptional nanny to work for you. Our agency was nominated the "Best Canadian Nanny Agency of 2005" by the Canadian Caregivers Association (CCA). **Look for our ad in this section. See coupon section for valuable savings.**

Elite Nannies
416-789-7300 • pamela.sodhi@elitenannies.ca
Finding the right fit. As a former British nanny with over 15 yrs experience I understand the needs of your family.

ELMA Bee Nannies
2733 Lakeshore Blvd. W, Unit 111 , Toronto, Ont, M8V 1G9. • 416-354-2834 •
www.elmabeenannies.com
Looking for a qualified nanny? Live-in, live-out, full-time or part-time. A high quality service to families and caregivers.

EO HomeCare
5 Clarence Square , Scarborough, Ont, M5V 1H1. • 416-256-7776 • www.eohomecare.ca
The ideal nanny is waiting for you! We personally interview all applicants - only the most qualified will be introduced to you. We have an exceptional selection of live-in or live-out nannies, housekeepers and caregivers available now.

Excellent Placement Agency
269 Finch Ave W, Toronto, Ont, M2R 1M8. •416-222-4912 •
Philipino Nannies and Housekeepers from Hong Kong, Singapore, Israel, Middle East and Taiwan. Live In /Out. Excellent References. No fee for employer to sponsor overseas.

Execu-Nannies Inc.
100 Sheppard Ave W, Ste102, North York, Ont, M2N 1M6. • 416-221-6000 •
www.execunannies.com
Revealing profiles, deep reference checks, skills/style assessment, job description template, Human Resource Professionals. Live in/out, full/part time, temp/permanent. **Look for our ad in this section.**

Family Matters Caregivers Inc
416-633-0017 • www.familymatterscanada.com
Nannies, housekeepers & caregivers - all interviewed and prescreened. We also personally interview candidates in Hong Kong. Full time or part time. Live in or live out. Don't settle for anything less than the best for your family. **Look for our ad in this section.**

execunannies
FAMILY HOMECARE AGENCY SINCE 1988

Executive level care for children, elders and households
Live In • Live Out • Caregivers
Nannies • Household Managers
Helping you find 'Peace of Mind' and
'The right fit' Extraordinary detailed assessments,
written by our candidates

**100 Sheppard Ave West Suite 102
Toronto On M2N 1M6
416-221-6000**

www.execunannies.com
Open 2 weeknights, Saturdays and weekdays

HOME HELPERS
"The Agency that Cares"
(Giving excellent service since 1978)

Nannies, Housekeeper, House-couples
& Elderly Cargivers. Live-in & live-out.
All candidates have been carefully
interviewed & screened. Overseas
applicants are personally selected
for your specific needs.

416-596-0855
www.homehelpers.com

Family Ties Canada Inc.
108 Atlas Avenue, Toronto, Ont, M6C 3P3. • 416-264-6767 • www.familytiescanada.com
Looking for a nanny? Family Ties Canada provides highly personalized service and ensures that all
our placements are made with heart.

$COUPON$ Gini Caring Helpers; Nannies From Quebec
3-1750 The Queensway, Suite 314, Etobicoke, Ont, M9C 5H5. • 416-255-3838 •
Caring, competent, & trustworthy, legal, live-in nannies available. 6 months, year-round or summer
term. Thoroughly & personally interviewed. Since 1989. The safety & well-being of your children is
our priority! **Look for our ad in this section. See coupon section for valuable savings.** • Cheque.

Healthy Home (THHcanada) CareGiver Services
143 Westmount Road East, Kitchener, Ont, N2M 4Y6. • 519-894-4772 •
MISSION: Helping overseas nannies & local families connect.

$COUPON$ Helping Hands Caregiver Services
309 Davis Drive, Newmarket, Ont, L3Y 2N6. • 905-853-4752 • www.helpinghandscanada.com
Helping Hands is a premiere nanny placement agency. As our motto states , we focus on
"Putting Your Family First". We offer a personalized selection process, providing professional
nannies to employers. NO FEES for Oversees Hiring. Appointments available to fit your schedule. **Look for our ad in this section. See coupon section for valuable savings.**

$COUPON$ Home Helpers Placement Service
2 Carlton St #1422, Toronto, Ont, M5B 1J3. • 416-596-0855 • www.homehelpers.com
Placement agency for nannies, housekeepers for the elderly and house couples. All staff have
been personally interviewed and screened. We also bring in nannies from overseas, mostly from
Hong Kong, Singapore and Philippines. We're the agency that cares. **Look for our ad in this section.
See coupon section for valuable savings.** • Cheque • Mon-Fri: 9-5:30.

iCaregivers
416-945-9670 • www.icaregivers.ca
iCaregivers.ca provides personalized in-home care solutions by assisting our employers find a
Caregiver with the right skills and personality to match their needs. A surprisingly affordable
option, iCaregivers.ca, offers reliable care in the comfort of your own home.

$COUPON$ International Nannies & Homecare Inc
416-351-8777 • www.internationalnannies.com
Canada's leading Nanny agency with offices between Victoria & Halifax. Free instant access to
hundreds of nanny profiles on our website. Reliable, caring service with full support and follow
up. **Look for our ad in this section. See coupon section for valuable savings.**

Childcare

Jack & Jill Nanny Services
416-781-5993 •
An agency specializing in UK Nannies. Over 27 years first hand Nanny Experience. Placing full-time, part-time, live-in or live-out. Professional experienced Nannies with excellent references.

Just Like Mom Nanny Agency
526 Glengarry Ave, Toronto, Ont, M5M 1G3. • 416-784-5434 • www.justlikemom.ca
Voted "TORONTO'S TOP NANNY AGENCY" & 1 of "BEST" Nanny Agencies" by City Parent Magazine! Available 24 hours. Most selective agency representing only the highest calibre of nannies. Reference checks & a perfect track record equals incredibly pleased moms!

Childcare

Helping Hands
Caregiver Services
Putting Your Family First!

Live-In Nannies
An Affordable Childcare Option
▸ Professional Service
▸ Domestic Care

Benefits of Hiring a Nanny
Individual attention, no daycare illnesses, your child's own schedule, consistent care, familiar environment, no rushed mornings, expenses tax deductible.

905-853-4752
(Newmarket/Aurora)
905-294-2499
(Markham)
905-851-5733
(Vaughan)

No Agency Fees for Overseas Hiring
To discuss your childcare requirements, contact us 3 to 5 months prior to returning to work
OR
Local nannies are available for immediate childcare needs.

1-877-636-6437 www.helpinghandscanada.com

Marilyn's Nannies Inc.
150 Moore Ave, Toronto, Ont, M4T 1V8. • 416-487-4828 • A family run placement agency.

My Special Nanny & Personnel
905-849-3878 • www.internationalchildrenscare.com
My Special Nanny provides live in/live out and overseas nannies and home care. Now in York, Peel and Halton Regions. Subsidy available.

Nannies4Tots
115 Pondview Road, Thornhill, Ont, L4J 8P6. • 905-764-6255 • www.nannies4tots.com
Live in/out nannies and caregivers. Highly screened. All qualified and professional. Local or sponsored available.

$COUPON$ Nanny Providers Canada - division of Be International Recruiting Inc.
45 Sheppard Ave East, Ste 900, Toronto, Ont, M2N 5W9. • 416-590-7429 •
www.nanny-canada.com
Live-in nannies. The $195 fee to employer waived if you use the coupon at the end of the book. Amazing experience and educational background. 6-month to 3-year contracts. Availability for rural areas as well. **Look for our ad in this section. See coupon section for valuable savings.**

Nannyhood - Training & Workshops
523 Douglas, Toronto, Ont, M5M 1H7. • 416-274-9306 • Nanny training/workshops. Training/consultations for employers.

Ontario Employment Agency
1986 Mississauga Road , Mississauga, Ont, L5H 2K6. • 416-699-6931 • www.oeanannys.com
Extensive experience & honest, reliable service has resulted in hundreds of satisfied clients. We pride ourselves on professionalism & the ability to satisfy each client's individual needs. No fee to employer. Nannies, Eldercare or Special Needs Care, we take care of all your caregiving needs!

FREE childcare
for a week
Low placement fee of only $195.00 waived if you use the coupon at the end of the book.
Wonderful nannies and a unique chance for a free week of childcare (valued at $350*).

416 590 7429 / 1 877 242 7706
www.needananny.ca/free
*Estimate only. Please contact our placement coordinators for details.

Personal Care Employment Agency
46 St Clair Ave E, Ste 203, Toronto, Ont, M4T 1M9. • 416-922-1189 •
www.personalcareontario.com
Experienced quality service for all your domestic needs. Childcare in particular. Our personal touch has helped care for Canadian families for over 35 years. Trial period and guarantee.

Professional Care Personnel Inc
540 Mt Pleasant Rd, Ste 203, Toronto, Ont, M4S 2M6. • 416-504-8589 •
Household help & nanny specialists. Screened. Guaranteed. CPR, First Aid training.

R&R Caregiver
22 Rosseau Road, Suite 1, Toronto, Ont, M3H 3G2. • 416-901-7435 •
Honest, reliable & hardworking nannies for nurturing childcare and meticulous household work. Local or Abroad (Hongkong, Singapore, Israel). Full-time or part-time. Call for consultation.

Shelly's Nannies
124 Glenvale Blvd, Toronto, Ont, M4G 2V9. • 416-932-3815 • www.shellysnannies.com
Professional nannies for professional people. An established professional agency to help you find the right caregiver for your family.

Wee Care Placement Agency
416-789-3070 • www.weecareplacement.ca
Dedicated to caring since 1996. Live-in or live-out, f/t & p/t, local or overseas. Dependable, caring nannies. Interviewed, prescreened, guaranteed. Low finders fee. **Look for our ad in this section.**

Z's Domestics
905-731-1845 •
Great nannies! Live in or live out, F/T, P/T, weekends and nights. Screened. Certified & Guaranteed. Immediately available or free Sponsorship of Filipinas from Israel and Europe. Hundreds of satisfied clients. Call Zipi. **Look for our ad in this section.**

One of our children walked at 10 months and one at almost 16 months…both were perfectly normal. And both these two and our other four have now worked their way up from first walkers to stylish big kid shoes. In this section, we only include those stores that are specifically focused on selection and expertise targeted at kids. From traditional to funky and from school shoes to party ones, these stores will make sure your children's feet are well shod!

Make sure you check your children's shoes often to ensure they have not outgrown them. Small children can outgrow their shoes as often as every 2-3 months if they are going through a growth spurt. Here are some guidelines to use when checking to see if your child's shoes still fit.

1. Leave 1/2" of room in front of the toes.
2. Make sure the toe box isn't too tight; check when the child is standing.
3. The child's heel shouldn't slip out of the shoe.
4. Make sure there is no pressure on the baby toe as this means the shoe is not wide enough

$COUPON$ Look for this company's coupon at the back of the book

Adrian's - Stride Rite

3228 Yonge St, Toronto, Ont, M4N 2L4. • 416-485-6203 • www.adrianshoes.ca
Personalized service. We keep records of your child's growing feet. All major brands available.
When it's time for the next pair of quality footwear for your little one, trust us to take the time
and care to find the perfect fit. Ask about our Frequent Buyer Program. • Other Locations
Humbertown Shopping Centre 416-237-9757 • Ages: 0-Teen • VISA, ⊕, ▧, Interac • ⅊.

Bon Lieu/Petit Pied

2651 Yonge Street, Toronto, Ont, M4W 3P4. • 416-322-6067 • www.petitpied.com
Superb selection of fashionable European children's footwear from crib shoes and first walkers
to platforms and the newest athletic footgear. Come see where comfort is combined with top
quality and looks that can't be beat! **Look for our ad in the Children's Wear section.** • Other
Locations 890 Yonge St 416-963-5925, Bayview Village 416-225-3238, 2390 Bloor St W 416-767-
8366 • Ages: Size 18-40 • VISA, ⊕, ▧, Interac • Mon-Wed: 10-6, Thu-Fri: 10-8, Sat: 10-6, Sun:
12-5 • ⅊.

Browns Shoe Shops

Locations: Yorkdale 416-787-0313, Square One 905-566-0842, Promenade 905-764-1444,
Sherway Gardens 416-620-1910 , Toronto, Ont, M6A 2T9. • www.brownsshoes.com
A wide selection of casual and dressy, high quality, fashion designer and private label shoes for
children newborn+. Boogie Browns, Bcool, Rockstone, Baby Botte, Minibel, Tommy Hilfiger,
Kickers, Sorel, Maniqui The Look, Superfit, Cougar, Reebok. Also Invicta school and leisure bags.
Ages: Newborn+ • VISA, ⊕, ▧, Interac, Cheque • Mon-Fri: 10-9, Sat: 9:30-6, Sun: 12-5 • ⅊.

Children's Shoes

Need a copy for a friend?

Help!... We've Got Kids
is available at bookstores and
kids' stores everywhere OR use
the coupon at the back of this book
and we'll mail one right to you!

...WE'VE GOT KIDS
Tel. (416) 444-7678 • Fax: (416) 444-1289
Email: info@helpwevegotkids.com
www.helpwevegotkids.com

Need an extra copy for yourself?

CHIRO-PED - Custom Made Shoes & Foot Orthotics
North York, Richmond Hill, Thornhill & Scarborough locations, • Main No: 905-889-1600 •
Custom made Orthopedic Shoes, Foot Orthotics and Biomechanical Assessments.

Comfy Shoe Gallery
9665 Bayview Ave, Unit 9, Richmond Hill, Ont, L4C 9V4. • 905-883-0260 •
Quality children's footwear. School uniform shoe specialist. • &.

Kiddie Kobbler
Fairview Mall, 1800 Sheppard Ave, Toronto, Ont, M2J 5A7. • 416-499-3556 •
Expert fitting, service & selection. Athletic, school oxfords & 1st walking shoes. • Ages: Newborn+.

Kids Club Toronto
3377 Bathurst St, Toronto, Ont, M6A 2B8. • 416-398-4676 •
We expertly fit children for shoes. Friendly service. • Ages: infant-teen • &.

Little Squeaky Feet
416-909-1421 • www.littlesqueakyfeet.com
Fun kids shoes that squeak with each step. Encourages pre-walkers to walk and an great way to
keep track of your child. Canvas and leather styles for boys and girls from $17.99 to $27.99.

Naturino Children's Shoes
High quality children's footwear, specifically designed for children's feet. • Other Locations:
Woodbridge, 28 Roytec Rd. Unit 1c 905-264-9539, Oakville, 302 Lakeshore Rd. E. Unit a 905-
845-5437. • Ages: birth-teen • *VISA*, ⊕, ▓, *Interac*.

$COUPON$ Olly -Shoes Fit for a Kid

2600 Yonge St, Toronto, Ont, M4P 2J4. • 416-487-3100 • www.ollyshoes.com
OLLY specializes in expertly fitting children's shoes in a fun and friendly store. Quality brands in athletic, casual and school shoes. Computerized OLLYfit© technology. Membership Savings Program. **Look for our ad in this section. See coupon section for valuable savings.** • Other Locations: Sherway Gardens Mall, Etobicoke 416-622-6522, 1070 Major Mackenzie, Richmond Hill •
Ages: newborn to 'tweens • *VISA*, ⊕, ▦, *Interac*, Cheque.

$COUPON$ Shoe Company, The

1.88.88.SHOECO • www.theshoecompany.com
Each store has 20,000 pairs of men's, women's & kids' brand name shoes up to 50% off every-day. Featuring a huge selection of kids' shoes from infant/toddler sizes 6-13 to youth sizes 1-6. Brands like Osh Kosh, Stride Rite, Kangaroo & many more. 25 stores to serve you in the GTA. Check on line for a location near you or call us. **Look for our ad in this section. See coupon section for valuable savings.**

Tajo Shoes

1723 Bayview Ave, Toronto, Ont, M4G 3C1. • 416-486-1588 •
Specializing in fitting quality shoes for infants and children.

Zonas II: The Children's Shoe Shoppe

16925 Yonge St, Unit 5, Quaker Hill Marketplace, Newmarket, Ont, L3Y 5Y1. • 905-830-9737 •
Specializing in the correct fitting of children's shoes.

Children's Wear

Children like to express their independence and style through their clothing. We're inclined to let them since it is a very non-permanent way of doing so. We only wish they would still wear their "I dressed myself" butttons! In Toronto, there are clothing stores to suit every child's taste, every occasion and every parent's budget. From every day wear to special occasion clothing - you can find the perfect outfit for your function.

We also list specialty items such as Sun protective clothing for kids (and adults) which has come a long way and is now stylish as well as protective, dancewear and costume stores.

You will find the following sub-categories in this section:
Children's Wear Stores; Costumes, Dress up & Dancewear; Special Occasion Wear; Sun Protective Clothing.

$ COUPON$ Look for this company's coupon at the back of the book

■ Children's Wear Stores

A Perfect Fit Innerfashions Boutique
17 Frontenac Ave, Toronto, Ont, M5N 1Z4. • 416-782-8378 •
The place to come for your first, second, & third bra! Get a proper fitting bra by a trained & experienced specialist. From crop tops to "real" bras. Sports, support, cotton, minimizers, padded, & more. For all your bras, underwear & swimwear needs. • Ages: Girls of all ages.

Babywear Boutique
1-877-778-3884 • www.babywearboutique.com
Visit our online babywear boutique to shop for wraps, slings, shoes, toys and more!

be tween... Pre-teen Clothing
2097 Yonge St, Toronto, Ont, M4S 2A4. • 416-544-9626 •
Fun, Fashionable Pre-teen clothing for girls.

$ COUPON$ bean sprout
616 Mount Pleasant Rd, Toronto, Ont, M4S 2M8. • 416-932-3727 • www.beansprout.ca
We now feature only new clothing and accessories for children ages newborn to ten years. Mim-Pi, Blu, Deux par Deux, Mexx, Point Zero and more. Generous return policy, same friendly service, free cookies. **Look for our ad in this section. See coupon section for valuable savings.** • *VISA*, ⊖⊕, ▓, *Interac* • Mon-Sat: 10:30-5:30 • &.

Bon Lieu/Petit Pied
890 Yonge St (Bloor/Yorkville District), Toronto, Ont, M4W 3P4. • 416-963-4322 •
www.petitpied.com
Newly renovated boutique offers everything a mother needs from nursery accessories and European strollers to a wide selection of European children's fashions. We fit Moms too! **Look for our ad in this section.** • Other Locations: 890 Yonge St 416-963-5925, Bayview Village 416-225-3238, 2390 Bloor St W 416-767-8366 • Ages: 0-20 • *VISA*, ⊖⊕, ▓, *Interac* • Mon-Wed: 10-6, Thu-Fri: 10-8, Sat: 10-6, Sun: 12-5 • &.

Boutique Lyson
100 King St W, The Exchange Tower, Concourse Level, Box 274, Toronto, Ont, M5X 1C8. •
416-364-4148 •
Boutique Lyson gives you so many choices. Casual and formal clothing with quality and style at affordable prices. First Communion, Flower Girl, Boys' Suits and Tuxedos and wonderful everyday clothing too. Newborn to sixteen, girls and boys. Come visit us! • Ages: newborn - 16 • *VISA*, ⊖⊕, ▓, *Interac* • Mon-Fri: 8-6, Sat: 12-4 • &.

Crawlies - Clothing for Babies on the Move
1-866-222-1512 •

Cutie Patootie - Creative Hairwear
416-631-6092 • Creative hairwear for girls of all ages.

Europe Bound /Hikers Haven
383 King St W, Toronto, Ont, M5V 1K1. • 416-205-9992 • www.europebound.com
Toronto's largest selection of kids' gear. North Face, Columbia, Merrell, Teva, Kelty & Europe
Bound. Along with a great selection of well-priced Baby Joggers, child carriers, bikes and accessories and an extensive selection of camping gear. • Other Locations 47 Front St E 416-601-1990, 166 South Service Rd E, Oakville 905-849-8928 • Ages: 0+ • Mon-Wed: 10-7,
Thu-Fri: 10-9, Sat: 9-6, Sun: 11-5.

Funky baby
2116A Queen St E, Toronto, Ont, M4E 1E2. • 416-691-0980 •
Unique clothing for children birth-ten.

Grandma's Little Darlings
67 Bronte Rd., Oakville, Ont, L5K 1P9. • 905-465-2195 •
Weddings. 1st Communion. Christening. Boys suits.

Growing Image
3028 Bloor St W, Toronto, Ont, M8X 1C4. • 416-239-4989 •
European and Canadian designs in sizes 0-16.

Higher Ground For Kids
2511 Yonge St (4 bl. N. of Eglinton), Toronto, Ont, M4P 2H9. • 416-485-9228 •
Designer children's clothing, outerwear and accessories. Labels include Burberry, Diesel, Juicy
Couture, Lacoste, Miniman, Petit Bateau and more! Sizes NB-14yrs. Since 1988. • Mon-Sat:
9:30-6, Sun: 12-5.

Jacadi Children
Bayview Village Shopping Centre, 416-733-1717, Hazelton Lanes Centre, 416-923-1717 •
www.jacadi.fr • JACADI, a leader in children's clothing within everyone's budget, offers top-of-the-line clothing & shoes from 0-12 years. Expectant mothers will love the baby gift registry as
JACADI has a complete line of nursery furnishings, accessories & strollers including Bugaboo. •
Ages: 0-12.

La Senza Girl
1-888-LA SENZA call us for a location closest to you •
Canada's #1 fashion retailer for girls! • Ages: 8-14.

Children's Wear

Little Ones Fashions
372 Eglinton Ave W, Toronto, Ont, M5N 1A2. • 416-483-5989 •
Unique and up-to-date fashions and shoes. • Ages: 0-preteen • &.

Love Child
2523 Yonge St, Toronto, Ont, M4P 2H9. • 416-486-4746 • Gorgeous clothes for kids.

Mushee kids
848-123 Scadding Ave., Toronto, Ont, M5A4J3. • 416-359-8795 • Designer of quality kids clothing.

Piccolina Children's Wear
2901 Bayview Ave, Toronto, Ont, M2K 1E6. • 416-222-5493 •
Designer trends for the modern child. - DKNY, JuicyCouture, Ugg & more!

Planet Kid
960 Queen St W, Toronto, Ont • 416-537-9233 •
Funky clothes, cowboy jackets, luscious quilts & coordinated cushions.

$COUPON$ Snug
348 Danforth Ave, Unit #8, Toronto, Ont, M4K 1M9. • 416-463-6133 •
A Snug kind of boutique for moms and their kids. **Look for our ad in this section. See coupon section
for valuable savings.** • Ages: NB+ • *VISA*, ⊕, ▒▒, *Interac* • Mon-Sat: 10-6, Sun: 12-5.

Snug As A Bug Kids' Clothes
91 Brandon Ave, Toronto, Ont, M6H 2E2. • 416-534-6881 • www.snugasabug.com
Fun, functional children's clothing made in Canada. Warehouse sales. Shop online! • Ages: 0-
6yrs • *VISA*, ⊕, ▒▒, *Interac*.

Snugabye Factory Outlet
188 Bentworth Ave, Toronto, Ont, M6A 1P8. • 416-783-0300 •
Sleepwear, playwear, underwear, bedding. Factory prices. • &.

▪ Costumes, Dress-Up & Dancewear

509 Dancewear
509 Parliament Street, Toronto, Ont, M4X 1P3 • 416-924-9533 •
Dancewear and accessories for children and adults.

Canada's National Ballet School's The Shoe Room®
404 Jarvis St, Toronto, Ont, M4Y 2G6. • 416-964-5100 • www.nbs-enb.ca
Offers the best fit in pointe shoes and the latest in dancewear and accessories.

Costume Witch
975 Eglinton Ave W, Toronto, Ont, M6C 2C4. • 416-785-5553 •
Costumes and accessories ready-to-wear or made to order. • Ages: 2-14.

Fairyland Theatre
1183A Finch Ave W, Unit 1 & 2, Toronto, Ont, M3J 2G3. • 416-663-1700 •
Big selection of theme and dance kids' costumes for rent.

Kids Costumes
539 Mount Pleasant, Toronto, Ont, M4S 2M5. • 416-484-1940 • www.kidscostumes.ca
Costumes are toys providing hours of valuable play time. Costumes hats, make-up, tiaras,
wands, capes, wigs & accessories. Custom made for school plays and presentations. Mondor
tights & leotards. • Ages: newborn - 14 yrs • &.

...what a great store!

348 Danforth Ave. (at Chester) ★ 416 463-6133

Ms Dress-Up

1461 Dundas Street West, Toronto, Ont, M6J 1Y7. • 416-532-3337 • www.msdress-up.com
Ms Dress-up is a Toronto costume retailer providing kids and adult costumes for themed parties
and events.

Recycle Your Used Dance Shoes

416-566-7412 •
Used dance shoes consigned and sold.

■ Special Occasion Wear

Beatties

430 Eglinton Ave W, Toronto, Ont, M5N 1A2. • 416-481-4459 •
One of the largest boy's wear stores in Toronto. Sizes 3-20.

Carmen's Designs for Children Inc

1274 St Clair Ave W, Toronto, Ont, M6E 1B9. • 416-656-1022 •
Custom made special occasion clothing for children.

Crawford Boys

Lawrence Plaza, 508A Lawrence Ave W, Toronto, Ont, M6A 1A1. • 416-782-8137 •
Specialists in boys' clothing and Husky sizes. • Ages: 4+.

Kidstreat

The Promenade, 1 Promenade Circle, Store B 221, Thornhill, Ont, L4J 1P8. • 905-771-9906 •
Specializing in children's formal wear for all occasions. • Ages: 0-18yrs.

Misdemeanours & Fashion Crimes

322 1/2 Queen St W, Toronto, Ont, M5V 2A2. • 416-592-9001 •
Special occasion wear from Infant to Tweens. Bat Mitzvah, Prom, Bridal.

Peach Berserk Cocktails

507 Queen St W, Toronto, Ont, M5V 2B4. • 416-504-1711 •
Wonderful hand-printed clothes. Casual and party wear (Bat-Mitzvahs).

Children's Wear

▪ Sun Protective Clothing

Snug
348 Danforth Ave, Unit #8, Toronto, Ont, M4K 1M9. • 416-463-6133 •
Swimwear for kids, teens and moms including full line of UV protective suits. **Look for our ad in
this section. See coupon section for valuable coupons.** • *VISA*, ⊖, ■, *Interac* • Mon-Wed: 10-6,
Thu-Fri: 10-7, Sat: 10-6, Sun: 12-5.

SUNSENSE Sun Protection Products
905 576-7535 • www.sunsense.net
Protect children from outdoor elements! 99% UV blocking and water resistant stroller covers,
blankets, carseat covers and hats. All-season accessories. Made in Canada. • Ages: 0-6yrs.

SunSmart - UV Swim/Play All Day Wear
(866) 726-1827 • www.Sunsmart.ca
UV protection for your kids. One piece swim/play wear and cover ups. Superman™ & Supergirl™
& Superbaby - our 3 newest images. Kids think it's magic...we call it SunSmart! List of Quality
Retailers on website or call 1-866-726-1827. • Ages: NB-Youth.

Circumcision

People choose to circumcise their sons for a variety of personal reasons. The practice of circumcision has been performed since ancient times. For some people, circumcision is not only a medical procedure, but also a religious ceremony. In this section, you will find several doctors and rabbis who can make this event both a medically safe and, if desired, a spiritually meaningful one. Ask about making the procedure pain-free.

Adler, Rabbi Sholom H - Certified Mohel
27 Ridgevale Dr, North York, Ont, M6A 1K9. • 416-256-BRIS •
Rabbi Sholom H Adler, certified mohel. Free information package. • By appointment

Borden, Dr Barry S (Mohel)
1333 Sheppard Ave E #336, North York, Ont, M2J 1V1. • 416-494-7442 •
Ritual Circumcision (B'rit Milah). • By appointment

Diamond, Dr. Aubie, MD: Mohel
905-738-6699 or 905-889-2517 •
Ritual circumcision by appointment.

Greenberg, Dr. Mark. Family Physician & Certified Mohel
4700 Jane St, Ste 202, Toronto, Ont, M3N 2L3. • 416-661-0004 or 416-702-8990 •
www.drgreenberg.ca
Ritual and non-ritual circumcision. Mogen circumcision in combination with local anesthetic. **Look for our ad in this section.**

Jesin, Dr Aaron: Family Physician & Certified Mohel
203-4256 Bathurst St, North York, Ont, M3H 5Y8. • 416-635-5012 • www.drjesin.com
The JESIN CIRCUMCISION CLINIC: Expertise in ritual and non- ritual circumcision. Orthodox certified, yet sensitive to the entire community. Use of analgesics. 28 years experience. Performed over 10,000. By Appointment.

Langer, Jacob C, MD: Pediatric Surgeon and Certified Mohel
416-813-7269 •
Ritual Circumcision (b'rit milah). Traditional or Creative Services. • By appointment

Schwartz, Dr. Rochelle - Family Physician & Certified Mohel
905-760-1415 work or 416-457-9033 cell or pager: 416-328-4335 •
Effective "Pain Prevention Protocol" including Local Anesthesia, for infant circumcision. Beautiful, warm and customized Brit Milah circumcision ceremonies and Baby Namings for girls. Non-ritual circumcisions performed in the comfort of my clinic. Providing over 20 years of experience. **Look for our ad in this section.**

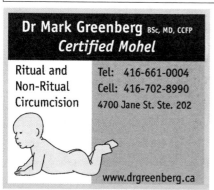

Counselling & Support Services

Both kids and parents have a lot to deal with these days and sometimes, it can all be a little overwhelming. There are many experienced professionals out there who can help you over both the little bumps and the bigger hills. Specialists can assist kids with things like anxiety and phobias, or with peer, school or social issues. With parents, counselling can work on family dynamics, behaviour, your relationship with your spouse or even just offer support to a parent feeling alone or overwhelmed. Reach out and make the first phone call - you'll be glad you did.

You will find the following sub-categories in this section:
Counselling & Support Services; Children's Mental Health Centres

$ COUPON $ **Look for this company's coupon at the back of the book**

▪ Children's Mental Health

Aisling Discoveries Child & Family Centre
325 Milner Ave, Ste 110, Scarborough, Ont, M1B 5N1. • 416-321-5464 •
Supporting children & families with emotional, behavioral and social problems. • Ages: NB-12.

Canadian Association of Psychoanalytic Child Therapists
Referral service: 416-288-8689 (ext. 1) • www.tcpp-capct.ca
Specialized psychotherapists work with children, adolescents and families with issues such as adoption, anxiety, attachment, bereavement, behavioural disorders, depression, eating disorders, learning disabilities, physical/sexual abuse and parental consultation.

Child Development Institute
197 Euclid Ave, Toronto, Ont, M6J 2J8. • 416-603-1827 •
Services for preschool children and families who have social, emotional and behavioural problems and/or are at risk of physical or sexual abuse. • &.

George Hull Centre for Children & Families, The
600 The East Mall, 3rd Fl, Etobicoke, Ont, M9B 4B1. • 416-622-8833 •
www.georgehullcentre.on.ca
Children's mental health centre offering comprehensive treatment services for children, adolescents and their families. Best Start program for young mothers and infants. Residential programs. Prevention, education and research. Residents of Etobicoke age 0-19. No fee for service. • &.

Hincks Dellcrest Center, The
Main location: 440 Jarvis St, Toronto, Ont, M4Y 2H4. • 416-924-1164 •
Outpatient & Residential services for children with emotional and/or behavioural problems and their families. (former City of Toronto Families Eligible Only). • Multiple locations throughout the GTA • Ages: 0-18 • Free • &.

Integra Children's Mental Health Centre
25 Imperial St 4th Fl, Toronto, Ont, M5P 1B9. • 416-486-8055 • www.integra.on.ca
Serving children and adolescents with learning disabilities. • Ages: 8-18.

Willow Centre
45 Sheppard Ave E, Ste 202, North York, Ont, M2N 5W9. • 416-250-1540 •
www.thewillowcentre.com
A centre providing psychological services for infants, children, adolescents and their families. Assessment and drug-free treatment for all types of behavioural, emotional and learning difficulties. Not all children "grow out of it". We can help. • Ages: 0-18 • _VISA_ • Mon-Sat: 9-5.

■ Counselling & Family Mediation

Assessment, Counselling & Coaching Centre; Dr. S. Jane Margles
29 Alvin Ave, Toronto, Ont, M4T 2A7. • 416-428-1600 •
Individual counselling and coaching for optimal performance. Psychological assessments for children, adolescents & adults. Specializing in learning disabilities, ADD/ADHD, underachievement, motivational difficulties, giftedness & stress management.

Breakthrough Communications
416-823-5343 •
1:1 in-home language/behaviour/social programmes for children 3-12 yrs.

Centre for Health, The
307 Sheppard Ave W, Toronto, Ont, M2N 1N6. • 866-241-9880 •
Individual, family, couples counselling; Naturopathic medicine; Massage.

Collaborative Therapy & Assessment Group, Dr. Stacey Berman, Dr. Ruth Slater & Ruth Benedikt DCS
118 Eglinton Ave W, Ste 405, Toronto, Ont, M4R 2G4. • 416-644-0983 •
Counselling services using a variety of treatment approaches to support change and growth for individuals, couples & families. Counselling available in English, Spanish & Hebrew. Covered by many extended health care plans. Comprehensive psycho-educational assessments available.

Dimerman, Sara - Psychological Services & Parent Education
Thornhill Square 300 John St, Ste 320, Thornhill, Ont, L3T 5W4. • 905-882-7690 •
www.helpmesara.com
Individual, couple, family counselling. Fees covered by extended health care plans. Nationally renowned parent educator, therapist and writer. • VISA, Cheque • By appointment • &.

Dr Tracy Friedman MSW, EdD
3219 Yonge St, Ste 139, Toronto, Ont, M4N 2L3. • 416-638-5575 •
Family therapist, divorce/parenting specialist.

Families in Transition: Family Service Association of Toronto
420A-700 Lawrence Avenue West , Toronto, Ont, M6A 3B4. • 416-585-9151 •
Works with separating, divorcing and remarrying families. Focus is helping children adjust to family changes. Counselling, support groups, seminars and mediation of parenting plan disputes.

Healing Through Play
650 Queens Quay W, Ste 101, Toronto, Ont, M5V 3M3. • 416-812-9734 •
Play therapy and psychotherapy for children. • Ages: 2-12yrs • By appointment.

Kendal, Dana MSW, RSW
416-789-9375 •
Family and child therapist. Families, couples and individuals.

Kids Help Phone
Toll-free 1-800-668-6868 • www.kidshelpphone.ca
Confidential counselling service for kids aged 4-25.

Counselling & Support Services

Lieberman, Susan: Family Therapist, HonBA, DCS

3292 Bayview Ave, Ste 202, Toronto, Ont • 416-512-6356 • www.familysupport.net
Counselling for families experiencing difficulty with children/adolescents in areas such as discipline, anxiety, ADD, communication and depression. Individual & marital counselling. Comprehensive psychoeducational assessments also offered. Self-help tools and baby blankets available on our website. Visit us online! • [VISA], Cheque.

Marcovitch & Associates: Drs. Sharon & Howard Marcovitch, Registered Psychologists

491 Lawrence Ave W, Ste 405, Toronto, Ont, M5M 1C7. • 416-780-0909 •
Parent counselling for preschool and school-age children with a range of difficult behaviours.
Individual counselling for school-age children and adolescents with issues of anxiety, attention, or underachievement. • By appointment • &.

Moscovitch, Dr. Jill, Psychologist

416-787-0883 Ext.1 •
Psychological assessment, consultation and counselling.

Natalie Orenchuk Msw.B.A.

93 Castlewood Rd, Toronto, Ont, M5N 2L3. • 416-480-2150 •
Specialist in Challenging, Bright, Gifted Children. Socio-emotional /academic performance issues.
Look for our ad in the Education section.

Parent Education Resource Centre

Thornhill Square 300 John St, Ste 320, Thornhill, Ont, L3T 5W4. • 905-882-7690 •
www.helpmesara.com
Counselling, parenting programs, psychoeducational assessments. • [VISA], Cheque •
By appointment • &.

Parental Guidance

677 Carlaw Avenue, Toronto, Ont, M4K 3K7. • 416-816-2254 • www.parentalguidance.ca
At-home, customized parenting advice and strategies to assist parents with issues such as meal-time/bedtime battles, tantrums, homework and sibling rivalry. • Ages: 0-14.

Parenting Insight - Parenting workshops

416-256-7472 •
Parenting counselling & workshops. Infant massage classes.

Sheri Betel: Counselling & Parenting Groups

1395 Bayview Avenue, Toronto, Ont, M4G 3A6. • 416-322-9005 •
Offering specialized individual, couple and family counselling.

TVOKids, Milton's Hotline

1-800-613-0513 • www.tvokids.com
Milton's Hotline on TVOKids lends a friendly ear to kids aged 6 to 9 who may be experiencing issues ranging from bullying to family conflict. Between 3 and 7 pm on the last Monday of each month, Milton and a counsellor from Kids Help Phone open up the phones to let kids talk freely and openly.

Custom Room Design: Murals, Bedding Etc.

This section contains listings of companies that can help you create themed rooms, murals, custom bedding and décor for your child's room and family spaces. If you need some assistance in coming up with concepts or design, we even list talented designers to help you put it all together.

Baby Decor Ltd
2104 Highway 7 W, Unit 19, Concord, Ont, L4K 2S9. • 905-738-1575 •
Custom designed linens for infant/toddler rooms..

Bonnie Pascal Designs, Interior Designer/Artist
416-654-6116 • Develop your ideas! Create a fabulous space! Amazing murals.

Cherry Hill Design
416-509-9030 • www.richardartstudio.net
Canada's most unique design team turns your child's bedroom into any environment they can imagine. From their favorite sports team's dressing room to creating a fairytale castle for your princess, we make fantasies come true. Our work will blow them away!

Dania's Keepsakes & Wall Murals
136 Woodcroft Lane, Woodbridge, Ont, L4L 6T4. • 416-505-2052 • www.daniaskeepsakes.com
Helping bring your child's dreams to life. Personalized handpainted accessories & wall murals. Unique and unforgettable keepsakes. Also offering prenatal casting.

Halstead & Company
83 Kenneth Ave, Toronto, • 416-760-9853 • Gorgeous mural and decorative painting for walls and furniture.

Mount 'N Seal
1947 Leslie St, Toronto, Ont, M3B 2M3. • 416-423-9975 • mountnseal@canada.com
Lightweight, colourful, low-cost picture framing alternative. Ideal way to preserve and display kids' artwork. Perfect for hanging posters in kids' rooms. • Ages: 7+ • Mon-Wed: 11-6, Thu-Fri: 11-9, Sat: 10-6, Sun: 12-6.

Murals by Liz
416-528-9047 • Transform walls - personalized murals. Art objects. Furniture.

Nestings Kids/The Pod
418 Eglinton Ave W, Toronto, Ont, M5N 1A2. • 416-322-0511 • www.nestingskids.com
Design trained staff can help you create anything from custom gift baskets to complete room design. Full design services in everything from unique accessories, lamps, linens to furniture. Newborn to Teen. **Look for our Ad in the Furniture and Accessories section**. • Mon-Sat: 10-6, Sun: 12-5.

PaintFX Kids - Natalie L. Herman, Decorative Artist
905-201-6231 • www.paintfxkids.com • Painted environments for children. Wonderful "one-of-a-kind" nurseries and children's rooms. Free consultation.

PeterPam Designs
416-322-5176 • www.peterpamdesigns.com
Customized, hand-painted children's murals, portraits, and toy boxes. Experienced, skilled, imaginative artists. Design consulting included. Free, no obligation, in-home consultation.

Red Square Murals
10 Rondeen Road, Concord, Ont, L4K 5S4. • 905.303.4005 • Specializing in hand-painted customized murals.

Rosanna's Creations
1967 Bur Oak Ave, Markham, Ont, L6E 1W4. • 416-414-0917 • www.mymurals.com
Beautiful airbrushed/handpainted murals. Airbrushed clouds on ceilings a specialty! Any subject matter or cartoon can be painted as well as trompe l'oeil, borders, fabric matching, painted furniture, canvas wall hangings & more. Professional quality work, extensive portfolio & references available.

Wonderwall Custom Children's Murals
237 Osmond Cres, Newmarket, • 416-277-2410 • Amazing murals for all ages - free consultation!

Diaper Stores & Services

The type of diaper you use is one of the first decisions you have to make regarding the care of your new baby. There is no right answer to this one and no wrong answer either. It is purely a matter of personal choice.

The disposable route is starting to be less of an environmental compromise now that many Toronto municipalities are moving to composting diapers. There are several stores and services to help with either choice. There are environmentally friendly cloth diaper stores that carry diapers and baby accessories. There are diaper services that pick up and deliver either cloth or disposable diapers. There are also several discount or bulk diaper stores which sell brand name diapers at greatly reduced prices.

$COUPON$ Look for this company's coupon at the back of the book

ABC Diaper Depot

1656 Eglinton Ave W, Toronto, Ont, M6E 2H2. • 416-787-0058 •
Factory outlet prices on disposable diapers. Free delivery within Metro.

$COUPON$ Comfy Cotton Diaper Service

905-940-8118 or 888-759-3945 • www.comfycotton.ca
18 years in business, thousands of happy customers & 5 environmental awards are vivid proof this is the best diapering system for your baby. Highest quality standards on the laundering of 100% cotton diapers. Free weekly pick-up & delivery. **Look for our ad in this section. See coupon section for valuable savings.**

$COUPON$ Diaper-Eez

2309 Bloor St W, Toronto, Ont, M6S 1P1. • 416-604-0916 • www.diaper-eez.com
Fun and exciting store to find all your baby's layette needs from large, hooded terry towels, cotton diapers, clothes, toys, mobiles to nursing supplies. We deliver all over the GTA and worldwide. Catalogue available and gift registry. **Look for our ad in this section. See coupon section for valuable savings.** • _VISA_, ⊕, ▦|, _Interac_.

Diaper Stores & Services

WE REALLY CARE ABOUT YOU AND YOUR BABY

baby carriers
breast pumps
cotton diapers
diaper bags
nursing bras
layette

inspiring **confidence**, *giving* **answers** *and delivering*
quality products *to* **new** *and* **expectant** *families*

FREE Catalogue
DELIVERY Everywhere
GIFT Registry

diaper-eez

2309 Bloor Street West • Toronto, Ontario M6S 1P1
416-604-0916 / 416-762-5811 / 1-888-420-0222
www.diaper-eez.com / diapers@diaper-eez.com

Diapers Direct

720 Burnhamthorpe Rd W, Unit 14, Mississauga, Ont, L5C 3G1. • 905-270-8888 •
Quality disposable diapers. Bulk. Free delivery GTA.

For Baby With Love

1-888-729-1934 or 905-633-9018 • www.forbabywithlove.ca
Cloth diapering today is easier than ever! It's fun, economical, healthier for baby and environmentally responsible. Give cloth diapering a try - you'll be surprised! We offer a variety of cloth diapers for your baby, including pocket diapers, AIO's and fitteds.

Happy Nappy Inc

3899 Bathurst St, Toronto, Ont, M3H 5V1. • 416-398-0845 •
Disposable diaper and baby gift delivery service.

$ COUPON $ Mr. Case Inc

416-661-CASE (2273) • www.mrcase.com
Celebrating our 21st year in business! Over 5000 brand name supermarket products delivered by the case. Diapers, bottled water, pop & juice, paper products, cleaning supplies and much more! Next day delivery. Call for your free catalogue or order online. **Look for our ad in this section. See coupon section for valuable savings**. • 𝗩𝗜𝗦𝗔, ▨, Cheque.

SUPERMARKET ITEMS DELIVERED BY THE CASE

mr.case
never run out

Make your life easier!

- Serving the Greater Toronto area for over 21 years
- We carry over 5,000 Brand name products
- Next day delivery to home or office
- Cash, cheque, VISA, AMEX & MasterCard

- Diapers
- Baby formula & food
- Pop & juice
- Bottled water
- Paper products
- Cleaning supplies
- Pet supplies

Call Mr.Case at 416-661-2273
for your free Catalogue today!

order on-line www.mrcase.com

Diaper Stores & Services

My Lil' Miracle & Indisposables™

1-877-218-0112 • www.mylilmiracle.com
Affordable, environmentally sympathetic products for babies & children including
Indisposables™ cotton baby products. Quote webpass AD0003 for 10% savings. • Ages: 0-6 •
$VISA$, ⊖, Cheque.

$COUPON$ smallplanet Inc. : smallplanet Home and smallplanet Community Diaper Recycling Service

800-566-9278 • www.smallplanetinc.com
smallplanet will pick up your baby's soiled disposable diapers and recycle them to reclaim their
valuable raw materials therefore diverting them from landfill. Look for our new website and products launching in spring of 2006! **Look for our ad in this section. See coupon section for valuable savings.** • $VISA$, ⊖, ▓, *Interac.*

Top Quality Diapers

416-499-8517 •
Delivery service for bulk disposable diapers. Baby & adult.

$COUPON$ With Child

705 Pape Ave, Toronto, Ont, M4K 3S6. • 416-466-9693 • www.withchildonline.com
Comprehensive selection of cotton diapers and related products. Call for store hours. **Look for our
ad in the Breastfeeding section. See coupon section for valuable savings.** • $VISA$, ⊖, *Interac.*

We have learned over the years that it is important look at each child as an individual. What is right for one of your children may not be right for another, and frankly, what is right this year may no longer be right next year. Education is a matter of ongoing evaluation.

Intervention can make all the difference in the world - there is enrichment as well as tutoring, and sometimes an assessment can tell you where the difficulties and opportunities lie.

With respect to the private schools listed here, some offer an alternative educational environment or learning methodology. Some offer specialized math, language or religious training. Don't assume that just because they're private that they are out of range financially. Several schools have subsidy or even scholarship programs available. You never know until you ask. Public schools are a great option too - there are multiple public boards and you can talk to all of them about your child.

Our biggest piece of advice…be proactive when it comes to your child's education. Although the teachers and schools want your child to succeed, they have many children to look after. If you have questions or concerns, bring them up with the teachers and ask for assistance. You are the parent - trust your instincts.

<u>You will find the following sub-categories in this section:</u>
Educational Assessments & Consultation; Educational Resources & Supplies; Education savings Plans; Private Schools & Preschools; Public Schools; Special Education; Tutoring & Enrichment; Uniforms

$ COUPONS $ Look for this company's coupon at the back of the book

■ Educational Assessments & Consultation

Ages, Dr. Kathryn, Psychoeducational Consultant
1 Promenade Circle, Ste 301J, Thornhill, Ont • 416-407-2796 •
Psychoeducational assessments, behaviour management, consultation, study skills training. • Ages: 6+.

Angus Lloyd Associates
8 Lawton Blvd., Toronto, Ont, M4V 1Z4. • 416-944-8185 •
Basic skills instruction, assessment, tutoring, direct instruction.

Assessment, Counselling & Coaching Centre; Dr. S. Jane Margles
29 Alvin Ave, Toronto, Ont, M4T 2A7. • 416-428-1600 •
Individual counselling and coaching for optimal performance. Psychological assessments for children, adolescents & adults. Specializing in learning disabilities, ADD/ADHD, underachievement, motivational difficulties, giftedness & stress management.

Collaborative Therapy & Assessment Group, Dr Stacey Berman & Dr Ruth Slater
118 Eglinton Ave W, Ste 405, Toronto, Ont, M4R 2G4. • 416-644-0983 •
Registered psychologists. Psycho-educational assessments - We do the testing! • Ages: 5-19yrs.

Dr Tally Bodenstein-Kales
250 Lawrence Ave W, Ste 211, Toronto, Ont, M5M 1B2. • 416-435-4496 •
Practice in children's behaviour and learning issues. • Ages: 3-18.

Education

Lieberman, Susan: Family Therapist, HonBA, DCS
3292 Bayview Ave, Ste 202, Toronto, Ont • 416-512-6356 • www.familysupport.net
Comprehensive, psychoeducational consulting & assessments including programming, team/parent meetings, classroom observations, etc. Interactive with a personal touch. Covered by private insurance/health care plans. • ▭, Cheque.

Marcovitch & Associates: Drs. Sharon & Howard Marcovitch, Registered Psychologists
491 Lawrence Ave W, Ste 405, Toronto, Ont, M5M 1C7. • 416-780-0909 •
Psychological assessments, school consultation, program planning & parent counselling for preschool & school-age children, adolescents and young adults with: communication disorders, developmental delays, attention deficit disorder, learning disabilities, advanced abilities & talents & behaviour difficulties. • By appointment • ♿.

Natalie Orenchuk Msw.B.A. Specialist in Performance Issues
93 Castlewood Rd, Toronto, Ont, M5N 2L3. • 416-480-2150 • htttp://pages.sprint.ca/gifted2000
Creative, gifted /alternative styles/L.D. ADD Consultation, psychotherapy, parenting, school meetings. **Look for our ad in this section.**

Options in Education- Educational Consulting by Judy Winberg M.Ed.
2100 Avenue Rd, Toronto, Ont, M5M 4A8. • 416-932-1168 • www.optionsineducation.com
School overview - public independent, private. Special needs and Special Education programs. Referrals for psychoeducational assessments, tutorial, remedial and enrichment programs. Personalized relocation service for families with school aged children moving to Toronto. • Ages: Preschool-Gr. 12.

Toronto A.D.D. Support Centre
416-924-2090, cell 416-567-5791 • www.torontosupport.ca
NEW. Offering services and information for families contending with A.D.D. and Attention Deficit/Hyper Activity Disorder. Stop in to have a free discussion or phone for brochure of services. Located near St. Clair/Yonge Subway.

▪ Educational Resources & Supplies

Alpha Textbooks Inc.
3709 Chesswood Dr., Toronto, Ont, M3J 2P6. • 416-461-3542 •
Educational, reference, Children's books, backpacks, Free Delivery.

Bookman Textbook and Educational Outlet, The
4910 Yonge St, side door, North York, Ont, M2N 5N5. • 416-BOO-KMAN or 1-800- 461-8398 • www.thebookman.ca
The Bookman carries textbooks used in all public and parochial schools, grades pre-K to 12 plus thousands of supplementary workbooks in all subjects. Parent and teacher resources. Huge selection of novels. Mail order across Canada. • Other Locations 124 Portland St, Etobicoke • Ages: 2+ • ▭, ⊕, *Interac* • Mon-Tue: 10-6, Wed: 10-8, Thu-Sat: 10-6, Sun: 12-5.

Discovery Toys - National Sales Director
416-630-0138 or 905-417-4514, •
Award winning educational books, toys, games & computer software. • Ages: 0-12 • ▭, ⊕, ▭, Cheque.

Gumdrop Books Canada
2005 Sheppard Ave E, Ste 109, North York, Ont, M2J 5B4. • 416-756-3327 or 800-433-3719 •
Quality library books from preschool to high school. • Ages: NB-18.

Louise Kool & Galt Ltd
10 Newgale Gate Unit 1, Scarborough, Ont, M1X 1C5. • 416-293-0312 •
Specialists in toys, teaching aids and educational materials.

Positive Strokes
416-446-2903 •
Callirobics - Handwriting exercises to music.

School Years Albums - Do you know where your Grade 1 report card is?
416-201-9877 • www.SchoolYearsAlbums.com
An album to organize & display children's school records & pictures.

■ Private Schools & Preschools

1st Step Montessori Centre
3385 Lawrence Ave E, Scarborough, Ont, M1H 1A8. • 416-438-8103 •
Enriched bilingual Montessori curriculum for children 18 mos - 6 yrs. • Mon-Fri: 7 - 6.

A.C.H.S. College Schools
11191 Keele St N, Maple, Ont, L6A 1S1. • 905-832-8121 • www.achscanada.com
Established in 1990 the ACHS College Schools offers high quality education for athletic boys and girls grades JK -8. • Ages: 6-13 • Cheque.

Education

A Guide to the Best Private Schools: www.ourkids.net
905-272-1843 •
Profiles more than 195 of the leading Canadian private schools- Our Kids helps you find the right one for your child.

Academy For Gifted Children- P.A.C.E.
12 Bond Cres, Richmond Hill, Ont, L4E 3K2. • 905-773-0997 •
Private school for intellectually gifted students. • Ages: 6-17.

Alan Howard Waldorf School
250 Madison Ave, Toronto, Ont, M4V 2W6. • 416-962-AHWS (2497) • www.ahws.org
Co-educational elementary education using worldwide Waldorf curriculum integrating the academic with the creative . • Ages: Nursery-Gr 8.

Bayview Glen School
275 Duncan Mill Rd, North York, Ont, M3B 3H9. • 416-443-1030 •
Co-educational, balanced, well-rounded programme.

Beach School, The
42 Edgewood Avenue, Toronto, Ont, M4L 3H1. • 416-693-0110 •
Self-directed learning for independent children.

Birchwood Elementary & Preschool
1146 Clarkson Rd, Mississauga, Ont, L5J 2W2. • 905-855-3800 •
Alternative, Individual programs. Nursery to Grade 8.

Branksome Hall
10 Elm Ave, Toronto, Ont, M4W 1N4. • 416-920-9741 •
Leading girls' independent school in the heart of Toronto.

Canada's National Ballet School
400 Jarvis St, Toronto, Ont, M4Y 2G6. • 416-964-3780 • www.nbs-enb.ca
Professional Ballet Program: full-time ballet/academic training to students from Grade 6 to post-secondary. • Cheque.

Central Montessori Schools
416-250-1022 • www.cmschool.net
Happy, stimulating environment. Emphasis on math & language. French, science, music, gymnastics. Enhance concentration & establish good work habits. Discover the joy of learning! **Look for our ad in this section.** • Other Locations 72 Steeles Ave W 905-889-0012, 157 Florence Ave 416-222-5097, 200 Sheppard Ave E 416-222-5940, 18 Coldwater Cres 416-510-1200, 157 Willowdale Ave 416-250-1022 • Ages: 18mos-14yrs.

Children's Garden Junior School
670 Eglinton Ave E, Toronto, Ont, M4G 2K4. • 416-423-5017 •
Small, nurturing, enriched, progressive, co-ed, JK-3.

Children's Garden Nursery School
1847 Bayview Avenue, Toronto, Ont, M4G 3E4. • 416-488-4298 • www.childrensgarden.ca
Children's Garden Nursery School offers half day programs for both pre-school and kindergarten children. French, Music, Gym, Art and Drama are just a sample of the wonderful programs that the children enjoy. • Ages: 2.5-5yrs.

Coulter's Mill Preschool

1401 Clark Ave W, Thornhill, Ont, L4J 7R4. • 905-660-5152 • www.uppercanadachildcare.com
Combines education with full day child care. Enriched Kindergarten programs provide reading readiness, mathematics and literacy skills. Low child:teacher ratios ensure individual attention and guidance. Snacks and lunch provided. Licensed, non-profit. **Look for the Upper Canada Child Care ad in the Childcare section.** • Ages: 2.5-6.

Creative Preschool of East Toronto, The

14 St Matthews Rd, Toronto, Ont, M4M 2B5. • 416-465-3865 • www.creativepreschool.ca
Superior teachers encourage active learning with child initiated activities. Intergenerational program integrates children and patients. Morning preschool, lunch, afternoon kindergarten.

Crestwood School

411 Lawrence Ave E, Don Mills, Ont, M3C 1N9. • 416-444-5858 •
Coeducational, small classes, French from JK, music, drama, computers, etc.

Discovery Private School

21 Ascot Ave, 3rd Fl, Toronto, Ont, M6E 1E6. • 416-916-0057 • www.discoveryps.com
Optimizing every child's potential through the development of self esteem, self-confidence and customized programming. Children advance at their own pace in a safe, joyful and loving environment. Ages: JK to Gr. 8.

e.p.i.c. School

111 Manor Rd E, Toronto, Ont, M4S 1R4. • 416-489-0132 • www.epicschool.com
Building a solid foundation for future learning. Enriched, outstanding creative Pre-K to S.K. programs for the critically formative years.

Goulding Preschool
46 Goulding Avenue, Toronto, Ont • 416-222-3640 •
Drop-in and drop-off programs available. • Ages: 2 1/2 - 4.

Hillcrest Progressive School - Private Jewish Preschool
59 Plymbridge Rd, Toronto, Ont, M2P 1A2. • 416-489-8355 •
Nursery to SK. Where every day is a special day. • Ages: 2 1/2 - 5.

Howlett Academy
15 Madison Ave, Toronto, Ont, M5R 2S4. • 416-921-7225 •
An individually guided Private School for grades 1-8.

Junior Scholars Preschool
1400 Lakeshore Rd W, Mississauga, Ont, L5L 1J1. • 905- 823-7575 •
We offer French program, dance and martial arts. • Ages: 16mos-6yrs.

Kidz Castle Indoor Playground & Childcare
2338 Major Mackenzie Dr, Unit 7, Maple, Ont, L6A 3Y7. • 905-417-2626 •
Preschool Nursery class & Summer day camp. Spacious & clean.

Kinder Connection/The Reading Connection
8707 Dufferin St, Unit 9, Thornhill, Ont • 905-709-8600 • www.thekinderconnection.net
Welcome to The Kinder Connection! Highly regarded Kindergarten & Nursery Enrichment
Programmes combining academics and hands-on fun! Certified teachers, low ratios, and a stimulating environment make us the perfect choice for your child. Ages 3-6. Reading programme for
5-9 yr olds also available. • Other Locations: 333 Wilson Ave 416-636-3000 • Mon-Sat: 9-3:30.

Kingsley Primary School
516 The Kingsway, Etobicoke, Ont, M9A 3W6. • 416-233-0150 •
Non-profit primary school Gr JK-5.

Laugh Learn and Grow Preschool
416-635-7222 •
Programs designed to stimulate education through play.

Lyndhurst Day Nursery and Kindergarten
1 Lyndhurst Dr, Thornhill, Ont, L3T 6T5. • 905-886-7455 • www.uppercanadachildcare.com
Combines education with full day child care. Enriched Kindergarten programs provide reading
readiness, mathematics and literacy skills. Low child:teacher ratios ensure individual attention and
guidance. Snacks and lunch provided. Licensed, non-profit. **Look for the Upper Canada Child Care ad
in the Childcare section.** • Ages: 3 mos-6yrs.

Mabin School
50 Poplar Plains Rd, Toronto, Ont, M4V 2M8. • 416-964-9594 •
Small, independent, co-ed school for 150 children in JK - Grade 6.

Maple Preschool " Where learn & play go hand in hand."
9954 Keele St, Maple, Ont, L6A 5O3. • 905-832-CARE (2273) • www.maplepreschool.com
Established in 1998. This unique and warm setting welcomes children ages 2.5-5 years to
engage in play with an educational influence. Qualified, ECE caregivers help maintain a clean &
safe atmosphere, along with providing a stimulating program & meeting children's individual
needs. Summer program available.

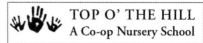

Montcrest School

4 Montcrest Blvd, Toronto, Ont, M4K 1J7. • 416-469-2008 • www.montcrest.on.ca
Montcrest School, overlooking Riverdale Park in Toronto, is a co-educational elementary day school. The challenging, core curriculum integrates the arts and co-curricular activities. Classes for children with learning disabilities are offered for Gr 2-8. Student/Teacher ratio 16:1. •
Ages: JK-gr8.

My First Preschool Children's Programs

7 Edithvale Dr, Rm 219, Toronto, Ont, M2N 2R4. • 416-663-5948 •
1 teacher - 5 children. Fun outdoor/indoor, educational activities. Co-op. Air Conditioned. • Ages: 3-5yrs.

Noah's Ark Nursery School

375 Melrose Ave, North York, Ont, M5M 1Z6. • 416-789-5749 •
An interactive, creative, fun and educational program. Enhance learning through music, tactile adventures, crafts, cooking, science experiments and discussions. Multicultural based, half-day program. • Ages: 2 1/2 -5.

North Toronto Early Years Learning Centre

416-544-0133 • www.earlyyearslearning.com
An Adlerian Preschool offering innovative enriching programs for Toddlers, Preschoolers, and Kindergarten students. An Enrichment Program that Nurtures your Child's IQ and EQ. Now two locations: 11 Bedford Park Ave and 27 Castlefield Ave. • Ages: 18mos-6yrs.

$COUPON$ Northwood Academy - Montessori Plus!

6 Locations covering North York, Thornhill & Markham: 416-492-7812 •
www.northwoodmontessori.ca
An enriched bilingual Montessori program. Parent/tot, preschool and camp. **Look for our ad in this section. See coupon section for valuable savings**. • Ages: 1.5-5yrs.

Oriole Nursery School

1570 Yonge St, Toronto, Ont, M4T 1Z8. • 416-960-1293 • www.oriolenurseryschool.com
Cooperative preschool since 1948. We offer enriched morning and afternoon classes and a fun-filled summer camp. ECE teachers, music and drama specialists. • Ages: 2.5 - 5.

Prepskills ®

416-200-SSAT (7728) •
Applying to Private School? Canada's Industry Leader in Private School Preparation.

Spanish Schoolhouse

180 Steeles Ave West, Unit 202, Thornhill, Ont, L4J 2L1. • 905-771-1136 •
www.thespanishschoolhouse.ca
Learn Spanish the fun way! We offer Spanish immersion programs for preschool and kindergarten children. After school, Saturday and summer programs are offered for school agers. Adult
and parent and tot classes also available. • Ages: 0-12.

St. Philips Community Preschool

201 Caribou Rd, Toronto, Ont, M5N 2B5. • 416-782-8026 •
A fun place where a love of learning starts to grow. Quality Early Childhood program, specialized
music and French program, after school programs. Well-equipped learning centres, creative art,
field trips; fantastic outdoor playground. 9am - 11:45am. • Ages: 21/2 - 4 yrs..

Sterling Hall School, The

99 Cartright Ave, Toronto, Ont, M6A 1V4. • 416-785-3410 • www.sterlinghall.com
The Sterling Hall School est. 1987.   Preparatory Boys School JK to Grade 8: maximum of 18 per
class, dedicated faculty, challenging academics, character and leadership program. • Ages: 4 - 14.

The York School

20 Glebe Rd E., Toronto, Ont, M4T 1X2. • 416-926-1325 • www.yorkschool.com
Coed Early Years Programme - ages 3 to 5 - combines International Baccalaureate inquiry-based
learning with hands-on Montessori. Extended daycare. Grades 1-12 at 1320 Yonge St.

Top o' the Hill Co-op Nursery School

10030 Yonge St, Richmond Hill, Ont, L4C 1T8. • 905-884-7012 • www.topothehill.ca
Our child centered program incorporates creative themes, crafts, playtime, circle time, gym, outdoor play and field trips allowing the child to develop socially, emotionally, cognitively and physi-
cally. Our teachers are qualified, experienced and caring. Parents are involved and love the experience. **Look for our ad in this section.** • Ages: 2.5-5 yrs.

Toronto French School

306 Lawrence Ave East, Toronto, Ont, M4N 1T7. • 416-484-6533 x4247 • www.tfs.on.ca
A bilingual, co-educational, non-denominational school from pre-kindergarten to university
entrance. No previous knowledge of French necessary through grade 7. We offer the
International Baccalaureate Diploma and a strong co-curricular program. We also have a
Mississauga campus (PK - Grade 7). • Other Locations Mississauga campus, 1293 Meredith Ave.

Toronto Montessori Schools

8569 Bayview Ave, Richmond Hill, Ont, L4B 3M7. • 905-889-6882 •
Toronto Montessori Schools. For children 18 mos to Grade 10.

Toronto Waldorf School

9100 Bathurst St, #1, Thornhill, Ont, L4J 8C7. • 905-881-1611 •
TWS educates the whole child: mind, body and heart.

Unionville Day Care and Kindergarten Programs

4171 Highway 7 E, Unionville, Ont, L3R 1L5. • 905-477-4778 • www.uppercanadachildcare.com
Combines education with full day child care. Enriched Kindergarten programs provide reading
readiness, mathematics and literacy skills. Low child:teacher ratios ensure individual attention and
guidance. Snacks and lunch provided. Licensed, non-profit. **Look for the Upper Canada Child Care ad
in the Childcare section.** • Ages: 18mos-6yrs.

Upper Canada College

200 Lonsdale Rd, Toronto, Ont, M4V 1W6. • 416-488-1125 •
UCC - a leading independent school for boys. • Ages: SK-gr12.

Uptown Yonge Preschool & Child Development Centre

1 Lord Seaton Road (North of Yonge&York Mills), Toronto, Ont • 416-602-9541 •
www.uptownyongepreschool.com
Enriched North Toronto preschool offering half-day toddler & preschool programs. Creative, cognitive,
sensory, & motor activities, enhanced by specialized music & field trips. Ages: 18 months to 5 years

Willow Academy

250 Davisville Avenue 2nd floor, Toronto, Ont, M4S 1H2 • 416-972-6717 •
Enriched academics in a nurturing environment.

Wilmington Tiny Tots

205 Wilmington Ave, Toronto, Ont, M3H 6B3. • 416-395-7892 •
Motivated and loving teachers create a stimulating, enjoyable environment for your preschooler.
Children participate in an educational and recreational program. Parent & Tot and Co-Op options
available. Am. Open year-round. Air conditioned. Ages: 0-4 years.

Yes I Can! Nursery School of Toronto

100 Ranleigh Avenue, Toronto, Ont, M4N 1W9. • 416-486-4911 •
www.yesicannurseryschool.com
Award winning school recognized for outstanding achievement in Early Childhood Education.
Sparks creativity, nurtures self confidence & cultivates a love for learning. Hands-on discovery
through cooking, science & creative arts. Curriculum nurtures exploration, builds social skills in a
welcoming atmosphere of acceptance and respect. • Ages: Preschool & Kindergarten.

▪ Public Schools

Toronto Catholic District School Board

80 Sheppard Ave E, North York, Ont, M2N 6E8. • 416-222-8282ext. 5314 • www.tcdsb.org
TCDSB's publicly funded Catholic schools teach more than the basics. Through a Christ-centered
vision, and in partnership with parents, parishes and the community, we serve students from
diverse cultural, linguistic and ethnic backgrounds in Canada's largest and most dynamic city. •
Ages: JK - Gr. 12.

Toronto District School Board

5050 Yonge St, Toronto, Ont, M2N 5N8. • 416-397-3000 • www.tdsb.on.ca
New to Toronto? Check the website to find your neighbourhood school. Our goal is to provide
your family with a positive learning environment, the finest educational programs, and services
that promote outstanding student achievement.

▪ Special Education

C.H.I.L.D. Neurodevelopmental Treatment Center

2200 Rutherford Rd #4, Maple, Ont, L4K 5V2. • 905-417-3111 • www.childmdim.com
Learning center, social skills groups, summer/winter camp, home based and centre based IBI
therapy, after-school instruction for children with Neurodevelopmental disabilities (Autism, LD,
ADD, CP, GDD, communication disorders). • Ages: 0-15yrs.

Centennial Infant & Child Centre

1580 Yonge St, Toronto, Ont, M4T 1Z8. • 416-935-0200 •
Infant development and preschool program for children with delays in development.   No charge
for infant program, birth to five. •

Dunblaine School for Children
21 Deloraine Ave, Toronto, Ont, M4M 2A8. • 416-483-9215 •
Elementary school for children with learning disabilities. • Ages: 6-14.

Exceptional Learning Centre
570 Westney Rd South, Suite 25, Ajax, Ont, L1S 6V6. • 905-686-4800 • www.exlcentre.com
Small, full day elementary level school for students with special learning needs. Focus on founda-
tional subjects, social skills, community awareness. Find success in our warm, nurturing environment. • Other Locations: Richmond Hill.

Giant Steps Toronto
9600 Keele St, Maple, Ont, L6A 1R7. • 905-832-5270 •
Education/Therapeutic Centre Servicing Children with Autism. • ♿.

Kohai Educational Centre
41 Roehampton Ave, Toronto, Ont, M4P 1P9. • 416-489-3636 • www.kohai.ca
Kohai is a unique day school for students with neurodevelopmental and genetic disorders, including Autism, LD, ADD, ADHD, developmental delays. Enthusiastic, committed teachers use
direct instruction and intensive behavioural intervention within a caring environment. kohai@bell-
net.ca. • Ages: 4+.

Montcrest School
4 Montcrest Blvd, Toronto, Ont, M4K 1J7. • 416- 469-2008 • www.montcrest.on.ca
The objective of the Learning Disability program is to provide intensive instruction in specific
areas while promoting integration into the regular classroom. Student/Teacher ratio 7:1. •
Ages: JK-gr8.

Play Haven
100 Ranleigh Avenue, Toronto, Ont, M4N 1W9. • 416-486-4911 •
www.yesicannurseryschool.com
Offering a free Friday morning Parent & Child playgroup specific to youngsters who are medically
fragile. • Ages: 3 mos. - 5 yrs..

Spark Learning Centre
1118 Centre St, Unit 20A, Thornhill, Ont, L4J 7R9. • 905-709-1806 •
The Learning Disabilities Specialists. Full time/Part time program.

Step By Step Academy
44 Upjohn Rd, Toronto, Ont • 416-449-7624 • www.sbslg.com
Effective education for children with individualized programming needs. Direct Instruction, behavioural teaching, specialized curriculum and Precision Teaching. Programs designed & supervised by
a psychologist/certified behaviour analyst. Skillbuilding & assessment available. • Ages: 3-13yrs.

We Care Tutorial Services Inc
416-691-8554 • www.wecaretutorial.com
Experienced in working with people with learning disabilities. Since 1977. • Ages: 4+ • Cheque
By appointment.

Education

Three A+ students. Which one has ADD?

*You can't change the wind...
but you can adjust the sails.*

Underachievement?
- Attention Span is Short
- Distractibility
- Difficulty Organizing and Completing Work
- Impulsivity
- Learning Difficulties

Improve your child's learning and achievement through Neurofeedback (brainwave training) plus Learning Strategies.
Director: Dr. Lynda M. Thompson
Co-author with Dr. Wm. Sears of The A.D.D Book

(416) 488-2233 • (905) 803-8066
www.addcentre.com
Toronto & Mississauga locations.

Yes I Can! Nursery School of Toronto

100 Ranleigh Avenue, Toronto, Ont, M4N 1W9. • 416-486-4911 •
www.yesicannurseryschool.com
Yes I Can! is a warm, language enriched environment where children of different abilities learn together. We offer: • Inclusive preschool morning class • Special classes for communication delayed preschoolers and a Yes I Can! Build My Social Skills class • Enriched Kindergarten • Preschool summer camp. • Ages: preschool & kindergarten.

Zareinu Educational Centre

905-738-5542 • www.zareinu.org
A day treatment and educational centre for children with mild to complex special needs. Programs delivered in a caring environment rich in Jewish culture and tradition. Full/half day treatment and special education programs available. Certified and licensed teachers and therapists. Programs for children 6 wks (Infant Intervention) - 21 yrs. (High School). •

■ Tutoring & Enrichment

A Muse Tutoring Service

416-704-7069 •
All grades and subjects. Satisfaction guaranteed! • Ages: 6-20.

A+ Tutoring

(905) 896-1663 •
Grades 1-8. Preschool reading program (age 3-6).

$COUPON$ ADD Centre

905-803-8066 or 416-488-2233 • www.addcentre.com
Improve grades! Improve self-esteem! The ADD Centre combines instruction in thinking skills with computerized EEG training (Neurofeedback) to empower students to improve their attention span, concentration & school performance. Also effective with Asperger's. Director is Dr. Lynda Thompson, co-author with Dr. Sears of "The A.D.D. Book". **Look for our ad in this section. See coupon section for valuable savings.** • Cheque • Mon-Fri: 9:30-9, Sat-Sun: 9-5.

Adventure Phonics: Language Enrichment Program
416-657-1696 • http://adventurephonics.puppetadventure.com
Fabulous in-home phonics program. Give your kids a head start! Creative, comprehensive reading and writing. New! Shakespeare for Kids. Guaranteed. Ages 3+.

Autism Children's Intervention Services
8171 Yonge St, Ste 226, Thornhill, Ont, L3T 2C6. • 416-219-2316 • www.aciscanada.com
Tutoring & Test prep. ADD, LD, Autism, Language delays Educational Assessments (IEP). •
Ages: 0-15 yrs • Parking: 2/20/2006.

Bright Sparks Tutoring & Early Literacy Program
Ridge Hill Dr, Toronto, Ont • 416-787-6966 •
Multi-sensory techniques, standardized testing, results oriented.

Carol Ruskin - Remedial Reading Tutor
78 Montressor Dr, Toronto, Ont, M2P 1Z4. • 416-221-6924 •
Fast track action reading program provides outstanding results in reading, spelling, comprehension. Proven success with students with learning difficulties & those in immersion programs. Private sessions. Available all year. "I thought I was the dumbest kid in my class & now I think I'm the smartest." April 2006, Post Newsmagazines. • Ages: SK-adult.

Central Learning Centre
477 Mount Pleasant Rd, Ste106, Toronto, Ont, M4S 2M9. • 416-486-4545 •
One on one remedial tutorials. Kindergarten to University.

ClubZ In-Home Tutoring Inc
416-515-7755 • Affordable One-On-One Tutoring in the comfort of your own home.

Don Valley Academy
4576 Yonge St. Suite 408, North York, Ont, M2N 6N4. • 416-223-6284 •
www.donvalleyacademy.com
Don Valley Academy is an accredited, ministry-inspected private high school, offering credit courses, from grades 9-12. Classes are available days, evenings, and weekends, on a full-time or part-time basis. Private instruction is also available.

English Maniac
3080 Yonge Street, Ste 6000, Toronto, Ont, M4N 3N1. • 416-225-4566 • www.engmac.com
Personalized one-on-one or small group study programs for children of all ages and abilities. Supported by the highest quality instructors, your child will develop enthusiasm, self confidence and clear understanding in Math, English, Science, Computer, French, Spanish and/or Mandarin.

Exceptional Learning Centre
570 Westney Rd South, Suite 25, Ajax, Ont, L1S 6V6. • 905-686-4800 • www.exlcentre.com
Specialists in assessments and individual programming. Weekly tutoring, part-time studies and full day elementary level school available. Find success in our warm, nurturing environment! • Other Locations Richmond Hill.

$COUPON$ Explanations Unlimited: In-Home Tutoring Specialists
Toronto: 416-730-9323; York: 905-707-7339; Mississauga: 905-828-0233;
Toll Free: 1-866-EXU-4-YOU • www.ExplanationsUnlimited.com
Affordable private tutoring in your home since 1980. Specialists for all subjects & grades. Homework support, study skills, & entrance exam preparation. Customized remedial & enrichment programs for improved confidence & results. Year-round, city-wide. Progress reports & tax receipts. Government Certified. **Look for our ad in this section. See coupon section for valuable savings.** • Ages: 4+ • VISA, ⊜, Cheque.

Flex Tutoring
416-986-8334 • Offering tutoring at home for all ages.

Kids' Clinic
416-858-7827 •
Problems in school? Coaching kids to be successful. • Ages: 4-18 yrs.

Kinder Q
416-544-0133 •
A Kindergarten Enrichment Program that Nurtures your Child's IQ and EQ. • Other Locations 27 Castlefield Ave. • Ages: 18mos-SK.

Kumon Canada Inc
1-800-ABC-MATH (222-6284) •
An after-school Math and Reading supplemental program. • Ages: 4-15.

Math Masters Tutoring
4576 Yonge St. Suite 408, North York, Ont, M2N 6N4. • 416-223-MATH (6284) •
www.mathmasters.ca
Math Masters offers individualized, one-to-one instruction for all levels and all subjects. Our program emphasizes effective study skills and memory training. Tutoring is available days, evenings, or weekends.

$COUPON$  Oxford Learning Centres
Royal York 4195 Dundas St W, 416-234-1054; North York Lawrence, 201A-3130 Bathurst St 416-781-1225; Scarborough Willowdale, 2810 Victoria Park Ste 110, 416-502-9628, •
www.oxfordlearning.com
We also offer programs for 3-6 year olds, high-school students, French students and summer camps. • *VISA*, Cheque • Mon-Thu: 9-8, Fri-Sat: 9-5. **Look for our ad in this section. See coupon section for valuable savings.**

Phonic Beginnings
416-469-3163 • Basic reading skills taught in your home.

Prepskills ®
416-200-SSAT (7728) • www.prepskills.com
Canada's Industry Leader in Private School Preparation. SSAT/ISEE/UTS/CAT/CTBS Tests.
Prepwrite® Essay Course. Locations throughout the GTA. • Ages: gr5-10.

$COUPON$ Qualified Tutors: We Come to You
905-763-7134 or 1-877-818-1811 •
Home tutoring specialists with proven results at affordable prices...all subjects, all grades. **Look for our ad in this section. See coupon section for valuable savings.**

Reading Connection
8707 Dufferin St, Unit 9, Thornhill, Ont • 905-709-8600 •
Certified teachers. Saturday programmes. Remediation and enrichment. • Other Locations: 333 Wilson Ave 416-636-3000 • Ages: 5-9.

Reading Lab for Kids
65 Latimer Ave, Toronto, Ont, M5N 2M1. • 416-544-0888 • www.readinglab.ca
Certified Phono-Graphic Reading Therapist. 2-year average gain in reading and comprehension scores in 12 hours of instruction. • Ages: JK-Gr 12.

Scholars Education Centre
North Toronto 3293 Yonge St. (north of Lawrence) • 416-488-9301 • www.scholarscanada.com
Premium individualized tutoring services. Also: Grade 9-12 OSS credits, (S)SAT Preparation, "Grade 1 Preparation", and ESL programs. Summer Programs available.

Spirit of Math® Schools
North York, North Toronto, Mississauga, Markham, Richmond Hill, • 416-223-1985 •
www.spiritofmath.com
After school math classes for high performing students. Focus on problem solving. A place where students can discover the thrill of a challenge. SMS has produced many of the top math students in the Nation. • Ages: 5-17.

Sunporch Tutoring Inc
275 Kerrybrook Dr, Richmond Hill, Ont, L4C 3R2. • 905-883-1459 •
Primary Specialist designs individualized programs. Make learning fun! • Ages: 3-12 yrs.

Sylvan Learning Centre
13+ locations in the GTA, • (800) EDUCATE (338-2283) •
Personalized programs, Certified teachers, Guaranteed results. After School and Saturdays.

Sylvan Learning Centre North Toronto
3370 Yonge St, Toronto, Ont • 416-487-2875 • www.educate.com/centers/m4n2m7
Premium supplemental education services, JK-Gr12. Proven results, cost effectively. Ask about result guarantees. Reading, writing, math, study skills, special programs, homework support, Johns Hopkins University Middle School Writing and Math, SSAT Prep For Private School Entrance.

Teachers On Call
905-881-1931 • Tutoring at your home with qualified teachers. • Cheque.

Toronto SAT & SSAT Prep
416-351-0909 • Yale and Havergal graduate. Ivy League acceptances.

Tutor Doctor
5863 Leslie Street, Suite #350, Toronto, Ont, M2H 1J8. • 647-218-1661 • www.tutordoctor.com
"ONE ON ONE TUTORING AT HOME TO HELP YOU BUILD CONFIDENCE AND GET BETTER GRADES WITH EASE". All subjects from JK to University. SAT and SSAT are now available. Our online tutoring is available at all hours. Call now for a free assessment.

Education

Reading | Writing | Math | Spelling | Grammar | French | Study Skills

Oxford Learning is the only after-school learning program of its kind. First, we pinpoint how your child learns. Then, we create an individualized program that goes beyond tutoring to teach your child to **learn** and **study** more effectively. Better grades, motivation and confidence follow.

Give your child a lifetime of learning success.
Contact Oxford Learning today.

"I CAN DO IT!"

Skills for Success, Lessons for Life.

www.oxfordlearning.com

Etobicoke- Royal York	**North York- Lawrence**	**Scarborough- Willowdale**
4195 Dundas Street West	201A-3130 Bathurst Street	2810 Victoria Park Suite 110
Phone: (416) 234-1054	Phone: (416) 781-1225	(Victoria Park and Van Horne)
royalyork@oxfordlearning.com	nyork@oxfordlearning.com	Phone: (416) 502-9628
		Willowdale@Oxfordlearning.com

TutoringWorks Inc
416-782-2071 •
Developing Successful Learners. In-home and in-school tutoring of academic subjects, study skills and remedial help for students with learning disabilities.

Village Learning Centre
10055 Keele St, Maple, Ont, L6A 1R7. • 905-417-3560 •
Individualized programs. Homework help. Home or centre tutorials.

Wall, Adele: Educational Consultant
10 West Pearce St, Ste 3, Richmond Hill, Ont, L4B 1B6. • 905-881-8400 •
32 yrs teaching experience. Primary Specialist. ESL. Educational assessments. • Ages: Senior K to Gr. 8.

We Care Tutorial Services Inc
416-691-8554 • www.wecaretutorial.com
We Care Tutorial Services Inc specializes in in-home, individualized or group academic tutoring sessions for all levels and ages. Creative learning programs adapt to the needs of the student. Serving Toronto and the surrounding area since 1977. • Cheque • By appointment.

▪ Uniforms

Uniform Basics
255 Industrial Pkwy S, Unit 10, Aurora, Ont, L4G 3V5. • 1-877-7BASICS •
Wholesale school uniforms. We make it. We sell it.

Festivals, Fairs & Carnivals

This section has lots of fun things to do but it is by no means exhaustive. We recommend perusing both the book and our website (www.helpwevegotkids.com) as well as our other publication Summer Fun Guide and website www.SummerFunGuide.ca for many additional festivals and fairs posted in our online calendars. Notices of local fairs and festivals are often posted on signs, at community centres, and in community papers so check there too.

40th Annual Cavalcade of Lights Festival
6th floor West tower Toronto City Hall
100 Queen St W., Toronto, Ont, M5H 2N2. • 416-338-0338 • www.toronto.ca/special_events
A month-long calendar of spellbinding events including spectacular fireworks, sparkling lighting displays and a one-of-a-kind holiday tour of Toronto's picturesque neighbourhoods. Beginning Nov 18/2006.

Amanda's Lemonade Stand for the Heart & Stroke Foundation
10 Briancliff Drive, Toronto, Ont, M3B 2G2. • www.lemonade4heart.org
Lemonade, hot chocolate, jumping castle, pony rides, concert, balloon art, etc.

$ COUPONS $ Baby & Toddler Show
Metro Toronto Convention Centre, North Building. Toronto, Ont, • 416-691-2852 •
www.thebabyandtoddlershow.com
Oct 27, 28 & 29, 2006. The ultimate event for mums, dads, babies and toddlers! Packed with expert pregnancy and parenting advice, fantastic shopping, great entertainment and inspiring features. **Look for our ad in this section. See coupon section for valuable savings.** • Ages: 0-5yrs.

Canadian International Air Show
CNE Waterfront, Toronto, Ont • 416-263-3650 •
September-Labour Day Weekend. Free with admission to CNE. International military and civilian performers.

Canadian National Exhibition (CNE)
Exhibition Place, Toronto, Ont • 416-393-6300 • www.theex.com
One of the largest annual fairs in North America with a unique variety of entertainment and fun for all ages. Aug. 17-Sept. 3, 2007. **Look for our ad in this section.** • Ages: Adults 25-49 with kids 6-13.

Celebrate Toronto Street Festival
Toronto City Hall, 100 Queen St. West
6th Floor, West Tower, Toronto, Ont, M5H 2N2. • 416-338-0338 •
www.toronto.ca/special_events
Celebrate Toronto Street Festival, July 6 - 8, 2007. World's longest street transformed into a curb-to-curb celebration of tastes, talent and all that is Toronto. • Free • &.

City Parent Camp Fair
467 Speers Rd, Oakville, Ont, L6K 3S4 . • 905- 815-0017 • www.cityparent.com
City Parent's annual Camp Fair: At the International Centre in February. **Look for our ad in the Parentstuff section.**

Harbourfront Centre: World Routes Summer 2007
235 Queens Quay W, York Quay Centre, Toronto, Ont, M5J 2G8. • 416-973-4000 •
www.harbourfrontcentre.com
Experience the world at a different festival every summer weekend! Mid- June to Labour Day.

Magic Hill Farms Haunted Adventure
PO Box 1298, Stouffville, Ont, L4A 8A3. • 905-640-2347 • www.magichill.com
Weekend evenings in October. Not for wimps, pregnant people or children under 8 years!

Milk International Children's Festival of the Arts
Harbourfront Centre, Toronto, Ont, M5V 2Z3. • 416-973-4000 •
www.harbourfrontcentre.com/milk
May 14-21, 2007. The world's best theatre, dance, visual art, music, architecture, design, and more! • *VISA*, ⊖, ▓, Cheque • &.

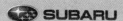

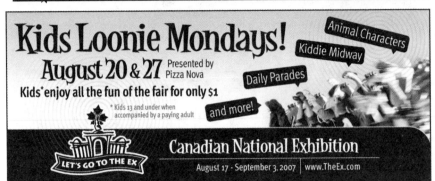

Our Kids; Private School Fair
905-272-1843 • :www.ourkids.net
Canada's most successful annual private school fair. Fall dates. Oakville and Toronto locations.

Port Elgin Pumpkin Festival
Port Elgin District Chamber of Commerce , 559 Goderich St, Port Elgin, Ont, N0H 2C4. •
1-800-387-3456 • Family Fun Second to None! Oct 7, 8, 2006.

Royal Agricultural Winter Fair
Exhibition Place, Coliseum, Toronto, Ont, M6K 3C3. • 416-263-3400 • www.royalfair.org
November 3rd - 12th, 2006. Petting Farm, Giant Vegetables, Entertainment, Education, etc.

Santa Claus Parade, The
139 Wendell Ave, Toronto, Ont, M9N 3K9. • 416-599-9090 #500 for route info (Sept- Nov) •
Sunday, November 19, 2006.

Sugarbush Maple Syrup Festival
416-667-6299 • www.trcaparks.ca
During March & April. Tap into Spring! Maple Syrup demonstrations at Kortright Centre (9550
Pine Valley Dr) & Bruce's Mill (Stouffville Rd E of Hwy 404). Tours, samples, activities and more!

Toddle For Tots at the Metro Toronto Zoo
416-977-0458 •
Toddle for Tots in support of Toronto's Ronald McDonald House. Sept 30, 2006. Call for 2007 dates.

Toronto International Circus Festival
416-469-1440 • www.TOcircusfestival.com
Expect to experience side-splitting comedy, eye-popping acrobatics and mind-bending daredevil
stunts! A one-of-a-kind event that is great fun for the whole family! Free admission. Ticketed
indoor shows. Friday, July 14th: 6:00 pm - 11:00 pm, Saturday, July 15th: 11:00 am - 11:00 pm,
Sunday, July 16th: 11:00 pm - 6:00 pm.

WinterCity
416-338-0338 • www.toronto.ca/special_events
WinterCity Festival, Feb 2 - 11, 2007 Award-winning 14-day city-wide celebration of Toronto's
culture, creativity and cuisine.

Word on the Street
416-504-7241 •
Canada's largest book & magazine festival. Last Sunday in Sept. 11am-6pm. Queen's Park.
Special kids section.

Have you ever taken the kids, a picnic and a Frisbee to Toronto Island? It is a fabulous place to spend the day without spending the money! There is small fee for the ferry ride but the kids love it! We are very lucky to be living in Toronto ... a city with many great Fun For Free options. See live animals in summer (High Park) or climb ice sculptures in winter. Look at the listings in this section and don't forget about calling some of the places in the Attractions section for more low cost ideas.

Allan Gardens Victorian Greenhouses

19 Horticultural Ave (Jarvis & Gerrard), Toronto, Ont, M5A 2P2. • 416-392-7288 • http://collections.ic.gc.ca/gardens/
16,000 square feet of tropical oasis in historical greenhouse. Goldfish, Palm trees, ponds and more! Great for learning about plants and our environment. Downtown. Mon-Sun: 10am-5pm, all year long. FREE.

$COUPON$ Bata Shoe Museum, The

327 Bloor St W, Toronto, Ont, M5S 1W7. • 416-979-7799 • www.batashoemuseum.ca
Find the smuggler's shoes, chestnut crushing spiked clogs and space boots in our shoebox! Free for kids under 5. **Look for our ad in the Attractions section. See coupon section for valuable savings.** • ♿.

CBC Museum

Canadian Broadcasting Centre, 250 Front St W, Toronto, Ont, M5V 3G5. • 416-205-5574 • www.cbc.ca/museum
UNCOVER behind the scenes secrets of CBC's classic children's programs and EXPLORE Canadian broadcasting history at the CBC Museum! • Mon-Fri: 9-5, Sat: 12-4.

Cummer Skateboard Park - Toronto's First

6000 Leslie St, Toronto, Ont, M2H 1J9. • 416-395-7803 •
Jumps, ramps, half-pipe, etc. Built for skateboarding. Public, free, unsupervised.

Douglas Snow Aquatic Centre North York Parks and Recreation

5100 Yonge St, North York, Ont, M2N 5V7. • 416-395-7585 •
Excitement year round. FREE Leisure swims with a Tarzan rope or a giant, 3-story, tubular slide.

Far Enough Farm - Toronto Island Park, City of Toronto Parks & Rec

Centre Island, Toronto, Ont, M5J 1X9. • 416- 398-BOAT •
Free outdoor petting farm on Centre Island. Runs all year round if the ferry is running. For Ferry Schedule call 416-392-8193 • Ages: 1-13.

High Park Zoo

Deer Pen Rd (Bloor & High Park), Toronto, Ont • 416- 392-1111 •
See deer, yaks, llamas, peacocks and many more animals in our paddocks. Large, unique children's play area too. Nature walks available all year round. FREE. Entrances at Bloor St West (West of Keele St) and High Park Blvd and Parkside Drive. Follow signs to Grenadier Cafe (parking available) then walk across the street to Deer Pen Rd. Zoo is located at the end of the road. Open 7:30 - dusk every day.

Mississauga Skateboarding Park

located beside the Iceland Arena on Matheson Blvd,

Riverdale Farm

201 Winchester St (3 bl. E. of Parliament, 3 bl. N. of Gerrard St. E.), Toronto, Ont, M4X 1B8. • 416-392-6794 •
Kids look eye-to-eye with pigs, goats, cows, horses, rabbits, swans and chickens housed in a farm-like setting. Admission free. Arts & crafts, events, demonstrations & activities daily. Call for details. • Free • ♿.

Toronto Botanical Garden

777 Lawrence Ave E (at Leslie), North York, Ont, M3C 1P2. • 416-397-1340 •
www.infogarden.ca
Nature mid-town! Bike paths, picnics, gardens. Free guided tours: July & August, Tues & Thurs
at 11 am. Call ahead. Check out our website. • &.

Toronto Island Park

416-397-BOAT (2628) • www.toronto.ca/parks
Hike, bike, blade, fish, paddle or picnic. Ferry terminal located at foot of Bay Street at Queen's
Quay West. Call for ferry schedule (fee for ferry).

Toronto Parks and Trails

416-392-1111 • www.toronto.ca/parks
Explore ravines, parks, gardens, the waterfront and neighbourhoods with Discovery Walks, self-
guided walks. Guided tours available through Toronto Field Naturalists, 416-593-2656. For High
Park Walking Tours call 416-392-1748.

Toronto Police Museum & Discovery Centre

Located in Police Headquarters, 40 College St, Toronto, Ont, M5G 2J3. • 416-808-7020 •
Bring a camera and take a pictures of a jail cell. Learn about police work using interactive displays. View police equipment, and REAL evidence from famous Toronto cases. Flash the lights in
a police cruiser, listen to live police radio. Guided tours for school/daycare groups. Public welcome. Free admission. • Mon-Fri: 10-4:30.

Toronto Special Events

Toronto City Hall, 9th Floor, East Tower, Toronto, Ont, M5H 2N2. • 416-338-0338 •
www.toronto.ca/special_events
Fabulous FREE events for families and kids - year round. Cavalcade of Lights, WinterCity,
Celebrate Toronto Street Festival, Canada Day Celebrations, Toronto Kid's Tuesdays and more.
Call to find out what's happening now. • Free • &.

WinterCity

416-338-0338 • www.toronto.ca/special_events
WinterCity Festival, Feb 2 - 11, 2007 Award-winning 14-day city-wide celebration of Toronto's
culture, creativity and cuisine. • Free • &.

Furniture & Accessories

Sometimes we wonder if our babies/kids' rooms are nicer than ours. There are so many fabulous & creative options these days ... for every budget. The stores listed here will provide you with anything from a crib or bed to an entire room, complete with design consultations. You will also find one-of-a-kind, personalized items for you or for a gift.

Whether you are furnishing your child's whole room or just looking for that special finishing touch, you will be able to find it here. There are choices for every budget and every taste.

You will find the following sub-categories in this section:
Baby Accessories, Furniture & Accessories Stores, Handpainted Furniture, Rentals & Repairs.

$COUPON$ Look for this company's coupon at the back of the book

▪ Baby Accessories

Baby Cocoon
416-567-9833 •
Fits all newborn carseats. Original, practical, cozy! • Ages: infant - 1 year • **VISA**, Cheque.

BabySteps Children's Fund
905-707-1030 or 1-866-334-4666 • www.babystepsgiftshop.com
Unique gifts for all ages. Personalized puzzle stools & more. Baby's 1st Year & School Frames for monthly/annual photos. All proceeds to Hospital for Sick Children. • Ages: NB+ • **VISA**, ⊖, ▦.

Babywrappers
Box 28510, Aurora, Ont, L4G 6S6. • 905-841-8906 •
The most innovative baby bath towel ever made.

Bon Lieu/Petit Pied
890 Yonge St (Bloor/Yorkville District), Toronto, Ont, M4W 3P4. • 416-963-4322 •
www.petitpied.com
Nursery accessories and European strollers and a wide selection of European children's fashions. **Look for our ad in the Children's Wear section.** • Other Locations 890 Yonge St 416-963-5925, Bayview Village 416-225-3238, 2390 Bloor St W 416-767-8366 • Ages: 0-20 • **VISA**, ⊖, ▦, *Interac* • Mon-Wed: 10-6, Thu-Fri: 10-8, Sat: 10-6, Sun: 12-5 • ♿.

"Buggy Bagg" by Kreative Kidzstuff
416-737-6721 • Shopping cart seat cover, highchair cover & diaper bag in one.

Cuddle Karrier...baby carrier/sling
1(877) CUDDLEKARRIER (283-3535) •
"World's top rated baby carrier" the 8-in-one Kinder Mobility System.

$COUPON$ K.I.D.S. - Kid's Interior Design Store
201 Millway Ave, Unit 1 (N of Hwy 7 off Jane), Concord, Ont, L4K 5K8. • 905-738-7121 •
www.kidsroomscanada.ca
Welcome to K.I.D.S., Kid's Interior Design Store, featuring a huge selection of the finest quality cribs, change tables, gliders and accessories. All at kid's size prices. Visit K.I.D.S. today! **Look for our ad in this section. See coupon section for valuable savings.** • **VISA**, ⊖, ▦, *Interac* • Mon: closed, Tue-Wed: 10-6, Thu: by appt, Fri: 10-6, Sat: 10-5, Sun: 12-5.

Furniture & Accessories

We offer an extraordinary selection of quality furniture, bedding, rugs, lamps and decor for babies, children and teens.

Whether you are looking for one item or want to complete the entire room - this is the store for you.

PetitePosh
416-575-1886 •
Online baby boutique. Gifts and essentials.

Sit'n'Stroll: The Strolex Corporation
20 Bermondsey Rd, Toronto, Ont, M4B 1Z5. • 905-794-9359 •
The world's only 5-in-1 carseat/stroller.

SUNSENSE Sun Protection Products
905-576-7535 •
99% UV blocking. Stroller covers. Hats. Blankets. All-season accessories.

Wunder Blankets
41 Ridelle Ave, Toronto, Ont, M6B 1H9. • 416-780-1997 •
Custom fleece blankets, monogrammed towels and apparel.

■ Baby Equipment Rentals & Repairs

Away WEE Travel Inc Baby Equipment Rentals
156 Dalemount Avenue, Toronto, Ont, M6B 3C9. • 416-737-1622 •
Baby equipment rentals and delivery. Toronto Vancouver.

Crayons
974 Kingston Road, Toronto, Ont, M4E 1S9. • 416-694-9733 •
Stroller repairs available. Most brands. • 𝗩𝗜𝗦𝗔, ⊖, ▮, Interac.

gogoBaby Inc
716 Dufferin Street, Toronto, Ont, M6K 2B7. • 647-895-BABY (2229) • www.gogobaby.ca
Rent high quality baby/toddler equipment including Maclaren and Peg Perego. Our equipment is in new condition, cleaned after each use and replaced often. Delivery available.

Kiddie Travel Inc - Baby Equipment Rentals
www.kiddietravel.com
Carseats, strollers, etc. We provide safe, clean and quality equipment for all your children's travelling needs.

Macklem's Baby Carriage
2223 Dundas St W, Toronto, Ont, M6R 1X6. • 416-531-7188 • www.macklems.com
Specialists in REPAIRING carriages. We REPAIR strollers and refurbish English prams. • ♿.

Furniture & Accessories

Mr. Convenience Furniture Rentals

3400 Pharmacy Ave, Scarborough, Ont, M1W 3J8. • 416-497-2511 or Toll Free 877-497-2511 •
www.mrconvenience.com
Furniture rentals available for infant, juvenile and adult. Strollers, cribs, high chairs, car seats,
change tables, bedroom sets etc.

V.I.P. Child Car Seat Rentals Inc

29 Steckley St, Aurora, Ont, L4G 7K6. • 905-713-0326 • www.vipchildcarseat.com
Renting children's car seats, play pens, strollers, and high chairs, we are your first stop for the
rental of children's equipment in the Greater Toronto Area. Our equipment is safety checked and
our car seats come with clean slip covers. • Ages: 0-8.

▪ Furniture & Accessories Stores

$ COUPONS A Kids Corner

609 Ford Dr, Oakville, Ont • 905-849-4222 • www.akidscorner.com
Fine furniture and unique décor for babies, kids and teens. Complete furniture collections directly
from the manufacturer complement the accessories such as bedding, rugs, lamps, art and more.
Look for our ad in this section. See coupon section for valuable savings. • Ages: 0 - 18.

$ COUPONS A Room of My Own

2111 Dunwin Dr, Unit 9, Mississauga, Ont, L5L 3C1. • 905-828-2525 • www.aroomofmyown.net
Visit our 14 fully decorated bedrooms featuring quality furniture, linens, wallpaper, decor and accessories. Focusing on service, our courteous and knowledgeable staff are here to help you make the
best choices for decorating your child's room. **Look for our ad in this section. See coupon section for
valuable savings.** • Ages: 2+ • VISA, ⊖, *Interac* • Mon-Wed: 9:30-5:30, Thu-Fri: 9:30-9,
Sat: 9:30-5:30, Sun: 12-5 • ♿.

Furniture & Accessories

Fourteen fully decorated bedrooms featuring:

- Quality Canadian furniture.
- Unique gift ideas, wooden table & chair sets, beanbag chairs, lamps
- Wide selection of custom linens, wallpaper and accessories for children's rooms.
- Set-up and delivery within the GTA.

Come in and see us at
2111 Dunwin Dr (facing Dundas), Mississauga, Ontario
(2 blocks west of Erin Mills Parkway)
(905) 828-2525
Visit us at www.aroomofmyown.net

a room of my own

Fine Children's Furniture,
Linen and Decor

Baby & Teen Furniture Warehouse
2673 Steeles Ave W, Toronto, Ont, M3J 2Z8. • 416-288-9167 •
Great selections - many floor models to choose.

Baby's Corner
762 College St, Toronto, Ont, M6G 1C4. • 416-534-3166 •
Everything your baby needs. Strollers, cribs, clothing, etc. • Ages: 0-2yrs.

Backpro Plus; The Portable Seating Aid for Kids & Adults
167 Spadina Rd, Richmond Hill, Ont, L4B 2Z2. • 905-770-8215 or 416-918-6502 •
Indoor/Outdoor portable floorseat with back support!

$ COUPONS Bunk House Kids
1911 Avenue Rd (4 lights south of the 401), Toronto, Ont, M5M 3Z9. • 416-789-7088 or
800-588-8339 • www.bunkhousekids.com
Canada's largest selection of bedroom furnishings for kids with 6000 ft of space on 3 floors.
Families can outfit an entire kid's/baby's bedroom - cribs, beds, beanbags, linens, mattresses,
duvets, bedding, lamps, etc. Expert service & delivery to cottage country. **Look for our ad in this
section. See coupon section for valuable savings**. • Ages: 2+ • *VISA*, ⊕, ▦, *Interac*, Cheque •
Mon-Fri: 10-5:30, Sat: 10-5, Sun: phone for hours.

www.bunkhousekids.com

Juvenile bedroom

suites, cottage furniture,

bunk beds, cribs, linens,

mattresses and more.

kids
bunkHouse

1911 AVENUE RD, SOUTH OF 401, TEL 416 789 7088

Crayons

974 Kingston Road, Toronto, Ont, M4E 1S9. • 416-694-9733 • crayonsstore@msn.com
Full selection of Peg Perego, Phil & Teds, Zooper, Maclaren, Britax & many more bestsellers. Excellent selection of gently used name brand clothing up to size 6. Baby registry. Stroller repair. Delivery available. Parent package deals. Call for store hours. The Baby Experts! • *VISA*, ⊕, *Interac*.

$COUPON$ Dear-Born Baby

72 Doncaster Ave, Thornhill, Ont, L3T 1L3. • 905-881-3334
• www. dearbornbaby.com
Visit the GTA's leading baby store! Huge selection of specialty and brand names in cribs, furniture, linens, strollers, car seats, high chairs and much more - everything for your child. Expert staff will answer all your questions. Computerized Baby Registry. **Look for our ad in this section. See coupon section for valuable savings.** • Ages: Infant Toddler • *VISA*, ⊕, ▓, *Interac*, Cheque • Mon-Wed: 10-6, Thu-Fri: 10-9, Sat: 10-6, Sun: 12-5 • ♿.

$COUPON$ Dick & Jane Inc.

2582 Yonge Street (N. of Eglinton), Toronto, Ont, M4P 2J3. • 416-483-7400 •
www.dickandjane.ca
The children's shop with irresistible style! Beautiful bedding, furniture, strollers, diaper bags, unique toys, blankets and more...for the discerning shopper. Come and experience our fine assortment of merchandise for babies and toddlers. Online shopping, Baby registry, & Gift wrapping available. **Look for our ad in this section. See coupon section for valuable savings.**

Direct Interiors

2005 Clarke Blvd, Brampton, Ont, L6T 5E7. • 905-791-9660 • www.directinteriors.com
Complete line of discount children's furniture, from modern to traditional. Great prices.
Impeccable service. We can help you put together the room: rugs, accessories and linens. •
Cheque • Mon-Sat: 9:30-5:30.

Jacadi Children

Hazelton Lanes 416-923-1717, Bayview Village 416- 733-1717, Toronto, Ont, M5R 3R9. •
Nursery furniture [cribs,cradles or complete rooms] nursery accessories & strollers. • Ages: 0-12.

Kiddiesworld Of Furniture

1911 Dundas St E, Mississauga, Ont, L4X 1M1. • 905-624-9092 • www.kiddiesworld.ca
Family operated since 1980. 13,000 sq. ft. of furniture and accessories from newborn to teens.
On display, 85 cribs, all Perego and Bugaboo strollers and highchairs, Dutailier gliders, bunkbeds
and bedroom sets. We feature Ragazzi, Natart, Pali, Morigeau Lepine and many more. •
Ages: 0-Teen • ♿.

Your kids are one of a kind. So are we

The city's most eclectic collection
of fabulous furnishings, funky
bedding and accessories. We have great
stuff for kids of all ages. So drop by
with the kids and get inspired.

Kids at Home - Home Furnishing and Design
2086 Queen St E, Toronto, Ont, M4E 1E1. • 416-698-9726 • www.kidsathome.com
Featuring the most eclectic collection of one-of-a-kind furnishings, fabulous beddings and funky
accessories you'll find anywhere. We have great stuff for all kids - Tiny Kids, Little Kids and Big
Kids. Visit us and get inspired! **Look for our ad in this section.**

Li'L Niblets & Baby Sprouts
1654 Avenue Road, Toronto, Ont, M5M 3Y1. • 416-249-9881 • www.lilniblets.com
Does "your" baby store offer a private nursing room and a test track for demonstrating strollers?
If not, why not drop by to see what we're all about. **Look for our ad in this section.** • *VISA*,
Interac • Mon-Tue: 10-6, Wed-Fri: 10-9, Sat: 10-6, Sun: 11-6 • &.

Macklem's Baby Carriage
2223 Dundas St W, Toronto, Ont, M6R 1X6. • 416-531-7188 • www.macklems.com
Specialists in carriages and baby furniture. Family business since 1945. Full line of strollers, cribs,
juvenile furniture, bedding and baby accessories. Very competitive pricing. Experienced, knowledgeable staff. We repair strollers and refurbish English prams. • Ages: 0-6 • *VISA*, *Interac* •
Mon-Wed: 9:30-6, Thu-Fri: 9:30-8, Sat: 9:30-5 • &.

Marlene's Just Babies
631 Dupont St, Toronto, Ont, M6G 1Z4. • 416-534-4900 •
Quality baby furniture and accessories. Furniture from Dutailier - E.G. , Morigeau-Lepine, &
Natart. Strollers from Bugaboo, MacLaren, Perego and Silver Cross. • Ages: 0-3 • *VISA*,
Interac, Cheque • Mon-Sat: 10-6 • &.

thank you
for mentioning
you found it in

HELP!
...WE'VE GOT KIDS

A different kind of baby store
Stroller test track • Private nursing room
Gift Registry • And more

1654 Avenue Road, north of Lawrence
416 249 9881 • www.lilniblets.com

Furniture & Accessories

Moms To Be ...and More

1642/1644 Bayview Avenue, Toronto, Ont, M4G 3C2 . • 416-489-3838 or 416-488-9907 • www.momstobeandmore.com
Toronto's #1 baby store for service and selection, with a wide variety of products such as Bugaboo, Perego, Skip-Hop, Bjorn, Dutalier, Natart furnishings etc. Other services include registry, car seat installation and delivery. **Look for our ad in this section.**

■COUPONS■ Mother Hubbard's Cupboards Factory Direct Children & Baby Furniture

14 Brisbane Rd, Toronto, Ont, M3J 2J8. • 416-572-0486 • www.mhcfurniture.com
Mother Hubbard's Cupboards offers the very best baby to teen furniture at factory direct prices. Visit us at our factory showroom. **Look for our ad in this section. See coupon section for valuable savings.**

■COUPONS■ Mother's Choice

1420 Kennedy Rd, Scarborough, Ont, M1P 2L7. • 416-755-2500 •
Baby Stuff for all of your baby's needs. **Look for our ad in this section. See coupon section for valuable savings.**

■COUPONS■ NeoSet Modular Furniture

Call or visit the website for closest location, • 905 405 8500 • www.neosetcanada.com
Just imagine the fun your child can experience by creating their own unique bedroom. Custom designed rooms can include a study area, a bed, a closet... a place for everything. Different colours, sizes & shapes combine to create the perfect solution for each individual child. Brighten up your space with Neoset - Designed, Delivered & Installed for you! **Look for our ad in this section. See coupon section for valuable savings.** • Ages: 2+ • VISA, ⊕, ▓, Cheque • �& .

FACTORY DIRECT SAVINGS OF 20-65%

Mother Hubbard's Cupboards

14 Brisbane Rd, Toronto

416-572-0486 · www.mhcfurniture.com

pottery barn kids

Specializing in unique home furnishings including bedding, bath products, rugs, accessories, window treatments and lighting for nurseries, children's bedrooms, playrooms and family spaces.

Baby & Gift Registry are Available.

100 Bloor Street West
Sherway Gardens
Yorkdale Shopping Centre

Visit us at www.potterybarnkids.ca

$COUPON$ Nestings Kids/The Pod
418 Eglinton Ave W, Toronto, Ont, M5N 1A2. • 416-322-0511 • www.nestingskids.com
Nestings extraordinary home furnishings store just for kids. Exclusive furniture & custom linens from newborn to teen. Check out The Pod, our lower level for everything hip and modern. Unique accessories, gifts, toy boxes and full baby registry. **Look for our ad in this section. See coupon section for valuable savings.** • Mon-Sat: 10-6, Sun: 12-5.

Potato Skins Inc
2073 Yonge St, Toronto, Ont, M4S 2A2. • 416-484-6299 •
The affordable custom and casual slipcover experts.

Pottery Barn Kids
100 Bloor Street West, Sherway Gardens, Yorkdale Shopping Centre, •
www.potterybarnkids.ca
Pottery Barn Kids specializes in unique home furnishings including bedding, bath products, rugs, accessories, window treatments and lighting for nurseries, children's bedrooms, playrooms and family spaces. Baby & Gift Registry are available. **Look for our ad in this section.**

▪ Handpainted Furniture

$COUPON$ K.I.D.S. - Kid's Interior Design Store
201 Millway Ave, Unit 1 (N of Hwy 7 off Jane), Concord, Ont, L4K 5K8. • 905-738-4055 •
www.kidsroomscanada.ca
Beautiful handpainted furniture at Kid's Interior Design Store. **Look for our ad in this section. See coupon section for valuable savings.** • *VISA*, ⊕, ▓▓, *Interac* • Mon: closed, Tue-Wed: 10-6, Thu: by appt, Fri: 10-6, Sat: 10-5, Sun: 12-5.

Madelaine's Mom
416-486-4743 •
Custom painted, personalized baby and children's gifts. • Ages: newborn+ • .

Rosanna's Creations
1967 Bur Oak Ave, Markham, Ont, L6E 1W4. • 416-414-0917 •
Beautifully painted room accessories and furniture to match any decor!

Gifts for Babies & Kids

The items in this section are so unique and special that we hesitate to restrict them to babies or kids. We have sent personalized stationery to adult friends or hand-embroidered towels to relatives. Everyone loves a gift custom made especially for them! That is what you will find in this category. Have you ever thought of having a portrait made of your child … or having a plaster cast made of your baby's hands & feet for your parents? There are many wonderful gifts listed here. You can also order lawn signs and surprise a friend who has just had a baby or a child who is turning "double digits". These are gifts that will be cherished for a lifetime. Go wild! Have fun.

You will find the following sub-categories in this section:
Gifts & Personalized Gifts, Lawn Sign Rentals, Prenatal & Baby Casting

▪ Gifts & Personalized Gifts

Admiral Road Designs
416-963-9891 •
Personalized blankets for babies and kids. • Ages: 0-10.

Ani's Handcrafts
3347 Yonge St, Toronto, Ont, M4N 2M6. • 416-481-6212 •
Personalized appliqué pillows, towels and blankets for babies.

ANY "WEAR" BABY CHAIR
56 Palomino Dr, Richmond Hill, Ont, L4C 0P9. • 905-508-0690 • www.morsweets.com
NEW! Portable baby chair. Folds to size of diaper. Machine washable/dryable. Patterns: girls/boys. 4-12 mths. MAKES A GREAT GIFT!

Baby Shoe Bronzers, The
12921 Keele St, King City, Ont, L7B 1G2. • 416-482-6713 •
Mounted. Unmounted. We can bronze almost anything.

BabySteps Children's Fund
905-707-1030 or 1-866-334-4666 • www.babystepsgiftshop.com
Unique gifts for all ages. Personalized puzzle stools & more. Baby's 1st Year & School Frames for monthly/annual photos. All proceeds to Hospital for Sick Children. Looking for something different? Check us out! • Ages: NB+ • 𝗩𝗜𝗦𝗔, ⊕, ▦.

Babywear Boutique
1-877-778-3884 •
Visit our online babywear boutique to shop for wraps, slings, shoes, toys and more!

Bug in a Rug Canada Inc.
866 766 2349 •
The "Bug" is a multi-purpose travel wrap from Australia.

Daniela Easter, Original Oil Portraits
Studio One 70-74 Main St. N. , Brampton, Ont, L6V 1N7 . • 905-460-1606 •
www.beaux-artsbrampton.com
Professional, realistic portraits and scenes, timeless treasured gifts. • Ages: 8-12.

Designs by Melanie
416-219-9892 • www.designsbymelanie.com
Custom designed, handmade scrapbooks, pregnancy journals, baby books, announcements, invitations, brag books and more. Scrapping parties and workshops also available.

$COUPON$ Dick & Jane Inc.

2582 Yonge Street, Toronto, Ont, M4P 2J3. • 416-483-7400 • www.dickandjane.ca
The finest selection of gifts for the discerning tot. **Look for our ad in the Furniture section. See coupon section for valuable savings**.

DreamKids

905-918-2861 •
Unique gifts celebrate, inspire and develop potential. • Ages: newborn +.

Eclectics Unique ArtWare

905-886-8843 •
Swarovski "HeartBead" Pendants and "Sign-in" Caricature Canvases.

Ellaine Feferman Personalized Keepsake Baby Blankets

416-443-8842 • www.thebabyblanketlady.com
Custom knit in 100% Cotton with your baby's name. $ 105.00. Call 416- 443-8842 or go to www.thebabyblanketlady.com. • By appointment

Fuzzy Buddies

382 Osiris Drive, Richmond Hill, Ont, L4C 2P9. • 905-508-0026 • www.fuzzybuddies.ca as
Individual stuff a buddy kits. $19.75 + shipping.

Gift Baskets by Design
905 763-1231 •
Specializing in Gift Baskets for Baby. Personal/Corporate orders welcome. Delivery Available.
Gift giving made Easy! To order call 905-763-1231.

Just For Me Music Inc
416-624-JAZZ • www.justforme.com
Customized CDs with 12 children's classics, revamped with your child's name in every song!
New lyrics teach concepts like safety, transportation, the ABCs, animals, colours and even different languages. Makes a great gift. Order online. • Ages: 0-7.

$COUPON$ K.I.D.S. - Kid's Interior Design Store
201 Millway Ave, Unit 1 (N of Hwy 7 off Jane), Concord, Ont, L4K 5K8. • 905-738-4055 •
www.kidsroomscanada.ca
Beautiful Handpainted Growth Charts, Toy Boxes and more. All can be custom designed and
personalized. **Look for our ad in the Furniture section. See coupon section for valuable savings.** • [VISA],
[image], [image], *Interac* • Mon: closed, Tue-Wed: 10-6, Thu: by appt, Fri: 10-6, Sat: 10-5, Sun: 12-5.

Kid's Juke Box Toronto
905-655-9113 •
Personalized music and books for kids.

Kiddy Chronicles Publishing
905-731-2933 •
Baby , School Year, Jr & High School Chronicles. • Ages: 0-18.

Kozy & Co. Inc. (KozyRoo)
416-909-5458 • www.kozyroo.com
The KozyRoo stroller bunting bag made of corduroy and fleece is the ideal solution for keeping
your child warm during the cooler months. • Ages: newborn-4 yrs.

Liandrea Company, the
2430 Park Row West, Montreal, Que, H4B 2G4. • 1-866-483-0045 • www.liandrea.com
The Liandrea Company produces how-to parenting DVDs. Bringing Baby Home covers newborn
care 0-6 months. Yummy in my Tummy is on nutrition 6-12 months. Make great gifts!

Lil' Miss Knits
650 Queens Quay W. Suite 901, Toronto, Ont, M5V 3N2. • 416-893-2737 •
Handmade blankets, booties, scarves, bags etc. for children.

Lilly Gold
905-508-6888 • www.lillygold.ca
The functional and innovative 3-in-1 Diaper Bag by Lilly Gold! A diaper bag, bassinet and change
station all in one! Great for traveling parents! Available in red or black. • [VISA].

$COUPON$ Mabel's Labels
866-306-2235 • www.mabel.ca
Dispatched within 24 hours! Mabel's Labels are the original Canadian-made Label! Iron-ons,
Stickies, Bag Tags & more. Lots of cute icons. Dishwasher, microwave, laundry & kid tested!
Look for our ad in the Camps section. See coupon section for valuable savings.

Madelaine's Mom

416-486-4743 • www.madelainesmom.ca
Personalized, brightly painted puzzle stools. Hand painted picture frames, jewellery boxes, coat racks, storage chairs and more! Also available - the ULTIMATE DIAPER bag for delivery and beyond. • Ages: newborn+ • Hours: Variable.

Margot's Smashing Designs

905-881-3565 •
Mosaic frames: customized, personalized - birth, bar/bat mitzvah.

Moments in Time by Lisa Husar

905-822-2567 • www.momentsbylisahusar.com
Art portraits (graphite, watercolour) from photographs; Personalized photo albums, memory boxes & tiles, invitations, announcement cards & DVDs; framed family photo montages.

mommy mia inc

213 Carmichael Ave, Toronto, Ont, M5M 2X3. • 416-789-4141 •
Sterling silver personalized bracelets & other unique gifts for kids & moms.

Name Beadz

416-787-8902 •
Sterling silver personalized name bracelets for everyone.

$COUPON$ Name Your Tune

905-508-3633 • www.nyt.ca
A personalized children's music compilation featuring your child's name more than 75 times throughout the 14-song CD. Songs includes much-loved favourites Wheels on the Bus and Old MacDonald. Proud to be fully Canadian. **Look for our ad in this section. See coupon section for valuable savings.** • Ages: 0-5yrs.

Nameography

416- 256-0539 •
Customized black and white framed photograph of a child's name. An original gift!

Namesakes - Personalized Music, Books and more

905-770-9509 •
Personalized, books, music, clocks and other gifts.

Nestings Kids/The Pod

418 Eglinton Ave W, Toronto, Ont, M5N 1A2. • 416-322-0511 • www.nestingskids.com
Unique accessories, handpainted furniture, toyboxes, rugs, lighting, one-of-a-kind gifts, blankets, baby registry and more. **Look for our ad in the Furniture & Accessories section.** • Mon-Sat: 10-6, Sun: 12-5.

Play at Home Music

905-881-3629 •
High quality musical instruments for kids.

Polka Dot Kids

917 Queen St W, Toronto, Ont • 416-306-2279 • www.polkadotlife.com
We offer a unique collection of timeless products to enrich your baby's and young children's lifestyle using natural fabrics and materials. Discover our passion for style, quality and simplicity in a distinctive Queen Street approach! • Ages: babies & toddlers • Mon-Wed: 12-6, Thu-Fri: 12-6:30, Sat: 11-6:30, Sun: 11-6.

Present Place
416-486-6332 •
Personalized Puzzle Stool. Treasure Boxes, Coat Racks too.

Princess Publishing Inc - Family Medical Journal
905-271-3546 • www.getorganizedjournals.com
GET ORGANIZED! Family Medical Journal is a Handy Book to record Parent's & Kid's Medical Info, all in one place. Makes a perfect baby shower gift - fits into diaper bag or purse. A must-have for new & experienced parents!

Quilt in a Pocket
416-489-9916 •
Children's blankets that fold into their own pockets.

Raintree Studio: Photo Montage
416-626-1932 •
Capturing your cherished moments with Photo Montage.

Sammy G's Personalized Blankets, & Towels
416-444-8272 • www.sammygs.com
Personalized Baby, Adult & Family size blankets. Available in primary colours and pastels. Mix & match these 2 layered polar fleece blankets. NEW! Personalized baby bibs, hats, onesies and towels. Delivery available. Call Samantha Graff for details.

Sew Cozy
416-531-4948 •
Handmade quilts, blanket+ - Fun, funky, functional.

Sew What?!
35 Edenbridge Dr, Thornhill, Ont, L4J 7V1. • 905-882-6558 •
Personalized polar fleece blankets and pillows.

Solo Para Ti Inc
905-508-6888 • www.soloparatigifts.com
Unique gifts at fantastic prices! Monthly specials! Specializing in Mexican Pewter serveware. Children welcome! Gift wrapping and delivery service available. • *VISA*, ⊕, 🖃, *Interac* • By appointment.

Sports Poster Warehouse
1947 Leslie St, Toronto, Ont, M3B 2M3. • 416-696-8353 • www.SportsPosterWarehouse.com
World's greatest selection of sports posters - over 3,500 different in stock! Perfect gifts for boys and girls who love to play or watch sports. Our giant showroom is fun for fans of all ages! • Ages: 7+ • Mon-Wed: 11-6, Thu-Fri: 11-9, Sat: 10-6, Sun: 12-6.

Sugar Sugar Creative Videos
647-200-7290 • www.sugarsugarvideos.com
Creative Videos of Children. Dust off your rarely watched home videos and gather your favourite photos....We'll transform them into something you'll watch over and over again.

Tag Along
416-481-7286 •
Personalized tags for diaper bags and more!

The Wrappers, Toronto's Fabulous Kids' Label Catalogue

416-250-6020 • www.thewrappers.ca
Address labels, notepads, notecards, stationery, luggage tags, fun labels, custom pillowcase, towels and more. All personalized with professionally created, funky and fabulous, colourful graphics that kids and adults love! Choose the graphic that best describes the child's favourite activities and unique personality. Perfect for school or camp. Great gifts!

Toys Toys Toys

Fairview Mall, 1800 Sheppard Ave, North York, Ont, M2J 5A7. • 416-493-5416 •
Fabulous gifts for babies and children. Fantastic assortment of toys, games & puzzles. Largest selection of Fisher Price products in the city. Great Gund toys. Our friendly staff provides personalized service to help you find that perfect gift they're sure to love! • Other Locations: Eaton Centre 416-979-1121, Square One 905-273-4148, 2654 Yonge St 416-486-3034, Hillcrest 905-883-3595, TD Centre 416-306-0045, Vaughan Mills 905-738-9664 • *VISA*, ⊝, ▦, *Interac* • Mon-Fri: 10-9, Sat: 9:30-6, Sun: 12-5.

Tulip Press

416-785-9700, Kathryn • kathrynklar@rogers.com
Personalized rubber stamps. Whimsical hand lettering and illustration: name, address, baby, child, family and more. Choose from 9 ink colours.

Windows of Memories

905-764-9722 •
Custom scrapbooks and paper bag albums.

Wunder Blankets

41 Ridelle Ave, Toronto, Ont, M6B 1H9. • 416-780-1997 •
Custom designed warm and cozy, non-pill, fleece blankets with your child's name...many colours and patterns to choose from. Monogrammed baby towels, bath sheets, bibs, hats, onesies and pillows. Great baby gifts and birthday presents. • Cheque.

You Name It, Baby!

365A Wilson Ave, Unit 211 (Bath/Wilson), North York, Ont, M3H 1T3. • 416-638-1227 •
www.younameitbaby.com
Funky Gifts for Babies and Toddlers. Personalized stools, growth charts, and blankets. Canvas art work and hand-painted letters. Unique room accessories. Stylish clothing. Get the same gifts the Celebrities are buying for their babies. • Ages: NB+.

ZACK & ZOE Bilingual (French/English) Educational DVD

www.zackandzoedvd.com
A one-of-a-kind children's BILINGUAL DVD that is both fun and educational. Whether your child speaks English and would like to discover French or speaks French and would like to be exposed to English, this DVD is perfect! • Ages: 0-7.

Zoodonyms

1-888-285-5512 •
Handcrafted name puzzles. Great baby or birthday gifts. Worldwide shipping.

▪ Lawn Sign Rentals

A True Expressions Lawn Greetings

416-757-5683 •
Baby Storks/lawn animals for all occasions.

Order a copy for a friend
OR
order an extra copy for yourself

Help!... We've Got Kids is available at bookstores and children's stores everywhere OR use the coupon at the back of this book and we'll mail one right to you!

Tel: (416) 444-7678 ▪ Fax: (416) 444-1289
Email: info@helpwevegotkids.com
Website: www.helpwevegotkids.com

All Original Lawn Signs
416-735-9167 •
Lawn signs for every special occasion.

Flamingos & Friends
416-255-8999 •
Storks, yard card, flamingos, penguins, since...1989.

Special Greetings
905-584-6990 • www.specialgreetings.ca
Don't just say congratulations! Say surprise ... Gotcha! with an 8 foot lawn sign/ornament rental. Storks, clowns, bride & groom cats, sheep, teddy bears, butlers, princesses, skunks, flamingos, penguins, pink elephants, pigs & cows. For birthdays, birth announcements and more! • VISA, 😊.

X-press Yourself Lawn Signs
14 Beamish Crt, Brampton, Ont, L6P 0X8. • 905-794-9075 • www.xpresslawnsign.com
Professionally airbrushed lawn signs. As unique as the person it is for. A great gift for any occasion from birthdays to birth announcements.

▪ Prenatal & Baby Casting

Handsies & Footsies Forever
416-233-0716 • www.handsiesandfootsies.com
Hand and feet castings for babies, toddlers and children. Safe. Clean. Non-toxic. In-home appointments and mommy groups. • Ages: 0-7 yrs.

$COUPON$ Snugabug Portrait & Art Studios
1160 Clarence St Units 3 & 4, Vaughan, Ont, L4H 2V3. • 905-264-2640 • www.snugabugportraits.com
Helping capture the miracle of pregnancy with prenatal castings. Personalized hand painted accessories and canvas art. Unique and unforgettable keepsakes. **Look for our ad in the Photography section. See coupon section for valuable savings.**

In theory, we should have enough time to casually shop for dinners, prepare our kids' lunches and plan for nutritious, elegant meals ... in reality, we do not! Although we may enjoy planning and preparing some of the time, many of us are too busy with daily responsibilities to spend time shopping and cooking every day. This section will help you save time and even money. You can order some of your daily groceries, drinks or diapers in bulk. You can order some nutritious meals or you can even have a chef come to your house for those special occasions when you really need it. Try these out ... we think you'll like them. They also make a wonderful gift for a new mom or sick friend.

$COUPON$ **Look for this company's coupon at the back of the book**

All Good Things... Delicious, Nutritious, Customized Dishes
122 Millicent St, Toronto, Ont, M6H 1W4. • 416 516-4680 •
Specializing in food allergies/sensitivities. Frozen meal delivery in the GTA.

Enjoy Not Cooking Inc
416-604-9035 • www.enjoynotcooking.com
Freshly prepared dinners packaged & labeled with reheating/storage instructions. New parents & busy families discover the joy of not cooking.

Front Door Organics
416-201-3000 • Certified organic groceries - delivered right to your front door.

Imperial Personal Assistant
PO Box 60011 RPO Glen Abbey, Oakville, Ont, L6M 3H2. • 1-866-642-5145 •
You decide schedule anywhere in North America.

$COUPON$ Mr. Case Inc
416-661-CASE (2273) • www.mrcase.com
Celebrating our 21st year in business! Over 5000 brand name supermarket products delivered by the case. Diapers, bottled water, pop & juice, paper products, cleaning supplies and much more! Next day delivery. Call for your free catalogue or order online. **Look for our ad in the Diaper Stores section. See coupon section for valuable savings**. • VISA, [ ], Cheque.

DID WE MISS YOU?
...WE'VE GOT KIDS

Would you like to be listed in the 2008 edition of Help!...We've Got Kids?

Help!...We've Got Kids has over 2000 listings, but inevitably some children's stores or services may be overlooked. If you provide a product or service for kids we would be delighted to include you free of charge. Display ads are also available.

Call (416) 444-7678, fax (416) 444-1289 or
Email info@helpwevegotkids.com and tell us who you are.

Hair Salons

A first haircut can sometimes be traumatic. That is why these hair salons are so valuable. Kids learn that haircuts can be fun, that new experiences can be enjoyable. The specialty Hair Salons listed in this section are experienced at cutting children's hair and making it fun! Kids can sit in special kids' chairs, play with toys or watch DVD's. There are also professional Head Lice removal services for times when you just don't know what else to do. Head Lice is very common among children everywhere. Don't panic but do take action immediately to avoid spreading.

$COUPON$ Look for this company's coupon at the back of the book

Beach Kidz Kutz

1826a Queen St E (3 blocks W of Woodbine), Toronto, Ont, M4L 1G9. • 416-698-3539 •
A friendly children's hair salon in the Beaches, specializing in cutting children's hair with over 15 years of experience. Special kids chair, T.V, train set with play area, toys, first haircut certificate, great hair accessories, etc. • Ages: 2mos + -Teens/Adults welcome • Tue-Fri: 10-6, Sat: 9-5, Sun: 11-3.

Circle of Friends

#5 - 16760 61st Ave. , Surrey, BC, V3S 3V3 . • 888-575-1947 •
Professional Hair and Body care created for kids. • Ages: 1-12yrs.

Little Tots Hair Shop®

Voted "Toronto's #1 Children's Hair Salon" by City Parent Magazine Poll

A Unique Children's Hair Salon & Toy Store
- Ballroom at the Bottom of the Sea
- Kid's Chairs • Toys, party favours
- First Haircut Certificate
- Great hair accessories
- Adult haircuts too

Open 7 days a week

Celebrating 19 years of cutting kid's hair at 2 great locations

Toronto (Beaches)   **Pickering (Mandarin Plaza)**
1926 Queen St.E. (416) 691-9190   1725 Kingston Rd. (905) 428-3484

www.littletotshairshop.com

HAIR SALON

- First Haircut certificate
- Special seats for haircut
- Children friendly atmosphere
- We do moms and dads too!

728 St. Clair Ave. West • **416-658-3271**
1010 Dreamcrest, Unit 10
Mississauga • **905-567-3476**

New Location!

$COUPONS$ Kids Kuts

728 St Clair Ave W, Toronto, Ont, M6C 1B3. • 416-658-3271 •
We specialize in kids and parents cuts! **Look for our ad in this section. See coupon section for valuable savings.** • Other Locations: 1010 Dreamcrest, Unit 10 Mississauga 905- 567-3476 • &.

Lice Squad Inc

1 866 838-LICE or 705-456-4440 • www.licesquad.com, www.nitpickers.ca
Providing professional head lice removal services. Pesticide free. Confidentiality guaranteed.
Parent and teacher trusted since 1999. Franchises available. Call the professionals today!

Melonhead™ children's hair care

10% off Your first visit with this ad!

Friendly experienced stylists
Cool toys and books

3215 Yonge Street • 416.483.7010
Promenade Mall • 905.731.6200
Markville Shopping Centre • 905.944.9098
Bloor Street West • 416.762.0800
Square One, Mississauga • 905.276.0004

MELONHEAD HAIR PRODUCTS FOR KIDS!
for Franchising info call 905.731.6280

"Best Kid's Haircut"-City Parent   www.melonhead.ca

Hair Salons

$COUPON$ Little Tots Hair Shop

1926 Queen St E in the Beaches, Toronto, Ont, M4L 1H5. • 416-691-9190 •
www.littletotshairshop.com
Celebrating our 19th year cutting kid's hair. Sit in a horse, train, boat or firetruck. Play in our ball-room at the bottom of the sea. Toys, party favours and birthday gifts. Open 7 days/week. **Look for our ad in this section. See coupon section for valuable savings.** • Other Locations: 1725 Kingston Rd
905-428-3484 • *VISA*, ⊕, *Interac*, Cheque.

$COUPON$ Melonhead Children's Hair Care

Yonge/Lawrence 416-483-7010, Promenade Mall 905-731-6200, Markville Shopping Centre
905-944-9098, Bloor West Village 416-762-0800, Square One Mississauga 905-276-0004, •
www.melonhead.ca
Top quality kids' hair salon and store. Dedicated to delighting kids and parents. Named "Best Children's Hair Salon" by The Globe and Mail and City Parent. Professional hair stylists. We sell cool toys and books. **Look for our ad in this section. See coupon section for valuable savings**. • Ages:
NB+ • *VISA*, ⊕, ▓, *Interac*.

Nit Pickers

416-391-5453 Jody or 416-447-7674 Lynn •
Headlice removal services.

ScoreCuts -Winning Haircuts for Men

250 Eglinton Ave W, Toronto, Ont, M4R 1A7. • 647-430-3755 •
Sports theme hair salon just for boys.

Shortcuts Hairplace For Kids

963 Eglinton Ave W, Toronto, Ont, M6C 2C4. • 416-789-1131 •
Specializing in children's hair care. Play area with video set-up. Unique tot chair. Experienced pro-fessionals. Friendly stylists. Parent/child specials. Kids' highlights. Glamour parties. • Ages: 6
mos+ • *VISA*, ⊕, *Interac* • Mon-Fri: 10-6, Sat: 9-4, Sun: 11-4 • ♿.

Comments? Questions?

HELP!
...WE'VE GOT KIDS

We'd love to hear from you!
Email us at info@helpwevegotkids.com

Health & Wellness

As parents, we have a heightened concern for the Health and Wellbeing of our families and ourselves. Whether it is a question about Allergies, the need to see a doctor at off-hours, a curiosity about the benefits of infant massage or an interest in First aid & CPR training ... you will find it here. This section will provide you with a start to keeping your family on the road to good health.

<u>You will find the following sub-categories in this section:</u>
After Hours Medical Care, Allergy/Asthma, Children's Massage & Infant Massage Instruction,   Family Dentistry, First Aid & CPR, Health Services for Kids, Nutrition for Kids, Optical Services

About Kids Health - The Hospital for Sick Children
555 University Ave, Toronto, Ont, M5T 1X8. • 416-813-5819 •
Provides child health and safety information. • Ages: 0-18yrs.

Ontario Medical Association "Find a Doctor" service
416-967-2626 •
Call for referrals to find a doctor in your area or visit the 'Find a Doctor Website: www.cpso.on.ca

■ After Hours Medical Care

Call Your Pediatrician
www.callyourped.com, •
This website is designed to give guidelines to common pediatric illnesses and what to do to treat them. It helps parents figure out when to call the doctor, especially in the middle of the night.

Children's After Hours Clinic
1100 Sheppard Ave E Suite 100 & 235 Danforth Ave Ste 100 , • 416-250-5000 or 416-461-3000 www.kidsafterhourscare.ca
No appointment required. Bring your child's health card. Staffed by Paediatricians. Open M-F 6-9:30 pm, 10am-6pm weekends & holidays. NOTE: Danforth clinic open M-F 6-9pm. 10am-6pm weekends & holidays.

Just for Kids Clinic at St. Joseph's Health Centre
30 The Queensway 1st floor Glendale Wing, Toronto, Ont, M6R 1B5. • 416-530-6611 •
M-F 10am-1pm and 2-8 pm. Open weekends/holidays 10-2.

Medvisit Doctors House Call Service Inc
416-631-3000 •
Medical Housecalls. Doctor's fee covered by OHIP. 8am-11:00pm, 7 days/wk.

Shoppers Drug Mart
800-746-7737 x1 •
Call to find the 24 hour pharmacy nearest you.

St. Clair & Avenue Pharmacy
200 St. Clair Avenue W., Toronto, Ont, M4V 1R1. • 416-324-8443 •
We FLAVOUR any prescription or over the counter liquid medication, within minutes.

Trillium Kidz Klinic
100 Queensway W, Mississauga, Ont, L5B 1B8. • 905-848-7174 •
After hours care - no appointment necessary. Bring your health card. • Mon-Fri: 6-9pm, Sat: 2-4, Sun: 2-5.

Health & Wellness

Zidel, Dr. Brian

416-402-2525 •
Does home visits for urgent care evenings and weekends. Covers area from Wilson to St. Clair and Yonge to Dufferin.

▪ Allergy/Asthma

Allergy/Asthma Information Association

416-679-9521 •
Education & support on allergies, anaphylaxis and asthma.

Allergypack

Toll free 1-877- 282-8070 •
Allergy & asthma medication carrying cases.

Anaphylaxis Canada

2005 Sheppard Avenue E, Ste 800, Toronto, Ont, M2J 5B4. • 416-785-5666 or 866-785-5666 • www.safe4kids.ca
Information, support, education and advocacy for individuals and families with life-threatening allergies. Charitable organization.

Asthma Action Helpline (The Lung Association)

573 King St E, Main Floor, Toronto, Ont, M5A 4L3. • 800-668-7682 • www.on.lung.ca
Staffed by certified asthma educators. Refers to local resources. Teaches what to ask doctors and how to be more informed & more proactive in managing asthma.

Centre for Home Environment Testing

(888) 633-1690 or (905) 726-1689 • www.buildinghealth.org
Creating healthier indoor environments for your family.

ENJO Cleaning - Lisa Borden

744 Briar Hill Ave, Toronto, Ont, M6B 1L3. • 416-785-3048 •
Reduce dust in your house by 30%. Clean every room with only water and ENJO. NO CHEMICALS. Cleaner. Less expensive. Healthier.

MedicAlert

2005 Sheppard Ave E, Ste 800, Toronto, Ont, M2J 5B4. • 416-696-0267 or 800-668-1507 •
Custom-engraved bracelets. Protecting the lives of children with health conditions. • Mon-Fri: 8-6.

Vermont Nut Free Chocolates

10 Island Circle, Grand Isle, VT, 05458. • (888) 468-8373 or (802) 372-4654 •
Gourmet nut free and peanut free chocolates.

▪ Children's Massage & Infant Massage Instruction

Bayview Sheppard R.M.T.

321 Sheppard Ave E., Toronto, Ont, M2N 3B3. • 416-222-3768 •
Massage therapy for pre natal, post natal and instruction on infant massage.

Bayview Village Wellness Centre, Melanie Kemper RMT & Carrie Reynolds RMT

Bayview Village Shopping Centre, 2901 Bayview Ave, Suite 201, Toronto, Ont, M2K 1E6. •
416-221-7724 •
Massage therapy for pre natal, post natal and instruction on infant massage. Increases muscle tone & digestion. Helps teething, colic, constipation and benefits overall health.

Coulter Clinic Infant Massage

2300 Yonge St, Ste 2902 Box 2325, Toronto, Ont, M4P 1E4. • 416-322-6506 •
www.coulterclinic.com
Infant Massage classes for mothers and/or fathers and their babies. Learn to give your child a
soothing, relaxing massage. Help strengthen the digestive, respiratory, circulatory, nervous and
immune systems. Special needs children are welcome. Infants: 1 month to crawling. Older children by appointment. • *VISA*, ⊖, ▣, *Interac*, Cheque.

■ Family Dentistry

Avenue Dental Office, Dr Marlene Morrow & Dr Samuel Mincer

1916 Avenue Road, Toronto, Ont, M5M 4A1. • 416-256-0907 •
Husband and wife dental team providing a full range of services for the entire family. Helping
kids feel at ease with a fully stocked kids playroom, and TV and video in each patient room.
Flexible hours. • *VISA*, ⊖, *Interac*.

Blitz, Dr Nathan, Dentist

3034 Bloor St W., Etobicoke, Ont, M8X 1C4. • 416-233-1234 •
We pamper patients of all ages.

Bobkin, Dr. Alan

8403 Yonge St, Thornhill, Ont, L3T 2C7. • 905-881-5787 • www.straightenteeth.com
Specializing in all types of orthodontic treatment for kids and adults. Over 20 years professional
experience. **Look for our ad in this section.** • Other Locations: 1013 Wilson Ave, Ste 204 , 416-245-
5155 • *VISA*, ⊖, Cheque • Mon-Fri: 9-5.

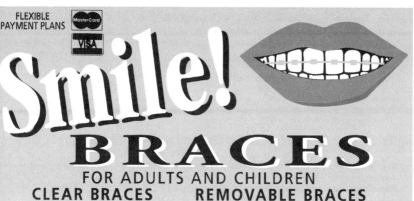

Chin, Dr. Joan; Family Dentist
1414 Lakeshore Rd W, Mississauga, Ont, L5J 1J1. • 905-823-9555 •
Gentle dental care for kids & families.

Dental Emergency Service
1650 Yonge St, Main Floor (N. of St. Clair), Toronto, Ont, M4T 2A2. • 416-485-7121 • www.dentalemergency.com
Emergency dental service offering emergency dental care from 8am-midnight, 7 days per week.

Kellerstein, Dr Jeremy; Orthodontist
935 Sheppard Ave W Unit 4, Toronto, Ont, M3H 2T7. • 416-630-0020
Orthodontist for children and adults. Sheppard at Allen Rd, steps from TTC (Downsview subway). Free parking. No headgears/bulky appliances - quicker, more accurate and esthetic treatment using latest technology. Free initial consultation. Payment plans available. Flexible hours. Ages: 8 - ADULT.

Leaside Children's Dentistry - Dr Katherine Ing
586 Eglinton Ave E, Ste 607, Toronto, Ont, M4P 1P2. • 416-486-6765 •
Specializing in dentistry for children in a comfortable, friendly environment. Kids of all ages and abilities welcome.

Linetsky, Dr. Laurel; Village Family Dental Care
551 Eglinton Ave West, Toronto, • 416-485-5000 •
Family Dental Practice. We make the dental experience fun! Your children will want to come back. Child friendly office. TVs in every room. Fabulous, experienced and patient staff. Laughing gas available. Check out our terrific treasure box!

Rosenberg, Dr. Miriam
1746 Bayview Ave, Toronto, Ont, M4G 3C4. • 416-488-0351 •
A visit to the dentist can be fun! Examine the instruments. Push a button or two. I will carefully and gently explain each step of the process. You will learn dental hygiene and leave with a smile and a little gift.

Stein, Dr. Howard & Associates - Children's Dental Specialists
4040 Finch Ave E, ste 201, Scarborough, Ont, M1S 4V5. • 416-298-3232 •
www.childrensteeth.com
Specialists in dentistry for children from infancy through teens. Our specialist approach gives kids a fun start to dental health. • *VISA*, ⊖, *Interac*.

Telch, Dr F; Charendoff, Dr M; Charendoff, Dr G; Michelberger, Dr D
2901 Bayview Ave, Ste 219, North York, Ont, M2K 1E6. • 416-224-1777 •
Our family dental clinic offers comprehensive case management. Whether you or your family require preventative, periodontic, restorative, cosmetic or orthodontic treatment, we will be most happy to discuss your individual requirements with you. • *VISA*, ⊖, *Interac*, Cheque.

York Mills Orthodontics, Dr. David Morrow
300 York Mills Rd, Ste 202, Toronto, Ont, M2L 2Y5. • 416-391-4222 • www.yorkmillsortho.ca
Specializing in orthodontic treatment for children and adults including mini braces, invisible braces and invisalign. Bright, friendly, open environment. Kids play area with video games, movies and books. Watch movies while getting your braces on. Flexible hours. • *VISA*, ⊖, *Interac*, Cheque.

▪ First Aid & CPR Instruction

2HEALTH First Aid & Child Safety
416-873-8606 • www.2health.com
A choking child is cardiac arrest in 60 seconds. Learn to rescue and be confident! Convenient, practical in-home training for 4-12 people. Training thousands of parents since 1992. We're Friendly, Recommended and Red Cross certified. Weekends or weeknights, all ages.

Allied First Aid/CPR Training
905-391-6118 Pickering • Alliedfact@aol.com
Be prepared for emergencies. Learn first aid and CPR in relaxed and fun-filled courses. In home or office locations. WSIB and Heart & Stroke certified.

Canadian Red Cross Society, The
1623 Yonge St, Toronto, Ont, M4T 2A1. • 416-480-2500 •
Learn CPR , rescue breathing, choking and much more.

Champion 1st Aid
150 Moore Ave, Toronto, Ont, M4T 1V8. • 416-487-4828 •
Your ultimate on-site first aid training.

F.A.S.T. Rescue Inc
905-751-0149 or 866-706-7283 •
First Aid & CPR Training. First Aid Kits.

First Choice First Aid Training
416-409-7439 •
First aid/CPR training. WSIB, HSFO approved.

Staying Alive
1229 Forestwood Drive, Mississauga, Ont, L5C 1H6. • 905-783-8523 •
First aid training for parents and caregivers of young children.

■ Health Services for Kids

Alexander Mostovoy - HD, DHMS, Doctor of Homeopathic Medicine
3910 Bathurst St, Ste 202, Toronto, Ont, M3H 3N8. • 416-638-7555 •
Safe, effective homeopathic treatment for children and families.

Bedwetting Help
Ste 800, 200 Yorkland Blvd, Toronto, Ont, M2J 5C1. • 416-490-0121 •
Bedwetting is a treatable medical condition.

Create Cord Blood Bank
790 Bay Street Ste 1130, Toronto, Ont, M5G 1N8. • 416-813-4700 •
A once-in-a-lifetime opportunity to collect and secure crucial cord blood.

Homeopathic Care by Elena Gribanova, HD, MD (rus)
1896 Avenue Road Suite 2B, Toronto, Ont • 416-565-3438
416-322-9550 • Homeopathic care for kids and families.

Insception Biosciences Inc.
1620 Tech Avenue Unit #1 , Mississauga, Ont, L4W5P4. • 866-606-2790 • www.insception.com
Canada's largest, most experienced cord blood bank.

Jill Kelner, Doctor of Naturopathic Medicine
100 Harbord Street, 2nd Fl, Toronto, Ont, M5S 1G6. • 416-923-4860 x2 •
Safe, effective naturopathic medical treatment for infants, children & families.

Public Health Nurses: Region of Peel
905-799-7700 • www.peelregion.ca
Public Health Nurses - answer parents' and caregivers' questions about children from birth to age 6. Discipline/behaviour, sleep, mealtimes, toilet learning, community programs and resources. Home visiting program.

Health & Wellness

TOMA Foundation for Burned Children
PO Box 754, 169 The Donway, Don Mills, Ont, M3C 4G5. • (877) 410-8662 (TOMA) • www.fondtomafound.org
Bringing concrete and material help to burned kids. Volunteer psychologists, counselling, parent support and victim support. Visit us online for more information.

Upper Canada Naturopathic Clinic
Unit 200-7089 Yonge St, Thornhill, Ont, L3T 2A7. • 416-720-9670 •
Naturopathic medicine for the whole family. Nutrition, homeopathy, acupuncture, herbal medicine, focus on pediatric and special needs.

Young Travellers Clinic
2100 Finch Ave W, Ste 202, North York, Ont, M3N 2Z9. • 416-661-5997 • www.cdc.gov
Travel related counselling and immunizations for children and families. • By appointment

■ Nutrition for Kids

House of Nutritional Wellness
171 Seabreeze Ave, Thornhill, Ont, L4J 9H2. • 905-709-9771 •
Baby food cooking classes and private consultations.

Lytle, Dr. Millie ND
502-111 Peter St., Toronto, Ont, M5V 2H1. • 416 923 4325 •
Family nutrition education. Food Introductions. Home visits.

Nutrition in Motion ... We do the diet, You lose the weight
801 Eglinton Ave W, Ste 105, Toronto, Ont, M5N 1E3. • 416-486-1646 •
Diet meals delivered to your door daily.

Real Food for Real Kids
1415 Bloor St W, Toronto, Ont, M6P 3L4. • 416-410-5437 •
Healthy food for kids at daycare.

Sprout Right ... nutrition from tummy to toddler
679 Beresford Ave, Toronto, Ont, M6S 3C4. • 416-471-9267 • www.sproutright.com
Nutrition Counselling services offering informative workshops and private consultations to health conscious mothers-to-be, new mothers and their babies and toddlers.

■ Optical Services

Josephson Opticians
566 Eglinton Ave E (at Avenue Rd), Toronto, Ont • 416-545-1845 • www.josephsonopt.com
Great selection of frames from Roots, Lafont, Adidas and Lindberg Air Titanium. Ask about our Kids Package. Eye appointments can be arranged. • Other Locations York Mills and Bayview 416-444-8485, Humbertown Centre 416-232-1222.

Squint Eyewear
286 Lakeshore Rd E., Oakville, Ont • 905-339-2227 • www.squinteyewear.com
Exclusive frames from European designers. Specializing in pediatric fittings. Eye appointments can be arranged. • Other Locations York Mills and Bayview 416-444-8485, Humbertown Centre 416-232-1222.

For quick reference, we have included both emergency numbers and some warm lines for various types of family, kid-related or personal assistance. Please show these to your kids – sometimes they need an objective outsider to listen when they need help.

211 Toronto (Findhelp Information Services)
211 • www.211toronto.ca
Dial 211 for FREE information about community, social, health and government services in Toronto. 211 is multilingual and open 24 hours a day.

Birth Certificates (Ontario Government)
416-325-8305 •

Catholic Children's Aid Society of Toronto
26 Maitland St, Toronto, Ont, M4Y 1C6. • 416-395-1500 • www.ccas.toronto.on.ca
Confidential child protection services, adoption, family counselling, child management, foster care, family support programs for Toronto Catholic families. • Other Locations 5230 Dundas St W, 30 Drewry Ave, 1880 Birchmount Rd, 900 Dufferin St, 2494 Danforth Ave • Ages: 0-16.

Child Find Ontario
440A Britannia Rd E, Mississauga, Ont, L4Z1X9. • 1-866-Kid-Tips (866-543-8477) • www.ontario.childfind.ca
Offers hope and help to families by teaching how to keep children safe, and helping find them should they go missing. Free. Recognized by police, Kidcheck safety clinics. Admin: 9am - 5pm. Hotline open 24/7.

Child Tax Benefit (Automated Line)
(800) 387-1193 • www.ccra.gc.ca/benefits

Children's Aid Society of Toronto
416-924-4646 • www.torontocas.ca
Child protection services; family counselling and supervision; foster care services; adoption; adoption disclosure; pregnancy counselling and support services for adolescents.

Children's Safety Association of Canada
385 The West Mall , STE 250, Etobicoke, Ont, M9C1E7. • 416-620-1584 •
Safety questions? Call (888) 499-4444 for information on topics such as: carseat information, poisonous plants & household products, drowning prevention, sun safety, playgrounds & much more! FREE. Every caller gets a free safety pack. • Ages: 0-5.

consumerinformation.ca
Canada's one-stop shop for comprehensive consumer information - featuring financial calculators as well as tips on safe shopping on-line and protecting yourself from fraud. Includes Toy Report, electronic birth certificates and other consumer information about children and families.

Distress Centre (24 Hours)
416-408-4357 •
Call 24 hours. Help available for family related issues.

Information and Referral for Addictions and Mental Health
416-595-6111 •
Information on addiction and mental health. Referral for treatment. Support line from Tuesday - Saturday 3pm - 9 pm. • Mon-Sun: 9-9.

Jewish Family & Child Service

4600 Bathurst St, Toronto, Ont, M2R 3V3. • 416-638-7800 • www.toronto.com/jfcs
24 hour emergency service. • ♿.

Justice For Children & Youth

415 Yonge St Suite 1203, Toronto, Ont, M5B 2E7. • 416-920-1633 • www.jfcy.org
Legal clinic serving kids younger than 18. • Ages: 0-17 • ♿.

Kids Help Phone

Toll-free 1-800-668-6868 • www.kidshelpphone.ca
Confidential counselling service for kids aged 4-25.

Kids' Line: Regional Municipality of York Community Services & Housing Dept

(888) 703-KIDS (5437) or (905) 830-9487 (Newmarket) •
Info on Childcare, Early Intervention Services, Preschool Speech & Language, Childcare Fee
Assistance, Infant Hearing.

La Leche League Of Metropolitan Toronto

416- 483-3368 •
Specially trained experienced, breastfeeding mothers (volunteers) will answer breastfeeding
questions or give information on local groups. Call for the volunteer nearest you.

Maternity Benefits (Canada Employment & Immigration) Automated Service

1-800-206-7218 •

Metro Police General Information (for non-emergencies)

416-808-2222 •

Motherisk

416-813-6780 •
Information for expectant or new mothers on a variety of topics including nutrition and medication.

National Eating Disorder Information Centre

416-340-4156 • www.nedic.on.ca
Information on eating disorders, referrals and help. Distress centre hotline (416) 408-4657.

PhoneFriend - A befriending line for kids

905-459-4590 •
We are here to: comfort and support you, listen when others won't, understand when others
can't, pray with you when asked, provide information and referral, respect your choices and
needs. 4pm-7pm Mon-Fri. 10am-6pm in summer.

Poison Information Hotline

416-813-5900 •
Call immediately if your child has ingested any poisonous substance.

Police, Fire and Ambulance Emergency

911 •

Public Health Nurses: Toronto Health Connection / York Region Health Connection

5100 Yonge St, 2nd Fl, Toronto, Ont, M2N 5V7. • 416- 338-7600- Toronto or 1-800- 361-5653 or 905-895-8004- York Region • www.city.toronto.on.ca/health • www.region.york.on.ca
Public health nurses answer questions on breastfeeding and caring for newborns and school-aged children. Immunization, feeding, toilet training, community programs and resources, etc. Free, confidential counselling. • Ages: 0-19.

Reference Canada

1-800-O-CANADA • www.canada.gc.ca
Do you have a question for the federal government but you're not sure who to call? We can help.

Region of Peel - Public Health:Family Health

905-799-7700 • www.peelregion.ca
Nurses answer parents' questions about children from birth to age 6. Discipline/behaviour, immunization, sleep, mealtimes, toilet learning, community programs & resources. Home visits.

Telehealth Ontario

Ministry of Health and Long -Term Care, 10th Fl Hepburn Block, 80 Grosvenor St, Toronto, Ont, M7A 1S3. • 1-866-797-0000 • www.health.gov.on.ca
24 hour, 7 day a week, FREE, confidential service that you can call to get health advice or general health information. Staffed by qualified Registered Nurses. In English and French with translation support for other languages and TTY access.

Toronto Transit Commission Information Line

416-393-4636 • www.city.toronto.on.ca
Complete transit information 24 hours a day.

Modelling and acting can benefit children in more ways than one. Acting can teach kids how to speak clearly, with proper inflections and how to present effectively. These are lifeskills that will benefit them throughout their careers. If your child is interested in modeling or acting and you are ready to commit to taking them to auditions, you should consider getting an agent or at least some professional advice. It should not require a substantial monetary commitment up front. Call the various agencies listed here and ask as many questions as you can. You can also ask for references and check with AMIS. They can give you objective advice about what to look for and what to watch out for. Good luck!

AAB Talent

512 King St East, Ste 108, Toronto, Ont, M5A 1M1. • 416-594-0222 •
Promoting kids into commercials, television, movies and more.

Acting and Modelling Information Service (AMIS)

c/o 215 Spadina Ave, Ste 210, Toronto, Ont, M5T 2C7. • 416-977-3832 • www.amisontario.com
Your child could be a star - or you could be ripped off. Before you spend a cent, call AMIS for free advice on getting started in the fashion and entertainment industry. • Free.

Applause Model & Talent Management

499 Main St S #208, Brampton, Ont, L6Y 1N7. • 905-457-7571 •
Our kids have appeared in numerous advertisements, catalogues, fashion shows, commercials and film work including: Eatons, The Bay, Kelloggs, KFC, Hyundai, Huggies, Fisher Price and Doc. Ages: 0-18yrs • *VISA*, ⊕, Cheque • Mon-Thu: 11-7, Fri-Sat: 10-2.

Baby Face Talent Agency

1498 Yonge St , Toronto, Ont, M4T 1Z6. • 416-922-9906 •
Representing babies & kids from 0-12yrs. Print, commercials, movies.

Carolyn's Model & Talent Agency Ltd

1965 Britannia Rd W #210, Mississauga, Ont, L5M 4Y4. • 905-542-8885 or 416-544-0232 •
www.carolynsonline.com
Represents all ages for television commercials, movies, fashion and lifestyle print. Our models are seen in catalogues, tv commercials and print ads. In business over 20 years. Member of the Better Business Bureau. • Other Locations Toronto.

Eleanor Fulcher International Ltd

615 Yonge St #200, Toronto, Ont, M4Y 1Z5. • (416) 922-1945 •
Model & talent agency and school since 1960. • Ages: 3+.

Kamera Kids

174 Spadina Ave, Ste 100, Toronto, Ont, M5T 2C2. • 416-504-5433 •
Reputation! Reputation! Reputation! Commercials, catalogues, and more. • Ages: 0-16.

Max Agency

2063 Yonge St, ste 202, Toronto, Ont, M4S 2A2. • 416-482-5392 •
Principal TV/Film Modeling agency.

Toronto Kids Talent

477 Richmond St W Ste 601, Toronto, Ont, M5V 3E7. • 416-504-7833 •
With over 30 years collective industry experience, we can help you discover your child's showbiz potential. • Ages: 6-16.

Nearly New

Nearly New shops are a great way to purchase beautiful, designer outfits, baby accessories, furniture, outerwear and special occasion wear. They are also great for finding that extra high chair, stroller or crib for Grandma's house or the cottage and for the stuff that you want, but don't really need.

Nearly new does not mean old or worn out. Most resale or consignment shops are very selective with their clothing, equipment and accessories. If you have something you no longer need, ask because some stores also accept consignments.

$ COUPON $ **Look for this company's coupon at the back of the book**

Ages & Stages
1552 Danforth Ave, Toronto, Ont, M4J 1N4. • 416-465-7777 •
We offer good quality gently used children's wear, maternity fashions, equipment and accessories at affordable prices. Sizes NB - 16. Change facilities onsite. • [VISA], [card], [card], *Interac*.

Double Take
310 Gerrard St E, Toronto, Ont, M5A 2G7. • 416-925-6069 (223) •
Nearly new for the entire family.

Fashion Go-Round
6 Brentwood Rd S , Etobicoke, Ont, M8Z 3N2. • 416-236-1220 •
Ladies' and kidswear on consignment. Household treasures also available.

Hand Me Downs
Markham 905-479-1869, Newmarket 905-836-7701, •
Quality new & used children's clothing & maternity wear. • Ages: 0-16 • [VISA], [card], *Interac* &.

$ COUPON $ Kaleidoscope
159 Lakeshore Rd E, Mississauga, Ont, L5G 4T9. • 905-891-8530 • www.kaleidoscopekids.ca
A-1 CONDITION New and gently used Children's Designer Clothing. PLUS: Brand New Toys & Gift Items. Size newborn - 14. **Look for our ad in this section. See coupon section for valuable savings.**

Little Treasures Clothing Co Inc, The
265 Church St, Oakville, Ont, L6J 1N7. • 905-844-8466 •
Secondhand maternity and children's fashion boutique.

Mulberry Bush
376 Kingston Rd, Pickering, Ont, L1V 6K4. • 905-509-6750 •
Kids, teen, maternity, toys, baby equipment on consignment.

$COUPON$ Once Upon A Child
Ajax: 905-427-4194, Brampton: 905-792-4347, Toronto (north): 416-661-0678, Toronto (south): 416-485-2776, Newmarket: 905-898-2002 • www.ouaccanada.com
"Kid's Stuff With Previous Experience" - We buy and sell new and "gently used" children's items 7 days a week. Furniture, equipment, toys, books and clothing. Please check our web site for all the information on your nearest store. **Look for our ad opposite the Copyright page at the front of the book. See coupon section for valuable savings.** • &.

$COUPON$ Play 'n' Wear
1986 Avenue Rd, Toronto, Ont, M5M 4A4. • 416-782-0211 • www.playnwear.com
Children's consignment shop specializing in new and lightly used clothing (infant - teen), toys, books, sports equipment, maternity fashions, baby furniture and accessories. Top quality. Consignments accepted. In business for over 25 years! Call for summer hours. **Look for our ad in this section. See coupon section for valuable savings.** • Ages: 0-18 • VISA, ⊕, Interac • Mon-Fri: 9:30-6, Sat: 10-5, Sun: 1-5 • &.

Precious Seconds
14 Oxford St, Unit 12, Richmond Hill, Ont, L4C 4L5. • 905-883-8885 •
Quality clothing, toys, books, videos, equipment, giftware. • &.

Roundabout Kids Inc
332 Lakeshore Rd E, Mississauga, Ont, L5G 1H4. • 905-274-9561 •
High quality children's resale merchandise. • Ages: 0 - 12.

Soldbymoms.com
www.soldbymoms.com
The best place to buy and sell used kids' stuff! Find everything including baby furniture, sports equipment, toys, maternity wear.

Twice as Nice
683 St Clair Ave W, Toronto, Ont, M6C 1A7. • 416-656-9969 •
Bright, cheerful children's resale store. Clothing, furniture, new and used equipment. Deux par Deux, Gap, Gymboree, New Yorker, Kindergo, Exersaucers... we've got it all! • &.

Wee Cycled Kids Stuff
389 Main St N, Unit 4, 1 block N of Vodden, Brampton, Ont, L6X 1P6. • 905-456-9220 •
Wee buy, sell, trade, consign new and pre-loved kids stuff! • Ages: 0-size 16.

This section contains a wide array of programs for babies, toddlers and preschoolers. Research has shown that children from birth to 5 years old gain significant value from age-appropriate stimulation and education. There are so many programs to choose from that there is something for everyone. Whether you and your child want to explore or experience Art, Music, Movement, Sports or a bit of everything, you will find it here.

You will also find companies offering fitness programs for new parents WITH their babies. What a great way to get back in shape and spend time with your baby! Another fun way for a new parent to spend an afternoon is to go to a movie theatre that makes special accommodations for young babies and their parents. Check out these listings for new and interesting things to do together.

You will find the following sub-categories in this section:
Art, Early Learning & Enrichment, Early Years Centres, Family Resource Centres, Fitness for Mom & Baby, Kindergym & Sport Programs, Multi-Program Centres & More..., Music & Movement, Parent & Baby Movies

---

$ COUPONS Look for this company's coupon at the back of the book

▪ Art

Art Garage Inc, The
2188 Queen St E, Toronto, Ont, M4E 1E6. • 416-686-0960 •
Parent/tot or Drop off programs for ages 1.5+. Special Kindercraft class for 3-5 year olds.

$ COUPONS MESSY HANDS Art Studio
2501 Rutherford Rd, Unit 27, Bldg B, Richmond Hill, Ont • 905-303-MESS (6377) •
www.messyhands.com
Play with paint! Pinch and pound clay! Collage with glue! Watch your child's little face light up as he/she manipulates and explores different art materials. Mom & Baby classes also available. **Look for our ad in the Birthday Parties section. See coupon section for valuable savings.** • Ages: 4-12.

▪ Early Learning & Enrichment

Baby Signs® with Karen
416-223-1993 • www.babysigns.com
Infant sign language. Parent workshop. Play classes. • Ages: 0-2.5yrs.

Bob Rumball Centre for the Deaf - Parent-Infant Program
2395 Bayview Ave, North York, Ont, M2L 1A2. • 416-449-9651 x105 or 416-449-2728 TTY •
www.bobrumball.org
Program for deaf/hard of hearing children and their parents. • Ages: 0-2yrs.

French The Fun Way!
416-518-9093 • www.frenchthefunway.com
Weekly lessons, playgroups, tutoring and help with homework. Children are exposed to French through creative play, songs, rhymes, arts & crafts, sign language, stories and educational games in a fun and stimulating environment. • Ages: 2 1/2 - 8.

Hebrew Fun Time
224 Faywood Blvd, Toronto, Ont, M3H 6A9. • 647-285-7045 or 416-638-2014 •
Learning Hebrew through art, drama, music and movement. Enrich the Jewish holidays and traditions. Enhance creative thinking and self expression with art. Groups and individuals 6-12 years.

Imagine If...Ingredients for Creating your Own Stories
416-787-2882 (V/TTY) • www.thumbprintadventures.com
5 time award winning 'choose your own adventure story book'. A brand new story every time! Ages: 3 +

Parent/Tot Drop & Off Programs (0-6yrs.)

Kinder Connection, the
8707 Dufferin St, Unit 9, Thornhill, Ont • 905-709-8600 •
Kindergarten & Nursery Enrichment. Certified Teachers. • Other Locations 333 Wilson Ave 416-
636-3000 • Ages: 3-6.

Laugh Learn and Grow Preschool
416-635-7222 • www.laughlearnandgrow.com
A program for children and parents/caregivers to participate in an environment which provides
activities that stimulate education through play. • Ages: 18mos-4yrs.

Little Hands Talking - Sign Language Programs
1013 Woodward Ave, Milton, Ont, L9T 5Y2. • 905-876-2547 • www.littlehandstalking.ca
Sign language for your hearing family! Workshops, classes, sign and sing-a-long programs and
more! Our instructors are certified. • Ages: 6mos-12yrs.

MLK - Multi Lingual Kids
416-223-3382 •
Italian, French, Spanish, Mandarin or English circle time – songs, poems, rhymes & stories.

North Toronto Early Years Learning Centre - KinderQ ™
416-544-0133 • www.earlyyearslearning.com
KinderQ™ is our half-day enriched learning program that complements a child's regular
Kindergarten program. Available two or three days per week. A Program that Nurtures Your
Child's IQ and EQ. Now available at two locations: 11 Bedford Park Ave and 27 Castlefield Ave.
Ages: 18mos-SK.

Northview Height Early Learning Centre
550 Finch Ave W, Toronto, Ont, M2R 1N6. • 416-739-0987 •
Childcare centre servicing our local community for 20 years. For further information or scheduling
a tour, contact the centre supervisor. • Ages: 0-5yrs.

Parenting Programs - Toronto District School Board
4th fl, 2 Tretheway Dr, Toronto, Ont, M6M 4A8. • 416-394-2104 •
Free play-based family Literacy/Numeracy Program.

Small Talk
416-238-7676 • www.smalltalktoronto.com
Specializing in fun second language immersion for young children aged 6 months to 4 years
through songs, rhymes, creative play.

Spanish Schoolhouse
180 Steeles Ave West, Unit 202, Thornhill, Ont, L4J 2L1. • 905-771-1136 •
www.thespanishschoolhouse.ca
Learn Spanish the fun way! Spanish programs for preschool and kindergarten children. Parent
and tot classes also available. • Ages: 0+.

Thumbprint Adventures
Central Toronto: 416-787-2882; Oakville: 905-845-6789 Bloor West Village: 416-787-2882, •
416-787-2882 (V/TTY) • www.thumbprintadventures.com
An 'educationally balanced' curriculum that boosts innovative thinking, creativity, and confi-
dence…one adventure at a time! Learning was meant to be this much fun! **Look for our ad in the
Parent/Tot section.** • Ages: 18 mos. - 3 (adults stay & play) Drop -off: Ages 3 - 6; Gr. 1 - 3

▪ Early Years Centres

Central Eglinton Community Centre
160 Eglinton Ave E, Toronto, Ont, M4P 3B5. • 416-392-0511 x0 •
Parent/child programs, drop-in, toy library, clothing exchange.

Parent/Tot & Drop Off Programs (0-6yrs.)

Scarborough East Ontario Early Years
4218 Lawrence Ave E, Scarborough, Ont, M1E 3E6. • 416-282-7284 •
Free programs for families with children 0-6 years old. • Mon-Fri: 9-8, Sat: 10-3.

Toronto Danforth Ontario Early Years Centre
Massey Centre, 1102 Broadview Ave , Toronto, Ont, M4K 2S5. • 416-425-3636 •
For families with children aged 0-6. • Ages: 0-6yrs.

▪ Family Resource Centres

Applegrove Community Complex
60 Woodfield Rd, Toronto, Ont, M4L 2W6. • 416-461-8143 •
Parent/child drop-ins (2 locations) year round plus summer day camp. • Other Locations
Edgewood Ave, 416-461-3060 • Ages: 0-12.

Birchmount Bluffs Neighbourhood Centre
93 Birchmount Rd, Scarborough, Ont, M1N 3J7. • 416-396-4310 •
Nursery school. Ontario Early Years Centre. Family resource. • Ages: 0-5 • Mon: 9-3, Wed: 9-3,
Fri: 9-12, Sat: 9:30-12:30.

Cecil Community Centre
58 Cecil St, Toronto, Ont, M5T 1N6. • 416-392-1090 •
Parent/child drop-in with toy library. • Ages: 0-6 • Tue: 10-1, Thu: 10-1, Sat: 10-1.

Parent/Tot Drop & Off Programs (0-6yrs.)

Family Resource Centre, The
1 Promenade Circle, Ste 313, Thornhill, Ont, L4J 4P8. • 905-882-8509 •
www.thefamilyresourcecentre.ca
Drop-in program for parents/caregivers and their children age 0-5. Songs, crafts, stories, workshops, parenting library, resources and referrals. M-F and Sunday.

Family Resource Connection
21 Swanwick Ave (N. of Kingston Rd, S. of Gerrard), Toronto, Ont, M4E 1Z2. • 416-690-0102 •
Drop-in. Activities for parents and caregivers with young children. Childcare lending library.
Workshops. • Ages: NB-6.

$COUPON$ Jewish Family Institute
1072 Eglinton Ave West, Toronto, Ont, M6C 2E2. • 416-785-1107 x204 •
www.jewishfamilyinstitute.com
We provide amazing family focussed seminars, speakers and workshops. We help make good families great! Everyone welcome so give us a call. **Look for our ad in this section. See coupon section for valuable savings.**

Metro Association Of Family Resource Programmes
1117 Gerrard St E, Toronto, Ont, M4M 1Z9. • 416-463-7974 •
Information about family resource programmes in your area, toy libraries, emergency childcare and parent relief programmes.

Next Door Family Resources
95 Mimico Ave, Ste 101, Etobicoke, Ont, M8V 1R4. • 416-259-0333 •
Home childcare referral service, serving Western Toronto. • Ages: 0-6 • &.

Ontario Early Years Centre; Scarborough Agincourt
416-491-1466 • www.ontarioearlyyears.ca
Early Childhood Development Programs, Parent/caregiver support & education, Resources,
Toy/book libraries, School readiness, Breakfast Program, parking. Fully accessible. • &.

Ontario Early Years Centre; Scarborough Southwest
2555 Eglinton Ave E., Suite 212, Toronto, Ont, M1K 5J1. • 416-266-8289 •
www.ontarioearlyyears.ca
Early Childhood Development Programs, Parent/caregiver support & education, Resources,
Toy/book libraries, School readiness, parking. Fully accessible. • &.

West Scarborough Neighbourhood Community Centre: Creative Child/Parent Program
313 Pharmacy Avenue, Scarborough, Ont, M1L 3E7. • 416-755-9215 • www.ontarioearlyyears.ca
Early Childhood Development Programs, Parent/caregiver support & education, Resources,
Toy/book libraries, School readiness, parking. Fully accessible. • &.

YMCA Family Development Centre
15 Breadalbane Street, Toronto, Ont, M4Y 1C2. • 416-513-9622 • www.ymcatoronto.org
Membership, programs and services for children and families.

YMCA Family Resource Centres
416-928-9622 • Drop-in programs, toy lending, resources for parents. 5 locations across the GTA.

■ Fitness for Mom & Baby

BABY & ME FITNESS (est. 1987)
416-604-2249 •
Baby & me classes: yoga, fitness, aquafit, strollerfit, pilates. Workshops. Guest speakers.

Parent/Tot & Drop Off Programs (0-6yrs.)

TORONTO
(416) 920 - 5262
andrea@fitmomcanada.com

DURHAM
(416) 908 - 4127
mbasic@fitmomcanada.com

OAKVILLE REGION
(416) 821-7240
bwestmaas@fitmomcanada.com

PRENATAL
★ *Yoga for Birth*
★ *Fitmom 2 B Fitness*

POSTNATAL
★ *Fitmom & Baby classes*
★ *Stroller Classes*
★ *Fitmom Bootcamp*
★ *Personal Training*
★ *Birth Services*

Becoming Maternity and Parenting Centre

505 Eglinton Ave W Suite 401, Toronto, Ont, M5N 1B1. • 416-440-4020 • www.becomingmaternity.com
Variety of classes for new moms and babies including a six week course facilitated by an RN/lactation consultant (topics include sleep, feeding, developmental activities, massage), yoga, music, baby signing, and classes for moms and older babies.

Diaper-Fit for Moms & Tots by H2O-FIT (est. 1984)

416-449-0900 • www.h2ofit.com
30 minute aquafit workout for mom, 30 minutes swimming for tot. • Ages: 5 - 18 mos.

$COUPON$ Ella Centre Fitness

105 Vanderhoof Ave, Ste #2, Toronto, Ont, M4G 2H7. • 416-425-6500 • www.ellacentre.com
Pre and postnatal yoga and fitness. Mom + baby classes. Onsite childcare. **Look for our ad in this section. See coupon section for valuable savings.**

$COUPON$ Fitmom - PreNatal, PostNatal & Beyond

416-920-5262 • www.fitmomcanada.com
Pregnancy and Mom & baby fitness, Yoga, Stroller Classes, Running Clinics, Couples Yoga, Personal Training & Birth services. Mom & baby interaction, infant stimulation, corporate/public workshops. Beginner to athlete. Goal & result oriented programming for today's active woman. Many locations. **Look for our ad in this section. See coupon section for valuable savings.**

• Post Natal Fitness classes with baby
• Stoller fitness
• Aquaplay
• Mommy and Baby Yoga

Songs, rhymes, kneebouncers, fingerplays and much more.

We offer the largest variety of fun, innovative postnatal fitness programs for mom and baby, PLUS a huge assortment of infant stimulation and activities.

Many locations across the GTA

905 770-3400
www.mommyandbabyfitness.com

$ COUPON $ Mommy and Baby Fitness

905-770-3400 • www.mommyandbabyfitness.com
Workout and play with your baby. Adding good health and wellness to your family and life. Fitness, Yoga, Aquafitness, Stroller Fitness all include mom and baby activity session. Group discussions. Guest speakers. Baby song and rhyme booklet and much more. **Look for our ad in this section. See coupon section for valuable savings**. • Other Locations Many locations • Ages: 6wks-36 mos.

ORANGE DOT - Studio of Discovery

260 St. Germain Ave, Toronto, Ont, M5M 1W3. • 416-486-4614 • www.orangedotinc.com
ORANGE DOT artistic programs are designed to unleash your creative energy, spontaneity and passion. Prenatal Classes (the truth about the big day and beyond), Prenatal Yoga & Dance, Postnatal Body Conditioning for weight loss, Cooking Classes & Book Clubs for Moms, and Jazz Dance for Adults and Toddlers.

Pilates for Life

247 Yorkville Ave, Toronto, Ont, M4W 1L1. • 416-922-0387 •
Pilates and yoga for mommies and babies.

Salsa Babies - Latin Beat for Tiny Feet!

416-919-4851 • www.salsababies.com
Latin Beat for Tiny Feet! New moms dance back into shape with the best partner of all - your baby! Salsa Tots classes. All levels of fitness and dance experience. Many locations. Ask about licensing opportunities! • Ages: 2mos-3 yrs.

▪ Kindergym & Sport Programs

All Children's Progressive Gym

20 Glebe Rd E (3 Bl. N. of Davisville, S. of Manor), Toronto • 416-480-9826 •
A recreational and non-competitive program which provides the maximum variety of exercises and equipment, challenging and encouraging physical activity. Since 1959. Now serving 2nd Generation students! September-May program. **Look for our ad in this section.** • Ages: 2-7 • Cheque • Mon-Thu: 9-5.

Gyros Gymnastics: Ready, Get Set, Go!

2301 Keele St Unit 105, North York, Ont, M6M 3Z9. • 416-614-0521 •
Gymnastics for 2 to 6 year-olds, for 2 -3 yr olds parent participation required. • Ages: 2yrs - 6 • ♿.

My Gym Children's Fitness Center

Opening Fall 2006 in Richmond Hill, • 905-780-7700 • www.my-gym.ca
170+ worldwide locations offering structured weekly classes, birthday parties, camps and other fantastic fun filled programs. Low student/teacher ratio. • Ages: 3 months to 13 years.

$ COUPON $ Sportball Canada

39 Glen Cameron Rd, Unit 8, Thornhill, Ont, L3T 1P1. • 905-882-4473 or 1-8-Sportkids •
www.sportball.ca
Programs are designed to teach Parents how to assist their children in learning the skills of Hockey, Soccer, Tennis, Baseball, Basketball, Volleyball and Golf. **Look for our ad in this section. See coupon section for valuable savings**. • Ages: 16mos to 8 years.

$COUPON$ Sportplay Multi-Sport Weekly Classes

Locations around the GTA, • 905-940-9481 or 1-866-940-9481 • www.sportplay.ca
Fun, positive, supportive multi-sport program teaching 2-8 year old kids general athletic skills & specific skills for the major sports. Ball hockey, baseball, basketball, cooperative games, soccer, tennis, touch football, track & field, volleyball and much more! Mom & Baby Fit too! **Look for our ad in this section. See coupon section for valuable savings.**

Wonderkids Sports Center Inc

34 Doncaster Ave Unit 9, Thornhill, Ont, L3T 4S1. • 905-881-8499 •
Parent and Tot gymnastics classes. • Ages: 2-3.

$COUPON$ YogaBuds: Yoga for Kids, since 1997

416-785-7888 • www.yogabuds.com
YogaBuds pioneered kids & family yoga in Canada 10 years ago. Offers yoga classes, workshops & private sessions for parent & child (age 4 yrs+) together. Unique classes include partnering and assisting to enhance bonding & connection. **Look for our ad in the After School Activities section. See coupon section for valuable savings.**

■ Multi-Program Centres & More...

Adath Israel Congregation Pre-school Programs

37 Southbourne Ave, Toronto, Ont • 416-635-5340 •
Exciting preschool programs (0 - 6yrs). Afternoon drop-offs (3-5yrs).

$COUPON$ Animals with Whimz at Whimz Studio

784 St. Clair Ave. West (west of Bathurst), Toronto, Ont, M6C 1B6. • 416-656-7894 • www.whimzonline.com
Come meet the Whimz Live Animals: from hedgehogs, rabbits and chinchillas, to lizards and toads and snakes. Learn all about them, even how to hold them, while singing songs, reading books and colouring in some drawings. An amazing introduction into our natural world. Very busy- integrated arts and very upbeat. Also: Parties, Camps and Classes . **Look for our ad in the Birthday section. See coupon section for valuable savings.** • Ages: 2-5 • Cheque.

Armour Heights Community Centre: Tiny Tots Program

2140 Avenue Rd (corner Wilson), Toronto, Ont, M5N 4M7. • 416- 483-3840 •
Come and enjoy safe and quality children's programming at your neighbourhood community centre. 4 sessions per year. Programs include: Drama, music, playtime, arts & crafts, kindergym, cooking, summer camp and more. Call for info or pick up a brochure at the centre.

$COUPON$ Avenue Road Arts School

460 Avenue Rd, Toronto, Ont, M4V 2J1. • 416-961-1502 • www.avenueroadartsschool.com
High quality and innovative programming in the visual and performing arts - all in a warm and supportive environment. Programs for toddlers and preschool children, offered Monday-Saturday, integrate visual art, drama and music. Small class sizes, highly qualified artist/instructors. **Look for our ad in the Art section. See coupon section for valuable savings**. • Ages: 9mos-adult • *VISA*, ⊖, *Interac*, Cheque • Mon-Thu: 8:30-8, Fri: 8:30-6:30, Sat: 8:30-5:30.

Cookerydoo

325 Roncesvalles Ave. • Toronto, 416-532-2232 • www.cookerydoo.com
We offer a range of fun and uniquely creative cooking and craft classes for children ages 21/2 & up. Our truly inspired cookshops, craftshops and camps are tailored to various interests and seasonal themes. Daycares and schools welcome. **Look for our ad in the Birthday section.**

$COUPON$ Fun & Fitness Club at Candy Castle

1 DeLisle Avenue (Yonge & St. Clair), Toronto, Ont • 416-962-2639 • www.clubcandycastle.com
Programs for Toddlers (6 months to 3 years) and Little Monkeys (Ages 4 to 6). Classes include Toddler Art and Play, Creative Movement, Ballet, Whimz Animals, Music Together, Tumbling, Sportball, Intro to Woodworking and Wee Whizards (Early literacy computer class). **Look for our ad in the Birthday section. See coupon section for valuable savings**.

Lil' Explorers Clubhouse & Indoor Gym

190 Bullock Dr. Unit 10, Toronto, Ont, L3P 7N3. • 905-910-PLAY (7529) •
We have a variety of programs for kids and parent & tots.

$COUPON$ Mabel's Fables Children's Bookstore

662 Mount Pleasant Rd, Toronto, Ont, M4S 2N3. • 416-322-0438 • www.mabelsfables.com
Reading programs for babies & toddlers. Book talks with visiting authors for older children. Visit our website for event details. **Look for our ad in the Children's Books section. See coupon section for valuable savings.** • Ages: 0-12+ • *VISA*, ⊖, *Interac*, Cheque • ♿.

Mississauga Recreation & Parks - Preschool Programs

300 City Centre Drive, Mississauga, Ont, L5B 3C1. • 905-615-4100 •
www.mississauga.ca/rec&parks
Art, music and movement and physical activity programs for you and your child. Registered and drop in programs across the city. **Look for our ad in the Swimming section.** • Ages: 0-6.

Moms in the City

416-428-0867 • www.momsinthecity.ca
Enjoy grown up outings without sacrificing time with your little ones. Engage in the culture and history of the city. Join us for baby friendly gallery tours, neighbourhood walks, luncheons, and much more.

Multi-sport Classes

Boys & Girls 2-8 years old
1 hour classes weekdays & Saturdays
Fun, positive, supportive instruction
Locations across GTA & York Region

www.sportplay.ca
905-940-9481
866-940-9481

ALL CHILDREN'S PROGRESSIVE GYM INC. since 1959

CHRISTIANE von KLEIST

(416) 480-9826

CANADA'S FIRST GYM SCHOOL FOR CHILDREN
Our program and method is copied
but never duplicated!

Sept.-May   Mon.-Thurs.   Ages 2-7

20 Glebe Rd. E. UNITED CHURCH
(north of Davisville at Yonge)

$ COUPON $ Northwood Montessori Parent & Tot

6 Locations covering North York, Thornhill & Markham: 416-492-7812 •
www.northwoodmontessori.ca
Parent & Tot program introduction to Montessori plus music, art, drama, gym, French and playtime.
Look for our ad in the Private Schools section. See coupon section for valuable savings. • Ages: 1.5-2.5 yrs.

Pegasus Studios

361 Glebeholme Blvd (Danforth & Coxwell), Toronto, Ont, M4C 1T9. • 416-469-2799 •
www.pegasusdance.com
Childhood Expressions program for children aged 2.5-4 yrs combining music, dance and art. RAD
ballet, Jazz, Hip Hop, Tap, Modern dance, Musical Theatre & Yoga 4 Kids. Pilates and adult programs.
Summer Creative Arts Camps. In operation since 1986. • Ages: Birth+ • _VISA_, ⊖, ▣, Cheque.

Storytelling Programs for Young Children: Sally Jaeger & Erika Webster

416-465-5982 •
Lullabies and LapRhymes, Mr. Bear Says Hello, Jack in the Box Tales for Two's. Age appropriate
family storytelling. 8 week sessions start September, January and March. Central Toronto. Ages
0 - 3 with parent or caregiver. Celebrating 25 years! • Cheque.

$ COUPON $ Thumbprint Adventures

Central Toronto: 416-787-2882; Oakville: 905-845-6789 Bloor West Village: 416-787-2882, •
416-787-2882 (V/TTY) • www.thumbprintadventures.com
"Where are we going today? To a clubhouse or an island; to the desert or outer space?"   Our
'educationally balanced' curriculum boosts innovative thinking, creativity and confidence!
Learning was meant to be this much fun! **Look for our ad in this section.** • Ages: 18 mos. - 3
(adults stay & play) Drop -off: Ages 3 - 6; Gr. 1 - 3

How many more sleeps until **Thumbprint** ?
Adventures

Enrichment programs that are engaging, 'educationally balanced' and packed with fun!

Bathurst & Eglinton: (416) 787-2882
Yonge & Lawrence: (416) 787-2882
Bloor West Village: (416) 277-5075
Oakville: (905) 845-6789

www.thumbprintadventures.com

Parent/ Tot classes (1½ - 3 yrs.)   Drop-off Programs (3 - 9 yrs.)   Themed Birthday Parties

Giving children a chance to create, laugh and learn... one adventure at a time!

Parent/Tot Drop & Off Programs (0-6yrs.)

▪ Music & Movement

88 Keys - Kindermusik
1669 Bayview Ave, Unit 203, Toronto, Ont, M4G 3C1. • 416-932-8080 •
Creative music for newborn to age 7.

$ COUPONS All That Dance
630 Magnetic Dr Unit D, North York, Ont, M3J 2C4. • 416-663-1212 • www.allthatdance.ca
Fun, energy & music! Classes specially designed for 2, 3, 4 & 5 year olds. Inspiring instructors
welcome your youngster to the creative world of dance. Newly renovated facilities. **Look for our
ad in this section. See coupon section for valuable savings.** • Ages: 2+ • *VISA*, *Interac*, Cheque.

Beth Sholom Playtime Nursery
1445 Eglinton Ave W, Toronto, Ont, M6C 2E6. • 416-783-6103 •
Mommy & Me, Bubbie & Me Programs for toddlers/preschoolers. Playgroups.

$ COUPONS Bonjour, bébé!
12 Bannockburn Ave (Avenue Rd & 401), Toronto, Ont, M5M 2M8. • 416-789-7855 x308 •
www.frenchprogrammesfrancais.com
This programme allows mom/dad to spend quality time with their child ...EN FRANCAIS, dancing,
singing, playing and laughing together. **Look for our ad in this section. See coupon section for valuable
savings.**

Catching Fireflies Ltd -Kindermusik
Pickering/Whitby 905-420-6622 or 1-888-513-0004 •
Internationally acclaimed music and movement program. Newborn - 7 years. • *VISA*, ⊕, Cheque.

Children's Parties and Music Programs by Robyn (B.A., B.Ed.)
905-881-4699 • musicbyrobyn@sympatico.ca
Energetic singer/guitarist offering programs to groups (8 or more children) featuring interactive
musical activities: songs, movement, bubbles, instruments, parachute, FUN...!! • Ages: 6mos-7yrs.

$ COUPONS Drama Mamas, The
515 St. Germain Avenue, Toronto, Ont, M5M 1X3. • 416-256-1308 • www.thedramamamas.com
We offer an engaging program of creative exploration, storytelling, role playing, movement,
music and crafts. Our classes build confidence and self-esteem, strengthen communication skills
and foster the imagination - all in a fun & safe environment. **Look for our ad in this section. See
coupon section for valuable savings.** • Ages: 18 mos+.

$ COUPONS Ella Learn, Move and Play and Music Programs
105 Vanderhoof Ave, Ste #2, Toronto, Ont, M4G 2H7. • 416-425-6500 • www.ellacentre.com
Ella's seasoned Occupational Therapists teach parents how their child develops. Engage with
your child as you learn about gross motor, fine motor and cognitive development. Ella Music with
your Baby classes give parents a repertoire of songs, rhymes and instrumental play. **Look for our
ad in this section. See coupon section for valuable savings.** • Ages: 3 mos. - 36 mos.

Etobicoke Suzuki School Of Music - Toddler Programs & Lessons
416-239-4637 • www.etobicokesuzukimusic.ca
Suzuki toddler and parent classes for children up to 3 years. Ability development through songs
and rhythmic games. Also offering violin and cello instruction for ages 3 and up. Parent attends
lesson with child. Qualified Suzuki method teachers. • Cheque • ♿.

The DRAMA MAMAS

DRAMA CLASSES FOR AGES 18 MONTHS +
Engaging young minds through...
CREATIVE EXPLORATION · STORYTELLING
ROLE - PLAYING · CRAFTS · MOVEMENT · MUSIC

416-256-1308 · www.thedramamamas.com

MUSIC TOGETHER **rosedale** the annex
forest hill midtown

Music for infants, toddlers, preschoolers
• Sing move chant listen explore
• Take home cd and songbook
• Try a free demonstration class

musictogetherrocks@rogers.com
www.musictogetherrocks.com
416-272-5263

Families Makin' Music
5 locations, • 416-225-5655 •
SIBLINGS come to the same music/movement class. • Ages: Birth-5yrs.

Front and Centre Dance Academy
875 Eglinton Ave W, Unit 7, Toronto, Ont, M6C 3Z9. • 416-916-3687 •
Fun and creative daytime classes for 3-5 yrs.

Fun with Music Together
Beaches, Roncesvalles & Bloor West, • 416-406-0160 • www.funwithmusictogether.ca
Music Together is an internationally recognized early childhood music program based on the
premise that all children are musical. Mixed age classes include songs, rhythmic rhymes, movement and instrument play. New music each semester - 9 collections in all! • Ages: 0-5yrs.

$COUPON$ Groove School of Dance - Preschool Programs
53 Burnaby Blvd (St Margaret's Church - Avenue Rd/Eglinton); Bayview/Lawrence; East York, •
416-919-2914 •
An introduction to performing arts - Imagination, Creativity, Dance, Music, Drama. **Look for our ad
in the After School Activities category. See coupon section for valuable savings.** • Ages: babies-5 yrs.

·ALL·THAT· Dance

Introductory and specialty
classes in dance starting at
age 2, 3, 4 & 5 years old.

630 Magnetic Dr. Unit D,
North York
416-663-1212

www.allthatdance.ca

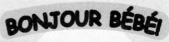

BONJOUR BÉBÉ

Your little one learns, claps, dances
and sings **in French... with you.**

Spend quality time with
your baby or toddler en français.

Experience the French language in a way
that is fun for both kids & adults!

416-789-7855 x308

www.frenchprogrammesfrancais.com

$COUPONS Gymboree Play and Music Programs

Central Toronto 416-410-6FUN, Thornhill 905-707-1420, Bloor West/Etob/Miss/Oakville 905-542-PLAY • www.gymboree.com
Gymboree - the world leader in parent-child interactive play, music & arts programs. Our trained, knowledgeable teachers focus on your child's social, intellectual and physical development. Play classes feature 40 pieces of unique Gymboree play equipment. Music classes emphasize exploration and enjoyment of many musical styles and instruments. Great Birthday parties too! **Look for our ad in this section. See coupon section for valuable savings.** • Other Locations Call: 1-800-520-PLAY. • Ages: 0-4 • *VISA*, 🏧, *Interac*, Cheque.

$COUPONS Kayla's Music Circles

905-709-0234 • www.kaylamusic.ca
Enriched, educational, energetic, exciting and entertaining. These are words that parents use to describe "Kayla's Music Circles". Programs are in-home, in your neighbourhood. **Look for our ad in this section. See coupon section for valuable savings.** • Ages: 3mos-4 years • Cheque.

Kinderdance

105 Vanderhoof Ave, #1, Toronto, Ont, M4G 2H7. • 416-696-7466 • www.turningpointe.ca
Designed for 3 year olds beginning their dance experience, creativity and free movement are explored. Children develop coordination, body awareness and foundations for ballet & jazz. Fun & surprises for all students.

Kingsway Conservatory of Music

3086 Bloor St W, Toronto, Ont, M8X 1C8. • 416-234-0121 • www.kingswayconservatory.ca
Music for You & Your Baby (0-3 yrs) - Early Childhood Musicianship (Eurhythmics/Kodály/Orff, from 3 yrs) - Kingsway Children's Chorus (from 6 yrs) - Suzuki Violin (from 4 yrs) - Musical, social, emotional, intellectual development through speech, singing, instrument-play, movement.

Parent/Tot & Drop Off Programs (0-6yrs.)

Ella Centre for Pregnancy & Parenting

- Pre- and Postnatal Fitness and Yoga
- Childbirth Education Classes
- Parenting Workshops
- Massage Therapy and Spa Services
- Learn, Move & Play Classes
- Parent & Tot Programs
- Doula Services and Breastfeeding Support
- Drop-In and Drop-Off Childcare

www.ellacentre.com
416.425.6500/105 Vanderhoof Ave.

from belly to baby
and beyond

Let's Get Started Presents Kindermusik
1550 16th Ave, Building "A" - Units#11 & #12, Richmond Hill, Ont, L4B 3K9. • 905-737-2335
or 1-877-737-2335 • www.letsgetstartedltd.com
Through Kindermusik, enhance your child's thinking, reasoning, creativity, expression and overall
development. Internationally recognized music and movement program. Music is an essential
part of your child's life. Other programs also available. • Ages: 0-7 years.

"Little Voices Dancing Feet" with Jodie Friesen
416-461-9989 • www.littlevoices.ca
Music & Movement. 3 Beaches locations. Qualified, caring teacher with 15 years experience.
Age specific, Interactive, Educational and FUN! Start your child on the road to making music an
enriching part of their life. Summer Camps, Birthday parties also available. Ages: NB - 8 yrs.

Making Music Together
Leaside, Forest Hill, North Toronto, Cedarvale, • 416-833-1231 • www.makingmusictogether.com
Music Together® is an internationally celebrated program of Music & Movement for Young
Children and the Adults Who Love Them! Songs, chants, movement & instrument play in a
relaxed, fun & creative environment! 9 Different Song Collections, 2 new CDs each semester!
Birth - 5yrs. Mixed age & babies classes.

Mammakin Mom & Baby Music and Art Classes
905-556-0333 • Music and craft classes for mom and baby - infant to toddler.

Kayla Music Circles

- **In-Home Music & Drama classes**
- **Enriched, Interactive, Educational & Fun!**
- **For kids 3 mos. - 4 yrs.**

Birthday Parties and Corporate & Community Concerts also available

"As seen on Treehouse TV"

ph. (905) 709-0234
www.kaylamusic.ca

Parent/Tot Drop & Off Programs (0-6yrs.)

Martha Hicks School of Ballet
2384 Yonge St, 2nd Fl, Toronto, Ont, M4P 2E0. • 416-484-4731 x224 • www.mhsb.ca
Energetic, imaginative fun and creative daytime dance classes for pre-school and kindergarten
children. Qualified instructors. Warm and personable. Ages 3+. 7 Locations in North Toronto.
Check out our website for details.

$COUPON$ Music for Young Children
1-888-474-1556 • www.myc.com
A keyboard-based music program that includes piano, singing, rhythm, theory, and composing. Group lessons with adult participation. Teachers throughout Canada and the USA. Wonderful introduction to
music! **Look for our ad in the After School, Music section. See coupon section for valuable savings.** • Ages: 3+.

$COUPON$ Music Together ROCKS
416-272-5263 • www.musictogetherrocks.com
Newborn and mixed age classes up to 5 years. Children sing, move, chant, listen and explore
musical instruments. Take home CD and songbook. The Annex, Rosedale, Forest Hill Village,
and Midtown. **Look for our ad in The After School Music section. See coupon section for valuable savings.**

Music with Jayne Harvey
905-731-0625 •
Mommy, Daddy, or Nanny & Me home music circles. Fun, interactive, guitar accompaniment.
Baby safe instruments and puppets. Since 1984. CD available.

Music with Nancy
255-61 Shaftsbury Ave., Richmond Hill, Ont, L4C 0L9. • 905-787-8363 •
Movement, fun, guitar! AMAZING! Schools, Birthdays, Events.

Music With Simone
416-450-6391 •
Fun, interactive, age appropriate, music classes for kids aged 6 mos. - 5 yrs.

Musica Music School; Music for Young Children® Program
88 Laird Drive, Toronto, Ont, M4G 3V1. • 416-696-0905 •
Parent & Tot introduction to the exciting world of music through an interactive, keyboard-based, group
program that includes singing, rhythm and listening activities. Classes offered 7 days a week.

North Toronto Institute of Music
550 Eglinton Ave E, Toronto, Ont, M4P 1N9. • 416-488-2588 •
Educational, interactive, quality parent & tot music programs. • Ages: Birth-5yrs..

North York Suzuki School of Music
348 Sheppard Ave East, North York, Ont, M2N 3B4. • 416-222-5315 •
www.northyork-suzuki. com
Dance with your darling, sing with your sweetheart! Classes are relaxed sessions of happy, musical exploration for parent and child. Excellent Suzuki preparation. Suzuki instrumental instruction
offered as well. • Ages: 0-5yrs • Cheque.

Pia Bouman School for Ballet and Creative Movement
6 Noble St, Toronto, Ont, M6K 2C6. • 416-533-3706 • www.piaboumsnschool.org
Music & Movement for 2 1/2 to 4 year olds. Discover a rich music vocabulary and movement
ideas. Develop physical skills. Use singing, voice and rhythm instruments. Sessions of 16 weeks.
Teacher qualified in Music, Dance and Early Childhood Training. Sept to June .

Parent/Tot & Drop Off Programs (0-6yrs.)

Did we miss you?

Would you like to be in the 2008 edition of Help!... We've Got Kids?

If you provide a product or service for kids we would be delighted to include you free of charge. Display ads are also available.

Call (416) 444-7678 or fax (416) 444-1289 or email info@helpwevegotkids.com & tell us who you are.

Sugar Beat
Music for Children
4 months to 6 years

Join our group classes with songs, instruments, puppet shows, and creative movement.

Bloor West Village & Bathurst/St.Clair

www.sugarbeat.ca • (416) 767-5535

Rainbow Songs Inc
3-182 Wright Ave, Toronto, Ont, M6R 1L2. • 416-535-5247 •
Music classes for babies and young children.

Reach Dance Academy
70 Newkirk Road Unit 38 , Richmond Hill, Ont, L4C 3G3. • 905-918-4900 •
www.reachdanceacademy.com
Join us for Toddler Grooves - a dance/movement class specially designed for toddlers 18 months - 3yrs. All classes are taught by our Artistic Director (B.ED and B.A Hons) in a warm, supportive environment. 8wk sessions and full year available.

Movies for MOMMIES
THE ORIGINAL PARENT & BABY FILM EVENT

Weekly Screenings Throughout the GTA

Dads, Grandparents & Caregivers Welcome too!

On Site: Change Tables & Wipes, Stroller Parking, Bottle Warming, Welcome Gift & More!

Reduced sound to protect little ears

For weekly listings visit: **www.moviesformommies.com** or call 905.707.8866

Parent/Tot Drop & Off Programs (0-6yrs.)

Sesaya! Featuring Kindermusik (North York)

647-439-6346 • www.sesaya.com
Full range of Kindermusik programs. Ages 0-7. Weekday and Saturday classes. Exceptional tailored programs and events for schools and daycares. Dynamic FUN instructors! • Ages: 1mon-8yrs.

Sing Out

416-385-3311 •
Upbeat music classes for preschoolers in your home. Central Toronto.

$ COUPON $ Sugar Beat Music for Children

locations: Bloor West Village & St. Clair/Bathurst, • 416-767-5535 • www.sugarbeat.ca
Sugar Beat offers age-appropriate music classes filled with song, instrument play, and creative movement. Come to inspire your child's lifelong love of music! Twelve week sessions begin in September and in January, with continuous enrolment. **Look for our ad in this section. See coupon section for valuable savings**. • Ages: 4 mos. - 6 yrs..

Tots'nTunes

115 Pondview Road, Thornhill, Ont, L4J 8P6. • 905 764 6255 •
Music lessons, group and private, all ages.

Yamaha Music Schools

5075 Yonge St, 10th Fl, Toronto, Ont, M2N 6C6. • 416-224-5590 • www.yamaha.ca
Yamaha Music Schools offer quality music programs throughout the week: "T42" for 2 year olds; "Music Wonderland" for 3 year olds and the world renowned "Junior Music Course" for 4 and 5 year olds. • Ages: 2+ • VISA, ⊕, ▥, Cheque • ♿.

■ Parent & Baby Movies

Cineplex Entertainment - Stars and Strollers Program

416-323-6600 • "The Big Screen With Your Little One."

$ COUPON $ MOVIES for MOMMIES - Canada's Original Parent & Baby Film Event!

905-707-8866 • www.moviesformommies.com
Weekly matinees of current films. Infant friendly environment. Stroller parking, Change table, Bottle warming, Reduced sound to protect "little ears", welcome gift and weekly promotions. Infants (0-18 mos) Free of charge. Rainbow Cinemas - Promenade, Rainbow Cinemas - Market Square, Fox Cinema, & Rainbow Cinemas- Fairview. Visit us online. **Look for our ad in this section. See coupon section for valuable savings.**

PCITY Parent

Published monthly, City Parent offers today's busy family a showcase of children's activities, family oriented events, what's new in products and services, health issues and timely advice on a variety of parental concerns.

Pick up your free copy at:

TORONTO PUBLIC LIBRARY

- Banks
- Libraries
- Grocery Stores
- Cultural Centres
- Shopping Malls
- Professional Offices
- Children's Stores
- Recreation Centres
- Schools
- Bookstores
- Drugstores

- Maternity, Birth & Early Education Facilities

For advertising or home delivery service call

905-815-0017

467 Speers Road, Oakville • www.cityparent.com

While most of this book is targeted at your children, there are many resources that can be found in Toronto for parents. Parenting classes are always beneficial ... look for classes that are appropriate for your child's age as parenting information differs according to age/stage. You will find listings here that offer adult companionship with new Moms/Dads groups or help with some of our ever-present parental challenges. Don't put it off ... if you are thinking of calling for help or information, do it today!

<u>You will find the following sub-categories in this section:</u>
General ParentStuff, Homebased Businesses; Moms/Dads Groups; Multiples, Parenting Classes; Private Kids' Transportation

$ COUPON $ Look for this company's coupon at the back of the book

▪ General Parentstuff

Aloha Mobile Car Care
647-388-4186 •
Convenient car cleaning service for parents with imperfect children.

Association for Bright Children of Ontario
416-925-6136 •
Information, support and advocacy for parents of bright & gifted children.

Babbling Bananas
416-428-0867 • www.babblingbananas.com
Innovative perspectives on caring for you and your family. Expert strategies and advice from trusted professionals. Subscription is FREE.

Babies Best Start
325 Milner Ave, Ste 110, Scarborough, Ont, M1B 5N1. • 416-447-2885 •
Community home visiting parenting program. Scarborough only.

Bereaved Families Of Ontario
416-440-0290 or 800- 236-6364 •
Group support for children whose parent or sibling has died. Evenings by appointment. • Ages: 4+.

Breast is Best - Clothing for Nursing Mothers
905-837-5439 or (877- 837-5439 • www.breast-is-best.com
Offering Quality Breastfeeding Clothing at Affordable Prices Since 1995.

City Parent Newsmagazine
467 Speers Rd, Oakville, Ont, L6K 3S4. • 905-815-0017 • www.cityparent.com
A valuable source of information for every family; Pick up your free copy each month at libraries, pharmacies, grocery stores, retail and cultural centres. **Look for our ad on the previous page.**

Forever Organized Plus
905-737-2485 • Reliable home organizer. Friendly, honest service.

Invest in Kids
416-977-1222 •
A national charitable organization providing parenting resources (birth to age five).

Jewish Family & Child Service

4600 Bathurst St, North York, Ont, M2R 3V3. • 416-638-7800 • www.toronto.com/jfcs
Group educational programs on parenting, single and step parenting, stress and anger management, etc. Child protection service. • Other Locations: Downtown Branch 416-961-9344,
Promenade Mall in York Region 905-882-2331, Jerome D. Diamond Adolescent Centre
416-482-3023 • ⅋.

Orderly Lives

416-461-8018 • www.orderlylives.net
We create order out of chaos in playrooms, family rooms, kitchens, closets and bedrooms. As
seen in Style At Home. Our new concierge service is like having an extra pair of hands when
you need it most. • Cheque • Mon-Sat: 9-6.

Organized Zone Inc Professional Organizers

125 Robert Hicks Drive, North York, Ont, M2R 3R2. • 416-665-2165 • www.organizedzone.com
Creating systems & solutions for all your family's organizing challenges. There is nothing that
can't be overcome! Get organized today!

Princess Publishing Inc - Family Medical Journal

905-271-3546 • www.getorganizedjournals.com
Family Medical Journal is a Handy Book to record Parent's & Kid's Medical Info.

Savvy Mom Media

416-488-6667 • www.savvymom.ca
Sign Up and Get Savvy! SavvyMom Today is a free online publication for moms, full of fun and
practical solutions for mom's busy lives. Stay informed, connected and entertained - go to
www.savvymom.ca and sign up now. You don't want to miss another article!

UJA Federation - Jewish Information Service of Greater Toronto

4588 Bathurst Street, ste 115 (BJCC), Toronto, Ont, M2R 1W6. • 416-635-5600 •
www.jewishtoronto.com
Everything you need to know about Jewish Toronto - schools, daycares, synagogues and tem-
ples, organizations, services and programs.

www.childrensinfo.ca

Information about children & youth programs & services provided by the Government of Ontario.

▪ Home-based Businesses

Discovery Toys - National Sales Director

416-630-0138 or 905-417-4514, • www.discoverytoyslink.com/WendyLitvak
Fun; flexible; earn extra $$; replace a full time income! Earn while you train, save $$ on future
purchases, enjoy free vacations every year! • Ages: 0-12 • VISA, ⊜, ▓, Cheque.

Epicure Selections

647-885-0367 • bette.lewin@rogers.com
Epicure Selections is expanding. Consultants needed for home parties & catalogue sales selling
gourmet spices, dip mixes & kitchen tools. Fundraisers also available. Great commissions &
incentives. Contact Bette Lewin, Independent Consultant. "Turn your everyday into gourmet…simply by opening a jar."

$ COUPONS $ Stayin' Home and Lovin' It!

1842 Emmaus Dr, Corpus Christi, Texas, 78418. • 877-216-1940 code HELP • www.GetWah.info
Perfect for Parents. Work from Home. Amazing opportunity! FREE training! FREE website!
Complete support. No selling, delivering or stocking products! **Look for our ad in this section. See
coupon section for valuable savings.**

Yummy Mummy Careers

647-288-3170 • www.yummymummycareers.com
A service for working mothers to assist with their careers. Job postings and resources available online.

■ Moms/Dads Groups

A Morning Out (AMO)

c/o Richmond Hill United Church, 10201 Yonge St, Richmond Hill, Ont, L4C 3B2. • 905-884-1301
Break for parents. Guest speakers. Childcare provided. • Wed: 9-11.

Book Clubs by Janna

905-762-0109 •
Mommies' Book Clubs - Child care on site!

Breastfeeding Support - Region of Peel

905-799-7700 • www.peelregion.ca
Breastfeeding mothers' groups - free, drop-in group for breastfeeding mothers and children of all ages, with opportunity to speak with a public health nurse. Breastfeeding Companions - a mother-to-mother volunteer support program.

Metro Mothers Network (MumNet)

416-487-MUMS (6867) •
Weekly fitness and discussion groups with childcare. • Cheque.

$COUPON$ Mommy and Baby Fitness

905-770-3400 • www.mommyandbabyfitness.com
More than just fitness. Group discussions. Guest speakers. Infant stimulation. **Look for our ad in the Parent/Tot section. See coupon section for valuable savings.** • Other Locations Many locations • Ages: 6wks-36 mos.

ORANGE DOT - Studio of Discovery

260 St. Germain Ave, Toronto, Ont, M5M 1W3. • 416-486-4614 • www.orangedotinc.com
Programs designed to unleash your creative energy, spontaneity and passion.

■ Multiples

Durham Region Parents Of Multiple Births Association (D.R.POMBA)

PO Box 70607, 1801 Dundas St E, Whitby, Ont, L1N 2K0. • 1-888-358-5145 •
Support group for families with multiples.

Maxine's Multiple Birth Newborn Care

188 Parkview Cres, Newmarket, Ont, L3Y 2C8. • 416-668-9957 •
ECE Specializing in Newborn-Infant care for Twins and Triplets.

MPOMBA (Miss. Parents of Multiple Births Assoc.)

P.O. Box 42016, Mississauga, Ont, L5M 4Z0. • 416-620-3470 •
Supporting parents of multiples for 25+ years.

Toronto Parents Of Multiple Births Association (TPOMBA)

Regional Women's Health Centre, 790 Bay St, 8th Fl, Toronto, Ont, M5G 1N9. • 416-760-3944 • www.tpomba.org
TPOMBA is a not-for-profit self-help support group for parents of twins, triplets, and more. We are experienced parents ready to lend our experience and tricks of the trade. Social events, clothing & equipment sales, support groups, "Bulletwin", info nights etc.

▪ Parenting Classes

$COUPON$ 5 Elements Camps & Workshops

416-423-8456 • www.5elements4girls.com
Raising adolescent girls is a challenge for any parent. Understanding their moods, their relationships and the pressures they deal with is a tall order. 5 Elements offers workshops that afford the opportunity to learn from and discuss relevant issues with parenting experts. **Look for our ad in the Camp section. See coupon section for valuable savings.**

After Baby Comes - Sandi Cole

416-447-1719 • www.afterbabycomes.com
7- week course for new mothers with their babies (aged 1 week-4 months). Topics include infant crying, nutrition, sleeping, baby massage and more. In conjunction with Prenatal and Family Life Education Mount Sinai Hospital. York Mills and Bayview area.

Baby & Birth Support

905-882-9805 •
"Happiest Baby On The Block™" instructor. Tried & true method to soothe, calm and help even colicky babies to sleep longer and better. As seen on Oprah & Dr Phil.

Becoming Maternity and Parenting Centre

505 Eglinton Ave W Suite 401, Toronto, Ont, M5N 1B1. • 416-440-4020 •
www.becomingmaternity.com
Parenting workshops for parents of babies, toddlers and preschoolers including positive discipline, nutrition, toddler development, first aid, making homemade baby food, infant care. Centre also offers classes for parents and children, and lactation consulting.

$COUPON$ Ella Centre Education

105 Vanderhoof Ave, Ste #2, Toronto, Ont, M4G 2H7. • 416-425-6500 • www.ellacentre.com
Everything you need to be a confident and relaxed parent. Small class size, expert advice, personal attention. Childbirth Education programs, New Mom's Groups, and Ella Experts Workshops on everything from CPR to power struggles. **Look for our ad in the Parent-Tot section. See coupon section for valuable savings.**

$COUPON$ Jewish Family Institute

1072 Eglinton Ave West, Toronto, Ont, M6C 2E2. • 416-785-1107 x204 •
www.jewishfamilyinstitute.com
The Jewish Family Institute promotes positive relationships between parents and children and between spouses. The aim is to provide families from all segments of our community with useful family-focussed learning opportunities. We help make good families great! **Look for our ad in the Parent/Tot section. See coupon section for valuable savings.**

Parent Stuff

Joys of Parenting
905-764-3514 • www.joysofparenting.com
Coaching courses and workshops. Making positive and practical parenting solutions come together to create the harmony and joy you want to have in your home.

Ontario Parenting Education
56 Carrington Dr, Richmond Hill, Ont, L4C 8A4. • 905-508-5240 •
Non-profit organization providing parenting workshops and education.

Parent Education Network
605 Royal York Road, Suite 108, Toronto, Ont, M8Y 4G5. • 416-255-8969 •
Parenting Classes Parenting skills: Discussion Groups. One night workshops.

Preparing for Parenting - E Revivo
164 Codsell Ave, Toronto, Ont, M3H 3W6. • 416-543-7974 •
Having a baby? Learn what to expect - new roles, communication techniques, how to become a healthy family. 1 day workshop or 6 week sessions.

Young, Randi, M.S.W., R.S.W.
3335 Yonge St, Ste 404, Toronto, Ont, M4N 2M1. • 416-440-0408x2 •
Parenting expert as seen on City-Line.

■ Private Kids' Transportation

Alexander Limousine Service
235 Queen's Drive, Weston, Ont, M9N 2H8. • 416-614-0786 •
Limousine carpool packages available. Call Sandy.

Dignity Transportation Inc
280 Midwest Rd,Unit B, Toronto, Ont, M1P 3A9. • (416) 398-2222 •
Largest accessible fleet. Programs, schools, etc. Seatbelts in all vehicles.

kidskoolTrans - Transportation for Kids
309 Major Mackenzie Dr E, Unit 716, Richmond Hill, Ont, L4C 9V5. • 905-508-1801 •
Since 1994, providing safe, reliable, person to person transportation for kids to and from school and activities. Integrated car seats & boosters. Service now available in Toronto,York, Peel & Halton Regions.

Little Peoples Transportation Corp
905-660-4414 •
Private transportation for children.

Magic Bus Company, The
26 Roncesvalles Ave, Toronto, Ont, M6R 2K3. • 416-516-7433 •
Toronto's transporTAINMENT. Magic School Bus themed transportation! Fun, safe, reliable and memorable. Voted Best Bus Company. Be on the bus!

Royal Taxi Inc - School Transportation Division
620 Wilson Ave, Ste 100, Toronto, Ont, M3K 1Z3. • 416-785-3322 • www.royaltaxi.ca
Now servicing Toronto, Richmond Hill, Markham, Aurora & Newmarket. Reliable & Efficient Child/Student Transportation. With almost 750 taxis, school buses, mini vans & wheelchair vans and growing... Royal will be able to handle any transportation request. Call Jonathan for more information.

Photography for Children & Families

Hanging a professional photographer's photos on your wall at home is a constant tug at the heartstrings ... every time you pass by. Professional photographers have the ability to capture that impish grin, the still-innocent gleam in their eye or the hearty laugh that we all see in our kids. Don't put it off, make an appointment with a photographer and capture those irreplaceable smiles for you, and eventually your grandchildren, to cherish.

$COUPON$ **Look for this company's coupon at the back of the book**

A Fitting Image Digital Photography - Mummy Tummy to Tiny Toes
info@AFittingImage.com, • 416-488-3372 • www.AFittingImage.com
In home maternity, baby, child and family portraits by patient woman photographer. Negatives on CD. Lab prints. Photo birth announcements. Thank-you cards. Colour, b&w, sepia, selective colour. Beautiful photo samples, packages and costs on extensive website.

Andrea Rees Photography
416-907-9827 or 905-908-0662 • www.andrearees.com
Creating images that are full of emotion. Portraits that speak to your heart with an artistic edge. Relationship (family) and maternity sessions. Programs include: New Mommy (maternity & newborn) and Baby's First Year. From Newborn to Graduate.

Art & Design by Tara Sinclair Hingco
905-999-4278 •
Artist specializing in studio or location photography.

Ashley and Crippen Photography
200 Davenport Rd, Toronto, Ont, M5R 1J2. • 416- 925-2222 •
Fine photography for children of all ages.

Baby's 1st Pictures
RPO Bay Ridges, PO Box 22007 713 Krosno Blvd., Pickering, Ont, L1W 4B8. • 905-831-5834 •
Specializing in newborn and baby in-home photography.

Creative Kids by Piper Studio
238 Supertest Rd, Toronto, Ont, M3J 2M2. • 416-650-1868 • www.piperstudios.com
Imagination, originality and expression; 3 ingredients for exciting and fun photography. Available in vibrant colours or dramatic Black & White portraits. Custom work available. • **VISA**, ⊖,
Interac • Mon: 10-6, Tue: 10-8:30, Wed: 10-6, Thu: 10-8:30, Fri-Sat: 10-6.

DAVID BECKETT
P H O T O G R A P H Y

SPECIALIZING IN
CHILDREN'S
PORTRAITURE

416/588-8864

www.beckettphoto.com

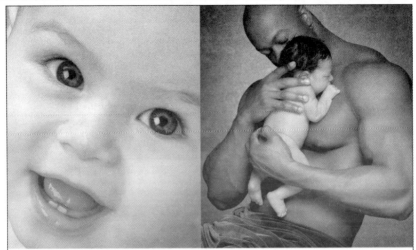

Here's My Baby!
fine portraits

By Appointment 905-893-9292 www.heresmybaby.ca
10465 Islington Ave. Downtown Kleinburg

David Amoils Photography
72 Doncaster Ave, Thornhill, Ont, L3T 1L3. • 905-882-6770 •
A true children's portrait studio. Regular sittings or 5 year "Watch Me Grow" Program.

David Beckett Photography
224 Wallace Ave, Ste 421, Toronto, Ont, M6H 1V7. • 416-588-8864 • www.beckettphoto.com
Children's specialist. David's distinctly playful approach has led to his success in capturing the spirit and personalities of his subjects. **Look for our ad in this section**. • Cheque • By appointment.

Gemini Photography
1817 Queen St E, Toronto, Ont, M4L 3Z6. • 416-469-4552 • www.geminiphotography.com
Family, newborn and maternity portraits that capture the true character of each member of your family. Studio, location, colour and black & white available.

Go Big Images
29 - 2021 Sixth Line, Oakville, Ont, L6H 4S2. • 416-456-2444 •
We provide exceptional quality, large format digital printing.

Gurgles and Giggles Photography
416-466-9723 • www.gurglesandgiggles.ca
Photography for children, families and moms-to-be, all in the comfort of your own home. Colour or Black & White. Custom designed birth announcements too.

Heather Rivlin Photography
416-782-6482 •
Photographic artist specializing in B&W portraiture for newborns, children & maternity.

Photography for Children & Families

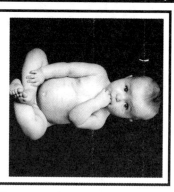

STEVE STOBER PHOTOGRAPHY

659 Mount Pleasant Road
Toronto, Ontario M4S 2N2
telephone: 416-322-6855
web: www.stevestober.com

Here's My Baby! Fine Portraits
10465 Islington Avenue, P.O. Box 838, Kleinburg, Ont, L0J 1C0. • 905-893-9292 •
www.heresmybaby.ca
Specializing in children and family portraits. We create a portrait that captures the uniqueness of
your family & child's personality, their traits, and their relationships. Whether they are best seen
through our Relationship Black & White Studies or our Classic Colour Studies. By Appointment
Only. *VISA* or MC required to reserve appointment. **Look for our ad in this section.**

Horvath Photography
24 Centre St, Thornhill, Ont, L4J 1E9. • 905-707-5770 • www.horvathphoto.com
Award winning creative portraiture in the warmth of a turn of the century home environment
with both indoor and outdoor studio facilities.

Irving Posluns Photography
100 Broadview, Ste 417, Toronto, Ont, M4M 3H3. • 416-461-9143 •
Specializing in black & white studio portraits of children and families.

JA Pearson Photography
416-892-3493 •
Photographer specializing in colour and black and white children's portraiture. • Ages: newborn
and up.

Photography for Children & Families

Julie Broadbent Photography
647-668-4356 • www.juliebroadbentphotography.shutterfly.com
Capture the moment with a different approach to photography! Photojournalism is great for birthdays and celebrations. Maternity photos also available!

Macy Mills Photography
416.250.8782 • www.macymills.com
Renowned for creating artful, beautiful, lifestyle portraits of children and families. Macy photographs children just as they are - honest, spirited, and soulful - creating visual biographies, which your family will cherish as art and heirlooms forever. By Appointment Only.

Manuela Stefan
250 St George Unit #306, Toronto, Ont, M5R 3L8. • 416-924-7457 • www.manuelastefan.com
Children are full of expression. They carry the world in their eyes. A child's face is a canvas on which emotions are displayed each and every second. I want to write little stories of their days.

Michelle Bjork Photography
416-995-4470 •
Specializing in pregnancy, child and family images in B&W and colour.

Paula F Photography
416-636-9466 • www.paulafphotography.com
"Photography Capturing Life" Specializing in children and families, casual poses and candid moments, bar/bat mitzvahs, social events and children's parties.

$COUPONS Snugabug Portrait & Art Studios
1160 Clarence St Units 3 & 4, Vaughan, Ont, L4H 2V3. • 905-264-2640 •
www.snugabugportraits.com
Snugabug specializes in milestones. From an expectant mother, to the spontaneity of children and the fun family moments. Pet friendly studio! **Look for our ad in this section. See coupon section for valuable savings.**

$COUPONS Steve Stober Photography
659 Mt. Pleasant Rd, near Eglinton Ave. E., • 416-322-6855 • www.stevestober.com
Renowned for a spontaneous and intuitive approach, his hand-printed, authentic black and white portraits of children, pregnancy and families succeed in capturing the real spirit and energy of his subjects. Free e-cards on website. **Look for our ad in this section. See coupon section for valuable savings.** • VISA, ⊕, Cheque • Mon: closed, Tue-Fri: 10-5, Sat: by app't.

Studio Anka
2374 Bloor St West - Bloor West Village, Toronto, Ont, M6S 1P5. • 416-769-4488 •
www.studioanka.ca
We love working with children, parents, grandparents and pets. Celebrating our 30th year of capturing character and playfulness in all stages of life. Specializing in intimate classic, handprinted black and white fibre portrait. Digital capture also available.

Studio White Sauce Mussel
39 Karma Road, Markham, Ont, L3R 4S8. • 416-419-8848 •
Unique, artistic, B&W children's portraits.

Welcome Aboard Photography Studio
1715 Lakeshore Rd West, Studio 202, Mississauga, Ont, L5J 1J4. • 905-855-8905 •
Priceless newborn & black & white portraiture of your children.

Play equipment is an investment - no doubt about it - but having made the investment personally, we both think it is one that paid off in full! . While we love the park, there have been many days where we welcomed the opportunity to let them burn off steam without going anywhere. Our children have spent hours swinging, sliding and hanging from our equipment and we have even been able to add components to the systems as they got older.

Don't forget though, no matter how old your children, they still need supervision on play equipment. Please note that pressure treated wood cannot be sold as of December 2003. Also, be aware that grass is not an acceptable surface for injury prevention and consider checking some of the safer alternatives.

$COUPONS Look for this company's coupon at the back of the book

Everplay Installation Inc
18 Automatic Road Unit 12, Brampton, Ont, L6S 5M5. • 416-410-3056 • www.everplay.com
Play and recreation surfaces exceeding CSA requirements. 5 yr warranty & 3 yr warranty extension for total of 8 years available. Pigmented terra-cotta or green. Colored EPDM available. •
VISA, Cheque.

$COUPONS Kids Playground World Toronto
15190 Woodbine Ave, Gormly, Ont, L0H 1G0. • 905-713-1825 • www.kidsplaygroundworld.com
Our playsystems are a dream come true for all children! They are packed with plenty of fun and interesting features to keep your children occupied for hours. Choose from a comprehensive list of features including a 9' slide, Pirates Plank, Knotted Rope Climb, Sky-Glider, Rock Climbing Wall & more! We also carry high quality state of the art trampolines. **Look for our ad in this section. See coupon section for valuable savings.** • Ages: 1-13 • **VISA**, ⊖, Cheque • Mon-Sat: 9-6.

$COUPONS Rainbow Play Systems of Ontario
28 Fulton Way, Unit 7, Richmond Hill, Ont, L4B 1E6. • 905-795-3999 •
www.rainbowofontario.com
Rainbow has sold and installed thousands of Rainbow backyard play systems and offers superior sales consultation, installation, warranties and service on premier residential playgrounds equipment. **Look for our ad in this section. See coupon section for valuable savings.** • Other Locations 1795 Meyerside Drive Unit 607, Mississauga • **VISA**, ⊖, *Interac*, Cheque • Mon-Fri: 9-5, Sat-Sun: 10-5.

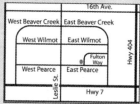
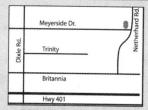

Many parents now buy their child's teacher a copy of this directory at the beginning of the year to help in planning new and different field trips for the year to come. Both the teachers and the parent council tell us they find Help! useful in organizing everything from hot lunch programs to school fun fairs.

The section has companies which will come to your school at lunch or after school for an extended period (once a week for a whole term or semester for example) as well as educational programming which is appropriate for a one time special event or seminar. Some of these companies do larger scale shows which are great for fairs, end of year parties, or other special days.

When planning school excursions, don't forget that many companies only list in one category so be sure to check the Attractions/Family Outings, Amusement Centres, Festivals, Fairs & Carnivals, and Fun for Free sections for other ideas.

Finally, almost all schools and daycares have at least one annual fundraising program in place. Here we have included some ideas to help your organization raise money.

<u>You will find the following sub-categories in this section:</u>
After School & Lunchtime Programs, Educational Workshops & Special Event Programming, Field Trips, Fundraising & Hot Lunch Programs

$ COUPONS Look for this company's coupon at the back of the book

■ After School & Lunch Time Programs

$ COUPONS Active Kids Programs Inc: AllSports, Crafts, & Ceramics
905-307-0707 • Sports, Crafts, Ceramics & Scrapbooking offered at lunchtime and afterschool.
Look for our ad in the Birthday and Camp sections. See coupon section for valuable savings. • Ages: Gr1-8.

Amazing Magic by Philip & Henry Productions
1-866-376-2033 • www.philipandhenry.com
Discover the "Secrets of Magic" ! Hands-on lessons. Bring the magic to your school!

$ COUPONS Animals with Whimz
784 St. Clair Ave West or we come to you, Toronto, Ont, M6C 1B6. • 416-656-7894 •
www.whimzonline.com
Featuring Small Mammals, Reptiles, Amphibians, Bug & Birds - from rabbits, hedgehogs and chinchillas to lizards, toads and snakes! Hands-On - Designed to Life Sciences Curriculum. We come to you or you to us. **Look for our ad in the Birthday Parties section. See coupon section for valuable savings.** • Ages: 1-16 • Cheque.

Arts Express
30 Twenty Eighth Street, Toronto, Ont, M8W 2Y6. • 416-239-3093 •
Dynamic in-school drama programming designed to build self- confidence.

$ COUPONS Bugs Without Borders
416-788-4542 Sabeena or 416-573-5234 Nadine • www.bugswithoutborders.com
Interactive & exciting presentations with our 'menagerie of wildlife'. Ontario Curriculum based.
Look for our ad in the Birthday section. See coupon section for valuable savings. • Ages: SK-Gr. 8.

Kids Fun Factory, The: Cooperative Learning Specialists
416-239-6047 • Team oriented Adventures in Science, DesignTech, and the Arts

Programs For Schools, Daycares & Special Events

$ COUPONS Mad Science
1170 Sheppard Ave W, Unit 14, Toronto, Ont, M3K 2A3. • 800-630-4403 •
www.madscience.com/toronto
After school and lunch time programs. Lasers, rocketry, slime, chemical magic and tons more!
Look for our ad in the Birthday Parties section. See coupon section for valuable savings. • Ages: 5-12 •
Cheque • By appointment.

$ COUPONS MESSY HANDS Art Studio
2501 Rutherford Rd, Unit 27, Bldg B, Richmond Hill, Ont • 905-303-MESS (6377) •
www.messyhands.com
Get messy! Get inspired! During school and Afterschool ART program which complies with the
Ontario Art Curriculum. Choose from drawing, painting, sculpture or multimedia classes! **Look for
our ad in the Birthday Parties section. See coupon section for valuable savings.** • Ages: 4-12.

PLASP Child Care Services
HO 121 Brunel Rd, Mississauga, Ont, L4Z 3E9. • 905-890-1711 • www.plasp.com
FUN programs Before School - starting 7:30 a.m., breakfast served daily; After School until 6:00
p.m.; Lunch and P.A. Days Ages 6-12.

$ COUPONS Pottery-A-Go-Go
416-658-4545 • www.potteryagogo.com
We bring the fun and creativity of handbuilding clay and painting ceramics to your School,
Community Centre, Camp, Daycare or Special Event. Choose from a wide range of after-school
and lunch time programs or in-class workshops. **Look for our ad in the Birthday Parties section. See
coupon section for valuable savings.** • Ages: 1+.

$ COUPONS Super Science
2600 John St, Ste 106, Markham, Ont, L3R 3W3. • 905-479-4459 •
www.supersciencetoronto.com
Science programs, workshops, special entertainment, presentations and shows. **Look for our ad in
the Birthday Parties section. See coupon section for valuable savings.**

TenTen Tennis Program
at your School or Community Centre, • 905-771-7511 • www.tententennis.com
Tennis made easy. An active, dynamic & progressive indoor mini-tennis program that teaches
the fundamentals of tennis in an entertaining, easy to learn way. Available at schools & community centres. • Ages: 3-12.

▪ Educational Workshops & Event Entertainment

Elise's Travelling Critters; We Come to You!
905-831-4470 • www.travellingcritters.com
Hands-on educational programs for all age groups.

Living Rhythm
45 Steepleview Cr, Richmond Hill, Ont, L4C 9R3. • 647-444-DRUM (3786) •
www.livingrhythm.ca
Interactive rhythm-based events, drums/percussion provided.

Living University
1 Copeland Ave, Toronto, Ont, M4S 1A9 . • 416-694-8444 •
Drum making, drumming circles, events, workshops. Ages 5+.

Masque Making
416-463-6162 •
Mask workshops, events and camps.

Movement Makers
416-651-4756 • www.movementmakers.ca
Creative movement encourages children to explore their imaginations through dance, play, story-telling, songs & music. • Ages: 2-13yrs.

Roseneath Theatre
Education Office, 59 Joseph Duggan Rd, Toronto, Ont, M4L 3X5. • 416-686-5199 •
First rate theatre for young people since 1982.

Arts For Children of Toronto
460 Avenue Rd, Toronto, Ont, M4V 2J1. • 416-961-1502 x302 • www.artsforchildren.org
Arts for Children of Toronto provides subsidized Outreach Programs in music, drama, visual arts and dance to under-serviced schools throughout the Greater Toronto Area. All workshops are hands-on and taught by professionals. Suitable for Nursery - Grade 8.

Chris McKhool Kids' Concerts!
49 Ashdale Ave, Toronto, Ont, M4L 2Y6. • 800-MCKHOOL •
Canada's fastest rising star. Sing-along fun!

Council on Drug Abuse (CODA)
111 Peter Street Suite 505, Toronto, Ont, M5V 2H1. • 416-763-1491 x223 • www.drugabuse.ca
CODA has been developing and providing age appropriate, interactive drug awareness programs to students, teachers and parents for over 35 years. Programs deal with issues such as self-esteem, friendship, being your own person, reaching out to others, as well as understanding drug and streetproofing concepts. • Ages: 4+.

$ COUPON $ Creepy Crawlers Express Educational Presentations
1 Promenade Circle, PO Box 943, Thornhill, Ont, L4J 8G7. • 416-456-0262 •
www.creepycrawlers.ca
Hands-On interactive presentations for students daycare to grade 9. Curriculum based and age appropriate. Choose from Bugs/Reptiles/Science/Furry Friends and more! **Look for our ad in the Birthday Parties section. See coupon section for valuable savings.**

$ COUPON $ Critters - Amazing Hands-on Animal Presentations
73 Baroness Cr, Toronto, Ont, M2J 3K4. • 416-494-0712 • www.critters.ca
An entertaining, educational, hands-on experience in your school or daycare. Touch and hold reptiles, bugs, birds, mammals, frogs and more. Curriculum based. Ideal for private, public and Montessori schools. Fun fairs, special events, camps too. **Look for our ad in the Birthday Parties section. See coupon section for valuable savings.** • Ages: 2-12.

$ COUPON $ Kayla
905-709-0234 • www.kaylamusic.ca
Ontario's popular children's entertainer available for all types of community concerts, programs. **Look for our ad in the Parent/Tot section. See coupon section for valuable savings on a Kayla Birthday Party.** • Ages: 1-6 years • Cheque.

Little Scientist Educational & Hobby Workshops
Unit #5, 801 Matheson Blvd W, Mississauga, Ont, L5V 2N6. • 905-755-1100 •
Science 101 Workshops for Schools and Home Schoolers.

Magic Mike
389 Manor Rd E, Toronto, Ont, M4S 1S9. • 416-322-1442 •
The Magic Mike Show as seen on TV. Professional family entertainment. Over 20 years experience.

Mystic Drumz
416-494-5485 •
Interactive, power-packed jam session. Over 60 percussion instruments. Schools, Daycares, Special Events. • Ages: 4+.

$COUPON$ Stories & Music From Around the World
416-652-9403 • www.worldplaytheatre.com
Children love these captivating, interactive performances with Music, Stories and Theatrical games. **Look for our ad in the Birthday Parties section. See coupon section for valuable savings.**

$COUPON$ Tom's Amazing Cats
416-347-1153 • www.tvpuppetree.com
14 different curriculum based shows ranging from Alphabet Show to Too Much Garbage. **Look for The T.V Puppetree ad in this section & Tom's Amazing Cats ad in the Birthday Section. See coupon section for valuable savings.**

▪ Field Trips

Bisque It Pottery Painting
8 - 9200 Weston Road, Woodbridge, Ont, L4H 2P8. • 905-303-6333 •
Inspire educational creativity with instructional pottery painting in our studio or at your location.

National Film Board of Canada - Mediatheque
150 John Street (at Richmond - Osgoode Subway), Toronto, Ont, M5V 3C3. • 416-973-3012 •
www.nfb.ca/mediatheque
Groups make their own films using professional techniques in hands-on workshops. Animation, documentary and Foley sound workshops all guided by professional instructors. $5 per child; free for leaders. Call for information and to book. • Ages: 3-16.

Ontario Science Centre " Sleepovers"
770 Don Mills Rd, North York, Ont, M3C 1T3. • 416-696-3256 • www.OntarioScienceCentre.ca
Sleepovers at the Ontario Science Centre make a perfect adventure for groups, Girl Guides & Scouts and families of all ages. Participants will explore the Science Centre after hours, take part in science workshops and shows, watch an IMAX® film and sleep overnight among the exhibits. Call for details and availability.

Programs For Schools, Daycares & Special Events

Pony Farm & Petting Zoo at Lionel's

11714 McCowan Rd, Stouffville, Ont, L4A 7X5. • 905-640-7669 • www.lionelsfarm.com
Introduce children to the sights, sounds, smells, culture, products and lifestyles of the farming community. A world beyond the classroom. Petting zoo. Hosting school tours for nearly 40 years.
Look for our ad in the Birthday Party (Party Places) section.

Toronto Police Museum & Discovery Centre

Located in Police Headquarters, 40 College St, Toronto, Ont, M5G 2J3. • 416-808-7020 •
www.TorontoPolice.on.ca
Bring a camera and take pictures of a jail cell. Learn about police work using interactive displays. View police equipment, and REAL evidence from famous Toronto cases. Flash the lights in a police cruiser, listen to live police radio. Guided tours for school/daycare groups. Public welcome. Free admission. • Mon-Fri: 10-4:30.

▪ Fundraising & Hot Lunch Programs

Alex Szwed Entertainment

905-893-4631 •
Free magic shows and carnival games.

Discovery Toys - National Sales Director

416-630-0138 or 905-417-4514, •
Receive free resources through reading programs and toyraisers. • Ages: 0-12 • VISA, ⊖, ▄▄, Cheque.

Food Forethought/ Food ForTots

754 Gordon Baker Dr, North York, Ont, M2H 3B4. • 416-502-3304 •
Fundraising without sacrificing nutrition.

Lunch Lady Group, The

1-800-603-6656 or 905-881-6408 •
Delivering GOOD HOT LUNCHES to kids throughout the GTA. • Ages: 6-13.

Scholars' Supplies

647-226-0817 or 705-431-1919 •
Helping schools fundraise - through student school supplies.

So Simple Designs

905-787-0569 •
Fundraisers featuring your child's artwork on cards.

Comments ?   Questions ?

We'd love to hear from you!
Email us at
info@helpwevegotkids.com

...WE'VE GOT KIDS

The internet has enabled many families to research medical or special needs information. Some of the information on the net is a bit too international sometimes, so we try to provide associations that can give more local information, contacts or medical updates. We also include schools that specialize in dealing with special children and sports and activities that can teach these children valuable skills in a fun environment.

You will find the following sub-categories in this section:
ADD/ADHD; Associations; Autism Spectrum Disorders; Special Needs Camps; Special Needs Sports; Speech & Hearing

$COUPON$ Look for this company's coupon at the back of the book

■ ADD/ADHD

A.D.D. Support Network
416-924-2090 • www.addsupport.org
A non-profit information website regarding attention differences (ADHD).

$COUPON$ ADD Centre
905-803-8066 or 416-488-2233 • www.addcentre.com
Improve grades! Improve self-esteem! The ADD Centre combines instruction in thinking skills with computerized EEG training (Neurofeedback) to empower students to improve their attention span, concentration & school performance. Also effective with Asperger's. Director is Dr. Lynda Thompson, co-author with Dr. Sears of The A.D.D. Book. **Look for our ad in the Education & Tutoring section. See coupon section for valuable savings.** • Cheque • Mon-Fri: 9:30-9, Sat-Sun: 9-5.

Brainworks; Programs for LD, ADD/ADHD Children & Their Parents
4 Paradise Blvd, #24, Brechin, Ont, L0K 1B0. • 1-866-807-3926 •
Non-Medical Solutions: Learning Disabilities, AD(HD) for the family. • Ages: 3+.

■ Associations

Canadian Cystic Fibrosis Foundation
2 Carlton St Unit 817, Toronto, Ont, M5B 1J3. • 416-932-3900 • www.ccfftoronto.ca
Fundraising and educational information.

Down Syndrome Association of Toronto
1580 Yonge Street, Suite 3D, Toronto, Ont, M4T 1Z8. • 416-966-0990 • www.dsat.ca
DSAT is a charitable, non-profit organization. We provide information, programs and mini-conferences.

Learning Disabilities Association Of Ontario
365 Bloor St E, Ste 1004, Toronto, Ont, M4W 3L4. • 416-929-4311 • www.ldao.ca
Information/referral for persons with learning disabilities and families. Lending library and video rental available. Local chapters across Ontario. Visit us online for the one nearest you. • Ages: Preschool+.

Muscular Dystrophy Canada
2345 Yonge St #901, Toronto, Ont, M4P 2E5. • 1-866-687-2538 • www.muscle.ca
MDAC provides equipment, funding, information, referral and research. • &.

Ontario Federation for Cerebral Palsy
1630 Lawrence Ave W, Ste 104, Toronto, Ont, M6L 1C5. • 416-244-9686 • www.ofcp.on.ca
A support, information and referral service which includes cerebral palsy information packages, videos, books, tapes and workshops for families.

Special Needs

Spina Bifida & Hydrocephalus Association of Ontario
555 Richmond St W, PO Box 103, Ste 1006, Toronto, Ont, M5V 3B1. • 416-214-1056,
1-800-387-1575 •
To build awareness & drive education, research, support, care & advocacy. To improve the quality of life of those with spina bifida and/or hydrocephalus. • ᕫ.

▪ Autism Spectrum Disorders

Aisling Discoveries Child & Family Centre
325 Milner Ave, Ste 110, Scarborough, Ont, M1B 5N1. • 416-321-5464 •
Supporting children & families with emotional, behavioral and social problems. • Ages: NB-12.

Autism Acceptance Project, the
416-932-3626 • http://joyofautism.blogspot.com
An annual event October 5-November 5, 2006 with writers, researchers and people with autism redefining autism and quality of life at Lonsdale Gallery at Al Green Theatre.

Autism Children's Intervention Services
8171 Yonge St, Ste 226, Thornhill, Ont, L3T 2C6. • 416-219-2316 • www.aciscanada.com
Infant, Preschool and school aged child development & IBI programs, Speech, OT, social skills, summer/winter camp for kids with developmental & learning disabilities (Autism, GDD, LD, ADD, communication delays/disorders). • Ages: 0-15 yrs.

Autism Society Ontario
416-246-9592 • www.autismsociety.on.ca
Providing support, information and resources to families of children and adults with Autism Spectrum Disorders in the province of Ontario. 31 Chapters. Publications include a quarterly magazine for members, plus Videos and Manuals available for purchase.

C.H.I.L.D. Neurodevelopmental Treatment Center
2200 Rutherford Rd #4, Maple, Ont, L4K 5V2. • 905-417-3111 •
Learning center, social skills groups, summer/winter camp, etc for children with Neurodevelopmental disabilities (Autism, LD, ADD, CP, GDD, communication disorders). • Ages: 0-15yrs.

Geneva Centre for Autism
112 Merton St, Toronto, Ont, M4S 2Z8. • 416-322-7877 • www.autism.net
Parent education & support. Direct service for kids. • Ages: 2-25.

Learning 2 Play
258 Wilson Ave, Toronto, Ont, M3H 1S6. • 647-436-5651 •
Social skills program for children ages 3 - 14.

Step By Step Learning Group
servicing GTA & surrounding area, • 905-877-9600 • www.sbslg.com
Effective education for children with individualized programming needs. Direct Instruction, behavioural teaching, specialized curriculum and Precision Teaching. Programs designed & supervised by a psychologist/certified behaviour analyst. Private school, centre & in-home programs, skill-building & assessment available. • Ages: 2 1/2-13yrs.

▪ Special Needs Camps

Camp Awakening Inc
150 Eglinton Ave E #204, Toronto, Ont, M4P 1E8. • 416-487-8400 •
Outdoor recreation promoting accomplishments, friendships and fun. • Ages: 8-18 yrs. • ᕫ.

Camp Kirk- "Working to Raise Self-Esteem"

378 Fairlawn Ave, Toronto, Ont, M5M 1T8. • 416-782-3310 •
Residential camp for children with learning disabilities and ADD/ADHD. • Ages: 6-14.

■ Special Needs General

Adapt-Able Design Inc

75 Dufflaw Rd, Ste 203, Toronto, Ont, M6A 2W4. • 416- 781-3335 •
Barrier-free design, construction and accessibility reports.

ARCH: Disability Law Centre

425 Bloor St E, Ste 110, Toronto, Ont, M4W 3R5. • 416-482-8255 or 1-866-482-2724 •
www.archdisabilitylaw.ca
Legal resource centre for persons with disabilities and their families. Call for information. TTY:
416-482-1254. • &.

Assessment, Counselling & Coaching Centre, The; Dr. S. Jane Margles

29 Alvin Ave, Toronto, Ont, M4T 2A7. • 416-428-1600 •
Counselling and coaching for optimal performance. Psycho-educational assessments.

Canadian National Institute for the Blind (CNIB)

1929 Bayview Ave, North York, Ont, M4G 3E8. • 416-486-2500 • www.cnib.ca
Counselling & referral, rehabilitation teaching, orientation & mobility training, vision rehabilitation,
technical aids, career development, library services. Early intervention (ages 0-6), services/activi-
ties for children. Visit our new Parents' Message Board to share information: www.cnib.ca/pmb.

Canadian National Institute For The Blind (CNIB) Library Resource Centre

1929 Bayview Ave, Toronto, Ont, M4G 3E8. • 416-480-7599 • www.cnib.ca
Library resource centre. Books and periodicals in Braille and other formats (talking books, electronic text, etc). • &.

$COUPON$ Canadiansitter.ca & Canadiannanny.ca

1-866-221-7918 •
70% of our babysitters/nannies want to care for children with special needs. **Look for our ad in the
Childcare section. See coupon section for valuable savings.**

Coordinated Information Peel

905-890-9432 or TTY - 890-8089 • www.cdrcp.com
Free information on services for children, families and people with developmental disabilities.

Coulter Clinic Infant Massage

2300 Yonge St, Ste 2902, Mail: Box 2325, Toronto, Ont, M4P 1E4. • 416-322-6506 •
www.coulterclinic.com
Infant Massage classes. Help strengthen your baby's digestive, respiratory, circulatory, nervous
and immune systems. Special needs children are welcome. • *VISA*, ⊖, ▓, *Interac*, Cheque.

Cyril Rehab/Kids FUNction

serving the GTA, • 416-995-6237 (Nadine) • www.cyrilrehab.ca
Occupational Therapy offered to children with varying levels of difficulty with e.g. Motor
Milestones (MEDEK), Writing, Organization, Sensory Integration, Life Skills and Attention.
Therapists see children in their own environment (school, home and/or daycare) or in clinic set-
ting. (Information disponible en français.) • Ages: 0-19yrs.

Erinoak Serving Young People With Physical Disabilities
2277 South Millway, Mississauga, Ont, L5L 2M5. • 905-820-7111 •
Paediatric habilitation, rehabilitation, and support services. • Ages: 0-19 • ♿.

Exceptional Behaviour Services
570 Westney Rd South, Suite 25, Ajax, Ont, L1S 6V6. • 905-686-4800 •
Behaviour therapy and ABA for children with special needs. • Other Locations Richmond Hill.

Extend-A-Family
200-3300 Yonge St, Toronto, Ont, M4N 2L6. • 416-484-1317 •
Building relationships for children with disabilities living in Toronto.

Family Day Care Services
710 Progress Ave. Ste. 1, Toronto, Ont, M1H 2X3. • 416-922-3434 • www.familydaycare.com
Family style childcare for your special needs child, infants to 12 years. Subsidy available. Since
1851. **Look for our ad in the Childcare section.**

Flaghouse
235 Yorkland Blvd Suite 105, Toronto, Ont, M2J 4Y8. • 800-265-6900 • www.flaghouse.com
300+ page catalogue for special needs children. • [VISA], [⊖], [▪], Cheque.

Hand Skills for Children
8201 Weston Road, Unit 1, Vaughan, Ont, L4L 1A6. • 647-889-2207 •
www.handskillsforchildren.com
Programs for children that address fine motor skills, pencil grasp, letter formation and writing
skills from pre-printing to cursive. • Ages: 3-16yrs.

HME Ltd Your Mobility Connection
124 St Regis Crescent S., Toronto, Ont, M3J 1Y8. • 416-633-9333 •
Home medical equipment, sales, rentals, supply, service.

Kids On The Block
510 King St E, Ste 224, Toronto, Ont, M5A 1M1. • 416-964-9095 •
www.kidsontheblocktoronto.com
Disability awareness puppet show that teaches children about accepting differences in others. • Ages: Gr 1-6.

Kortright Centre For Conservation
9550 Pine Valley Dr, Woodbridge, Ont, M3N 1S4. • 905-832-2289 • www.kortright.org
Guided nature walks for special needs groups. Scenic, hard surface, flat pathways. Barrier free
facilities - washroom, gift shop, cafe. To book call 416-667-6299 ext. 3.

Listening Centre, the
599 Markham St, Toronto, Ont, M6G 2L7. • 416-588-4136 • www.listeningcentre.com
Listening training to facilitate communication, language and learning. Recommended for children
with learning or developmental issues such as learning disabilities, ADD, ADHD, CAPD and
Autism Spectrum Disorders. Also appropriate as an early enrichment program. All ages. • [VISA],
Cheque • Mon-Fri: 11:00-7.

McCurdy Products
275 Jeffcoat Dr, Toronto, Ont, M9W 3E4. • 416-742-2310 •
Tricycles. Safe, fun, cool & inclusive. • Ages: 3+ • By appointment.

Natalie Orenchuk Msw.B.A. Specialist in Gifted /All Other Special Needs
93 Castlewood Rd, Toronto, Ont, M5N 2L3. • 416-480-2150/416-992-4409
htttp://pages.sprint.ca/gifted2000
Emotionally intense /sensitive children/adolescents gifted. L.D. ADD Aspergers, autism etc.
Assessments, school meetings, specialized psychotherapies, parenting strategies. **Look for our ad
in the Education section.**

respiteservices.com
112 Merton Street, Toronto, Ont, M4S 2Z8. • 416-322-6317 •
Connects families to respite workers and respite services.

Variety Village
3701 Danforth Ave, Toronto, Ont, M1N 2G2. • 416- 699-7167 • www.varietyontario.com
Variety Village is an integrated sports facility where the priority group is youths with disabilities.
Adapted physical education and aquatics programs offered daily. Summer hours closed Sundays.
Ages: 3+ • ♿.

York Paediatric Therapy Services Inc
2 locations: Richmond Hill & Toronto, • Head Office: 905-737-9680 • www.yorkpaediatrics.com
Providing Occupational and Physical assessments/therapy for children experiencing developmental and learning difficulties. Handwriting, Medek, Sensory Integration, Neurodevelopmental
Therapy focussed. Open 6 days. • Ages: 0-14 • Cheque • By appointment • ♿.

▪ Special Needs Sports

Community Association For Riding For The Disabled (CARD)
4777 Dufferin St, Toronto, Ont, M3H 5T3. • 416-667-8600 • www.card.ca
CARD promotes therapy and rehabilitation for people with physical and developmental disabilities
through horseback riding. Horse provides stimulus by creating a changed therapeutic and social
environment. • Ages: 5+ • ♿.

Horses of Course
416-691-8554 • Riding programs for kids. Adaptive sessions available for kids with special
needs. • Ages: 4+ • Cheque • By appointment.

Paralympics Ontario (partnered with Canadian Paralympics Committee)
1185 Eglinton Ave E #102, North York, Ont, M3C 3C6. • 416-426-7187 •
www.paralympicsontario.ca • Provide leadership, resources & opportunities to ensure a strong
community for persons with a disability in the Ontario sport and recreation community. Affiliated
with Ontario Amputee & Les Autres Sports Association, Blind Sports Association, Cerebral Palsy
Sports Association & Wheelchair Sport Association. • ♿.

Special Olympics Ontario
18 Wynford Dr, Ste 300, North York, Ont, M3C 3S2. • 416-447-8326 • www.osoinc.com
Year round sports training and competition for people who have an intellectual disability. Sixteen
official sports...become involved...join in and have fun! Toll free (888) 333-5515. • Ages: 8+.

Yoga 4 Kids
416-532-5988 • Private yoga therapy sessions for children with special needs available.

▪ Speech & Hearing

It is recommended that all children have their hearing tested. There is an infant hearing
screening program that all newborns should undergo - ask for it if it is not offered to you.
Even slight hearing impairments resulting from ear infections can have an impact on speech,
comprehension, development, movement and learning. And now, we are discovering that
playing too-loud music through headphones can also cause impairment. For additional information, call the Ontario Speech and Language Association (OSLA) at (416) 920-0361, which
can provide a referral to a registered therapist in private practice in your area, or the College
of Audiologists and Speech-Language Pathologists of Ontario.

Aaron Low - Speech Pathologist
200 St Clair Ave W, Toronto, Ont, M4V 1R1. • 416-922-0070x3 •
Voice, singing, nodules, hoarseness, autism.

Bob Rumball Centre for the Deaf - Happy Hands Preschool
2395 Bayview Ave, North York, Ont, M2L 1A2. • 416-449-9651 or 416-449-8859 TTY •
www.bobrumball.org
Preschool for deaf children and hearing children. Open all year round including summer. Qualified
ECE staff. Warm and friendly environment. Subsidy available. Communication in ASL/English. •
Ages: 2.5-5yrs • *Interac* • Mon-Fri: 7:30am-5:30pm.

Bob Rumball Centre for the Deaf - Parent-Infant Program
2395 Bayview Ave, North York, Ont, M2L 1A2. • 416-449-9651 x105 or 416-449-2728 TTY •
www.bobrumball.org
Program for deaf/hard of hearing children and their parents. • Ages: 0-2yrs.

Canadian Hearing Society
271 Spadina Rd, Toronto, Ont, M5R 2V3. • 416-928-2500, 416-964-0023 tty, 1(877) 347-3427 •
www.chs.ca
Hearing aids. Audiology for children over 2 years. Speech & Language for children 0-5 years.
Information for parents of children with hearing loss.

Clearly Speaking
517 Cranbrooke Ave, Toronto, Ont, M5M 1N9. • 416-410-8255 (Talk) •
Paediatric speech-language pathology assessment and treatment services. Hanen centre certified.

Hanen Centre
1075 Bay St, Ste 515, Toronto, Ont, M5S 2B1. • 416-921-1073 • www.hanen.org
Resources and programs for parents of children with language delays. • Ages: 1-6 • ♿.

Helen Turk Speech Clinic: Paediatric Services
1333 Sheppard Ave E, Ste 338, Toronto, Ont, M2J 1V1. • 416-499-2939 •
Assessment and treatment of childhood speech and language disorders including articulation/phonology,
language and fluency/stuttering. Hanen certified. Over 15 years of clinical experience.

Kidspeech & Family Rehabilitation
19 Larabee Cr, Don Mills, Ont, M3A 3E6. • 416-447-7325 •
Speech-language, learning disabilities, brain injuries, rehabilitation. • Cheque.

Kim Doron, Speech-Language Pathologist
31 Amberty Street, Thornhill, Ont, L4J 8W6. • 905-731-3400 • kimdoron@sympatico.ca
Assessment and treatment for preschool and school-age children with speech/language difficulties. Parental involvement encouraged. Dufferin and Highway 7.

Speech, Language & Learning Centre
570 Westney Rd South, Suite 25, Ajax, Ont, L1S 6V6. • 905-686-4800 •
Assessments and individual therapy. • Other Locations: Richmond Hill.

Toronto Preschool Speech & Language Services (TPSLS)
225 Duncan Mill Rd, Ste 201, Toronto, Ont, M3B 3K9. • 416-338-8255 (voice), 416-338-0025
(TTY), French 416-491-1230 • www.tpsls.on.ca
TPSLS offers FREE services to children and families living in Toronto. SPEECH AND LANGUAGE
PROGRAM provides assessment, parent training and intervention for children from birth to
Senior Kindergarten entry, who have trouble talking or understanding language. INFANT HEAR-
ING PROGRAM provides newborn hearing screening to identify babies born Deaf or Hard of
Hearing. Once a newborn is identified with a hearing loss, communication development services
are provided for the babies and information and counseling for their families. • Ages: 0-5 years.

Voice for Hearing Impaired Children
161 Eglinton Ave E, Ste 701, Toronto, Ont, M4P 1J5. • 416-487-7719 •
www.voicefordeafkids.com
Providing programs and services for deaf children. 17 chapters across Canada.

Sports

We feel very strongly that kids should be exposed to sports while they are young. Not only is it vital to get them active in this age of childhood obesity, but we have also found that the camaraderie and team support is a wonderful lesson for children of any ability. If your child happens to find a sport that he/she will love for a lifetime, that is even better!

Last year, we found a great website www.Sportalliance.com. Click on the "Links" button and you will be taken to a list of the associations for every sport you have heard of and some you haven't! Seriously, we suggest that this be the starting point for anyone looking to find teams or coaches for their child.

<u>You will find the following sub-categories in this section:</u>
General Sports & Multi-Sport Centres; Gymnastics, Trampoline & Circus Arts; Horseback Riding; Martial Arts; New & Used Sporting Goods; Skating & Hockey; Ski/Snowboard Lessons, Centres & Resorts, Soccer; Sports Associations; Swimming

$COUPON$ Look for this company's coupon at the back of the book

▪ General Sports & Multi-Sport Centres

$COUPON$ Active Kids Zone
2600 John St, Unit 116, Markham, Ont, L3R 3W3. • 905-307-0707 • www.activekidszone.com
Sports & Creative Movement programs for walking to age 12. **Look for our ad in the Birthday section. See coupon section for valuable savings.**

DASH Sports
53-1250 Marlborough Crt, Oakville, Ont, L6H 2W7 • 905-849-8837 •
Fun, unique multi-sport programming for kids.

Fizz Ed's Youth Fitness Club
9078 Leslie St. Unit 10, Richmond Hill, Ont • 905-881-8555 • Co-ed youth fitness club 10-18 yrs.

$COUPON$ North Beach Indoor Volleyball Academy
74 Railside Rd, North York, Ont, M3A 1A3. • 416-446-0777 • www.northbeachvolleyball.com
We offer fun and exhilarating sports on and off the sand. Beach volleyball, 4 on 4 beach soccer, boxing for teens, Fitness on the sand and beginner rock climbing. All age groups. **Look for our ad in this section. See coupon section for valuable savings.** • Ages: 4+.

$COUPON$ Sportball Canada
39 Glen Cameron Rd, Unit 8, Thornhill, Ont, L3T 1P1. • 1-877-678-5437 •
Multi-sport programs offered year round. Programs also available for children with special needs. **Look for our ad in the Parent/Tot section. See coupon section for valuable savings.** • Ages: 16mos - 9years.

$COUPON$ Sportplay Multi-Sport Weekly Classes
Locations around the GTA, • 905-940-9481 or 1-866-940-9481 • www.sportplay.ca
Sportplay is a fun, positive, supportive multi-sport program teaching 2-8 year old kids general athletic skills and specific skills for the major sports. Sports include ball hockey, baseball, basketball, cooperative games, soccer, tennis, touch football, track& field, volleyball and much more! **Look for our ad in this section. See coupon section for valuable savings.**

Top Spin Table Tennis School
7026 Bathurst St (at Steeles), Thornhill, Ont, L4G 8K3. • 905-326-9570 or 647-298-2243 •
Professional Instruction in Recreational and Competitive Table Tennis (Ping-Pong). • Ages: 6+.

Sports

Toronto Blue Jays Baseball Club - Kids Club
1 Blue Jays Way, Ste 3200 (Rogers Centre), Toronto, Ont, M5V 1J1. • 416-341-1000, for tickets call 416-341-1234 • www.bluejays.com
Jr Jays, sign up for the Toronto Blue Jays Kids Club today! For only $10, you will receive: a Kids Club knapsack, t-shirt, membership card entitling you to a 2 for 1 ticket discount, newsletters, contests and so much more! • Ages: all, Jr Jays 14 & under.

Toronto Flag Football League
136 Ledbury St, Toronto, Ont, M5M 4H9. • 416-485-7055 • www.torontoflagfootball.com
Toronto's One and Only Flag Football Experience! Fun, safe, exciting non-stop football action. Trained coaches & referee at every game. Spring session. 8 weeks. Includes games, practices and exciting playoffs! Please see our website for details. Ages 10-14.

Toronto Parks, Forestry & Recreation; Sports Programs
416-392-1111 • www.toronto.ca/parks
Community centres, fitness and aquatic centres, arenas, tennis courts, golf courses, children's water play areas, outdoor pools, skating rinks, parks, ski hills, camps, gardens and more!

University of Toronto Junior Blues
55 Harbord St, Toronto, Ont, M5S 2W6. • 416-978-3436 • www.juniorblues.ca
An exciting variety of sport and leadership programs. Experienced instructors, central location and small class sizes. Swimming, Water Polo, Gymnastics, Track, Skating, Tennis, Soccer, Yoga, March Break Camps and more! Have Fun and Get Active! • Ages: 6mos-16yrs.

Valley Tennis Club
Yonge & York Mills, • 416-440-0645 (April-Oct) • www.valleytennis.ca
Outdoor summer club. Children's programs & summer camps. Professional coaches.

▪ Gymnastics, Trampoline & Circus Arts

airborne trampoline
3 locations: Woodbridge 905-850-8477, Mississauga 905-828-2412, Newmarket 905-836-9091
Classes, March break & summer camps. Competitive team training & Birthdays. **Look for our ad in the Birthday Parties section.** • Ages: 4+ • *Interac*, Cheque.

All Children's Progressive Gym
20 Glebe Rd E (3 Bl. N. of Davisville, S. of Manor), • 416-480-9826 •
A recreational and non-competitive program which provides the maximum variety of exercises and equipment, challenging and encouraging physical activity. Since 1959. September-May program. **Look for our ad in the Parent/Tot section.** • Ages: 2-7 • Mon-Thu: 9-5.

Big Top School of Circus Arts
1105 Kerrisdale Blvd, Newmarket, Ont, L3Y 8W1. • 905-898-0699 •
Trapeze, Trampoline, Bungee, Tight-Wire, Stilts, Juggling etc. • Ages: 1.5yrs+.

$COUPON$ Birchmount Gymnastics Centre
1800 Birchmount Road, Toronto, Ont, M1P 2H7. • 416-292-4110 •
www.birchmountgymnastics.com
Gymnastics for all ages. After school, evening and weekend programs. New day time programs: parent & tot open play time, kindergym for pre-school ages, movement with music, parent strength and stretching classes while your child is doing kindergym. **Look for our ad in this section. See coupon section for valuable savings.**

Bramalea Gymnastics Club

255B Rutherford Rd S , Brampton, Ont, L6W 3J7. • 905-455-0105 •
Recreational, competitive programs and camps - all ages. • ♿.

Canadiana School of Rhythmic Gymnastics

905-760-0092 • Develop grace, poise and elegance practicing with ball, hoop, rope, ribbon. •
Other Locations North and Central Toronto, Thornhill, Woodbridge, Aurora, Richmond Hill and Ajax.

Discovery Gymnastics

205 Champagne Dr, Unit #5 (Finch & Dufferin), North York, Ont, M3J 2C6. • 416-638-3033 •
www.discoverygymnastics.com
Professional instruction in recreational and competitive gymnastics, trampoline, tumbling, dance
and yoga for boys and girls. 10,000 square feet of Olympic equipment, certified instructors, separate kindergym area. Viewing window. Birthday parties & seasonal camps. • Ages: 18mos+.

G.S. Aquatics (Georgina Shaw Aquatics Inc) - Gymnastics Programs

14 Carluke Cr., North York, Ont • 416-222-3745 • www.gsaquatics.com
Fun-filled gymnastics programme with specially designed, scaled down equipment for students
of all ages. We offer Toddlergym: 18 mos. - 3 years, Kindergym: 3-5 years and Senior Kindergym:
5-8 years. Low student/coach ratios of 6:1. All programmes are Gymnastics Ontario approved.

Sports

Gyros Gymnastics

2301 Keele St Unit 105, North York, Ont, M6M 3Z9. • 416-614-0521 •
Gyros offers recreational and competitive programs for every age and skill level. Our gym is fully equipped. Daytime, after school and weekend programs; March Break, Passover, Summer & Winter Camps available. Call to request a brochure be mailed to you. • Ages: 2yrs+ • *VISA*, *Interac*, Cheque.

Just Bounce Trampoline Club

3731 Chesswood Dr, North York, Ont, M3J 2P6. • 416-635-0206 • www.justbounce.ca
8 TRAMPOLINES - The biggest trampoline facility in Ontario! Trampoline Lessons for Tots, Children, Teens and Adults. Trampoline burns 600 calories/hour. A great way to keep in shape and have fun! 1:8 Instructor ratio.

Kidnasium

745 Mount Pleasant Rd, 2nd Floor, Toronto, Ont, M4S 2N4. • 416-480-2608 •
Recreational gymnastics programs for children aged 18 mos. - 8 years old.

Kids Super Gym Mississauga

3620A Laird Rd. Units 9 & 10, Mississauga, Ont • 905-607-5437 •
Recreational gymnastics, camp programs and birthday parties. • Ages: 18mos-teens.

"Ritmika" Rhythmic Gymnastics Centre

361 Four Valley Drive Unit # 3, Concord, Ont, L4K 5Z3. • 905-660-9535 • www.ritmika.ca
Rhythmic gymnastics programs for all ages and ability levels. A beautiful combination of dance and gymnastics performed to music using colorful ribbons, balls, hoops & ropes. Professional coaching staff. • 15 Toronto locations • Ages: 4+ • Cheque • &.

$COUPON$ Seneca College Community Sport & Recreation; Gymnastics Program

Newnham Campus, 1750 Finch Ave E, Toronto, Ont., • 416-491-5050 x2301 •
www.senecac.on.ca/home/kidstuff/comrec
Gymnastics at its best! For 34 years Seneca College has been providing children and adults with exceptional recreational programs. Our highly qualified staff, small class size and excellent facility foster fun and learning. **Look for our ad in the Camp section. See coupon section for valuable savings.** •
Ages: 2+ • *VISA*, ⊕, ▤, *Interac* • Mon-Tue: 6-9, Wed: 3:30-8:30, Sat: 9-4, Sun: 9:30-3:30.

Silhouettes of York Rhythmic Gymnastics Club

1105 Kerrisdale Blvd, Newmarket, Ont, L3Y 7V1. • 905-898-0699 •
Recreational and competitive ribbon and ball = FUN. • Ages: 3+.

Skyriders Trampoline Place

9094 Leslie St, #5A, Richmond Hill, Ont, L4B 3L9. • 905-731-0005 •
The exciting sport of trampoline. Summer, March Break and winter camps. • Ages: 8+ • Cheque.

Steeles West Gymnastics

601 Magnetic Dr, Unit 21, North York, Ont, M3J 3J2. • 416-736-8759 •
Children's gymnastics and tumbling lessons and camps.

Toronto Aspirals Rhythmic Gymnastics Centre

Locations in North & Central Toronto, R. Hill, Thornhill, Aurora, • 416-636-1880 # 457 or
905-760-0092 • www.aspirals.com
Quality recreational and competitive classes for girls age 4 & up. Where girls develop coordination, grace, and elegance practicing with hoop, rope, ball and ribbon in a safe and stimulating environment. Nationally certified experienced instructors.

University of Toronto Gymnastics Club
55 Harbord St, Toronto, Ont, M5S 2W6. • 416-978-3436 •
Sports skills. Professional instruction. Year-round program - competitive & recreational. • Ages: 4 -16 .

Vaughan Gymnastics Club
15 Connie Cres, Unit 9, Concord, Ont, L4K 1L3. • 905-660-7800 •
Gymnastics classes, birthday parties and summer camps. • Ages: 3+.

$COUPON$ Wonderful World of Circus
2600 John St, Unit 204-205, Markham, Ont, L3R 3W3. • 905-479-2411 •
www.wonderfulworldofcircus.com
Gymnastics, Acrobatics, Circus Arts, Trapeze, Aerial Hoop, Spanish Web. Classes are taught by professional circus performers from Moscow Circus and Cirque de Soleil. **Look for our ad in this section. See coupon section for valuable section.**

▪ Horseback Riding

Bertin Stables English Riding School
3445 Dundas W (hwy 5), Oakville, Ont, L6M 4J4. • 905-827-4678 •
English riding school lessons, camps. All ages.

Circle R Ranch
RR # 1, Delaware, Ont, N0L 1E0. • 1-877-844-8738 or 519-471-3799 •
Western horseback riding- Learn to Ride & Care for Your Own Horse. • Ages: 8-16 yrs.

Clairville Conservation Ranch
10309 McVean Dr, Brampton, Ont, L6P 0K3. • 905-794-0700 •
Come horseback ride on beautiful Clairville Ranch. • Ages: 10+.

Five Star Ranch
3340 Dundas St W, Oakville, Ont, L6M 4J3. • 905-827-7519 •
Western riding lessons, Camps, Clinics & trail riding.

Horses of Course
416-691-8554 •
Riding programs teach kids of all ages about riding and caring for the horse. Quiet, safe horses. Summer programs. Adaptive sessions available for kids with special needs. Adult beginners welcome. Ontario Safety Standards met. • Ages: 4+ • Cheque • By appointment.

Riding Academy at the Horse Palace
Exhibition Place, Toronto, Ont • 416-599-4044 • www.horsepalace.ca
Located on the Exhibition grounds and TTC accessible, The Horse Palace offers English instruction to beginner and experienced riders. • Ages: 8+ • Mon-Fri: 1-10, Sat-Sun: 9-6.

Sunnybrook Stables Ltd: Sunnybrook Park
1132 Leslie St (at Eglinton), Don Mills, Ont, M3C 2S7. • 416-444-4044 •
www.sunnybrookstables.ca
Specializing in both flatwork and jumping, Sunnybrook Stables has been teaching students of all ages to ride for over 25 years. • Ages: 9+ • Mon-Thu: 1-8, Sat-Sun: 9-6.

WES Equestrian School
Woodbine Ave at Aurora Rd & 404, • 905-713-9991 •
Year round riding lessons - indoor and outdoor arenas.

Sports

▪ Martial Arts

Classical Martial Arts Centre (CMAC)
Yonge/St. Clair 416-923-1501, Bathurst/College 416-535-1501, • www.cmac1.ca
Improved attention span has been shown to be the most obvious advantage to training in the Martial Arts, leading directly to improved academic performance. And the Development of Self Discipline, Self Confidence, Self Awareness & of course Self Defense. Specialized classes 6 days/week specifically targeted to your child's age range & attention span. Karate Do and Jiu Jitsu.

East West Karate
1107 Lorne Park Rd, Unit 16, Mississauga, Ont, L5H 3A1. • 905-891-9448 •
Intro Karate. $24.95 includes free uniform & 2 lessons. • Ages: 3+.

High Park Martial Arts
3094 Dundas St W, Toronto, Ont, M6P 1Z8. • 416-769-9222 • www.highparkmartialarts.ca
Self-Discipline. Self-Esteem. Self-Defense. Open since 1992. Classes divided by age groups. • Ages: 4+.

North Toronto Karate Schools
5 locations @ Yonge/Eglinton, • 416-875-9820 •
Kids 3+. Youth & adult classes too.

$ COUPON$ Northern Karate Schools
Toronto 416-651-6000, Don Mills 416-441-3648, Woodbridge 905-856-4047, Richmond Hill 905-508-5811, Markham 905-475-0044, Thornhill 416-999-9345 • www.northernkarate.com
Northern Karate Schools, Toronto's leading martial arts organization conducts classes for children, teens, adults and families, beginners to advanced, at 6 metro locations, 7 days a week. Special programs include Camp Black Belt™, Reality Check™ street-safety, Bully Proof™, Cardio Combat® martial fitness and Budo Bliss™ yoga+martial arts+zen fusion. Introductory program $19.95. Family discounts. **See ad in this section. See coupon section for valuable savings.** 30-day, money-back guarantee. • Ages: 3+ • *VISA*, ⊜, ▓, *Interac*, Cheque • ♿.

Salvosa BJJ Ascension - Academy of Mixed Martial Arts
31 Progress Ave Unit 19, Scarborough, Ont, M1P 4S6. • 416-677-2722 •
www.martialartstoronto.com
Our unique Brazilian Jiu-Jitsu program is both fun and effective. Children develop respect for their peers and gain tremendous confidence in their social and physical environment.

Superkids Karate
50 McIntosh Dr, #113, Unionville, Ont, L3R 8C7. • 905-470-7740 •
Awesome kids classes for the past 16 years. • Ages: 4-12 yrs.

Toronto Academy Of Karate, Fitness & Health
50 Poplar Plains Cres, Toronto, Ont, M4V 1E8. • 416-924-3123 •
Established in 1970. Featured in National Geographic.

▪ New & Used Sporting Goods

Hogtown Extreme Sports
401 King St W, Toronto, Ont, M5V 1K1. • 416-598-4192 •
Full selection of skateboards, snowboards, BMX, clothing, shoes, accessories.

Majer Hockey
4610 Dufferin St (North of Finch), Toronto, Ont, M3H 5S4. • 416-736-7444 •
Skate exchange. Graphite stick repair. Huge Goalie room. Laser sharpening & more!

Original STX Pro Shop
2015 Avenue Rd, Toronto, Ont, M5M 4A5. • 416-484-1105 •
We do hockey well! Filling your hockey needs year round.

Play It Again Sports
5863 Yonge St, North York, Ont, M2M 3T9. • 416-222-5713 •
Buy, Sell, Trade - New & Used Sports Equipment. • Ages: 3+.

▪ Skating & Hockey

Avenue Road Hockey Association
416-398-3825 •
House league & select hockey - ages 6-18.

Breakaway Skating Institute
905-881-6548 x3 • www.breakawayskating.com
Experience the fun of skating! Unique programs, enthusiastic instructors, and limited enrollment
create the environment & opportunity to learn and have fun! Programs offered: hockey skating &
skills or basic skating with intro to a variety of ice sports. No exp required; Age 2.5 yrs +

Sports

Forest Hill Figure Skating Club

Forest Hill Arena: 340 Chaplin Crcs (2 bl. N. of Eglinton), Toronto, • 416-481-7325 •
www.fhfsc.ca
It's never too early or too late to learn to skate. The FHFSC offers a wide array of versatile programs including Preschool, Start Right, CanSkate, Double Digit, Adult, Junior Development, Advanced and Competitive. Professional, caring coaches. September-May. • Ages: 2+.

Harbourfront Centre: Natrel Skating Rink

235 Queens Quay W, Toronto, Ont, M5J 2G8. • 416-973-4000 •
www.harbourfrontcentre.com/skating
Beautiful harbourside rink with rentals, sharpening and lessons available. Open 7 days/wk, 10am-10pm.

Hockey Toronto - www.hockeytoronto.com

416-631-4221 • www.hockeytoronto.com
Hockeytoronto.com is a comprehensive listing of all aspects of hockey in Toronto, the GTA and Ontario. Boys hockey, girls hockey, men's hockey, women's hockey and coed hockey. Hockey leagues, hockey tournaments, pickup hockey and hockey instruction. March Break hockey camps, Passover hockey camps and summer hockey camps.

Ice Nook Indoor Skating Rinks

905-940-2877 • www.pathcom.com/~mns
Our ice never melts! No refrigeration or water required. Install an indoor, year-round synthetic ice skating rink in your basement, garage or shed. It's easy. ICE NOOK is versatile and family fun for all ages and at all levels of ice skating.

North Toronto Hockey

www.nthockey.ca
Neighbourhood House League Hockey. No Skills Required! • Ages: boys & girls 5-19 yrs.

North York Storm Girls Hockey

1995 Weston Rd, PO Box 79508, Toronto, Ont, M9N 3W9. • 416-249-5361 •
Teams for girls 5-19. Affordable fun.

Performance Skating Schools Inc

905-430-3125 •
Serving private schools since 1994 •Locations Metro wide • Ages: 3+.

Saves Goaltending International

3978 Chesswood Dr, Toronto, Ont, M3J 2W6. • 416-633-7620 •
Professional goaltending instruction. Innovative training methods. Low student:instructor ratio. Fun for all.

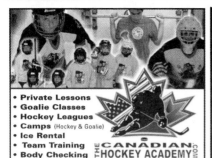

$ COUPONS $ Seneca College Community Sport & Recreation; Skating Program

Newnham Campus, 1750 Finch Ave E, • 416-491-5050 x2301 • www.senecac.on.ca/home/kidstuff/comrec

35 Years in the Business of offering exceptional skating programs for children & adults. Parent & Tot, Pre-Canskate, Canskate, Canpower, STAR Skate Program and Adult programs. NCCP and Skate Canada certified coaches, small groups and great facilities. **Look for our ad in the Camp section. See coupon section for valuable savings.** • Ages: 3+ • *VISA*, ⬡, ▓▓, *Interac* • Mon: 7-9, Thu: 5:15-9:10, Sat: 11-3:05.

Silver Blades Skating Club Inc

Central Arena, 50 Montgomery Rd, Etobicoke, Ont, M9A 4X1. • 416- 233-8331 • Skating programs from Canskate to competitive. • Ages: 4-17 • Cheque.

Skating Rink Hotline - Toronto Parks, Forestry & Recreation

416-338-RINK (7465) • www.toronto.ca
Indoor & outdoor skating rinks. Public skates, lessons & programs.

Universal Skating Academy

3299 Bayview Ave, P.O. Box 38597, Toronto, Ont, M2K 2Y5. • 905-731-2953 • Skating lessons - all ages, disciplines and levels. • Ages: 3-18.

▪ Ski/Snowboard Lessons, Centres & Resorts

Beginners Discover Skiing & Discover Snowboarding

905-212-9040 • All inclusive lesson/rental packages for new skiers & boarders.

Blue Mountain Resort

108 Jozo Weider Blvd, R.R. 3, Collingwood, Ont, L9Y 3Z2. • 416- 869-3799 • Ski programs for kids and families.

Canadian Ski Council: Grade 5 Snow Pass

5045 Orbitor Dr, Building 7, Suite 100, Mississauga, Ont, L4W 4Y4. • 905-212-9040 • www.snowpass.ca • Free skiing for kids in grade 5.

Earl Bales Ski Centre & Centennial Park Snow Centre- Ski and Snowboard Toronto

North York Ski Centre in Earl Bales Park, 4169 Bathurst St & Centennial Park Snow Centre, 256 Centennial Park Rd. • 416-33-TO-SKI (416-338-6754) • www.toronto.ca/parks
Alpine skiing & snowboarding. Lessons, camp programs, equipment rentals. Weather permitting, Dec. - Mar.

Glen Eden Ski & Snowboard Centre

5234 Kelso Rd , Milton, Ont • 905-878-5011 •
Lessons, snowmaking, night skiing, 12 slopes, snowtubing. • Ages: 4+.

Hockley Valley Resort

R.R. #1, Orangeville, Ont, L9W 2Y8. • 416-363-5490 or 519-942-0754 • www.hockley.com
Excellent ski programs and instruction. Perfect for your next family getaway. Open year-round.
Enjoy golf, spa, fine dining and more. Just 45 min north of Toronto.

Raven Snow Club

416-225-1551 • www.ravensnowclub.com
Ski and snowboard day camp. Christmas Break, 4 or 8 Saturdays or Sundays, March Break.
Transportation from GTA to Blue Mountain. • Ages: 6-17.

Snow Valley Resort

PO Box 46, Barrie, Ont, L4M 4S9. • 705-721-7669 • Ski & snowboard lessons. Snow tubing park.

Snowhawks Ski and Snowboard School

166 Lytton Blvd, Toronto, Ont, M4R 1L4. • 416-487-5271 • www.snowhawks.com
Certified instructors stress skill development and fun! Mid-winter travelling programs for kids,
teens and adults plus Christmas and Spring Break camps. • Ages: 6-99.

▪ Soccer & Baseball

Frozen Ropes Canada

2009 Wyecroft Road,Unit B, Oakville, Ont, L6L 6J4. • 905-847-7697 •
www.frozenropescanada.ca
Play ball! Frozen Ropes is open. Frozen Ropes opens in Oakville, having trained 30,000 baseball
and softball players. For Major League instruction and facilities, call 905-847-7697. **Look for our ad
in the Birthday section.**

Just for Kicks Soccer

38 Maida Vale, Scarborough, Ont, M1K 2X9. • 416-285-5425 •
Soccer for children 4-17 years old in Scarborough.

K.I.K. Soccer

53-1250 Marlborough Crt, Oakville, Ont, L6H 2W7. • 905-849-8837 •
Soccer league; instruction and games-3-7 yrs.

$COUPON$ Madskills Soccer Programs

101 Chester Avenue, Toronto, Ont, M4K 2Z8. • 416-705-9090 • www.madskillsinc.com
Through our Freestyle soccer shows & programs, we develop confidence, co-ordination & ball
control. The skills needed to play the worlds greatest game. **Look for our ad in the Birthday section.
See coupon section for valuable savings**.

Power Soccer School of Excellence

905-829-0562 or 1-888-883-6712 • www.powersoccer.ca
Professional soccer coaching clinics. Learn soccer in a fun, safe atmosphere! Fall, Winter &
Spring programs. March Break and Summer Camps also. **Look for our ad in the Camps section.**
Ages: 4-18.

▪ Swimming

Dafna's Swim Centre
4884 Dufferin St, Unit 8, North York, Ont, M3H 5S8. • 416-661-Swim (7946) •
Red Cross teaching program. Small classes (Max 3:1 ratio). Warm water pool (90 degrees F). •
Ages: 6 mos +.

Davina's Swim House
416-385-1005 • davinaswim@rogers.com
Swim lessons. Located in Toronto. Low 3:1 ratio. Kids' AquaRobics. All year round sessions. Red
Cross & Lifesaving Society Programs. • Ages: 5mos+.

Douglas Snow Aquatic Centre North York Parks and Recreation
5100 Yonge St (behind City Hall), North York, Ont, M2N 5V7. • 416-395-7585 •
Excitement year round. Group, semi-private or private swim lessons. Tarzan rope & 3-story, tubular slide.

$COUPONS Eunice's Swim School & Recreation Centre (Red Cross Program)
2 locations: Don Mills/Sheppard & Allen/Eglinton, • 416-410-SWIM (7946) •
www.euniceswimschool.com
The Best and Most Unique Swim School in Toronto. 100% Success Rate. Warm pool temperature.
All instructors trained carefully in our methods. Life Saving & I Can Swim awards. Our special meth-
ods and scientific approach and our Caring, Quality Instructors Make The Difference. Visit us online.
Look for our ad in this section. See coupon section for valuable savings. • Ages: 2 Mos. + • 🔲, 🔲, 🔲,
Cheque • ♿.

Extreme Fitness/ Extreme Kids
8281 Yonge St, Thornhill, Ont, L3T 2C7. • 905-709-9498 •
Private and semi-private swimming lessons for all ages. • Ages: 5-12 • 🔲, 🔲, 🔲, *Interac.*

Felix's Swim School
8403 Yonge St, Thornhill, Ont, L3T 2C7. • 905-731-3601 •
Low ratio. Qualified instructors. Nobody does it BETTER! • Other Locations 7026 Bathurst St.

G.S. AQUATICS

- Swimming (6 months-adult)
- Synchronized Swimming & Aquafit
- Gymnastics (Walking -8 years)

- I Can Swim (Esso Swim)
- Maximum Pupil - Teacher Ratio
  Swimming 3-1, Gymnastics 6-1

SWIM & GYM SCHOOL

Bayview/Eglinton • Bayview/401
ALL RED CROSS AND LIFESAVING SOCIETY LEVELS UP TO AND INCLUDING BRONZE CROSS

(416) 222-3745

SAFETY & FITNESS IS ALL YEAR 'ROUND
www.gsaquatics.com

$COUPON$ G.S. Aquatics (Georgina Shaw Aquatics Inc)
2 locations: Bayview/401 and Bayview/Eglinton., • 416-222-3745 • www.gsaquatics.com
Qualified, screened individually trained instructors - same teacher each week. All Red Cross and
Lifesaving Society levels. Synchro and I Can Swim (Esso Swim). Toddlergym and Kindergym.
Private pool instruction available. Instructional games/Lifeguarding. Fun & Learning! Classes
everyday. Call for schedule. **Look for our ad in this section. See coupon section for valuable savings.** •
Ages: 6mos+ • Cheque.

Mississauga Recreation & Parks - Swimming Program
300 City Centre Drive, Mississauga, Ont, L5B 3C1. • 905-615-3200 ext. 5349 •
www.mississauga.ca/rec&parks
Recreational swimming and lessons available at Mississauga indoor and outdoor pools. **Look for
our ad in this section.**

Neighbourhood Development Swim Club of Scarborough - NDSCS
416-267-SWIM (7946)
Give your child the lifesaving skill of swimming the "Olympic Way". Learn-to-stroke programs for
children 4-8 yrs. Build skill, speed and endurance for swimmers 6-19 yrs. Programs run from
September to July. Sessions are 10 weeks in length. • Ages: 4-19 • Tue: 11-5, Thu: 11-5.

$COUPON$ Shendy's Swim School
Central Toronto Location, • 905-763-7915 • www.shendys.com
Swimming lessons for all ages and levels in a warm and friendly atmosphere. Quality instruction
with a low student/instructor ratio. Creative and effective teaching methods. Red
Cross/Lifesaving program. Member of Ontario Camping Association. **Look for our ad in this section.
See coupon section for valuable savings.** • Ages: 6mos+ • Cheque • ♿.

Swimming in Mississauga

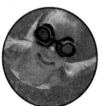

- 11 Indoor and 7 Outdoor Pools all heated to a minimum of 84 F
- Learn to Swim Lessons for children 3 months to adult
- Group, semi-private and private lessons available
- Qualified instructors offer all levels of the Lifesaving Swim
  and Canadian Swim Patrol programs
- Citi*Swim- introduction to competitive swimming program
- Recreational swim times for families and adults

Ask us about our LIfesaving Learn to Swim Program!

For more information, call 905-615-4100 or visit www.mississauga.ca

MISSISSAUGA
Leading today for tomorrow

Swim for Life Aquatics
647-296-7777 • We teach lessons in your own backyard!

$ COUPON $ Swim Time

Thornhill 905-707-9495, Woodbridge 905-856-9505, Pickering 905-683-9099, •
www.swim-time.com
A positive, fun, learning experience. Free assessment, multiple locations, flexible scheduling, experienced instructors, excellent facilities. **Look for our ad in this section. See coupon section for valuable savings.**

Swimming Pool Hotline - Toronto Parks, Forestry & Recreation
416-338-POOL (7665) •
Indoor & outdoor pools. Public swimming, lessons & programs.

Toronto Synchronized Swimming Club
647-285-4934 • www.torontosynchro.com
Toronto Synchronized Swimming Club offers recreational and competitive synchronized swimming at Leaside Pool and the U of T athletic centre.

$ COUPON $ Zodiac Swim School
Toronto, North York & Mississauga locations , • 416-789-1989 • www.zodiacswim.on.ca
High-quality, low-ratio classes specializing in Red Cross, Life Saving and many other fun programs. Aquafitness classes available. Convenient locations. Warm water. Qualified, caring instructors. **Look for our ad in this section. See coupon section for valuable savings.** • Ages: All ages •
VISA, ⊖, Cheque • Hours: Variable.

Theatre & Concerts For Kids

Toronto is a destination city for adults looking for theatre, music and dance, but it has become an equally impressive city in its offerings for kids - there are big productions like Lord of the Rings and the Nutcracker, but there are also wonderful smaller theatre companies and venues that expressly target children. Symphony, ballet, theatre...expose your children to the culture that Toronto has in abundance.

Air Canada Centre
40 Bay St, Ste 400, Toronto, Ont, M5J 2X2. • 416-815-5500 • www.theaircanadacentre.com
Call our Event Update Line for the latest information on upcoming events.

Cascade Theatre
39 Strathmore Blvd, Toronto, Ont, M4J 1P1. • 416-469-2878 •
Family theatre for ages 5 and up.

Famous People Players Dine & Dream Theatre
110 Sudbury St, Toronto, Ont, M6J 3T3. • 416-532-1137 •
This unique dinner theatre has an outstanding reputation for providing the only show of its kind. •
Ages: 3+.

Living Arts Centre
4141 Living Arts Dr, Mississauga, Ont, L5B 4B8. • 905-306-6000 •
Performances and art courses for the whole family!

Lorraine Kimsa Theatre for Young People
165 Front St E, Toronto, Ont, M5A 3Z4. • 416-862-2222 • www.lktyp.ca
Celebrating 41 years of young people's theatre! Our 2006/07 season includes Seussical – A Musical and Hana's Suitcase – plus five more wonderful shows the whole family can enjoy! •
VISA, ⬤, 💳, Interac • ♿.

Markham Theatre for Performing Arts
171 Town Centre Blvd, Markham, Ont, L3R 8G5. • Box office: (905) 305-SHOW (7469) or Toll free 1(866)768-8801 (not avail in 416/647 areas) • www.markhamtheatre.ca
See it, Hear it...Live. There's Nothing Better! Markham Theatre offers marvelous family shows for children aged 3 and up during our Professional Entertainment Season. Call for a FREE Season Brochure. • Ages: 3-8 • Mon-Sat: 11-6.

Meadowvale Theatre Family Entertainment
6315 Montevideo Rd, Mississauga, Ont, L5N 4G7. • 905-615-4720 •
Musical theatre for the whole family. Call for schedule of events.

Music with Bite, part of ZOOM! Family Sundays
Harbourfront Centre, 235 Queens Quay West, Toronto, Ont, M5J 2G8. • 416-973-4000 • www.harbourfrontcentre.com
Sing, dance, discover traditional instruments, or take a magical musical journey. Free. Select Sundays.

Rogers Centre- Events
Ste 3000, 1 Blue Jays Way, Toronto, Ont, M5V 1J3. • 416-341-1000 •
Kids events all year. Call for upcoming shows. • ♿.

Shrimp Magnet Theatre Company
Lagoon Theatre, Centre Island, Toronto, Ont • 416-262-1178 •
30-minute interactive musical for the whole family. • Ages: 4-9.

CELEBRATING 12 MAGICAL YEARS!

From treasured classics
to fresh music & plays,
we specialize in theatre for children aged 2 - 10!
Come discover us at our theatre at
100 Upper Madison Avenue

100 Upper Madison • Concourse Level • The Madison Centre, Toronto
Box Office: 416-368-8031 • School Shows: 416-368-4715
www.solarstage.on.ca • solarstage@bellnet.ca

$COUPON$ Solar Stage Children's Theatre
100 Upper Madison, Concourse Level (Yonge/Sheppard), • 416-368-8031 •
www.solarstage.on.ca
Join us in September 2007 for our exciting new season of children's theatre! Fun-filled
birthday/theatre packages also available. **Look for our ad in this section. See coupon section for valuable savings**. • Ages: 2-10 • ♿.

Stage West All Suite Hotel and Theatre Restaurant
5400 Dixie Rd, Mississauga, Ont, L4W 4T4. • 905-238-0042 or 800-263-0684 •
Stage West for families during school holidays. Buffet and live plays. • Ages: 5-12.

Toronto Symphony Orchestra: Concerts for Young People
Roy Thomson Hall, 60 Simcoe St at King St, Toronto, Ont, M5J 2H5. • 416-598-3375 •
Exhilarating and inexpensive live orchestral concerts! • Ages: 5-12 • ♿.

DID WE MISS YOU?
...WE'VE GOT KIDS

**Would you like to be listed in the 2008 edition of
Help!...We've Got Kids?**

Help!...We've Got Kids has 2000 listings, but inevitably some
children's stores or services may be overlooked. If you
provide a product or service for kids we would be delighted to
include you free of charge. Display ads are also available.

Call (416) 444-7678, fax (416) 444-1289 or
Email info@helpwevegotkids.com and tell us who you are.

Toys & Hobbies

Toy stores are filled with new toys and games as well as the traditional old standbys. Toys encourage your children's curiosity and allow them to express their creativity while playing. Staff are there to assist in selecting the ideal age-appropriate gift, from mobiles, plush stuffed animals and teething toys for infants to puzzles, building blocks and books for toddlers, to arts and crafts, building robots, magic kits or constructing ferris wheels for older kids.

Check out the toy warehouse outlets for great prices and selection and don't forget that there are online toy stores and home party opportunities that allow you to shop in the comfort of your living room.

You will find the following sub-categories in this section:
Catalogue/Online Shopping & Home Parties, Discount Toys, Dolls & Doll Repair, Toy & Hobby Stores

▪ Catalogue/Online Shopping & Home Parties

Discovery Toys - National Sales Director
416-630-0138 or 905-417-4514, • www.discoverytoyslink.com/WendyLitvak
Shop for FREE from home with friends! Learn how to stimulate & educate your child. Income opportunities available. Order by phone/on-line. Catalogues available. • Ages: 0-12 • VISA, ⊖, ▦, Cheque.

Grand River Toys
416-469-1946 •
Canada's online educational toy store. FREE catalogue available. • Ages: 0-13.

▪ Discount Toys

Mattel Toy Outlet
905-501-5147 •
Discontinued products & closeouts at value prices. Manufacturer warranties included. Mattel, Fisher-Price & Tyco.

Miko Toy Warehouse
60 East Beaver Creek Rd, Richmond Hill, Ont, L4B 1L3. • 905-771-8714 •
Name brand toys below wholesale prices. Only open mid-Sept to Christmas. Call for hours.

▪ Dolls & Doll Repair

Little Dollhouse Company
612 Mount Pleasant Rd, Toronto, Ont, M4S 2M8. • 416-489-7180 •
www.littledollhousecompany.com
MUST See! Largest Dollhouse Store in Canada. 65+ Wooden Dollhouses on Display. Furniture, Accessories. Custom Building to Order. • Ages: 18mos+ • ♿.

Martin House Store and Museum
46 Centre St, Thornhill, Ont, L4J 1E9. • 905-881-0426 •
Canada's largest selection of Dolls, Dollhouses, Bears, Miniatures. • Ages: NB+ • ♿.

▪ Toy & Hobby Stores

Animals Crackers
270 The Kingsway, Etobicoke, Ont, M9A 3T7. • 416-239-7474 •
Your neighbourhood toy store. Ages 0-14 yrs.

Browser's Den of Magic
875 Eglinton Ave West, Suite 10, Toronto, Ont, M6C 3Z9. • 416-783-7022 •
Magic tricks, juggling equipment, ventriloquist dolls. Lessons and mail order catalogue. • Ages: 5+.

Crossed Swords
722 Annette St, Toronto, Ont, M6S 2E2. • 416-604-9410 •
Miniatures. Gaming supplies. Historical, fantasy, sci-fi. Games workshop. Closed Sun/Mon. •
Ages: 7+ • &.

Discovery Toys - National Sales Director
416-630-0138 or 905-417-4514, , • 416-630-0138 or 905-417-4514 •
www.discoverytoyslink.com/WendyLitvak
More than a store! Award winning educational toys from birth - teens with a lifetime guarantee!
Also offering fun, flexible opportunities to earn extra $$ or replace a full time income. Shop for
FREE with a party or fundraiser. Gift baskets, corporate gifts available. Order by phone, cata-
logues available. • Ages: 0-12 • VISA, ⬤, ▓, Cheque.

EfstonScience: The Science & Astronomy Superstore
3350 Dufferin St (across from Yorkdale Mall), Toronto, Ont, M6A 3A4. • 416-787-4581 •
www.eScience.ca
Something for everyone in the family - from educational kits, toys, games and other smart sci-
ence fun to telescopes, binoculars and microscopes. A unique hands-on store for all ages. Look
for the huge telescope on the roof. Extended holiday hours (December). • Ages: 6-106 •
Mon-Wed: 9-6, Thu-Fri: 9-8, Sat: 10-6, Sun: closed.

Fun To Grow On
1077 North Service Rd, Mississauga, Ont, L4Y 1A6. • 905-896-3846 •
Toys, crafts, videos, books, puzzles and fun. • &.

George's Trains
510 Mount Pleasant Rd, Toronto, Ont, M4S 2M2. • 416-489-9783 •
Complete line of model trains & other hobbies. We carry wooden Thomas trains. • Ages: 3-93.

Hospital for Sick Children - 5 Fifty 5 Shop
555 University Ave, Toronto, Ont, M5G 1X8. • 416-813-8555 •
Sick Kids memorabilia, toys, books, handmades, bravery hearts...

Image Collections
181A Queen St S, Mississauga, Ont, L5M 1L1. • 905-542-8307 •
Comics, cards, gaming, posters and collectible fun!

John's Hobbies
2188 Danforth Ave, Toronto, Ont, M4C 1K3. • 416-421-1850 •
Toronto's award winning hobby shop. Come see!.

Kidding Awound
91 Cumberland St, Toronto, Ont, M5R 3N7. • 416-926-8996 •
"Toronto's Best Toy Store". Antique toys. • &.

Mastermind Toys & Books
10 stores to serve you. Find a location near you on our website., • 416-321-8984 press 3. •
www.mastermindtoys.com
Our toy & book specialists are ready to help find the perfect gift. • Ages: 0-12.

Mini Circuit Wheels for Kids
747 The Queensway, Toronto, Ont, M8Z 1M8. • 416-240-1988 •
Battery powered ride-on vehicles, also Perego strollers!

Planet X
2879 St Clair E, Toronto, Ont, M4B 1N4. • 416-285-4421 •
Comics, toys, collectibles, games, action figures.

Scholar's Choice
(800) 265-1095 • Canada's Neighbourhood Toy Store. Books, toys & more!

Smart Kids Toybox
2452 Bloor St W, Toronto, Ont, M6S 1R2. • 416-763-0794 •
Bloor West's neighbourhood toy store.

Top Banana
639 Mount Pleasant Rd, Toronto, Ont, M4S 2M9. • 416-440-0111 •
Traditional neighbourhood toy and book store. • Ages: NB+.

Toy Shop
62 Cumberland St, Toronto, Ont, M4W 1J5. • 416-961-4870 •
Unusual and imaginative playthings for children of all ages.

Toys "R" Us
905-660-2000 • 15 locations. Toys, bikes, video games, and more! • &.

Toys Toys Toys
Fairview Mall, 1800 Sheppard Ave, North York, Ont, M2J 5A7. • 416-493-5416 •
Toys, Toys, Toys is headquarters for all your toy needs. Barney, Thomas the Train, Barbie, Lego,
Brio, Gund and a fantastic assortment of Fisher Price toys are some of the wide variety of
games, puzzles and toys that are featured. • Other Locations: Eaton Centre 416-979-1121,
Square One 905-273-4148, 2654 Yonge St 416-486-3034, Hillcrest 905-883-3595, TD Centre
416-306-0045, Vaughan Mills 905-738-9664 • *VISA*, ⊕, ▆, *Interac* • Mon-Fri: 10-9, Sat: 9:30-6,
Sun: 12-5.

$ COUPONS $ Toytown
1754 Avenue Rd, Toronto, Ont, M5M 3Y9. • 416-783-8073 • www.toytown.ca
Toronto's oldest established toy store specializing in service and knowledgeable staff. We offer a
full range of toys, books, games, crafts and customized loot bags for children of all ages. Great
baby section. Full line Little Tikes dealer. **Look for our ad in this section. See coupon section for valuable savings.** • *VISA*, ⊕, *Interac* • Mon-Sat: 9:30-6, Sun: 11-4 • &.

Treasure Island Toys Ltd
581 Danforth Ave, Toronto, Ont, M4K 1P9. • 416-778-4913 •
Loot bags, educational toys, arts & crafts, art supplies, games, puzzles. • Ages: 0-14 • *VISA*, ⊕,
▆, *Interac* • Mon-Wed: 9:30-7, Thu-Fri: 9:30-9, Sat: 9:30-6, Sun: 11:30-5 • &.

Statistics show that the average child watches 3 to 5 hours of television every day. Television viewing accounts for more of a child's time than any other activity except sleeping!

In this section you will find TV shows for kids listed by network. While television watching time should be monitored, we are of the opinion that some TV is not a bad thing.

One proviso... experts agree that smart parents spend some of their time watching TV with their kids - that is the only way parents really know what their kids are taking in and gives them the opportunity of helping children interpret what they see.

Family Channel
BCE Place, 181 Bay St, PO Box 787, Toronto, Ont, M5J 2T3. • 416-956-2030 • www.family.ca
100% commercial free programming for the whole family!

TELETOON Canada Inc
BCE Place, 181 Bay St, PO Box 787, Toronto, Ont, M5J 2T3. • 1-888-884-8666 •
www.teletoon.com
TELETOON is Canada's first and only, 24-hour animation station dedicated to audiences of all ages. With English and French language services, the network offers viewers classic cartoons and new animation from Canada and around the world.

Treehouse TV
64 Jefferson Ave, Toronto, Ont, M6K 3H4. • 416-534-1191 •
#1 preschool children's network in Canada.

TVO
1-800-613-0513 • www.tvokids.com
Voted Best Family Station by City Parent for two years in a row, TVO offers TVOKids, a safe and friendly television environment of engaging programming with no commercials!
www.tvokids.com provides an array of fun and innovative games and activities online that further inspire and enhance kids' learning.

YTV
416-534-1191 • www.ytv.com
YTV is a major force in Canadian kids' entertainment with an interactive website, a kids' entertainment magazine and entertaining, educational shows for children.

Order a copy for a friend
OR
order an extra copy for yourself

Help!... We've Got Kids is available at bookstores and kid-related stores everywhere OR use the coupon at the back of this book and we'll mail one right to you!

Tel: (416) 444-7678 ▪ Fax: (416) 444-1289
Email: info@helpwevegotkids.com

We have learned an enormous amount about this category over the course of research-ing our other publication Summer Fun Guide. What we have discovered is that there is so much to do in this wonderful province of ours. Sometimes when we plan our holidays, we forget about investigating stuff close to home. There are resorts and hotels that special-ize in family holidays, with everything from waterparks to kids programs to cookies and milk at bedtime. Check out those listed here and have a look on our website www.summerfun-guide.ca as well.

Bayview Wildwood Resort
RR #1, 1500 Port Stanton Pkwy, Severn Bridge, Ont, P0E 1N0. • 1-800-461-0243 •
Ontario's best family vacation value!

Blossom the Clowns B & B
1-888-627-6690 •
In Bradford near Holland Marsh. Bed & Breakfast. Kids welcome! • _VISA_.

Briars Resort & Spa, The
55 Hedge Rd, RR 1, Jackson's Point, Ont, L0E 1L0. • 800-465-2376 •
Lake Simcoe resort one hour from Toronto.

Cartier Place Suite
180 Cooper St, Ottawa, Ont, K2P 2L5. • 613-236-5000 • www.suitedreams.com
Downtown Ottawa. Located between Rideau Canal and trendy Elgin St. 250 spacious suites, one and two bedrooms, full kitchens, dining & living room. Indoor pool, whirlpool, sauna, exer-cise & games room, outdoor playground & patio.

Clevelands House
PO Box 60, Minett, Ont, P0B 1G0. • (888) 567-1177 •
Giant play village. 4 Outdoor pools. Extensive children's programming.

Cranberry Golf Resort
19 Keith Ave RR4, Hwy 26 W, Collingwood, Ont, L9Y 4T9. • 800-465-9077 •
Great family getaways year-round. Kids Club, skiing, golf, tennis and more. • _VISA_, ⊕, ▨.

Deerhurst Resort
Peninsula Lake, 1235 Deerhurst Dr, Huntsville , Ont, P1H 2E8. • 1-800-461-4393 •
Visit Ontario's premiere resort.

Delawana Inn Resort
Honey Harbour, Ont (888) DELAWANA (335-2926) or (705) 756-2424 •
Creating vacation memories for over 100 years! Ideal for families.

Delta Chelsea Hotel
33 Gerrard St W, Toronto, Ont, M5G 1Z4. • 416-595-1975 or 1-800-CHELSEA (243-5732) •
www.deltachelsea.com
Family Fun Zone features a Children's Creative Centre, Teen Starcade, pool & 4-story indoor waterslide. Camp Chelsea keeps your little ones entertained with an exciting line-up of fully-supervised activities, giving Mom & Dad the option to explore the city on their own.

Events Barrie
800-668-9100 •
Events, Attractions, Accommodations for Great Family Getaways!

Fern Resort
R.R. #5, 4432 Fern Resort, Orillia, Ont, L3V 6H5. • 800-567-3376 •
No one treats families like Fern.

Hidden Valley Resort
1755 Valley Rd, Huntsville, Ont, P1H 1Z8. • 800-465-4171 •
Affordable Muskoka accommodations on the lake.

Hockley Valley Resort
R.R. #1, Orangeville, Ont, L9W 2Y8. • 416-363-5490 or 519-942-0754 • www.hockley.com
Perfect location for your next family getaway. 5 years and up!

Horseshoe Resort
PO Box 10, Horseshoe Valley, RR #1, Barrie, Ont, L4M 4Y8. • 800-461-5627 •
www.HorseshoeResort.com.
A family-oriented golf and ski resort.

Nottawasaga Inn Resort
6015 Hwy 89, Alliston, Ont, L9R 1A4. • 416-364-5068 or 705-435-5501 •
Readers' Choice Gold Award - favourite Ontario Resort.

Ontario Travel
800-668-2746 • www.ontariotravel.net
Trip planning ideas. Reservations. Camping. Provincial park info. Special events. Road info.

Pow-Wow Point Lodge
207 Grassmere, Resort Road, Huntsville, Ont, P1H 2J6. • 800-461-4263 •
Relaxed, friendly and carefree Muskoka family resort.

Severn Lodge
116 Gloucester Trail, P.O. Box 250, Port Severn, Ont, L0K 1S0. • 800-461-5817 •
Lakeside family resort in Muskoka-Georgian Bay. 90 min. from Toronto.

Sheraton Fallsview Hotel
6755 Fallsview Blvd, Niagara Falls, Ont, L2G 3W7. • 800-267-VIEW •
Stay just 300 yards from the Falls.

Talisman Mountain Resort
150 Talisman Mountain Dr., Kimberley, Ont, N0C 1G0. • 800-265-3759 •
Famous year-round resort & Kids Klub program.

Wheels Inn
615 Richmond St , Chatham, Ont, N7M 5K8. • 1-800-265-5257 • www.wheelsinn.com
350 Room hotel resort and the home of Wild Zone Adventures...Ontario's largest indoor amusement park, open year round for family fun. The hotel features 4 eateries, central atrium, indoor/outdoor pool, twin 100' waterslides, and spa/fitness centre.

Wigamog Inn Resort
1701 Wigamog Road R.R. #2 , Haliburton, Ont, K0M 1S0. • 1-800-661-2010 or 705-457-2000 •
www.wigamoginn.com
Ontario's Best Family Resort Value!

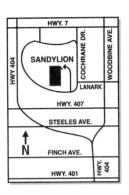

CLIP AND SAVE!!

283

www.helpwevegotkids.com

www.helpwevegotkids.com

www.helpwevegotkids.com

www.helpwevegotkids.com

www.helpwevegotkids.com

www.helpwevegotkids.com

CLIP AND SAVE!!

285

www.helpwevegotkids.com

www.helpwevegotkids.com

www.helpwevegotkids.com

www.helpwevegotkids.com

www.helpwevegotkids.com

www.helpwevegotkids.com

www.helpwevegotkids.com

www.helpwevegotkids.com

www.helpwevegotkids.com

www.helpwevegotkids.com

www.helpwevegotkids.com

www.helpwevegotkids.com

www.helpwevegotkids.com

www.helpwevegotkids.com

www.helpwevegotkids.com

www.helpwevegotkids.com

www.helpwevegotkids.com

www.helpwevegotkids.com

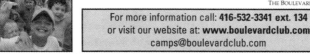

www.helpwevegotkids.com

www.helpwevegotkids.com

www.helpwevegotkids.com

www.helpwevegotkids.com

www.helpwevegotkids.com

www.helpwevegotkids.com

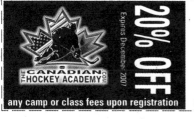

CLIP AND SAVE!!

COUPONS LISTED ALPHABETICALLY

www.helpwevegotkids.com

www.helpwevegotkids.com

www.helpwevegotkids.com

www.helpwevegotkids.com

www.helpwevegotkids.com

www.helpwevegotkids.com

296

www.helpwevegotkids.com

www.helpwevegotkids.com

www.helpwevegotkids.com

www.helpwevegotkids.com

www.helpwevegotkids.com

www.helpwevegotkids.com

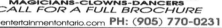

www.helpwevegotkids.com

www.helpwevegotkids.com

www.helpwevegotkids.com

www.helpwevegotkids.com

www.helpwevegotkids.com

www.helpwevegotkids.com

CLIP AND SAVE!!

www.helpwevegotkids.com

www.helpwevegotkids.com

www.helpwevegotkids.com

www.helpwevegotkids.com

www.helpwevegotkids.com

www.helpwevegotkids.com

www.helpwevegotkids.com

www.helpwevegotkids.com

www.helpwevegotkids.com

www.helpwevegotkids.com

www.helpwevegotkids.com

www.helpwevegotkids.com

www.helpwevegotkids.com

www.helpwevegotkids.com

www.helpwevegotkids.com

www.helpwevegotkids.com

www.helpwevegotkids.com

www.helpwevegotkids.com

www.helpwevegotkids.com

www.helpwevegotkids.com

www.helpwevegotkids.com

www.helpwevegotkids.com

www.helpwevegotkids.com

www.helpwevegotkids.com

CLIP AND SAVE!

www.helpwevegotkids.com

www.helpwevegotkids.com

www.helpwevegotkids.com

www.helpwevegotkids.com

www.helpwevegotkids.com

www.helpwevegotkids.com

www.helpwevegotkids.com

www.helpwevegotkids.com

www.helpwevegotkids.com

www.helpwevegotkids.com

www.helpwevegotkids.com

www.helpwevegotkids.com

CLIP AND SAVE!!

313

www.helpwevegotkids.com

www.helpwevegotkids.com

www.helpwevegotkids.com

www.helpwevegotkids.com

www.helpwevegotkids.com

www.helpwevegotkids.com

...WE'VE GOT KIDS
www.helpwevegotkids.com

...WE'VE GOT KIDS
www.helpwevegotkids.com

...WE'VE GOT KIDS
www.helpwevegotkids.com

...WE'VE GOT KIDS
www.helpwevegotkids.com

...WE'VE GOT KIDS
www.helpwevegotkids.com

WE'VE GOT KIDS
www.helpwevegotkids.com

www.helpwevegotkids.com

www.helpwevegotkids.com

www.helpwevegotkids.com

www.helpwevegotkids.com

www.helpwevegotkids.com

www.helpwevegotkids.com

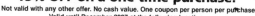

See ad on page 136
See ad on page 87,117
See ad on page 267
See ad on page 173
See ad on page 150
See ad across from copyright pg.

CLIP AND SAVE

www.helpwevegotkids.com

www.helpwevegotkids.com

www.helpwevegotkids.com

www.helpwevegotkids.com

www.helpwevegotkids.com

www.helpwevegotkids.com

CLIP AND SAVE!!

321

www.helpwevegotkids.com

www.helpwevegotkids.com

www.helpwevegotkids.com

www.helpwevegotkids.com

www.helpwevegotkids.com

www.helpwevegotkids.com

www.helpwevegotkids.com

www.helpwevegotkids.com

www.helpwevegotkids.com

www.helpwevegotkids.com

www.helpwevegotkids.com

www.helpwevegotkids.com

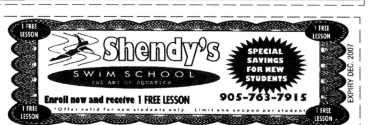

www.helpwevegotkids.com

www.helpwevegotkids.com

www.helpwevegotkids.com

www.helpwevegotkids.com

www.helpwevegotkids.com

www.helpwevegotkids.com

CLIP AND SAVE!

327

www.helpwevegotkids.com

www.helpwevegotkids.com

www.helpwevegotkids.com

www.helpwevegotkids.com

www.helpwevegotkids.com

www.helpwevegotkids.com

CLIP AND SAVE

331

www.helpwevegotkids.com

www.helpwevegotkids.com

www.helpwevegotkids.com

www.helpwevegotkids.com

www.helpwevegotkids.com

www.helpwevegotkids.com

CLIP AND SAVE!!

333

www.helpwevegotkids.com

www.helpwevegotkids.com

www.helpwevegotkids.com

www.helpwevegotkids.com

www.helpwevegotkids.com

www.helpwevegotkids.com

Index

Index

Index

Index

342

Index

Index

Readership Survey

 ...WE'VE GOT KIDS

Help! ... We've Got Kids
P.O. Box 47563, 939 Lawrence Ave. E.
Don Mills, Ont. M3C 3S7
416-444-7678 info@helpwevegotkids.com

We are constantly striving to improve the directory
Please help us understand your needs better by filling out this brief questionnaire.

Enter to WIN!
Return this survey to us and we'll enter your name
to win a great birthday party for your child.

VALUE $150.00

Return it to us by fax or mail for your chance to win.
Random draw will be held April 15, 2007.

Part 1:

Help! is an annual directory. Which copy (ies) do you have?

1995___ 1996___ 1997___ 1998___ 1999___ 2000___ 2001___ 2002___ 2003 ___ 2004 ___ 2005___ 2006 ___2007___

Where did you obtain your most recent copy?

_____

Help! ... We've Got Kids also has an online directory, www.HelpWeveGotKids.com
How often, on average do you refer to each directory per month?
Book: apprx. _____ times/month   Online: apprx. _____ times/month

Which resource directory do you prefer?
Help!...We've Got Kids, print directory _____
Help!...We've Got Kids, online directory _____
Both _____
Why? _____

_____

Which sections have you found most useful?

_____

Please specify companies that you have called/visited/used or found
through **Help!...We've Got Kids/www.helpwevegotkids.com**
1. _____ 2. _____
3. _____ 4. _____

Who in your household, uses your book most?
Mother _____   Father _____   Other, please specify _____

Some companies have placed an ad in the directory. Do the ads have any
impact on your decision to call or visit one company over another?
No _____ Yes _____ if yes, how so? _____

Some listings have boxes around their text. Do the boxes have any impact on
your decision to call or vist one company over another?
No _____ Yes _____ if yes, how so? _____

Readership Survey

...WE'VE GOT KIDS

Part 2: Demographics

1. How many children do you have?

    1. Age ____ M____ F____   4. Age ____ M____ F____
    2. Age ____ M____ F____   5. Age ____ M____ F____
    3. Age ____ M____ F____   6. Age ____ M____ F____

2. In what year were you born? _____

3. You are: Male/Female

4. Occupation: _____

5. Spouse's Occupation: _____

Comments or Suggestions: _____

_____

_____

_____

_____

Thank you very much for your cooperation

The undersigned will be entered into a random draw to win the prize listed above.
The draw will be held on April 15, 2007. Winners will be notified by mail or phone. Please c
Help!...We've Got Kids for the names of the winners. Employees of Help! and the
immediate families are not eligible to win. Good luck!

    Name: _____

    Address: _____

                 _____

    Phone: _____

Mail or fax to: **Help!...We've Got Kids** P.O. Box 47563, 939 Lawrence Ave. E. Don Mills, Ont. M3C 3S7

                 tel: (416) 444-7678   fax: (416) 444-1289   info@helpwevegotkids.com

Order A Book

SAVE $4.00
AND
we pay the
taxes & shipping

Help! is available at all major bookstores (Chapters/Indigo, etc.) as well as over 100 kids' stores near you.

Call 416-444-7678 for a location or fill in the coupon below and mail it to us. If it is a gift, we'll mail it directly to them with best wishes from you.

ORDER FOR YOURSELF OR SEND A FRIEND A COPY

For **$10.95** (including taxes & shipping), we'll send a copy of the **2007** edition to yourself or a friend/relative with best wishes from you.

Mail this coupon with your payment to:
Help! ... We've Got Kids
P.O. Box 47563, 939 Lawrence Ave. E. Don Mills, Ont. M3C 3S7
Phone: (416) 444-7678 • fax: (416) 444-1289 • info@helpwevegotkids.com

To: Name: _____
Address: _____

Phone #: _____

From: Name: _____
Address: _____

Phone #: _____

Paid by: ☐ **Cheque** (Payable to **Help! ... We've Got Kids**)
☐ **Visa** Name on card: _____
Number: _____
Expiry Date: _____
Amount: _____

RESERVE YOUR 2008 COPY!

For **$10.95** (including taxes & shipping), we'll send a "Hot Off The Presses" copy of the **2008** edition right to your front door. (available Sept. 2007)

Mail this coupon with your payment to:
Help! ... We've Got Kids
P.O. Box 47563, 939 Lawrence Ave. E. Don Mills, Ont. M3C 3S7
Phone: (416) 444-7678 • fax: (416) 444-1289 • info@helpwevegotkids.com

To: Name: _____
Address: _____

Phone #: _____

From: Name: _____
Address: _____

Phone #: _____

Paid by: ☐ **Cheque** (Payable to **Help! ... We've Got Kids**)
☐ **Visa** Name on card: _____
Number: _____
Expiry Date: _____
Amount: _____

Order A Book

Help! is available at all major bookstore (Chapters/Indigo, etc.) as well as over 100 kid: stores near you.

Call 416-444-7678 for a location or fill in th coupon below and mail it to us. If it is a gift, we' mail it directly to them with best wishes from you

ORDER FOR YOURSELF OR SEND A FRIEND A COPY

For **$10.95** (including taxes & shipping), we'll send a copy of the **2007** edition to yourself or a friend/relative with best wishes from you.

Mail this coupon with your payment to:
Help! ... We've Got Kids
P.O. Box 47563, 939 Lawrence Ave. E. Don Mills, Ont. M3C 3S7
Phone: (416) 444-7678 • fax: (416) 444-1289 • info@helpwevegotkids.com

To: Name: _____
Address: _____

Phone #: _____

From: Name: _____
Address: _____

Phone #: _____

Paid by: ☐ **Cheque** (Payable to **Help! ... We've Got Kids**)
☐ **Visa** Name on card: _____
Number: _____
Expiry Date: _____
Amount: _____

RESERVE YOUR 2008 COPY!

For **$10.95** (including taxes & shipping), we'll send a "Hot Off The Presses" copy of the **2008** edition right to your front door. (available Sept. 2007)

Mail this coupon with your payment to:
Help! ... We've Got Kids
P.O. Box 47563, 939 Lawrence Ave. E. Don Mills, Ont. M3C 3S7
Phone: (416) 444-7678 • fax: (416) 444-1289 • info@helpwevegotkids.com

To: Name: _____
Address: _____

Phone #: _____

From: Name: _____
Address: _____

Phone #: _____

Paid by: ☐ **Cheque** (Payable to **Help! ... We've Got Kids**)
☐ **Visa** Name on card: _____
Number: _____
Expiry Date: _____
Amount: _____